B. F. Bray Jr

1919 "A. B. P. S."

given to E. C. Wilkie
by Jack Neilson - his
pastor at Mills Home

BAPTIST CONFESSIONS OF FAITH

BAPTIST
CONFESSIONS
OF
FAITH

By
W. J. McGLOTHLIN, Ph. D., D. D.

Professor of Church History in the
Southern Baptist Theological Seminary

Author of
"A Guide to the Study of Church History," etc.

"Die warhayt ist untödtlich."—Hubmaier

PHILADELPHIA
AMERICAN BAPTIST PUBLICATION SOCIETY
BOSTON   CHICAGO   ST. LOUIS
TORONTO, CAN.

PREFACE

An effort has been made to bring together in the following pages the most important statements of doctrine put forth by the various bodies of Baptists scattered throughout the world. Material was in hand to make the volume more complete, but the limits of space forbade the incorporation of a few Confessions and catechisms which might have been expected. It is believed, however, that no Confession of much importance which had any large circulation in any language has been omitted. The volume presents all the material necessary to acquaint one with the doctrinal position of the Baptists throughout the world, and makes an impressive presentation of their substantial unity, with some exceptions, on the more important points of our religion. It is also noteworthy that doctrinal differences have been melting away until there is probably a greater measure of agreement at present than ever before.

Special thanks for valuable assistance are due to the management of Colgate Library, Hamilton, N. Y., which contains the best collection of the sources of Baptist history which can be found in this country; to Rev. W. T. Whitley, D. D., Preston, England; to Rev. Claus Peters, Hamburg, Germany; to Rev. C. E. Benander, Stockholm, Sweden; to Rev. H. Andru, Compiègne, France; and to others who have in one way or another aided in the discovery of material or the gathering of information. Some details as to editions of some of the English Confessions have been gleaned from the unpub-

v

lished work of the late John Taylor, of Northampton, on " European Confessions of Faith." In the case of the English Confessions whose original editions could be found the effort has been made to reproduce the text as nearly as possible exactly, in all its inconsistencies of spelling, punctuation, capitalization, etc. The desire has been to let the reader see the Confession as it first appeared to the world. It would be vain to hope that the work is wholly without mistakes where the reproduction of such a mass of details is involved; but no labor has been spared in an effort to make it as accurate as possible. The translations, except that from the Swedish, are by the author.

W. J. McGLOTHLIN.

SOUTHERN BAPTIST THEOLOGICAL SEMINARY,
Louisville, Ky., October, 1910.

TABLE OF CONTENTS

PAGE

INTRODUCTION ....ix-xii

PART ONE

THE ANABAPTISTS 1-23
    Earliest Anabaptist Articles............. 2-9
    Other Articles from Bern............... 9-13
    Peter Riedemann's Rechenschaft........13-18
    Appeal to the Lords of Lichtenstein.....18-23

PART TWO

THE MENNONITES 24-49
    Earliest Confession, Circa 1580..........24-25
    A Brief Confession, etc.................26-48
    Other Confessions 48-49

PART THREE

THE ENGLISH BAPTISTS......................50-291
    A. Arminian Baptists 54-167
    A Short Confession of Faith......... 54-66
    Confession of Faith of Certain English
        People Living at Amsterdam...... 66-84
    A Declaration of Faith of English Peo-
        ple Remaining at Amsterdam..... 85-93
    The Faith and Practice of Thirty Con-
        gregations 95-109
    The Standard Confession of 1660......109-122

PAGE

The "Orthodox Creed," 1678........122-161
Somerset Confession 161
Trinitarian Articles 162
Present Doctrinal Position............ 163
The New Connection.................164-167
B. *Calvinistic Baptists* 168-291
First London Confession..............168-201
A Confession of the Faith of Several
    Churches of Christ...............202-215
Assembly or Second London Confession.215-289
Private Confessions 289-290
Present Doctrinal Position of the Eng-
    lish Baptists 290-291

PART FOUR

AMERICAN BAPTISTS 293-329
    A. *Calvinistic Baptists* 293-307
    The Philadelphia Confession..........293-299
    The New Hampshire Confession......299-307
    Catechisms 307
    B. *Arminian Baptists* 308-329
    A Treatise on the Faith of the Free Will
        Baptists 310-329

PART FIVE

CONFESSIONS OF OTHER NATIONALITIES........330-368
    German Baptist Confession...........330-354
    French Baptist Confession............354-364
    Swedish Baptists 364-367
    In Other Lands..................... 368

INTRODUCTION

PRIMITIVE Christianity drew up no Confessions of Faith. Its interests and efforts were religious, ethical, and practical rather than theological. Repentance toward God, faith in the Lord Jesus Christ, and right living were the requirements of early days. As time passed the intellectual aspects of Christianity came into more and more prominence as a result of its contact with Greek philosophy and the various religions of the Greek and Roman world. As a consequence of the struggle with this thought without and within the church the first great group of creeds was produced in the third, fourth, fifth, and sixth centuries. The earliest is the so-called Apostles' Creed, which is not the product of any ecclesiastical council, but grew up in the daily needs of practical Christian work. Traces of this creed can be found as early as A. D. 200, and it reached substantially its present form in the fourth century. It is almost wholly a Confession of concrete facts rather than of doctrines.

The next creed was drawn up by the first world council of Christians, held at the call of the Emperor Constantine at Nicæa in Asia Minor in A. D. 325. It defined the doctrine of the Trinity, the internal relations of the Godhead, in that form which has been called orthodox by all parties to this day.

The third important creed was formulated by the Ecumenical Council of Chalcedon in Asia Minor in A. D. 451. It defines the interrelation of the human and divine natures in the person of Jesus Christ in that form which, with some variations, has been regarded as the orthodox doctrine of the person of Christ to the present time.

The so-called Athanasian Creed is a sort of epigrammatic expansion of that of Nicæa, and was widely influential. Its origin is obscure, but it was probably formulated in the sixth century.

These are the important creeds of the patristic period. They are all Oriental and Asiatic in origin. They are brief, dealing with only one phase of doctrine, making no attempt to present a complete system of theological truth. They are the product of the Greek mind, written in the Greek language; but at the time of their production they expressed the convictions of the great majority of Christians in the then known world. They were the proclamation of the great church, excluding heathendom, Judaism, and the smaller Christian parties. They have commanded the assent of the great majority of Christians throughout the centuries.

Creed-making now ceased for nearly a thousand years, till the beginning of the theological controversies aroused by the Reformation. Beginning with the Augsburg Confession in 1530, the next century and a half saw the formulation of most of the important modern Confessions. This group differs widely from the former. They are almost without exception of European origin, written in Latin or modern languages. They are long, presenting a more or less complete system of doctrine; they are all sectarian, representing the views of only a party of Christians, and intended to differentiate that party from the rest of Christendom and to justify its existence. The Catholic creeds of this period, both Greek and Roman, were drawn to meet Protestantism. Protestant creeds were drawn to meet the Roman Catholics and also other Protestant parties.

The Baptist Confessions were among the last to be produced, coming out of the latter part of the Reformation period, and even more recent times. Most of them were formulated in England after Catholicism had practically ceased to be a religious force in that country; they are, therefore, drawn against the background of English Protestantism. They constitute the latest group of denominational Confessions, most of the Lutheran, Reformed, Presbyterian, and Congregational Confessions having preceded them. They are not independent productions, but are the result of grafting Baptist views of baptism, church-membership, church government, and the relation between Church and State upon a Calvinistic or Arminian stock. Such in brief is the relation of Baptist Confessions to those of other denominations.

Being congregational and democratic in church government, Baptists have naturally been very free in making, changing, and using Confessions. There has never been among them any ecclesiastical authority which could impose a Confession upon their churches or other bodies. Their Confessions are, strictly speaking, statements of what a certain group of Baptists, large or small, did believe at a given time, rather than a creed which any Baptist must believe at all times in order to hold ecclesiastical position or be considered a Baptist. In the latter sense there has been no Baptist creed. Churches at their constitution have made their own Confessions, adopted an old one in its original or in a modified form, or, as in the case of the First Baptist Church of Providence, R. I., the oldest Baptist church in America, have had no doctrinal statement whatever. District Associations have sometimes adopted one Confession, sometimes another, have modified the oldest and most notable Confessions to suit their views, have formulated new statements, or have made no doctrinal deliverance of any sort. No Baptist individual, church, Association, or larger body has ever felt permanently bound by any Confession of Faith in its original, historical, or any other form. And yet the Baptists have preserved a remarkable degree of doctrinal agreement throughout their history. This is no doubt due to their insistence upon a converted church-membership, the authority of the Scriptures, and the right and duty of every individual Christian to decide doctrinal questions for himself by a study of the Scriptures under the guidance of the Holy Spirit.

Baptist Confessions are almost numberless, but comparatively few of them have any historical significance. It is manifestly impossible and undesirable to reproduce any but the most important ones in this work.

Some Waldensian and Bohemian articles, as representing the most evangelical forms of Christianity with which we are acquainted just prior to the Reformation, might have been reproduced had such been in existence. But nothing that can justly be called a Confession came from these parties before the Reformation. Accordingly, the work begins with the Anabaptists, who were in many respects the forerunners of the Baptists.

Part One

THE ANABAPTISTS

The Anabaptists were not Baptists in the modern acceptation of that term, since they did not insist upon immersion as the only acceptable mode or form of baptism. Some of them practised immersion at least occasionally, but none of them required it as a term of communion, and apparently a majority practised affusion. They held, however, so many fundamental Baptist doctrines that their Confessions deserve a place here. So far as known the mode of baptism was never a matter of discussion among them.

The question of their relation to earlier evangelical sects, as for example the Waldenses, is still under discussion. They betray no consciousness of dependence, stoutly maintaining the view that their distinctive doctrines were drawn from a direct and faithful study of the word of God under the guidance of the Holy Spirit. So far as the life history of early individual Anabaptists has been traced, they all came out of the Catholic Church, rather than from the sects. This is certainly true of all their leaders, many of whom had been priests or monks in that church. Nor did they ever, so far as known, enter into union or communion with the Waldenses. These considerations seem to point almost irresistibly to an independent origin. On the other hand, the similarity between some of their peculiarities and those of the Waldenses points strongly to some dependence. The most that can be asserted with confidence in the present state of

A

investigation is that they may have been influenced in their peculiar doctrinal views by older parties, but were entirely independent in the origination of their ordinances and other ecclesiastical matters.

Being the radicals and individualists of their time, they naturally broke up into many parties, differing more or less widely among themselves about various matters. Moreover, they were chiefly interested in practical Christianity, the following and imitation of Christ, the reformation of the lives of the people. Theology and ecclesiastical affairs with them took a much more subordinate place than among the Lutherans and other reformers; consequently they devoted little attention to creed-building. In general they were anti-Augustinian, *i. e.*, Pelagian or Arminian in their views of the plan of salvation, and were in agreement in their opposition to infant baptism and to the State church. Their fundamental principle, from which all else sprang, was a church composed of the regenerate only. On almost every other possible point of doctrine there were among them wide differences of opinion. These differences the various articles which have been preserved to us reflect. As sources for a knowledge of their views we have, in addition to their Articles of Faith, court records, writings of Hübmaier, Denck, and others, published accounts of disputations, their songs, and finally the writings of their opponents. The most important of their articles follow. The fact that they were written in old, and sometimes incorrect, German, makes the exact meaning of some passages uncertain.

I. Earliest Anabaptist Articles

The earliest were a set of seven articles drawn up by the Swabian and Swiss brethren, at Schlatten am Randen, near Schaffhausen, in 1527. So far as known, they were never printed, but Zwingli says (Wks. III, 387) that almost every Anabaptist had a copy in German. A manuscript copy in German is found in the Pressburg Cathedral Chapter, and has been published, somewhat condensed, by Beck, " *Geschichtsbücher der Wiédertäufer,*" p. 41f. The title, as it appears in this MS is " The VII Articles from Schlatten am Randen, drawn up Feb. 24, 1527." The conclusion of this manuscript, not given by Zwingli, is as follows:

Dear brethren and sisters, these are the articles which certain brethren hitherto in error and —— have not understood alike and thereby many weak consciences have been confused, so that the name of God has been grossly blasphemed; there has been, therefore, need that we be agreed in the Lord. To God be the praise and glory.

A copy is also found in Bern, and is reproduced somewhat condensed by Müller, " *Bernische Täufer,*" pp. 38f. Zwingli translated them faithfully, he says, into Latin. A translation of his translation follows:

" The Articles, which we have drawn up and in which we agree, are these: Baptism, abstention, breaking of bread, avoidance of abominable pastors in the church, sword, swearing.

First learn concerning baptism! Baptism ought to be administered to all who have been taught repentance and a change of life and in truth believe their sins to have been blotted out through Christ, and who wholly wish to walk in the resurrection of Jesus Christ, and who wish to be buried with him into death that they may be able to rise again with him. To all, then, who ask baptism after this manner and make the request of us for themselves we administer it. By these means are excluded all baptism of infants, the supreme abomination of the Roman Pontif. For this article we have the testimony and strength of Scripture; we have also the practice of the Apostles, which we shall preserve with simplicity and at the same time with firmness. For we have been made sure.

Second: With regard to excommunication we agree as follows: All ought to be excommunicated who, after they have given themselves to the Lord that they might follow him in his precepts and who have been baptized into one body of Christ and are called brethren or sisters, yet slip or fall into sin and are thrown headlong unawares. People of this sort ought, therefore, to be admonished twice in secret; the third time they ought to be corrected publicly before the church according to the precept of the Lord. Moreover, this ought to be done according to the ordinance or injunction of the divine Spirit before the breaking of bread, that all may be able to break and eat the one bread and drink from the one cup unanimously and with the same love.

Third: In the breaking of bread we agree and unanimously prescribe as follows: That those who wish to break the one bread in commemoration of the broken body of Christ and to drink from one cup in commemoration of the poured-out blood of Christ, should first be united into one, to-wit, into the one body of Christ, that is, into the church of God in which Christ is head. Moreover that is particularly through baptism. For, as the divine Paul teaches, we can not be at the same time participants of the table of the Lord and the table of demons; nor can we be at the same time participants in the cup of the Lord and the cup of demons. That is: all who have communion with dead works of darkness have no communion with those who have been called to God out of this world. All who are sunken in evil have no part with good. Thus, therefore, it must follow that those who have not the call of their God into one faith, into one baptism, into one Spirit, into one body with all the children of God, these cannot come together unto one bread; but beyond doubt this must be done if one wishes to break bread according to the precept of Christ.

Fourth: Thus we determine concerning the revolt, separation and avoidance which ought to be made from that evil which the devil has planted, so that we shall have no commerce with them nor concur with them in communication in those abominations. That is, since all who have not yet yielded to the obedience of faith and who have not yet given [their] name to the Lord that they wish to do his will, are exceedingly abominable in the sight of God; [therefore] nothing can be done by them which is not abominable. Now, moreover, in the world plainly there is nothing else, nor in all creation, than good and evil, faithful and unfaithful, shadows and light, people of the world and those who are now out of the world, the temple of God and idols, Christ and Belial, and no one of these can have part with the other. Known to us also is the precept of the Lord in which he commands that we be separated from the evil, for then he is willing to be our God and we shall be his sons and daughters. Again he prescribed that we should come out of Babylon and the Egyptian land lest we become partakers of the evils and punishments which the Lord is about to bring upon them. From all which we ought to learn that whatever is not united with our God and Christ is nothing else than an abomination which we ought to avoid. Here we perceive all papistical and *secundo-papistical* works and contentions of idolatry, processions to churches, houses of feastings, states and alliances of unbelief and many other things similar to these which are held in honor in the world, when nevertheless they fight and lead directly against the precept of Christ according to the measure of unrighteousness which is in the world. From all these we ought to be alien and separate, for they are pure abominations which render us hateful to Christ who liberated us from the bondage of the flesh and made us fit for the service of God through the spirit of God which he gave us. By the vigor of this regulation there fall away from us the diabolical arms of violence, such as swords and arms of this kind and all use of them whether for enemies or for friends in virtue of that word of Christ 'You ought not to resist evil.'

Fifth: Concerning pastors of the church of God we determine as follows: That the pastor *of the flock should be,* according to the order of Paul through all things, some one who has good testimony from those who are outside the faith. Let his office be to read, admonish, teach, instruct, exhort, correct or *communicate* in the church, and to preside well over all the brethren and sisters as well in prayer as in the breaking of bread, and in all things that pertain to the body of Christ to watch how it may be sustained and increased, that the name of God may be honored and praised through us, but the mouth of *blasphemy* may be stopped. But know that a support, *if* he is in need of it, ought to be supplied by the church which elects him. For he who serves the gospel ought to live of the gospel as the Lord ordained. But if a pastor has committed anything worthy of accusation or correction action ought not to be taken against him except on testimony of two or three witnesses. When they sin they ought to be reproved publicly, that the rest may have fear. But if a pastor be either *expelled* or led to the Lord through the cross another ought to succeed him at once that the people or flock of God be not scattered but preserved through exhortation and may receive consolation.

Sixth: We agree and determine concerning the sword in this manner: The sword is an ordinance of God, outside the perfection of Christ by which the evil man is punished and killed, but the good one defended. In law the sword is ordained against the evil for vengeance and death, and for this purpose the magistracy of the world was constituted. But in the perfection of Christ we use excommunication only, for the warning and exclusion of him who has sinned, for the destruction of the flesh alone, for warning and commendation, lest he sin further. Here it is asked by many who do not know Christ's will towards us, whether a Christian can or ought to use the sword against the evil for the defense of the good, or out of love. There was revealed, therefore, to us unanimously the following response: Christ teaches us that we should learn of him for he is meek and lowly of heart and we shall find rest to our souls. Christ, therefore, said to the woman taken in adultery, not that she should be stoned according to law; (who nevertheless said, 'As the Father commanded me, so I speak') but he spoke to her with pity and indulgence and warning that she should sin no more, and said, 'Go, sin no more.' That is to be equally observed by us according to the rule of excommunication.

Second, it is asked concerning the sword, whether a Christian can rightly pronounce or speak judgment in secular causes, between force and force, between suit and suit, in which unbelievers are at variance. To which we give this response: Christ was unwilling to decide between brothers who were contending about an inheritance, but drove them from him. Just so, therefore, it must be done by us.

Third, it is asked concerning the sword, whether a Christian ought to be an official or magistrate when he is chosen to it. To which we respond thus: Christ was about to be made king, but he fled and did not look back, in accordance with the ordinance of his Father. Thus we also ought to do, rightly to follow him, and we shall not walk in darkness. For he also says: 'If any man will follow me, let him deny himself and take up his cross and follow me.' He even interdicts the power of the sword and thus denounces it: 'The kings of the Gentiles exercise lordship, but ye are not so.' Further, Paul says, 'Whom God foreknew these he also predestined that they should be conformed to the image of his Son.' But Peter also says that He suffered, did not reign, and left us an example that we should follow his footsteps.

Finally, it is taught that a Christian is not permitted to be a magistrate by the things which follow: Magistracy is an office after the flesh but a Christian is after the Spirit. The home and corporal habitation of those [magistrates] is in this world, but that of all Christians in heaven. Their citizenship is in this world, that of the Christians in heaven. Their arms are carnal and against the flesh, those of the Christians spiritual against the bulwarks of the devil. Earthly magistrates are armed with brass and iron, but the Christians are clothed with the arms of God—truth, justice, peace, faith, salvation and the word of God. In short, in whatever way our head is disposed toward us, so ought the members of the body be disposed toward him in all things, lest there be any disagreement in the body by which it could perish. For every kingdom divided against itself perishes. Since, therefore, Christ is such as is written concerning him, necessarily the members ought also to be such, that the body may remain whole and united for its conservation and edification.

Seventh: We agree or determine

I. Concerning the oath in the following manner: The oath is a confirmation among those who are in litigation or make promises. And in the law it is taught II. That it be done by the *name of God alone*, truly not *fallaciously*. But Christ who teaches the perfection of the law, forbids all swearing to his [followers], that they swear neither truly nor falsely, neither by heaven nor by the earth nor by Jerusalem nor by themselves. And this for the following cause, III. which he adds, saying, 'Because ye can not make one hair white or black.' Notice, therefore, all swearing is prohibited, because we are able to perform nothing of those things which we promise with an oath since we are not able to change the least thing which pertains to us. But there are some who do not believe the simple precepts of God but say: IV. ' Since God swore to Abraham by himself who was God, when he promised to be benevolent to him and to be his God as long as he kept his precepts, why may not I also swear when I promise anything to any one?' We respond: Hear *then* what the Scripture says, when God wished to establish a promise to the heirs with certainty that his council would not vacillate he interposed an oath that we might have hope. Listen thou to the meaning of this Scripture: God has the power of taking an oath which he prohibits to thee, for to him all things are possible. God made an oath to Abraham, says Scripture, that he might show that his counsel would not vacillate; that is, because no man is able to resist his power, therefore, *it is necessary that he keep his oath.* But we are not able as was shown above by the word of Christ, to keep an oath or to perform what we have sworn; therefore we ought not to swear. Again, there are some who say that there is no prohibition against swearing by God in the New Testament, but in the Old; but in the New there is prohibition against swearing by heaven, the earth or Jerusalem. To which we reply: V. Hear thou the Scripture, he who swears by the temple or heaven swears by the throne of God and by him who sits upon it. Thou seest that to swear by heaven is prohibited *because it is the throne of God himself!* O fools and blind, which is the greater, the throne or he that sits upon it? But further there are those who dare to say, ' If it is wicked to swear even when the Lord's name is added to truth, Peter and Paul, the apostles, sinned, for they swore. To whom we reply thus: VI. Peter and Paul testify this only, that it was promised by God to Abraham by an oath; but they themselves promise nothing, as the examples clearly show. But to testify and to swear are different; for when an oath is taken future things are promised. VII. To Abraham as an old man was promised Christ whom we after a long time have received. But when one testifies, testimony is given concerning some present thing, whether it be true and good or not. Just as Symeon was saying and testifying to Mary concerning Christ: ' Behold, this one is set for the fall and rising again of many in Israel, and for a *sign to be spoken against.'* After this manner Christ taught us when he *says,* ' Let your speech be yea, yea, nay, nay, for whatever is added to this is of the evil one.' Thus Christ warns: ' Your speech ought to be nay, nay,' that we may not be willing to understand him as having permitted swearing. Christ is simply yea, and nay. And all who seek him with simplicity find him. Amen."

II. OTHER ARTICLES FROM BERN

Müller (" *Bernische Täufer,*" p. 37) found in the archives of Bern seven articles in manuscript without date which come out of the sixteenth century and describe the order of an Anabaptist congregation. A free translation follows:

" First. The brethren and sisters should come together at least three or four times a week, and exercise themselves in the doctrine of Christ and his apostles, and earnestly warn one another to remain steadfast to the Lord as they have covenanted.

" Second. When the brethren and sisters are together, they should select something to read; he to whom God has given the best understanding should expound it, but the others keep silent and hear, so that no more than one should speak at once and hinder the others. The Psalter should be read daily by them.

" Third. No one should be frivolous in the congregation of God, neither in word nor in work; and a good manner of life should be observed by them all, also before the heathen.

" Fourth. If a brother sees his brother going astray, he should, in accordance with the command of Christ, warn and chastise him in a Christian and fraternal way, as every one is obligated by love to do.

" Fifth. No brethren and sisters of this congregation should hold any property as their own, but hold all things in common as the Christians at the time of the Apostles; and in particular they should lay by a common store from which the poor can be helped as each one has need, and, as at the time of the apostles, no brother be allowed to suffer want.

" Sixth. All expenses should be avoided by the brethren when they are assembled in the congregation—soup, vegetables and meat be given in the most limited quantities, since the kingdom of heaven is not eating and drinking.

" Seventh. The Lord's supper should be celebrated as often as the brethren come together, thereby to proclaim the death of the Lord and warn every one to remember how Christ has given his body for us and poured out his blood for us, that we also might be willing to give our body and life for Christ's sake, that is for the brethren."

III. Anabaptist Articles from Moravia

As persecutions thickened in Germany and Switzerland, thousands of Anabaptists made their way to Moravia, where the political conditions made it possible for the lords Lichtenstein to protect them some years on their large estates. They settled at Nikolsburg and other places in great numbers. Soon the various opinions held by them began to clash, and the body was more than once rent by religious dissension. Out of these dissensions come some articles in German in MS form, found in the royal archives at Nuremberg among papers belonging to the years 1527 and 1528, printed by Cornelius, "*Münsterschen Aufruhr,* II, 279f. "*Beilag,*" VIII. Nothing further is known of their origin. A translation follows:

1. Some Brief Articles

"Eight articles of the preacher[s] at Nikolsburg, that one [or those] at Lichtenstein, now imprisoned at Vienna, with many others, who have had themselves baptized a second time.

"The gospel should not be preached publicly in the churches, but only in the ear and secretly in the houses.

"Christ was conceived in original sin, [that is by a natural birth].

"The Virgin Mary was not a mother of God, but only a mother of Christ.

"Christ is not God, but a prophet to whom the message or word of God was entrusted.

"Christ did not do enough for the sins of the whole world.

"Among Christian men there should be no power or magistracy.

"The last day is two years in the future.

"The angels were conceived with Christ and took flesh with Christ."

Another series at the same place:

"Articles of the Anabaptists.

"Those who can not hear and confess ought not to be baptized.

" He who has property, may not partake of the Lord's supper.

" He who is related to any magistracy can not be saved. One must understand that there should be no magistracy.

" Satan and the godless will also be saved finally.

" The holy Scripture was not given to believers, but to the godless that they might be overcome.

" Within two years the Lord will come from heaven and will deal and war with the worldly princes, and will root up the godless, but the pious and unworldly will reign with the Lord on earth.

" All who are learned and preach the gospel, are perverters of the Scriptures.

" In the Lord's supper is only bread and wine, although they [the Anabaptists] are not agreed about this.

" God strengthen them with visions."

Another series is as follows:

" Articles discussed by the congregation at Nikolsburg in Moravia.

" The gospel is not to be preached in the churches, but in the courts of princes and in their own houses.

" Christ was conceived in original sin [that is in a natural way].

" The blessed virgin Mary was not a mother of God, but only a mother of Christ.

" Christ is no God, but only a prophet to whom the secrets of God were entrusted.

" Christ did not do enough for the sins of the whole world.

" There should be no power or magistracy among the Christians.

" The last day is said to be two years in the future.

" The angels with Christ were without flesh and took flesh with Christ."

The same articles, with some Huterish additions, are found in the archives of the Thomas Church at Strasburg, under the title:

"Articles which the Anabaptists at Augsburg confessed (and which are learned by them with great joy), who still to the number of twenty-five lie imprisoned there and are well to do." [Language not clear.]

2. Peter Riedemann's Rechenschaft

Persecution of the Anabaptists broke out in Moravia in 1535. The brethren suffered not only physical violence, but also vile slander and misrepresentation. In order to meet and refute these false accusations, Peter Riedemann, one of their pastors and their ablest literary representative after the death of Hübmaier, drew up an account of their doctrines and practices which he called " *Rechenschaft unserer Religion.*" (Reprinted in Calvary's " *Mittheilungen,*" I, 256-417.) It is rather a treatise on doctrine and practice than a Confession, being the longest and most pretentious production the Anabaptists put forth in the whole course of their history. Riedemann belonged to the Huterite party which gradually won complete ascendency among the Anabaptists of Moravia and Eastern Europe. The " *Rechenschaft*" was drawn up about 1545, was printed probably before 1547, and a second edition appeared in 1565. It was never formally adopted by any ecclesiastical body so far as known, but gradually came into wide usage and great influence. It is diffuse, full of repetitions, and much too long for reproduction here.

It bears the title, " Justification (or account, ' *Rechenschaft*') of our religion, doctrine and faith, put forth by the brethren commonly called Huterish, through Peter Ryedemann." After a long preface stating the reasons for drawing up the Confession, the body of the work is divided into three parts—an exposition of the twelve articles of religion, then a somewhat orderly statement of distinctive Anabaptist doctrines and practices, and finally a third part, which is largely a repetition of the second, apparently by another hand. The whole is supplied with abundant Scripture references, the Apocrypha being constantly quoted as Scripture. Its general theological position is in agreement with the Protestants of that time, except that a general atonement and the salvation of all infants dying in infancy in virtue of that atonement, is taught. In these views they stood over against all the other reformers of the time. Only a brief summary of its chief teachings can be given here, and is as follows:

Only those who truly repent are to be baptized; the candidate kneels while the administrator pours water upon him, repeating the words " I baptize thee in the name of the Father, Son and the Holy Spirit, who according to thy faith hath forgiven thee thy sins and drawn [thee] into his kingdom and accepted [thee], therefore sin henceforth no more so that no worse thing befall thee; " baptism should be administered in the presence of the congregation since "the sins are remitted and forgiven the man in baptism, and the congregation has the key"; teaching and baptizing must not be done by all but only by those who have been called by the Lord and the congregation and set apart thereto; the choice is made by lot where more candidates are presented than are needed; ordination is in the presence of the congregation by the imposition of the hands of the elders; only those who have been tested are ordained.

The various officers of the church are apostles, bishops, pastors, helpers, rulers, elders—each of these classes having its own more or less distinct function;

The bread and wine of the supper are not the body and blood of Christ, but only reminders of his grace.

Community of goods is taught, because " communion of saints exists not only in spiritual but also in temporal things."

The true church is composed of true believers, separated from the world and ruled over by the Holy Spirit, where righteousness dwells; existing church buildings, having been put to idolatrous uses ought to be pulled down and utterly destroyed—Anabaptists never enter them; nor do they have anything to do with priests since these were not called of Christ nor do they preach the gospel as is shown by their evil deeds and their lack of the power of the Holy Spirit.

Marriage must be entered into " according to God's direction "; woman being the weaker is under the yoke of the man who should provide for her in temporal and spiritual things; the ceremony should be in the presence of the congregation by a qualified minister of the word.

" Magistracy is set up and ordained of God for a rod of his wrath wherewith to chastise and punish wicked, ruthless people. . . Therefore one should be obedient and subject to them as ordained of God . . . in so far as they do not act contrary to conscience or give commands against God. . . But when they command and act contrary to [the will of] God one must let their command remain unfulfilled and obey God rather than men, for the conscience is free and subject to God alone. . . Therefore wherever magistracy undertakes to attack the conscience and rule over the faith of men, it robs God of what belongs to him. Therefore it is improper to obey magistracy in such matters." Magistracy, wielding a worldly sword, is outside Christ. " Among Christians He alone will rule with his spiritual sword. . . God in Christ is alone king and overlord over his people . . . and as he is a spiritual king, so he also has spiritual ministers, wields a spiritual sword." In Christ's kingdom all are brethren on an equality in service, therefore " no Christian is a magistrate and no magistrate is a Christian, for the child of blessing can never be the minister of vengeance. . . no Christian can rule over the world."

Since Christ is the Prince of Peace who is building a peaceful kingdom, all earthly war ends in it. Therefore, " no Christian may either carry on war or exercise vengeance, and whoever does so has either deserted and denied Christ or the manner of Christ."

" Since magistracy is ordained of God and its office commanded, it is also ordained and commanded to pay the taxes necessary to it. . . But for making war, executing or shedding blood (when it is demanded especially for that purpose) we give nothing . . . that we make not ourselves partners in other men's sins."

Since Christians must not use the sword, so they must not make it for others to use. "Therefore we make neither swords, spears, guns, nor any weapons of this kind."

"In the matter of clothes we will make whatever ministers to the needs of our neighbors, but whatever ministers to pride and vainglory in dress we make for no man."

"Christians should not go to law with one another. . . From which it follows that no Christian can act as judge, for Christians do not go to law" and a Christian can not judge those who are without.

Christians must not swear since it is forbidden by Christ and others.

Greeting, that is wishing well in God's name, must occur only between Christians, and must be given and received solemnly and in faith, not thoughtlessly. Otherwise it is sin.

Giving the hand and embracing are signs of unity and fellowship, and are therefore to be practiced only in the church. But brother must embrace brother and sister embrace sister. Brothers and sisters must not embrace each other, but only give the hand.

Prayer must be made with a right heart, in faith and according to the Spirit.

The singing of spiritual songs is pleasing to God when it is done at the impulse of the Spirit and attention is given to the words. "We permit no other than spiritual songs to be sung among us."

"Keeping holy day as the world keeps it is an abomination before God, because the wickedness and shame they can not do the rest of the week (on account of work) that they do on holy days. . . But we have one day of rest in which we handle and hear the word of God, and with it awaken our hearts to abide in the grace of God. Now because it is customary for all men to observe Sunday, we also keep the same day so as to give nobody offense; but not because anything depends on it nor because of any commandment; for it is abolished in Christ (Col. 2c), but as was said [we keep it] to exercise ourselves in the word of God."

"Trading or merchandising is not permitted among us, because it is a sinful business. . . We permit nobody to buy in order to sell again. But one is suffered to buy for the needs of his house or hand-work so as to carry that on; also to sell and dispose of what one has made in his hand-work, we regard as not improper but right. But this alone we hold to be wrong, viz. when one purchases an article and then sells the identical article which he purchased, and takes from it his gain and thereby raises the price of the object for the poor and cuts off bread from their mouths."

"Nor do we allow any one among us to become keeper of a public house, or to sell beer or wine, because all manner of unchaste, ungodly and corrupt doings take place there; and all drunken and worthless scoundrels congregate there and carry on their shameful deeds; to whom place must be given, their orders taken and their blasphemy heard. Therefore we do not believe it is permitted to one who fears God to hear and permit such blasphemy for the sake of money." We render free hospitality to strangers who are in need.

We do not permit drinking among us for "drinking is wicked at the root, no matter how it occurs, invented of the devil with which to catch men and draw them into his net, make them dependent on him and fall away from God, and lead them into all sin."

Meetings for one, two, or three days are held in preparation for each celebration of the Lord's Supper.

Children were not allowed to attend any but Anabaptist schools. As soon as they were weaned they were put in the care of "sisters" selected by the congregation, who taught them to talk, read, and write, using Scripture as much as possible; at five or six they were put under schoolmasters who continued to make religious instruction prominent; they remained with the schoolmaster

B

till they were old enough to be taught to work at whatever they were fitted by nature to do.

They watch over each other, warn and admonish one another. Gross or incorrigible sinners are expelled. "When one is banned, we have nothing to do with him; avoid his company altogether, so that he may be made ashamed. But he is warned to repent, that he may be thereby moved the more rapidly to return to God." When he has genuinely repented, he is received back into the church. "But, as one is received into the church at the beginning through a sign, baptism, so must he who has fallen away and been cut off from the congregation, be received through a sign, the imposition of hands; this must be done by a minister of the gospel, by which it is indicated that he is again a partaker in the grace of God and rooted therein."

The true adornment of a Christian is not outward, but inward, as Peter says. Christians should not, therefore, indulge in expensive ornamentation, but avoid and shun it.

[END OF SECOND PART]

The third part, apparently written by another hand, is but a repetition in different form of some of the preceding articles, and is more polemical in spirit.

3. APPEAL TO THE LORDS OF LICHTENSTEIN

In 1545 persecution again threatened the brethren in Moravia. In order, if possible, to avert the impending calamity, they sent to the Moravian nobility Riedemann's "*Rechenschaft,*" and along with it the address which follows. It is found in Codex 215 in the library of the Pressburg Cathedral Chapter in MS form; also in a library at Grau, in MS, and is published in condensed form by Josef Beck, "*Geschichtsbücher d. Wiedertäu-*

fer," pp. 169-173. The following is a translation of Beck's text:

" Sent to the Moravian Nobility, in the year 1545.

We, brethren and true followers of the Lord Jesus Christ, who from many and various places, especially of the German nation, have been called through great grace and mercy to the wonderful light of divine knowledge which has arisen in these times and shone to all men, and now assembled in his holy name: wish you the true knowledge of God and of his eternal truth and righteousness. Amen!

Beloved Lords of the Land of Moravia! It is well known to you in part how we have come out of various places and lands into the land of Moravia for no other reason than that we desire to serve [God] according to the known truth of God, piously and agreeably; which heretofore has not been permitted to us in many lands on account of the tyranny of the governments which have taken our possessions from us by force, have plunged us into misery and hunted us away, have held many of us in long and wearisome imprisonment and have strangled a good part.

But because the Lord God has spied out for his people especially this place and has so favored them that they have assembled here, and we have received with thankfulness and have undertaken to serve him and walk before him blameless. Although we have been and are still diligent to do this, yet there has gone out from the fickle and especially from those who have gone out of our midst [and] have left the truth and made friends with the world, much evil report and much of such complaint has reached you, wherein we know ourselves to be blameless in all things.

Moreover because many of you are little acquainted with our doings or are in error on account of the slanders against us, we were moved to give you information concerning and justification of our doing, teaching and life, especially with regard to certain articles as for example, (a) magistracy, (b) taxes and (c) the assembly, which, we have been informed, are of special interest to you.

First, As the foundation and ground of our faith we unite to inform you, that we believe on the only, eternal, living God—who created and preserves heaven and earth and all that therein is—who has power over the hearts of all men and has begotten us again through the word of truth and made us his children through Jesus Christ who is one with God the Father in essence—made man in the virgin Mary in order to save the sinners who turn to God—who after his death again ascended to heaven to represent us and has poured out the promise of the Father in the Holy Ghost upon us his believers, which Spirit proceeded from the Father and Son and is, with the Son and Father in power and being, one God, who still today assembles the churches of Christ or his congregation, and makes therein the word of truth living, so that those who serve God with the heart, after they have finished their course, may rejoice in eternal life in peace with him.

With regard to magistracy and the obedience which we are under obligation to render it we say, first, that of course there must be in the world governments, and also that they are ordained of God. Further, if any man opposes magistracy in equitable matters he opposes the ordinance of God. Yet we say with Peter that one should obey God rather than men, as also many of you yourselves know, and at first, when we came into the land, in fact showed that you feared to demand of us anything contrary to the conscience.

With regard to taxes we say that if any one objects to paying the government taxes, interest or rent so that the office can be carried on, he would be found to oppose the ordinance of God. Therefore we also, as the governments under which we have sojourned and lived must themselves testify, have never opposed due annual taxes or interest, rent, toll and just socage. But if anything which God has not ordained be demanded [of us] as war taxes and hangman's wages or other things which are not becoming to a Christian and have no ground in Scripture, these we can by no means approve.

But in that by many we are compared in all points with the [Anabaptists] of Münster and are accused of

being of their kind [or spirit]; it is known to all men
who are acquainted with us that nobody has less of the
Münster kind [spirit] than we who hate the same most
intensely and testify that it is a work of the devil.

With regard to our communion, wherein we, as we
have heard, can not be tolerated and which is displeasing
to the king and his rulers, the cause is perhaps in part
(as people daily charge us) that when many of us were
together we did not act at all like those of Münster; but
we have never had that in mind and also hope not to
undertake it forever; again in part the cause is, and this
by far the most important, that we walk in the truth,
which, however, the world has never been willing to
receive. Therefore it is nothing strange to us that we
are hated for such love and unity. We, however, know
nothing else than that our purpose and assembly is of
God, who has also given us, as to the first churches, a
mind and heart after Christ Jesus.

But because many are moved whom God daily adds
[to us], many foolish souls with corrupt purposes are
mixed among them. After they have joined [us] under
a false pretense and have again given up the truth, they
shamelessly slander that which they have never yet
known, while the truth they have known they misrepre-
sent. They say they have been deprived of their possessions when as a matter of fact they had nothing, not even
enough food for them to move into this land if help had
not been given them. And even if some of them had
something, they gave it of their own accord for the support of the widows and orphans and needy. It is therefore our desire and request to you that you will not assent
to such unknown faultfinders in their complaint but will
also hear our answer.

Likewise with regard to the place [stett] which, as
we hear, has made complaint against us as if we were
cutting off bread from the mouth of country laborers,
we know nothing else than that in all true work we are
diligent to pay every man his penny, and our honesty is
now known among almost all the people. To God be all
the honor that the people are now coming to us in
great numbers. If now any man makes complaint un-

justly we can not, therefore, cease to push our work, but desire to live honestly and be blameless toward every man.

If any man would see other articles of our faith and religion we send you herewith a justification [" *Rechenschaft* "] and a complete summary of our faith and doing composed in the German language [Riedemann's " *Rechenschaft unserer Religion,*"] according to which rule we desire to serve the Lord with a good conscience in this land and by faithful work to be useful and helpful to every man; and we desire nothing more than that we with our children, old and sick may sojourn the short time we have yet to live here in the flesh. For we think that God did not without cause lead us into this land to which he has given very much more freedom in regard to faith than to many other lands, so that neither king nor emperor now has power to give it rules and orders, but every one may rest on his faith and serve God the best he knows how. If, however, any one misuses this freedom and does not obey God completely, he will also have his judge. Notwithstanding such freedom (you have now in response to) the steady effort and action of the king to destroy the pious and drive them apart, laid your hand upon the peaceable ones of the Lord and laid hold on God. Therefore now a faintheartedness has fallen upon you and [you] no more have so much earnestness to withstand his desire and demand with bravery and boldness, and are now inclined to lay hand anew on the people of the Lord and scatter them abroad at the demand of the king.

With regard to the multitude of our people who are reported to come together in great numbers, even in thousands as some say, we must ever declare that there are of us, adults without the children, in the land here and there somewhere about 2000 and that they live in some twenty-one places, and have more houses in one place than another according as it is better located for work. At Schäckowitz, however, about which there is special complaint, there are indeed several of us, [but] many sick, aged and children, who can do little or nothing. This, therefore, we have determined to lay before you and therewith we commend us to the care and protection of the Almighty and therewith have we warned you and all men that no one escapes the judgment of God by laying his hand on the pious.

For it has ever been the case that where sympathy with the people of God has been shown God has spared that place for the sake of his people, as happened even to this land as the Turk traversed Austria through and through but did not come into this land."

Part Two

THE MENNONITES

The Eastern Anabaptists, who came to be called Huterite Brethren, after Jacob Huter, were finally scattered and almost exterminated. Those of Western Europe held out through fearful persecutions. The terrible doings of the Münster Kingdom in 1535, increased their hardships and the disfavor from which they suffered. The name Anabaptist, already loaded with suspicion, fear, and opprobrium, became an intolerable stench in the nostrils of Europe. Persecution broke out with fresh fury, and princes who had not before persecuted, laid their hands to the sword. Frightful sufferings followed, but out of this night of their misfortunes came one great blessing—wild millenarian fanaticism received its death-blow. Henceforth they were the quiet in the land. They were gathered together and the work reorganized chiefly by a Dutchman, Menno Simons, a Catholic priest converted to Anabaptist views in 1536. He was a tireless and devoted worker, a popular and successful preacher, and a voluminous writer. Because of his great services in rehabilitating the Anabaptist cause in the Netherlands and North Germany, they came to be called Mennonites in Germany, Russia, and America, while they are usually called Doopsgezinde in the Netherlands and Taufgesinnte in Switzerland.

I. Earliest Confession c. 1580

For many years they drew up no Confession of faith, some of them being opposed to Confessions altogether, and others feeling that they were unnecessary. But about

24

the middle of the sixteenth century the body fell into disagreement and dissension, chiefly over questions of discipline and the proper view of the person of Christ, which finally resulted in serious divisions and much strife. After some time the various parties began to put forth statements of their views in the form of Confessions. The earliest one was that of the Waterlanders, or Mennonites of north Holland, the most liberal wing of the body. It has special interest for Baptists, because it was in the midst of this party that John Smith and other Englishmen became convinced of believers' baptism and began the General Baptist work; and, further, because Hans de Ries and Lubbert Gerrits, who drew up this first Mennonite Confession, were the pastors with whom Smith and his followers corresponded, and who probably drew up one of the so-called Baptist Confessions. In so far as the General Baptists originated from or were influenced by the Anabaptists, that influence was exerted by the Waterlanders, and especially by Ries and Gerrits, the authors of the following Confession. Naturally the early English General Baptists approximated very closely the views and practices expressed in this earliest Mennonite Confession. The following is a translation of the Latin text of Schyn, "*Historia Christianorum,*" etc., I, 172-220. (Compare the Confession signed by Smyth and his followers, p. 54.)

It will be observed that this and all subsequent Confessions are much more elaborate and complete and better fortified with Scripture references than those of the Anabaptists. This is due to the influence of the theological work of Luther, Calvin, and other Reformers, and to the great Protestant Confessions which had been formulated after the work of the Anabaptists had been completed, but before this Confession was drawn up.

A BRIEF CONFESSION OF THE PRINCIPAL ARTICLES OF THE CHRISTIAN FAITH.

Prepared by

John de Rys and Lubbert Gerrits, Ministers of the Divine Word among the Protestants who, in the Belgian Confederacy, are called Mennonites.

ARTICLE I.

OF THE UNITY AND ATTRIBUTES OF GOD.

We believe and confess, sacred Scripture preceding and proving it, that there is (a) one God (who is (b) a Spirit or (c) spiritual substance), (d) eternal (e), incomprehensible (f), immense (g), invisible (h), immutable (i), omnipotent (k), merciful (l), just (m), perfect (n), wise (o), wholly good (p), the fountain of life and (q) the spring of all good, (r) Creator and (s) Preserver of heaven and earth, of things visible and invisible.

a. Deut. 6 : 4; 32 : 39. b. John 4 : 24. c. Rom. 1 : 10. d. Gen. 21 : 33. Rom. 16 : 26. e. Ps. 129 : 6; Rom. 11 : 33. f. I Kgs. 8 : 27. Mat. 5 : 34. Act. 7 : 48. g. Col. i : 15. h. James 1 : 17. i. Gen. 17 : 1; 2 Cor. 6 : 18. k. Exod. 34 : 6, 7; Luc. 6 : 36. l. Ps. 11 : 7; Col. 3 : 24, 25. m. Lev. 19 : 2; Mat. 5 : 48. n. Tit. 1 : 17. o. Ps. 103 : 8; Mat. 19 : 17. p. Jer. 2 : 13. q. James 1 : 17. r. Gen. 1 : 1; Exod. 20 : 11; Act. 4 : 24. s. John 5 : 17.

ARTICLE II.

HOW THIS ONE GOD IS DISTINGUISHED IN SACRED SCRIPTURE.

This one God in sacred Scripture is revealed and distinguished into (a) Father, Son and Holy Spirit (b). There are three (and yet) only one God.

a. Mat. 3 : 16-19. b. John 5 : 7.

ARTICLE III.

HOW THE FATHER, SON AND HOLY SPIRIT, ACCORDING TO THIS DISTINCTION, ARE THREE AND ONE.

The Father is (a) the spring and principle of all things, who begat his Son from eternity (b), before all creatures (c), in a manner which the human mind cannot comprehend (d). The Son is the Father's eternal Word and Wisdom (e), through whom are all things (f). The Holy Spirit (g) is God's power, might or virtue (h), proceeding from the Father (i) and the Son (k). These three are neither divided (1) nor distinguished in respect of nature, essence, or essential attributes, such as eternity, omnipotence, invisibility, immortality, glory and similar things.

a. Rom. 11 : 36; I Cor. 8 : 6. b. Mic. 5 : 2. c. Col. 1 : 15; Heb. 7 : 2. d. Ps. 2 : 7. e. John 1 : 1. f. I Cor. 1 : 22; Col. 2 : 3. g. John 14 : 26. h. Luc. 1 : 31. i. John 15 : 26. k. John 16 : 7; Rev. 22 : 1. l. I John 5 : 7.

ARTICLE IV.

OF THE CREATION, FALL AND RESTITUTION OF MAN.

This one God created man, good (a), according to his own image and likeness (b), for salvation or safety, and in him all men for the same happy end (c). The first man fell into sins (d) and became subject to divine wrath, and by God was raised up again through consolatory promises (e) and admitted to eternal life at the same time with all those who had fallen (f); so that none of his posterity, in respect of this restitution, is born guilty of sin or blame (g).

a. Gen. 1 : 31. b. Gen. 1 : 27. c. Rom. 5 : 18. d. Gen. 3 : 6; Rom. 5 : 19. e. Gen. 3 : 15, 21. f. Gen. 12 : 3; 22 : 18; 26 : 4; Rom. 5 : 18. g. Col. 2 : 22.

ARTICLE V.

OF THE FACULTY OF MAN BEFORE AND AFTER THE FALL.

There was in man who was created good (a) and was continuing in goodness, a faculty of hearing, admitting

or rejecting evil which was offered to him by the spirit
of wickedness (b). Now in the same man, fallen and
perverted, was a faculty of hearing, admitting or rejecting good, occurring and offered by God (c). For just
as before the fall (d), hearing and admitting occurring
evil, he manifested the faculty of admitting it, so also
after the fall (e), by hearing and admitting occurring
good, he shows that he has the faculty of accepting it.
But that faculty of accepting or rejecting the grace of
God truly offered, remains, through grace, in all his
posterity (f).

a. Gen. 1 : 31. b. Gen. 3 : 1, 6. c. Gen. 38 : 10, 11, 12, 16, 17.
d. Gen. 3 : 1, 6. e. Gen. 3 : 8, 9, 10, 15. f. Gen. 4 : 6, 7; 6 : 23,
12; Deut. 11 : 26; 30 : 19; Ps. 81 : 14; Isa. 1 : 19, 20; 42 : 18,
19, 20, 21; Jer. 8 : 7; 25 : 4; Mat. 11 : 17; 22 : 3; 23 : 36; Luc.
13 : 32; Jhan 5 : 34, 40.

ARTICLE VI.

OF THE PROVIDENCE OF GOD.

God foresaw and foreknew (a) all things which have
come to pass, are coming to pass, and shall come to pass,
both good and evil, but since he is only perfect good (b)
and the fountain of life, we believe and confess that he
is the sole Author, Origin and Operator of those things
which are good, holy, sincere, pure and which agree with
his nature; but not at all of sins and damnable evils.
For God enjoins that which is good (d); he desires that
we obey him in that which is good (e); he consults for
and admonishes to it (f), and makes great promises to
those who obey (g). On the contrary he forbids evil (h),
exhorts against evil (i), threatens evil doers (k), and
punishes them not rarely in this life (l), and denounces
against them eternal punishment (m). And by this
means shows himself to be an enemy of sinners and that
all iniquity is contrary to his holy nature. And therefore,
not God who is good, but man who is evil, by voluntarily
choosing sin to which the spirit of wickedness leads him,
which is dominant in him, is the author (n), origin and
operator of sins and all wickedness, and for this reason is
worthy of punishment.

a. Job 28 : 24-27; Isa. 14 : 14-16; 48 : 3; Jer. 1 : 5. b. Ps.
103 : 8. Mat. 19 : 17. c. Ps. 36 : 9; Jer. 2 : 13. d. Exod. 20.
e. Deut. 5 : 29; 32 : 29; Luc. 19 : 42. f. Rev. 3 : 18. g. Deut.
28; Mat. 24 : 13. h. Gen. 2 : 17. i. Gen. 4 : 6; Deut. 27 : 15;
28 : 15. k. Ps. 7 : 12. l. Gen. 8 : 19, 24. m. Mat. 3 : 12; 25 :
47. n. Hos. 13 : 9; Mich. 9 : 2; Eph. 2 : 1-3.

ARTICLE VII.

OF GOD'S PREDESTINATION, ELECTION AND REPROBATION.

The cause, therefore, to which man owes his misery
and condemnation is man's voluntary choice of darkness
(a), agreement with sinners (b), and a life which is
spent in sins. Perdition, then, has its rise out of man but
not at all out of the good Creator. For God, since he is
the highest and most perfect good (c), and Love itself,
according to the nature of the highest love and goodness,
was not able not to have willed that felicity and salvation
should fall to the lot of his creatures. He did not, therefore, predestinate, ordain or create any one of them that
he should be condemned : nor did he wish nor decree that
they should sin or live in sins that he might subject them
to condemnation. But inasmuch as this good God, as
truly as he lives, does not delight in the destruction of any
(f), nor wish that any should perish, but that all men
should be saved (g) and attain to eternal salvation, so
also he decreed and created all men for salvation (h) ;
and when fallen, through his ineffable love (i) he
restored them in Christ and in him ordained and prepared for all a medicine of life (k), if indeed Christ was
given (l), offered (m) and died for a propitiation for
all. In confirmation of which thing God willed that this
universal grace, love and benignity should be announced
and offered, through the preaching of the gospel, to all
creatures or peoples. All who, being penitent and believing, admit or accept that gracious benefit of God in
Christ, (who appeared (o) as a propitiation for the world)
(p), and persevere in it (q), are and remain (r) through
his mercy the elect, concerning whom God decreed, before the foundation of the world was laid (s), that they
should become partakers of the heavenly kingdom and
glory. But those who disdain or reject that offered

grace (t), love darkness in place of light (v), persevere in impenitence and unbelief, render (w) themselves (through that wickedness) unworthy of salvation, and so on account of their own wickedness are justly rejected by God (x), and deprived of that end for which they were created and in Christ destined (y) and called (z), and therefore do not enjoy forever the Supper of the Lord to which they were invited and called.

a. John 3 : 19. b. James 1 : 15. c. Mat. 19 : 17. d. I John 4 : 8. e. Eze. 33 : 11. f. 2 Petr. 3 : 9. g. I Tim. 2 : 4. h. Gen. 1 : 27. i. Gen. 12 : 3; 22 : 18; Rom. 5 : 19. k. Col. 1 : 19, 20; I John 2 : 2; Hebr. 2 : 9. l. John 3 : 16. m. Eph. 5 : 2. n. Mat. 28 : 19; Marc. 16 : 15; Eph. 1 : 9. o. 1 John 2 : 2. p. Marc. 16 : 15, 16; John 1 : 12. q. Mat. 24 : 13; Rev. 2 : 10. r. Mat. 22 : 14; Eph. 1 : 4. s. Mat. 25 : 34. t. Mat. 22 : 5. v. John 3 : 19. w. Acts 13 : 46. x. 2 Chron. 15 : 2; I Kgs. 15 : 23, 30; 2 Thess. 2 : 10, 11. y. I Pet. 1 : 2. z. Mat. 22; Luc. 14 : 16, 17, 24.

ARTICLE VIII.

OF THE INCARNATION OF THE SON OF GOD.

In the fulness of time God has executed (a) the plan which was with him before the foundation of the world was laid, namely, that he would reconcile to himself the world which he saw would be subjected to divine wrath, and to this end has sent his eternal word, or Son (that the promise made by the Father might be fulfilled (b)) from heaven (c), who in the body of the virgin Mary was made flesh or man (e) through the admirable power of God and the incomprehensible operation of his Holy Spirit. Not indeed in such a manner that the divine Essence of the Word or any part of it was changed into visible and mortal flesh and thus ceased to be Spirit, Deity or God; but so, that, remaining the eternal Son of God (g), which he was before, namely God (h) and Spirit (i), he was made (what he was not before) namely flesh or man (k). And so this same Jesus is our Emmanuel (l), in the same person true God (m) and true man (n), born of Mary, visible and invisible, external and internal, and the true Son of the living God. (o).

a. Gal. 4 : 4. b. Gen. 3 : 15; 22 : 18; 26 : 4; Deut. 18 : 15; Isa. 7 : 14; 9 : 5; 11 : 1; Jer. 23 : 5. c. John 13 : 3; 16 : 28;

17 : 18. d. Luc. 1 : 27. e. John 1 : 14. f. Luc. 1 : 31. Mat.
1 : 20. g. Hebr. 1 : 10-12. h. Rom. 9 : 5. i. 2 Cor. 3 : 17. k.
John 1 : 14. l. Isa. 7 : 14. m. I John 5 : 20. n. John 8 : 40;
I Tim. 2 : 5. o. Mat. 19 : 16; John 6 : 69; 9 : 35-37.

ARTICLE IX.

OF THE FINAL CAUSE OF THE ADVENT OF CHRIST INTO THE WORLD AND OF HIS THREEFOLD OFFICE.

This person, God (a) and Man (b), Son of the living
God (c), came into this world that he might save sinners
(d), or that he might reconcile the world, polluted by
sins, to God the Father (e). On this account we confess
him to be our only Mediator (f), Prophet (g), Priest
(h), King (i), Lawgiver (k) and Teacher, whose mission into the world (l) God promised, to whom it is
necessary to hearken (m), in whom to believe (n), and
whom to follow (o).

a. I John 5 : 20. b. John 8 : 40. c. Mat. 16 : 16. d. Mat.
9 : 15; I Tim. 1 : 15. e. 2 Cor. 5 : 19; I John 2 : 2. f. I Tim.
2 : 5. g. Deut. 18 : 15. h. Ps. 110 : 4; Hebr. 3 : 1. i. Jer.
33 : 15; Mat. 22 : 5. k. Mat. 17 : 5; 28 : 20; Gal. 6 : 4. l.
Deut. 18 : 15. m. Mat. 17 : 5. n. John 3 : 36. o. John 8 : 12.

ARTICLE X.

OF THE ABROGATION OF THE LAW AND OF LEGAL THINGS.

The intolerable burden of the Mosaic law (a), with
all its shadows and types, was brought to an end in Christ
(b) and removed from the midst of his people; namely,
the sacerdotal office (c) together with temple, altar, sacrifices and whatever was typically connected with the
sacerdotal office; and then the royal office (d) and whatever adhered to that office, as kingdom (e), sword (f),
punishment agreeable to the law (g), war, and, in one
word, all that which typically looked to Christ's person,
function or office and was a shadow and figure of him.

a. Acts 15 : 10; 2 Cor. 3 : 11, 14. b. Col. 2 : 16, 17. c. Hebr.
8 : 4, 5; 10 : 1. d. Luc. 1 : 28, 29; John 18 : 33; Mat. 20 : 25-
27; Marc. 10 : 43-45. e. Isa. 2 : 4; Mich. 4 : 3. f. Mat. 5 : 38.
g. Zech. 9 : 10.

ARTICLE XI.

OF THE PROPHETIC OFFICE OF CHRIST.

And so this true promised prophet (a) revealed to us the will of God and announced all things (b) which God demands and requires from the people of the New Testament (c). For as God through Moses and other prophets spoke with the people of the old covenant and declared to them his will; so in the last days he has spoken to us through this prophet (Son) (d), and has announced to us the mystery which had been silent from the times of ages (e), and has made us certain of those things (f) which were to be spoken later. He has preached the promised gospel (g), instituted and ordained sacraments, functions and offices, prescribed by God to that end and at the same time, both by life (i) and doctrine (k), has demonstrated what the law of Christians is (l), what the rule and norm of life, and what sort of life and (m) path [leads] to eternal life.

a. Deut. 18 : 15. b. John 17 : 8; Heb. 1 : 2. c. Deut. 18 : 18. d. Hebr. 1 : 2. e. Mat. 13 : 35. f. Heb. 3 : 5. g. Mat. 1 : 14. h. Mat. 26 : 25, 26; 28 : 19. i. Matt. 5 : 6, 7. k. John 10 : 25, 28; I Pet. 2 : 21; I John 2 : 6. l. Gal. 6 : 4. m. John 8 : 12.

ARTICLE XII.

OF THE SACERDOTAL OFFICE OF CHRIST.

Moreover, as the only high priest (a) and mediator of the New Testament (b) he prayed his Heavenly Father for all believers (c), even for those who affixed him to the cross and killed him (d). And at last, most obedient to the Father (e), he underwent the most extreme and severe passion and offered himself to the Father (f) on the cross through death as a sacrifice (g) and gift for an odor of good fragrance, and indeed a universal sacrifice, which is of perpetual power (h).

a. Heb. 5 : 16, 20. b. 2 Tim. 2 : 5. c. John 17 : 9, 11, 15, 23. d. Lu. 23 : 33. e. Phil. 2 : 8. f. Matt. 27 : 49; Mark 15 : 39. g. Eph. 5 : 2. h. Heb. 10 : 12.

ARTICLE XIII.

OF THE EFFICACY AND DIGNITY OF THE OBEDIENCE AND
UNIQUE SACRIFICE OF JESUS CHRIST.

We confess that the obedience of the Son of God (a),
his bitter passion (b), death (c), effusion of blood (d),
and unique sacrifice on the cross, is a reconciliation (e)
and satisfaction for us all and for the sins of the whole
world: and therefore we, through the blood of his cross,
have reconciliation (f) and peace with God (g), and
at the same time a firm hope and certitude (h) of entering into eternal life (i) if indeed we persevere in faith,
and with unshaken faith place hope in the promise of
the gospel.

a. Phil. 2 : 8. b. I Pet. 3 : 18. c. Rom. 4 : 25. d. Heb. 9 : 13,
14, 28. e. 2 Cor. 5 : 19; I John 2 : 2. f. Col. 1 : 14, 19, 20. g.
Eph. 1 : 13. h. Heb. 10 : 19. i. Col. 1 : 23.

ARTICLE XIV.

OF THE KINGLY OFFICE OF CHRIST.

Jesus Christ, our prophet (a) and priest (b), as the
promised and only spiritual heavenly king of the New
Testament, has erected a spiritual kingdom and has collected many spiritual and faithful men, whom he has
provided with spiritual and royal laws (e), and whom
according to the nature of his kingdom he has clothed
with spiritual arms (f). And in it he has ordained law
(g), justice, and their ministers. Of this kingdom he is
the preserver (i), defender, strong tower (k), firmness
and rock (l), and in it he will remain King, ruling unto
eternity (m).

a. Deut. 18 : 15. b. Heb. 3 : 1. c. Jer. 23 : 6; Zech. 9 : 9. d.
Matt. 18 : 1; 3 : 23. e. Jer. 33 : 15. f. 2 Cor. 10 : 4; Eph.
6 : 13. g. Jer. 23 : 5. h. I Cor. 12 : 28. i. Ps. 121 : 4, 5. k.
Ps. 18 : 3; 19 : 2. l. Acts 4 : 11. m. Luke 1 : 19.

ARTICLE XV.

OF THE BURIAL AND RESURRECTION OF CHRIST, AND THEIR
UTILITY.

Christ, after he was dead by the office of the cross
in the earth, and it had imposed an end on him, was

c

buried (a), a certain indication that he was dead, and on
the third day after death he rose again (b). Thus he
conquered death and at the same time made it certain
that he was Lord of death, and could not be held in its
chains (c), which to all believers has been a consolatory
certainty (d) that they are to be liberated and so finally
raised from the dead.

a. Matt. 27 : 58, 59; I Cor. 15 : 4. b. Matt. 28 : 6; Acts 10 : 40.
c. Acts 2 : 24. d. I Cor. 15 : 12, 13, 21.

ARTICLE XVI.

OF CHRIST'S ASCENT INTO THE HEAVENS AND HIS GLORIFICATION AFTER THE RESURRECTION.

For forty days after the resurrection, he was seen by
his disciples (a) and manifested himself to them often,
lest anyone should in anywise be doubtful of his resurrection; and at length, being received by a cloud (b), he
ascended into the heavens and entered into his glory (c),
leading captivity captive (d) and openly making a spec-
tacle of spoiled empires and powers (e), he triumphed
over them and sat down at the right hand of the Majesty
of God (f), made Lord and Christ (g), glorified in body
(h), exalted (i) and crowned with glory and honor (k),
and so is priest (l) and king over Mt. Zion forever (m).

a. Acts 1 : 3.   b. Mark 16 : 19; Acts 1 : 9.   c. Luke 24 : 25.
d. Eph. 4 : 8.   e. Col. 2 : 15.   f. Mark 16 : 19; Heb. 8 : 1.   g.
Acts 2 : 36.   h. John 17 : 5; Phil. 3 : 21.   i. Phil. 2 : 9.   k. Heb.
2 : 7.   l. Ps. 2 : 6.   m. Ps. 110 : 2-4.   Heb. 7 : 2, 3.

ARTICLE XVII.

WHAT CHRIST, ACCORDING TO HIS SACERDOTAL OFFICE, PERFORMS NOW IN GLORY.

The function or holy office of this glorified priest (a),
king (b), Lord (c), and Christ, in that heavenly and
glorified state, consists in this, that he directs, rules and
guards through his Holy Spirit (d) his holy church in the
world through the tempests and billows of the sea of this
world. For by virtue of his sacerdotal office, (as minister

(e) of the sanctuary and of that true tabernacle) he is
our Intercessor (f), Advocate (g), and Mediator (h)
with the Father. He teaches (i), consoles, strengthens
and baptizes us with the Holy Spirit and fire (k), with
his heavenly gifts and fiery virtues; he sups with faithful souls spiritually (l), and makes them partake of food
and drink vitalizing to souls (m), the efficacious fruit
and worth of his merits acquired for us through the cross,
and also that true and peculiarly necessary good which is
shadowed forth through the sacraments.

a. Heb. 8 : 1. b. Rev. 1 : 5. c. Acts 2 : 36. d. Acts 2 : 33. e.
Heb. 8 : 2. f. Rom. 8 : 34. g. I John 2 : 1. h. I Tim. 2 : 5. i.
John 14 : 26; 16 : 13. k. John 1 : 33; Matt. 3. 11. l. Rev.
3 : 20. m. John 6 : 32-34.

ARTICLE XVIII.

WHAT CHRIST, ACCORDING TO HIS ROYAL OFFICE, PERFORMS NOW IN GLORY.

According to his royal office in that heavenly state (a),
he rules the hearts of believers through his Holy Spirit
and Word (b). He receives them into his tutelage (c),
covers them with the shadow of his wings (d), clothes
them with spiritual arms (e) for the spiritual struggle
against all their enemies, the spirits of evil under heaven
and whatever in earth fights against them. That glorious,
omnipotent (f), heavenly king bears to them in anxiety
succors, frees them from the hand of enemies (g), helps
them (h) that they may overcome and come off victors,
and has prepared for them in heaven a crown of righteousness (i). And these are the Lord's freedmen, who
dwell in the House of the Lord, and upon the holy Mt.
Zion (k), who beat their carnal weapons, their swords
(l) into hoes and their spears into pruning hooks, who
do not bear the sword, who neither teach the art of war
nor give assent to carnal wars.

a. Ps. 2 : 9. b. Rom. 8 : 11, 14. c. John 10 : 28. d. Matt.
23 : 36. e. 2 Cor. 10 : 4; Eph. 6 : 12, 13. f. Matt. 28 : 18. g.
Luke 1 : 69. h. 2 Cor. 2 : 16. i. 2 Tim. 4 : 8; Rev. 2 : 10. k.
Heb. 12 : 22. l. Isa. 2 : 4; Mich. 4 : 2, 3; 2 Cor. 10 : 4.

ARTICLE XIX.

OF THE KNOWLEDGE OF CHRIST ACCORDING TO THE SPIRIT AND ITS NECESSITY.

From that which has now been said concerning the ascension of Christ into heaven, his glorification, offices and functions in glory, we believe and confess that Christ must be confessed, not only according to the flesh (a), or literally according to history, as his holy incarnation, generation, revelation or appearance in the flesh, passion, death, cross and whatever refers to him; but we must ascend higher (b), know and acknowledge Christ according to the spirit, in his exaltation and glorification (c), according to his holy office in glory (d): what the holy scripture pronounces concerning all these things must be embraced with a faithful heart; and with earnest prayers God must be supplicated, that the knowledge of Christ and his holy office according to the spirit, through his love and kindness, may be consummated in us; *indeed* that the form and image of Christ (e) through him may be born and erected in us, that he may manifest himself to us (f), may live in us (g), may walk (h), teach (i), preach, that miracles done by him according to the flesh, he may consummate in us according to the spirit, heal us from the sickness of souls (k), from deafness, blindness, leprosy, impurity, sin and death; that he may baptize and wash us with the Spirit and fire (m), that he may nourish (n) and restore us (o) with heavenly food and drink and may make us partakers of his divine nature (p); that, indeed through his virtue the old man in us (q) may be crucified with him, so as to have communion with his sufferings and conformity to his death (r); and that through him we may rise and be restored to a new life (s) and may experience the power of his resurrection (t): And all these things for the glory and honor of God, our heavenly Father. This we call knowing Christ according to the spirit; without which knowledge, concerning which our conscience ought to be firmly persuaded, the knowledge of Christ according to the flesh does not at all suffice for obtaining salvation.

a. 2 Cor. 5 : 16.   b. Phil. 3 : 20; Col. 3. 1.   c. Phil. 2 : 9; John 17 : 5.   d. Heb. 8 : 1.   e. Matt. 12 : 50; Gal. 4 : 19; James 1 : 18. f. John 14 : 21.   g. Eph. 3 : 17; John 14 : 23.   h. 2 Cor. 6 : 16. i. Rev. 3 : 20.   k. Isa. 35 : 5.   l. Matt. 9 : 12; Isa. 53 : 4, 5. m. Matt. 3 : 11.   n. Eph. 5 : 30; John 6 : 48-50.   o. I Cor. 12 : 13.   p. 2 Pet. 3 : 4.   q. Rom. 6 : 5.   r. Phil. 3 : 10.   s. Rom. 6 : 5.   t. Phil. 3 : 10.   v. 2 Cor. 5 : 16, 17.

ARTICLE XX.

OF TRUE SAVING FAITH.

All goods and benefits which Jesus Christ, through his merits, has acquired for the salvation of sinners we graciously enjoy through true and living faith (a), which operates through love (b). This faith is a most certain cognition or knowledge acquired through the grace of God from the sacred scriptures, concerning God (c), concerning Christ and other heavenly things, the cognition and persuasion of which is necessary to salvation; and these things ought to be accompanied with the love of God (d) and with firm confidence in one God (e), who as a kind loving heavenly Father, will give and donate to us all things which, in respect of body and soul, are useful and effective for salvation (f), on account of Christ and his merits.

a. John 3 : 19, 36; Acts 15 : 2; Rom. 5 : 1, 2.   b. Gal. 5 : 6; Rom. 10.   c. John 17 : 3.   d. Gal. 5 : 6.   e. Heb. 11 : 1.   f. Matt. 7 : 12; John 16 : 23.

ARTICLE XXI.

OF JUSTIFICATION.

Through living faith (a) of this kind we acquire true righteousness (b), that is (c), pardon or remission of all our past, as well as present, sins (d), on account of the poured out blood of Jesus Christ; as also true righteousness which through Jesus, the Holy Spirit co-operating, is abundantly poured out upon or into us: moreover, as out of evil (g), carnal, avaricious, proud men, we are made good, spiritual, liberal, humble, and even out of unjust men, truly just. And this righteousness has its origin in regeneration.

a. Gal. 5 : 6. b. Rom. 5 : 1. c. Ps. 32 : 1. d. I John 1 : 7. e.
I Cor. 6 : 11; Rom. 4 : 25; I John 3 : 7. f. Tit. 3 : 5, 6. g.
I Cor. 6 : 11.

ARTICLE XXII.

OF REGENERATION.

Regeneration is a certain divine quality in the mind of
a man truly come to himself, an erection of the image of
God in man (a), a renovation of the mind or soul (b),
a true illumination of the mind with the knowledge of
the truth (c), bringing with it a change of will and of
carnal desires and lusts, a sincere mortification of internal
wickedness (d) and of the old man delighting himself in
lust, wickedness and sin: It is, moreover, a vivification
which manifests itself in an honest life according to God,
in true goodness, justice and holiness. It is a removal of
the stony heart (e), full of vanity, stolidity (f), blindness,
ignorance, sin and perverse pleasures, and, on the contrary, is the gracious gift of the promised heart of flesh
(g), replete with the law of God, light (h), sight, wisdom,
understanding, virtue and holy desires. This regeneration has its rise from God (i) through Christ (k). The
medium or instrument through which it is generated
in us, is the Holy Spirit (l) with all his fiery virtues,
apart from any co-operation of any creature. Here concerning the regenerate, we affirm that they are born not
out of anything whatsoever which the creature does, but
from God (m); and by it we become children of God
(n), divine, heavenly and spiritually minded, just and
holy. We believe and teach that this regeneration is
necessary to salvation according to the words of Christ:
(o) " Verily, verily I say to thee, except a man be born
again he cannot see the kingdom of God "; and " Except
a man be born of water and the Spirit, he cannot enter
the kingdom of God."

a. Eph. 4 : 24; Col. 3 : 9, 10. b. Rom. 12 : 2; Eph. 4 : 23. c.
John 8 : 32. d. Eph. 4 : 22-24; Col. 3 : 9, 10. e. Eze. 36 : 26. f.
Eph. 4 : 17, 18. g. Eze. 36 : 26. h. Jer. 31 : 33. Heb. 8 : 10.
i. John 8 : 47; I John 4 : 1, 2, 6, 7. k. I Pet. 1 : 3, 23; James
1 : 18. l. John 3 : 5, 6. m. John 1 : 13; I John 3 : 9. n. John
1 : 12. o. John 3 : 3, 5.

ARTICLE XXIII.

OF GOOD WORKS.

A man, in this way regenerated and justified by God through Christ, lives through love (a) (which is poured out into his heart (b) through the Holy Spirit) with joy and gladness (c), in all good works, according to the laws and precepts and customs enjoined on him by God through Christ. He watches, gives thanks (d) and blesses God (e) with a pure heart and holy life, for all his benefits and especially for those which pertain to the soul. Such are holy plants of the Lord (f), trees of justice who worship God with good works (g) and ardently expect the blessed remuneration promised them by God (h), through his abundant goodness (i).

a. John 14 : 23; Gal. 5. b. Rom. 5. c. Ps. 1 : 2; 10 : 2. d. Ps. 103 : 1. e. Matt. 5 : 8. f. Isa. 61 : 3. g. Matt. 5 : 16. h. Eph. 2 : 7. i. Luke 6 : 23; I Cor. 3 : 14.

ARTICLE XXIV.

OF THE CHURCH.

Such believing and regenerated men, dispersed throughout the whole earth (a), are the true people of God or Church of Jesus Christ in the earth, which he loved (b) and for which he gave himself up that he might sanctify it, which indeed he did sanctify through the laver, in the word of life. Of this church (c) Jesus Christ is the Foundation, Head (d), Shepherd (e), Leader (f), Lord (g), King, and Master (h). This alone is his adored (i) spouse (k), holy body, flock (l), and people and through regeneration (m) his flesh and bones. But even though a huge multitude of deceivers and hypocrites are hidden and live among this church (n), yet those alone who in Christ are regenerated and sanctified are true members of Christ's body (o), and for this reason heirs of his blessed promises of which great benefits the deceivers and hypocrites, on account of their own blame and wickedness, are deprived.

a. Matt. 8 : 11; 24 : 3; Rev. 7 : 9. b. Eph. 5 : 25. c. I Cor. 3 : 11. d. Eph. 5 : 23. e. John 10 : 11. f. Phil. 2 : 11. g. Matt. 21 : 5. h. John 13 : 15. i. John 3 : 29; Rev. 21 : 2. k. Eph. 5 : 23. l. John 10 : 16. m. Eph. 5 : 30. n. Matt. 13 : 24, &c. o. 2. Cor. 5 : 17. p. Luke 14 : 24.

ARTICLE XXV.

OF THE MINISTRIES TO BE EXERCISED IN THE CHURCH.

In this his holy church Christ has ordained an evangelical ministry, namely, teaching of the divine word (a), use of the holy sacraments, and the care of the poor (b), as also ministers for performing these ministries: and moreover the exercise of fraternal admonition (c), punishment and finally removal of those who persevere in impenitence: which ordinances, originating in the word of God, are to be performed only according to the meaning of the same word (d).

a. Matt. 28 : 19; Mark 16 : 15. b. Acts 6 : 2, 3, 4. c. Matt. 18 : 15; Luke 17 : 3. d. Matt. 17 : 5.

ARTICLE XXVI.

OF THE ORDER WHICH IS TO BE OBSERVED IN THE CHURCH ABOUT MINISTRIES.

Just as the body consists of divers members and each member performs its own work, for no member is [in turn] hand, eye or foot; in the same way (a) things are done in the Church of God. For although every believer is a member of the body of Christ, not everyone is for that reason a teacher, bishop or deacon: but those only who (b) have been set apart to those ministries according to order. Wherefore the administrations of those functions or offices do not pertain to every one, but to the ordained.

a. Rom. 12 : 4; I Cor. 12 : 12. b. Heb. 5 : 7.

ARTICLE XXVII.

HOW ELECTION TO THOSE MINISTRIES IS ACCOMPLISHED.

Calling or election to the aforesaid ministries is accomplished through the ministers of the church and its members conjointly (a), and by invocation of the name of God: for God alone knows hearts, walks in the midst of the believers (b), who are congregated in his name, and through his Holy Spirit directs their intellects and minds so that through them he manifests and calls forth such as he knows will be useful to his church.

, a. Acts 1 : 21; 14 : 2. b. Matt. 18 : 19, 20.

ARTICLE XXVIII.

OF CONFIRMATION TO THE AFORESAID MINISTRIES.

But although the election and call aforesaid are accomplished in the method [aforesaid], yet confirmation in the ministry itself is performed by the elders of the people in the presence of the church (a) and that for the most part by the imposition of hands.

a. Acts 6 : 6; 13 : 3; I Tim. 4 : 14; 2 Tim. 1 : 7.

ARTICLE XXIX.

OF THE DOCTRINE AND DOCTRINAL BOOKS OF THE SAME MINISTERS.

The doctrine which ordained ministers propose to the people ought to be or to agree with that which Jesus Christ brought from heaven (a), which he taught the people by word and work, that is, in doctrine and life, and which the apostles of Christ, at the mandate and according to the spirit of Christ, announced (c). It (as much as is necessary to us for salvation (d) is contained in the books of the New Testament to which we join all that which is found in the canonical books of the Old Testament and which is consonant with the doctrine of Christ and his Apostles and in accord with the administration of his spiritual kingdom.

a. Heb. 2 : 3; 12 : 25. b. Acts 1 : 1. c. Matt. 28 : 19; Mark 16 : 15. d. Deut. 4 : 1, 2; 2 Tim. 3 : 16.

ARTICLE XXX.

OF THE SACRAMENTS.

Jesus Christ instituted in his church two sacraments (whose administration he attached to the teaching office), namely, Holy Baptism (a) and the Holy Supper (b). These are external and visible actions, and signs of the immense goodness of God toward us; placing before our eyes, on the part of God, the internal and spiritual action which God accomplishes (c) through Christ (the Holy Spirit co-operating) by regenerating, justifying, spiritually nourishing and sustaining the souls which repent and believe (d); we on our part, by the same means, confess religion, repentance (e), faith (f) and our obedience (g) by earnestly directing our conscience to the service (or worship) of God.

a. Matt. 28 : 19; Mark 16 : 15. b. Matt. 26 : 25; Luc. 22 : 19. c. Tit. 3 : 5. d. Eph. 5 : 29; Rev. 3 : 23. e. Acts 2 : 38. f. Acts 8 : 36. g. Matt. 3 : 15.

ARTICLE XXXI.

OF EXTERNAL BAPTISM.

Holy Baptism is an external, visible and evangelical action, in which, according to Christ's precept (a) and the practice of the apostles (b), for a holy end (c), are baptized with water in the name of the Father and of the Son and of the Holy Spirit, those who hear, believe and freely receive in a penitent heart the doctrine of the holy gospel (d); for such Christ commanded to be baptized, but by no means infants.

a. I Pet. 3 : 21. b. Matt. 28 : 19; Mark 16 : 15. c. Acts 2 : 38, 41; 8 : 11, 36, 37; 10 : 45, 48; 16 : 15, 32-34; 18 : 8; 19 : 5. d. Matt. 3 : 15; Acts 2 : 38; Rom. 6 : 3, 4; Col. 2 : 12.

ARTICLE XXXII.

WHAT BAPTISM SIGNIFIES INTERNALLY.

The whole action of external, visible baptism places before our eyes, testifies and signifies that Jesus Christ baptizes internally (a) in a laver of regeneration (b) and renewing of the Holy Spirit, the penitent and believing man: washing away, through the virtue and merits of his poured out blood, all the spots and sins of the soul (c) and through the virtue and operation of the Holy Spirit, which is a true, heavenly (d), spiritual and living water, [washing away] the internal wickedness of the soul (e) and renders it heavenly (f), spiritual (g) and living (h) in true righteousness and goodness. Moreover baptism directs us to Christ and his holy office by which in glory he performs that which he places before our eyes, and testifies concerning its consummation in the hearts of believers and admonishes us that we should not cleave to external things, but by holy prayers ascend into heaven and ask from Christ the good indicated through it [baptism] (i): a good which the Lord Jesus graciously concedes and increases in the hearts of those who by true faith become partakers of the sacraments.

a. Matt. 3 : 11; John 1 : 33. b. Eph. 5 : 26; Tit. 3 : 5. c. I John 1 : 7. d. Isa. 44 : 3; Eze. 36 : 27; Joel 2 : 28; John 7 : 38. e. I Cor. 6 : 11; Tit. 3 : 5-7. f. Phil. 3 : 20. g. Rom. 8 : 9. h. Eph. 2 : 4, 5. i. John 7 : 31.

ARTICLE XXXIII.

OF THE HOLY SUPPER.

The Holy Supper (as also Baptism) is an external and visible evangelical action in which, according to the precepts of Christ (a), and the usage of the Apostles (b), for a holy end (c), we partake of bread and wine. The bread is broken, the wine is poured out and by them are sustained those who, believing, are baptized according to the institution of Christ. The bread is eaten by them, the wine is drunk. Thus Christ's death and bitter suffering are proclaimed (d), and all these things are done in commemoration of him. (e).

a. Luke 22 : 19. b. Acts 2 : 42; 20 : 11; I Cor. 11 : 22. c. I Cor. 10 : 15; 11 : 28. d. I Cor. 11 : 25. e. Luke 22 : 19; I Cor. 11 : 24.

ARTICLE XXXIV.

WHAT THE HOLY SUPPER SIGNIFIES.

The whole action of the external and visible supper places before our eyes, testifies and signifies that Christ's holy body was broken on the cross (a) and his holy blood poured out (b), for the remission of our sins; that he is now glorified in heaven, is the living bread, food and drink of our souls (c). It places before our eyes Christ's office or ministry in glory while he sups spiritually with believing souls (d) by nourishing and feeding souls with spiritual food (e). Through it we are taught, in that external action, to elevate our hearts on high with holy supplications (f), and to seek from Christ the true and highest good shadowed forth in this supper; (g) and finally it exhorts us to give thanks to God and to exercise unity and love among ourselves (h).

a. Luke 22 : 19; I Cor. 11 : 23. b. Mark 14 : 24. c. John 6 : 51, 55. d. Rev. 3 : 20. e. Eph. 5 : 29. f. Col. 3 : 1, 2. g. I Cor. 10 : 16. h. I Cor. 10 : 17.

ARTICLE XXXV.

OF EXCOMMUNICATION.

Ecclesiastical discipline or extreme punishment is likewise an external action among believers, by which an impenitent sinner, after Christian conversation (a) and sufficient admonition, is excluded from the communion of God and his saints, on account of sins; and against him the wrath and anger of God (until he comes to himself and amends) is denounced. By which external ecclesiastical exclusion is shown how God has already beforehand dealt with the excluded one on account of his sins, or judged concerning him. With God, therefore, the judgment upon the fallen sinner is antecedent (b), but with the church subsequent judgment. Wherefore special care must be taken, that no one be condemned in the church who has not beforehand been condemned by the word of God.

a. Matt. 18 : 15-18; I Cor. 5 : 2, 12. b. John 5 : 22; 12 : 48.

ARTICLE XXXVI.

OF WITHDRAWAL FROM PERVERSE APOSTATES.

Those excluded from the church are by no means admitted (as long as they persevere in sins) to the communion of the Holy Supper or other ecclesiastical actions, but we deprive them of these and all other privileges by which any communion, fraternity or spiritual participation in sacred things is signified. And since the life and daily conversation of wicked and perverse men offends and is hurtful (a), and not infrequently a stumbling block to the good, and subjects them to calumny; for these reasons, they withdraw themselves from them, nor do they wish to have any communion with them, their actions, words or works, lest their pure mind be polluted and contaminated and the name of God blasphemed: and all this in this manner, in accordance with the word of God as supreme law; the married do not separate themselves nor do they withdraw themselves from marital privileges, and so nothing is done in this matter which is contrary to love, mercy, Christian justice, want, promises and other similar things.

a. I Cor. 5 : 5; 2 Tim. 2 : 10, 17, 18; 2 Tim. 3 : 10; Tit. 3 : 10.

ARTICLE XXXVII.

OF THE OFFICE OF CIVIL MAGISTRATE.

Government or the civil Magistrate is a necessary ordinance of God (a), instituted for the government of common human society and the preservation of natural life and civil good, for the defense of the good and the punishment of the evil. We acknowledge, the word of God obliging us, that it is our duty to reverence magistracy (b) and to show to it honor and obedience in all things which are not contrary to the word of God (c). It is our duty to pray the omnipotent God for them (d), and to give thanks to him for good and just magistrates and without murmuring to pay just tribute and customs (e). This civil government the Lord Jesus did not institute in his spiritual kingdom, the church of the New Testament,

nor did he join it to the offices of his church (f) : nor
did he call his disciples or followers to royal, ducal or
other power; nor did he teach that they should seize it
and rule in a lordly manner; much less did he give to the
members of his church the law (g), agreeable to such
office or dominion: but everywhere they are called away
from it (which voice heard from heaven (h) ought to
be heeded) to the imitation of his harmless life (i) and
his footsteps bearing the cross (k), and in which nothing
is less in evidence than an earthly kingdom, power and
sword. When all these things are carefully weighed (and
moreover not a few things are joined with the office of
civil magistracy, as waging war, depriving enemies of
goods and life, etc., which [do not agree with] the lives
of Christians who ought to be dead to the world), they
agree either badly or plainly not at all, hence we withdraw
ourselves from such offices and administrations. And yet
we do not wish that just and moderate power should in
any manner be despised or condemned, but that it should
be truly esteemed, as in the words of Paul (l), the Holy
Spirit dictating, it ought to be esteemed.

a. Rom. 13 : 1, 3, 4, 6. b. Tit. 3 : 1; I Pet. 2 : 13, 17. c. Acts
4 : 19. d. Jer. 29 : 7; I Tim. 2 : 1, 2. e. Matt. 22 : 17; Rom.
13 : 7. f. I Cor. 12 : 28; Eph. 4 : 11. g. Matt. 20 : 25-28;
Luke 22 : 25-27. h. Matt. 17 : 5. i. John 8 : 12; 10 : 27. k.
Heb. 12 : 2, 3; I Pet. 2 : 21-23. l. Rom. 13 : 1-3.

ARTICLE XXXVIII.

OF THE OATH.

Jesus Christ, King and Lawgiver (a) of the New
Testament, has forbidden to Christians every oath (b),
and for this reason all oaths are unlawful to the believers
of the New Testament.

a. Matt. 28 : 20; Gal. 6 : 4. b. Matt. 5 : 34; James 5 : 10.

ARTICLE XXXIX.

OF MARRIAGE.

Marriage we profess to be an ordinance of God which
must be entered into according to the primal institution

(a) ; that each man have his own only wife (b) and each woman her own and one husband. This marriage cannot be dissolved except for the cause of adultery (c). Neither do we think it allowable that any of us should enter into marriage outside the Church of God, with wicked, unbelieving or carnal men (d), and we condemn that (as other sins) by the word of God, the state of the time and the reason of things.

a. Gen. 2 : 22; Matt. 19 : 4. b. I Cor. 7 : 2; Eph. 5 : 31. c. Matt. 19 : 9. d. Deut. 7 : 3; I Cor. 7 : 39.

ARTICLE XL.

OF CHRIST'S RETURN, OF THE RESURRECTION OF THE DEAD, AND OF THE LAST JUDGMENT.

Lastly, we believe and teach that Jesus Christ, our glorious King and Lord, visibly just as he ascended (a), will return from heaven (b) with power and great glory, and with him all the holy angels (c), that he may be glorified in his saints (d) and may be admired by all believers, and will manifest himself as the Judge of the living and the dead (e). At that time (f) all men, just and unjust, who have lived upon the earth and have died, will rise from the dead (with incorruption (g)) and live again, their souls being reunited with their own bodies in which they had lived evilly or well (h). But those who are alive in that day and have not died, changed in a moment and in the twinkling of an eye, will put on incorruption, (i) and the whole multitude of the human race will stand before the tribunal of Christ (k) to report (1) what each one has done in the body according to that which he has done whether good or evil. Then Jesus will separate the sheep from the goats as a shepherd separates the sheep from the goats (m), and will place the sheep on his right hand but the goats on the left (n), and will give sentence. The just who have lived here holily and have exercised all the works of charity and mercy (o), as the husband (p) of that Christian multitude, he will take to himself. They will enter with him into eternal life (q) and celestial joy and glory, where all

will always be with the Lord (r) and will possess forever
that kingdom (s) which God the Father had prepared for
them from the beginning of the world. But the unrighteous who have not known God (t) nor regarded the
gospel of our Lord Jesus Christ, will be condemned to
eternal fire (v), which was prepared for the Devil and
his angels, and there they will undergo sorrow and eternal
perdition (x), from the face of the Lord and the glory
of his power.

Preserve us, omnipotent God, full of grace and mercy,
from the punishment of the impious; and concede to us
grace and gifts for a holy life and happy death and a
joyous resurrection with all believers. Amen.

a. Acts 1 : 11. b. Matt. 24 : 30; 2 Thess. 1 : 7. c. Matt. 25 :
31. d. 2 Thess. 1 : 10. e. Acts 10 : 42; 2 Tim. 4 : 1. f. Matt.
25 : 32; John 5 : 28. g. I Cor. 15 : 42. h. 2 Cor. 5 : 10. i. I
Cor. 15 : 51, 52. k. Matt. 25 : 32. l. 2 Cor. 5 : 10. m. Matt.
25 : 32. n. Matt. 25 : 47. o. Matt. 25 : 35, 36, 37, 38. p. Matt.
25 : 10. q. John 5 : 29; Matt. 25 : 47. r. I Thess. 4 : 17. s.
Matt. 25 : 34. t. 2 Thess. 1 : 8. v. Matt. 25 : 42. x. Isa. 2 : 10;
2 Thess. 1 : 9.

II. Other Confessions

Other Mennonite Confessions were drawn up in the latter part of the sixteenth and early in the seventeenth centuries, chiefly by the Dutch Mennonites, in the Dutch language. They were, for the most part, union documents
drawn up in an effort to heal the schisms that so griev-
ously afflicted the body.

1. The Concept of Cologne, drawn up May 1, 1591, and
signed by the chief ministers of the Frisian and High German Mennonites. Schyn, " *Historia,*" II, 79.

2. The next Confession was drawn up at Amsterdam,
September 27, 1625, and was called " The Olive Branch."
It was an attempt to give a scriptural answer to the question, " What are the fundamental and unmistakable
marks " by which the children of God may be known? It
is found in a condensed Latin form in Schyn II, 85f, and

in English, translated directly from the Dutch in Van Braght's "Martyrs' Mirror," pp. 26-32.

3. A Confession treating only of the one God, the Father, Son, and Holy Spirit, and of the Incarnation of the Son of God, was presented to the deputies of Holland October 8, 1626, and was accepted by them as the basis of the policy of complete toleration of the Mennonites. Schyn, "*Historia*," etc., I, 79-85.

4. Another Confession in twenty-one articles was drawn up at Amsterdam, October 7, 1630, called "A Brief Confession of Faith and of the Principal Articles of the Christian Religion." Latin in full in Schyn II, 87-114; English translated from the Dutch in Van Braght, 32-36.

5. The Confession in use at present. The most important of all the Mennonite Confessions was drawn up in eighteen articles at a peace convention held in Dort, April 21, 1632, and was signed by fifty-one ministers, representing the Mennonite churches in sixteen of the leading cities of the Netherlands, and two from the upper country. It was afterward adopted by the German and French Mennonites of the Palatinate and Alsace and translated into their tongues. It was later translated into English and is still, with some verbal changes, the Confession of the Mennonites of America, by whom it is diligently circulated. It is found in Van Braght's "Martyrs' Mirror," pp. 36-42.

These later Mennonite Confessions had no direct influence on Baptist Confessions and, therefore, are not reproduced.

D

Part Three

THE ENGLISH BAPTISTS

English Baptists, from the beginning of their history, have been divided on the basis of the two great types of theology into two parties, Calvinistic and Arminian. With the exception of the Anabaptists, the theology of all parties of reformers was Augustinian, emphasizing predestination and personal election, a limited atonement, the final perseverance of the saints, and related doctrines. But in the beginning of the seventeenth century there was rising in the Netherlands a new theology, emphasizing the freedom of the will, the universality of the atonement, conditional election, possible apostasy, and related doctrines. This theology began as a criticism of Calvinism as it then existed in the Netherlands, and produced a tremendous sensation, little short of a national revolution. The English Baptists arose in the Netherlands, and possibly because of their contact with this new theology and their affinity with the Anabaptists or Mennonites, who held this type of doctrine, they adopted a theology which, from its leading representative, James Arminius, soon came to be known as Arminianism. Because they believed in a universal or general atonement they came to be known as General Baptists. Of the two parties or wings of English Baptists priority of origin belongs, therefore, to the Arminians, and these we shall study first. The other party, or wing, will be considered later. Of course, it will be understood that the whole matter is viewed historically.

50

I. Arminian or General Baptist Confessions

1. first group

No Baptist Confession before 1644, and none of the General Baptist Confessions till that of 1660, specifies immersion or dipping as the mode of baptism, and it is doubtful if the confessions prior to these dates ought to be called Baptist; but such is the custom, and it is followed here.

Some English Puritans came, in the latter part of the sixteenth century, to regard the English Church as unscriptural, hopelessly corrupt, and incapable of reform. They, therefore, left it and set up independent congregations, Calvinistic in theology and life, but congregational and democratic in church government. These views first appeared in eastern England where there had been Dutch Anabaptists for nearly half a century, to whose influence they may have been in some measure due. At any rate, about 1580, under the leadership of Robert Browne, the first independent congregation of this type was set up at Norwich. Similar congregations were soon gathered at London, Gainsborough, Scrooby, and possibly elsewhere soon afterward. The rigorous measures of the English government broke up all these bodies of Independents, or Brownists, as they were sometimes called. For safety and freedom most of them fled to the Netherlands. Browne and some of his followers went to Middleburg, whence he soon returned to England and ultimately reunited with the English Church. Barrow, Greenwood, and Penry, leaders of the London congregation, were hanged in 1593, and the congregation was broken up, a part fleeing to Amsterdam, where they again set up the congregation. In 1606 or the following year, John Smyth, Thomas Helwys, John Morton, and the Gainsborough congregation also fled to Amsterdam, where they set up a second congregation with John Smyth as pastor. In 1608, John Robinson, William Bradford, William Brewster, and the Scrooby congregation fled to Amsterdam, and thence in 1609 to Leyden, whence in 1620 a part came to America in the Mayflower and laid the foundation of New England. All these were what are now called Congregational churches. In Amsterdam they came in contact with the Anabaptists, or Mennonites, with whom they already had much in common. Both were suffering for their views, while they aspired largely for the same thing—a pure church of believers. These circumstances doubtless. drew the two parties together from the first. As early as 1606 we learn that " divers of them [English Independents in the Netherlands] fell into the errors of Anabaptism." In 1608 or 1609 John Smyth, the pastor of the second church at Amsterdam, and a large part of his congregation had come to recognize the unscripturalness of infant baptism and had determined to adopt believers' baptism. It might have been expected that they would go for baptism to the Mennonites with whom they had so much in common. But there were important differences about such questions as the oath, war, civil magistracy, and other things, and consequently these Englishmen began baptism anew. Smyth, apparently, baptized himself (probably by affusion, as was the custom of both the English Independents and the Dutch Mennonites at this time), and then some forty-one others, thus organizing the first English Baptist or Anabaptist church out of members of the second Congregational Church at Amsterdam. Along with infant baptism they also gave up Calvinistic theology and accepted the Arminian system, the type, as we have seen, which had been held from the first by the Anabaptists, and which was now greatly agitating the Netherlands.

Smyth soon came to feel that he had acted without Scriptural warrant in instituting baptism anew when the Mennonites, which he now regarded as a true church of Christ, were at hand to administer the ordinance. He did not believe they had succession from the apostles, for he distinctly asserts that succession had been " broken off "; nor did he believe succession was in any sense necessary to the existence of a true church or the validity of baptism. He held that one would be warranted in beginning baptism anew if there were no true church in existence, or at hand, to administer the ordinance; but where a true church existed, it was the duty of the individual to make application to it. He and some others, therefore, applied to the Mennonites for admission to their communion.[1] Helwys, Morton, and other members of his church disagreed with their pastor on this point, and the church was disrupted about 1609. Smyth and his party stood nearer the Mennonites, believing their own baptism to be unscriptural; Helwys and his party desired to be on a friendly footing with the Mennonites, but asserted the validity of their own baptism, and proposed to preserve their independent organization and identity. Smyth died August, 1612, and his party seem to have been absorbed by the Mennonites; Helwys and his party, in 1612, returned to England, but continued a friendly correspondence with the Mennonites, while they preserved their own identity and founded the General Baptists in England. The controversy between the two parties and the desire of both to retain the friendship of the Mennonites, produced the first group of General Baptist Confessions. These were all drawn up in the Netherlands, but their exact dates, origin, history, and relations are not entirely clear in most cases. Some of them were

---

[1] " Smyth's Retraction," in Barclay's Inner Life. Appendix to Chap. VI, p. 5.

never published, and none of them, it is likely, had any
wide circulation, since the entire Baptist body was at
this time very small.

1. What is perhaps the earliest of this group is a
brief Confession, consisting of twenty articles in Latin
(never printed) signed by John Smyth. It has been
supposed that this Confession was submitted by Smyth
and his party to the Mennonite church of Amsterdam as
the basis for their application for membership in that
body, though there is nothing in the manuscript to justify
the supposition. (Translated in Evans' " Early English
Baptists," I, 253f.)

2. Another Confession consisted of thirty-eight articles
in Dutch, signed by Smyth and forty-one others. It was
drawn up by Hans de Ries, a Mennonite; was then signed
by the English applicants for membership and sent by
Ries to other Mennonite churches, with the request for
advice as to whether the English ought to be received on
that basis. Recently it has been translated into English by
Professor Müller, and appears in Evans I, 45f. It is in
complete accord with the peculiar tenets of the Mennonites and probably did not properly represent the views
of the majority of the English General Baptists as to
oaths, war, civil magistracy, etc. It is almost a reproduction of the Confession of Ries and Gerrits, of 1580 (see
p. 26), with two articles, XIX and XXII, omitted. Prof.
Müller's translation follows:

A SHORT CONFESSION OF FAITH.

Article 1. We believe, through the power and instruction of the Holy Scriptures that there is one only God,
who is a Spirit, eternal, incomprehensible, infinite, almighty, merciful, righteous, perfectly wise, only good,
and only fountain of life and all goodness, the Creator of
heaven and earth, things visible and invisible.

2. This only God in the Holy Scriptures is manifested and revealed in Father, Son, and Holy Ghost, being three, and nevertheless but one God.

3. The Father is the original and the beginning of all things who hath begotten his Son from everlasting before all creation. That Son is the everlasting Word of the Father, and his wisdom. The Holy Ghost is his virtue, power, and might, proceeding from the Father and the Son. These three are not divided, nor separated in essence, nature, property, eternity, power, glory or excellency.

4. This only God hath created man good, according to his image and likeness, to a good and happy estate, and in him all men to the same blessed end. The first man was* fallen into sin and wrath and was again by God, through a sweet comfortable promise, restored and affirmed to everlasting life, with all those that were guilty through him so that none of his posterity (by reason of this institution) are guilty, sinful, or born in original sin.

5. Man being created good, and continuing in goodness, had the ability, the spirit of wickedness tempting him, freely to obey, assent, or reject the propounded evil: man being fallen and consisting (*sic*) in evil, had the ability, the T—himself moving freely to obey, assent or reject the propounded good; for as he through free power to the choice of evil, obeyed and affirmed that evil; so did he through free power to the choice of good, obey and reassent that propounded good. This last power or ability remaineth in all his posterity.

6. God hath before all time foreseen and foreknown all things, both good and evil, whether past, present, or to come. Now, as he is the only perfect goodness, and the very fountain of life itself, so is he the only author, original, and maker of such good things as are good, holy, pure, and of nature like unto him; but not of sin, or damnable uncleanness. He forbiddeth the evil, he forewarneth to obey evil, and threateneth the evil doer: he is the permitter and punisher. But evil men, through free choice of all sin and wickedness, together with the spirit of wickedness which ruleth in them, are the authors,

* Interlined.

originals, and makers of all sin, and so worthy the punishment.

7. The causes and ground, therefore, of man's destruction and damnation, are the man's free choice of darkness or sin, and living therein. Destruction, therefore, cometh out of himself, but not from the good Creator. For being perfect goodness and love itself (following the nature of love and perfect goodness) he willeth the health, good, and happiness of his creatures; therefore hath he predestinated that none of them should be condemned, nor ordained, or will the sinner, or means whereby they should be brought to damnation: yea, much more (seeing he hath no delight in any man's destruction, nor willing that any man perish, but that all men should be saved or blessed) hath he created them all to a happy end in Christ, hath foreseen and ordained in him a medicine of life for all their sins, and hath willed that all people or creatures, through the preaching of the gospel, should have these tidings published and declared unto them; now all they that with penitence and faithful hearts receive and embrace the gracious benefits of God, manifested in Christ, for the reconciliation of the world, they are and continue the elect which God hath ordained before the foundation of the world, to make partakers of his kingdom and glory. But they which despise and contemn this proffered grace of God, which love the darkness more than the light, persevere in impenitence and unbelief, they make themselves unworthy of blessedness, and are rejected, excluded from the end whereto they were created and ordained in Christ, and shall not taste forever of the Supper of the Lord, to which they were invited.

8. The purpose which God, before the foundation of the world, had for the reconciliation of the world (which he saw would fall into wrath and want of grace), he hath in the fulness of time accomplished; and for this purpose hath sent out of heaven his everlasting Word, or Son, for the fulfilling of the promises made unto the fathers and hath caused him to become flesh * . . in the womb of the holy virgin (called Mary) by his word, and power,

---

* Word wanting.

and the working of the Holy Ghost. Not that the essence of God, the eternal Word, or any part thereof, is changed into a visible mortal flesh or man, ceasing to be Spirit, God, or God's essence; but that he, the everlasting Son of God, continuing that he was before, namely, God or Spirit, became what he was not, that is, flesh or man; and he is one person true God and man, born of Mary, being visibly and invisibly, inwardly and outwardly, the true Son of the living God.

9. This Person, God and Man, the Son of the living God, is come into the world to save sinners, or to reconcile the sinful world to God the Father: therefore now acknowledge him to be the only Mediator, King, Priest and Prophet, Lawgiver and Teacher, which God hath promised to send into the world, whom we must trust, believe, and follow.

10. In him is fulfilled, and by him is taken away, an intolerable burden of the law of Moses, even all the shadows and figures; as, namely, the priesthood, temple, altar, sacrifice; also the kingly office, kingdom, sword, revenge appointed by the law, battle and whatsoever was a figure of his person or office, so thereof a shadow or representation.

11. And as the true promised Prophet he hath manifested and revealed unto us whatsoever God asketh or requireth of the people of the New Testament; for as God, by Moses and the other prophets, hath spoken and declared his will to the people of the Old Testament; so hath he in those last days, by his Prophet spoken unto us, and revealed unto us the mystery (concealed from the beginning of the world), and hath now manifested to us whatsoever yet remained to be manifested. He hath preached the promised glad tidings, appointed and ordained the sacraments, the offices and ministries, by God thereto destinated; and hath showed by doctrine and life, the law of Christians, a rule of their life, the path and way of everlasting life.

12. Moreover, as a High Priest and Mediator of the New Testament, after that he hath accomplished the will of his Father in the foresaid works, he hath finally given himself obediently (for the reconciliation of the sins of

the world) to all outward suffering, and hath offered up himself in death upon the cross unto the Father, for a sweet savor and common oblation.

13. We acknowledge that the obedience of the Son of God, his suffering, dying, bloodshed, bitter passion, death, and only sacrifice upon the cross, is a perfect reconciliation and satisfaction for our sins and the sins of the world; so that men thereby are reconciled to God, are brought into power, and have a sure hope and certainty to the entrance into everlasting life.

14. Christ, our Prophet and Priest, being also the promised, only spiritual, heavenly King of the New Testament, hath erected, or built, a spiritual kingdom, and united a company of faithful, spiritual men; these persons hath he endowed with spiritual, kingly laws, after the nature of the heavenly kingdom, and hath established therein justice, righteousness, and the ministers thereof.

15. Having accomplished and performed here upon the earth, by dying the death, his office of the cross he was afterwards buried, thereby declaring that he was truly dead; the third day he rose again, and stood up from the dead, abolishing death, and testifying that he was Lord over death, and he could not possibly be detained by the hands of death, thereby comfortably assuring all the faithful of their resurrection and standing up from death.

16. Afterwards, forty days spent, he conversed amongst his disciples, and ofttimes showed himself unto them that there might no doubt be had concerning his resurrection; after that, being compassed by a cloud, he was carried up into heaven, and entered into his glory, leading captivity captive, and making a show of his enemies, hath gloriously triumphed over them, and is sat at the right hand of the Majesty of God, and is become a Lord, and Christ, glorified in body, advanced, lifted up, and crowned with praise and glory, and remaineth over Mount Sion a Priest, and King for everlasting.

17. The holy office of this glorified Priest, King, Lord and Christ, in the heavenly glorious being is to help, govern, and preserve, by his Holy Spirit, his holy church

and people in the world, through the storm, wind, and troubles of the sea; for, according to his priestly office, as an overseer or steward of the true tabernacle, is he our Intercessor, Advocate, and Mediator by the Father. He teacheth, comforteth, strengtheneth, and baptizeth us with the Holy Ghost, his heavenly gifts and fiery victims, and keepeth his spiritual supper with the faithful soul, making it partaker of the life giving food and drink of the soul, the fruit, virtue, and worth of his merits obtained upon the cross; the only and necessary good signified in the sacraments.

18. And according to his kingly office, in his heavenly* being he governeth the hearts of the faithful by his Holy Spirit and Word; he taketh them into his protection, he covereth them under the shadow of his wings, he armeth them with spiritual weapons for the spiritual warfare against all their enemies, namely, the Spirit of wickedness, under heaven, and whatsoever dependeth on them in this earth. He, their most Glorious, Almighty, Heavenly King, standeth by them, delivereth and freeth them from the hands of their enemies, giveth them victory and the winning of the field, and hath prepared for them a crown of righteousness in heaven. And they being the redeemed of the Lord, who dwell in the house of the Lord, upon the Mount Sion, do change their fleshly weapons, namely, their swords into shares, and their spears into scythes, do lift up no sword, neither hath nor consent to fleshly battle.

19. All these spiritual good things and beneficial, which Christ, by his merits, hath obtained for the saving of sinners, we do graciously enjoy through a true, living, working faith. Which faith is an assured understanding and knowledge of the heart, obtained out of the Word of God, concerning God, Christ, and other heavenly things which are necessary for us to know, and to believe to salvation, together with a hearty confidence in the only God, that he, as a gracious and heavenly Father, will give and bestow upon us, through Christ, and for his merits, whatsoever is helpful and profitable for body and soul for salvation.

* Interlined.

20. Through such a faith we obtain true righteousness, forgiveness, absolution from sin through the bloodshed of Christ, and through righteousness, which through the Christ Jesus, by the co-operation of the Holy Ghost, is plentifully shed and poured into us, so that we truly are made, of evil men, good; of fleshly, spiritual; of covetous, liberal; of proud, humble; and through regeneration are made pure in heart, and the children of God.

21. Man being thus justified by faith, liveth and worketh by love (which the Holy Ghost sheddeth into the heart) in all good works, in the laws, precepts, ordinances given them by God through Christ; he praiseth and blesseth God, by a holy life, for every benefit, especially of the soul; and so are all such plants of the Lord trees of righteousness, who honor God through good works, and expect a blessed reward.

22. Such faithful, righteous people, scattered in several parts of the world, being the true congregations of God, or the Church of Christ, whom he saved, and for whom he gave himself, that he might sanctify them, ye whom he hath cleansed by the washing of water in the word of life: of all such is Jesus the Head, the Shepherd, the Leader, the Lord, the King, and Master. Now although among these there may be mingled a company of seeming holy ones, or hypocrites; yet, nevertheless, they are and remain only the righteous, true members of the body of Christ, according to the spirit and the truth, the heirs of the promises, truly saved from the hypocrites the dissemblers.

23. In this holy church hath God ordained the ministers of the Gospel, the doctrines of the holy Word, the use of the holy sacraments, the oversight of the poor, and the ministers of the same offices; furthermore, the exercise of brotherly admonition and correction, and, finally, the separating of the impenitent; which holy ordinances, contained in the Word of God, are to be administered according to the contents thereof.

24. And like as a body consisteth of divers parts, and every part hath its own proper work, seeing every part is not a hand, eye, or foot; so is it also the church of God; for although every believer is a member of the body of

Christ, yet is not every one therefore a teacher, elder, or deacon, but only such as are orderly appointed to such offices. Therefore, also, the administration of the said offices or duties partaineth only to those who are ordained thereto, and not to every particular common person.

25. The vocation or election of the said officers is performed by the church, with fasting, and prayer to God; for God knoweth the heart; he is amongst the faithful who are gathered together in his name; and by his Holy Spirit doth so govern the minds and hearts of his people, that he by them bringeth to light and propoundeth whom he knoweth to be profitable to his church.

26. And although the election and vocation to the said offices is performed by the aforesaid means, yet, nevertheless, the investing into the said service is accomplished by the elders of the church through the laying on of hands.

27. The doctrine which by the foresaid ministers must be proposed to the people, is even the same which Christ brought out of heaven, which he, by word and work, that is, by doctrine and life, hath taught, which was preached by the apostles of Christ, by the commandment of Christ and the Spirit, which we find written (so much as is needful for us to salvation) in the Scripture of the New Testament, whereto we apply whatsoever we find in the canonical book of the Old Testament, which hath affinity and verity, which by doctrine of Christ and his apostles, and consent and agreement, with the government of his Spiritual Kingdom.

28. There are two sacraments appointed by Christ, in his holy church, the administration whereof he hath assigned to the ministry of teaching, namely, the Holy Baptism and the Holy Supper. These are outward visible handlings and tokens, setting before our eyes, on God's side, the inward spiritual handling which God, through Christ, by the cooperation of the Holy Ghost, setteth forth i the justification in the penitent faithful soul; and which, on our behalf, witnesseth our religion, experience, faith, and obedience, through the obtaining of a good conscience to the service of God.

29. The Holy Baptism is given unto these in the name

of the Father, the Son, and the Holy Ghost, which hear, believe, and with penitent heart receive the doctrines of the Holy Gospel. For such hath the Lord Jesus commanded to be baptized, and no unspeaking children.

30. The whole dealing in the outward visible baptism of water, setteth before the eyes, witnesseth and signifieth, the Lord Jesus doth inwardly baptize the repentant, faithful man, in the laver of regeneration and renewing of the Holy Ghost, washing the soul from all pollution and sin, by the virtue and merit of his bloodshed; and by the power and working of the Holy Ghost, the true, heavenly, spiritual, living Water, cleanseth the inward evil of the soul, and maketh it heavenly, spiritual, and living, in true righteousness or goodness. Therefore, the baptism of water leadeth us to Christ, to his holy office in glory and majesty; and admonisheth us not to hang only upon the outward, but with holy prayer to mount upward, and to beg of Christ the good thing signified.

31. The Holy Supper, according to the institution of Christ, is to be administered to the baptized; as the Lord Jesus hath commanded that whatsoever he hath appointed should be taught to be observed.

32. The whole dealing in the outward visible supper, setteth before the eye, witnesseth and signifyeth, that Christ's body was broken upon the cross and his holy blood spilt for the remission of our sins. That the being glorified in his heavenly Being, is the alive-making bread, meat, and drink of our souls: it setteth before our eyes Christ's office and ministry in glory and majesty, by holding his spiritual supper, which the believing soul, feeding and* .. the soul with spiritual food: it teacheth us by the outward handling to mount upwards with the heart in holy prayer, to beg at Christ's hands the true signified food; and it admonisheth us of thankfulness to God, and of verity and love one with another.

33. The church discipline, or external censures, is also an outward handling among the believers, whereby the impenitent sinner, after Christian admonition and reproof, is severed, by reason of his sins, from the communion of the saints for his future good; and the wrath

* Word wanting.

of God is denounced against him until the time of his contrition and reformation; and there is also, by this outward separation of the church, manifested what God before had judged and fore-handled, concerning this secret sinner, by reason of his sin. Therefore, first before the Lord, the prejudging and predetermining of the matter must pass* . . in respect of the sinner* . . and the after-judging and handling by the church. Therefore the church must carefully regard that none in the church be condemned with it, and be condemned in the Word of God.

34. The person separated from the church may not at all be admitted (so long as he proceedeth in sin) to the use of the holy supper or any other* . . handling, but he must be avoided therein, as also in all other things betokening the communion of saints or brotherhood. And as the rebellious life, conversation, or daily company of the godless and perverse, or anything with them, is dangerous and hurtful, and oftentimes promoteth scandal and slander to the godly, so must they withdraw themselves from the same rebels, avoiding them in all works and ends whereby their pure souls might be polluted and defiled: yet so that always the Word of God take place, and that nothing take place or be performed that is contrary to love, mercy, Christian discretion, promise, or any other like matter.

35. Worldly authority or magistry is a necessary ordinance of God, appointed and established for the preservation of the common estate, and of a good, natural, politic life, for the reward of the good and the punishing of the evil; we acknowledge ourselves obnoxious, and bound by the Word of God to fear, honor, and show obedience to the magistrates in all causes not contrary to the Word of the Lord. We are obliged to pray God Almighty for them, and to thank the Lord for good reasonable magistrates, and to yield unto them, without murmuring, beseeming tribute, toll and tax. This office of the worldly authority the Lord Jesus hath not ordained in his spiritual kingdom, the church of the New Testament, nor adjoined to the offices of his church.

* Cannot decipher the word.

Neither hath he called his disciples or followers to be worldly kings, princes, potentates, or magistrates; neither hath he burdened or charged them to assume such offices, or to govern the world in such a worldly manner; much less hath he given a law to the members of his church which is agreeable to such office or government. Yea, rather they are called of him (whom they are commanded to obey by a voice heard from heaven) to the following of his unarmed and unweaponed life, and of his cross-bearing footsteps. In whom approved nothing less than a worldly government, power, and sword. This then considered (as also further, that upon the office of the worldly authority many other things depend, as wars* . . to hurt his enemies in body or good* . . which evilly or not at all will fit or consort with the Christ, and the crucified life of the Christians), so hold we that it beseemeth not Christians to administer these offices; therefore we avoid such offices and administrations, notwithstanding by no means thereby willing to despise or condemn reasonable discreet magistrates, nor to place him in less estimation than he is described by the Holy Ghost, of Paul.

36. Christ, the King and Lawgiver of the New Testament, hath prohibited Christians the swearing of oaths; therefore it is not permitted that the faithful of the New Testament should swear at all.

37. The married estate, or matrimony, hold we for an ordinance of God, which, according to the first institution, shall be observed. Every man shall have his one only wife, and every woman shall have her one only husband; those may not be separated but for adultery. We permit none of our communion to marry godless, unbelieving, fleshly persons out of the church; but we censure such (as other sinners) according to the disposition and desert of the cause.

38. Lastly, we believe and teach the resurrection of the dead, both of the just and the unjust, as Paul (1 Cor. 15) soundly teacheth and witnesseth: The soul shall be united to the body, every one shall be presented before the judgment seat of Christ Jesus, to receive in his own body

* Cannot decipher the word.

wages according to his works. And the righteous, whosoever hath lived holily, and through faith brought forth the works of love and mercy, shall enter into everlasting life with Christ Jesus, the Bridegroom of the Christian host. But the unsanctified, which have not known God, and have not obeyed the Gospel of Jesus Christ, shall go into everlasting fire. The Almighty, gracious, merciful God, preserve us from the punishment of the ungodly, and grant us grace and gifts helpful to a holy life, saving death, and joyful resurrection with all the righteous. Amen.

We subscribe to the truth of these Articles, desiring further information. [Forty-two names are attached to this document. We cannot decipher the whole, but the following are plain. A line is drawn through some of them. The * marks them. † Uncertain.]

*John Smyth,	*Matthew Pigott,
Hugh Broomhead,	Mary Smyth,
*John Grindall,	Janus ——,,
*Samuel Halton,	Margarett Staveley,
Thomas Piggott,	†Isabella Thomson,
John Hardie,	*Jane Argan,
*Edward Hawkins,	Mary Dickens,
Thomas Jessopp,	Bettriss Dickens,
Robert Staveley,	Dorothe Hamand,
*Alexander Fleming,	*Elnh. Buywater,
John Arnfeld,	Ann Broomhead,
Hannah Piggott,	Alexander Parsons,
Thomas Solphin,	*Joan Haughton,
Solomon Thomson,	*Joane Brigge,
Alexander Hodgin,	Alexander Pigott,
Ursula Bywater,	Margaret Pigott,
Dorothea Oakland,	Alexander Armfield,
John ——,	Elnh. White,
Fylis ——,	Dorothe Thomson,
*—— ——,	Margaret Morris.

[We judge the whole of these signatures autograph.]

3. A third Confession, consisting of one hundred and two articles, supposed to have been drawn up by Smyth

E

in Dutch (very imperfect Dutch, according to Professor Müller), and published, has also been translated in Evans I, 257f.

4. After Smyth's death, August 1612, and before 1614, this last confession, slightly modified, principally by a rearrangement of the articles and the omission of two of them, was published in English, along with Smyth's "Retraction of His Errors" and an account of his death. The "Epistle to the Reader" is signed "T. P." (probably Thomas Piggot, one of Smyth's party). The author states that he has "annexed a small confession of faith," without giving any information as to its origin or history. John Robinson, in commenting on certain articles of this confession in 1614, calls it "The Confession of Faith Published in Certain Conclusions by the Remainders of Mr. Smyth's Company after his death." (Cf. Robinson's wks., III, 237, Ashton ed.; Crosby, I, Appendix IV.) What is supposed to be the only copy in existence was discovered some years ago in the library of York minster, and reprinted entire in Barclay's "Inner Life," etc., Appendix to Chap. VI. Barclay's reprint of this Confession, which has the distinction of having been published in both Dutch and English, with slight differences, and which probably represents the final views of John Smyth, the founder of the English General Baptists, is reproduced below.

Propositions and Conclusions concerning True Christian Religion, containing a Confession of Faith of certain English people, living at Amsterdam.

1. We believe that there is a God (Heb. xi. 6) against all Epicures and Atheists, which either say in their hearts or utter with their mouths, that there is no God (Psal. xiv. 1; Isaiah xxii. 13.)

2. That this God is one in number (1 Cor. viii, 4, 6) against the Pagans or any other that hold a plurality of gods.

3. That God is incomprehensible and ineffable, in regard of His substance or essence that is God's essence can neither be comprehended in the mind, nor uttered by the words of men or angels (Exod. iii. 13-15, and xxxiii. 18-21).

4. That the creatures and Holy Scriptures do not intend to teach us what God is in substance or essence, but what He is in effect and property (Rom. i. 19, 22; Exod. xxxiii. 23).

5. That these terms, Father, Son, and Holy Spirit, do not teach God's substance, but only the hinder parts of God: that which may be known of God (Rom. i., Exod. xxxiii).

6. That God may be known by His titles, properties, effects, imprinted, and expressed in the creatures, and Scriptures (John xvii. 3).

7. That to understand and conceive of God in the mind is not the saving knowledge of God, but to be like to God in His effects and properties; to be made conformable to His divine and heavenly attributes. That is the true saving knowledge of God (2 Cor. iii. 18; Matt. v. 48; 2 Peter i. 4), whereunto we ought to give all diligence.

8. That this God manifested in Father, Son, and Holy Ghost (Matt. iii. 16, 17) is most merciful, most mighty, most holy, most just, most wise, most true, most glorious, eternal and infinite (Exod. xxxiv. 6, 7; Psalm xc. 2 and cii. 27).

9. That God before the foundation of the world did foresee, and determine the issue and event of all His works (Acts xv. 18), and that actually in time He worketh all things by His providence, according to the good pleasure of His will (Eph. i. 11), and therefore we abhor the opinion of them, that avouch, that all things happen by fortune or chance (Acts. iv. 27, 28; Matt. x. 29, 30).

10. That God is not the Author or worker of sin (Psal. v. 4; James i. 13), but that God only did foresee and determine what evil the free will of men and angels

would do; but He gave no influence, instinct, motion or inclination to the least sin.

11. That God in the beginning created the world viz., the heavens, and the earth and all things that are therein (Gen. i.; Acts xvii. 24). So that the things that are seen, were not of things which did appear (Heb. xi. 3).

12. That God created man to blessedness, according to His image, in an estate of innocency, free without corruption of sin (Gen. i. 27; ii. 17, 25); He created them male and female (to wit) one man and one woman (Gen. i. 27); He framed man of the dust of the earth, and breathed into him the breath of life, so the man was a living soul (Gen. ii. 7; 1 Cor. xv. 45). But the woman He made of a rib, taken out of the side of the man (Gen. ii. 21, 22). That God blessed them, and commanded them to increase, and multiply, and to fill the earth, and to rule over it and all creatures therein (Gen. i. 28; ix. 1, 2; Psal. viii. 6).

13. That therefore marriage is an estate honorable amongst all men, and the bed undefiled: viz. betwixt one man and one woman (Heb. xiii. 4; 1 Cor. vii. 2), but whoremongers and adulterers God will judge.

14. That God created man with freedom of will, so that he had ability to choose the good, and eschew the evil, or to choose the evil, and refuse the good, and that this freedom of will was a natural faculty or power, created by God in the soul of man (Gen. ii. 16, 17; iii. 6, 7; Eccles. vii. 29).

15. That Adam sinning was not moved or inclined thereto by God, or by any decree of God but that he fell from his innocency, and died the death alone, by the temptation of Satan, his free will assenting thereunto freely (Gen. iii. 6).

16. That the same day that Adam sinned, he died the death (Gen. ii. 17), for the reward of sin is death (Rom. vi. 23), and this is that which the Apostle saith, dead in trespasses and sins (Eph. ii. 1), which is loss of innocency, of the peace of conscience and comfortable presence of God (Gen. iii. 7, 11).

17. That Adam being fallen did not lose any natural power or faculty, which God created in his soul, for the

work of the devil, which is (sin), cannot abolish God's
work or creatures: and therefore being fallen he still
retained freedom of will (Gen. iii. 23, 24).

18. That original sin is an idle term, and that there
is no such thing as men intend by the word (Ezek. xviii.
20), because God threatened death only to Adam (Gen.
ii. 17) not to his posterity, and because God created the
soul (Heb. xii. 9).

19. That if original sin might have passed from Adam
to his posterity, Christ's death, which was effectual before Cain and Abel's birth, He being the lamb slain
from the beginning of the world, stopped the issue and
passage thereof (Rev. xiii. 8).

20. That infants are conceived and born in innocency
without sin, and that so dying are undoubtedly saved,
and that this is to be understood of all infants, under
heaven (Gen. v. 2; i. 27 compared with 1 Cor. xv. 49)
for where there is no law there is no transgression, sin
is not imputed while there is no law (Rom. iv. 15 and v.
13), but the law was not given to infants, but to them
that could understand (Rom. v. 13; Matt. xiii. 9; Neh.
viii. 3).

21. That all actual sinners bear the image of the first
Adam, in his innocency, fall, and restitution in the offer
of grace (1 Cor. xv. 49), and so pass under these three
conditions, or threefold estate.

22. That Adam being fallen God did not hate him, but
loved him still, and sought his good (Gen. iii. 8-15),
neither doth he hate any man that falleth with Adam;
but that He loveth mankind, and from His love sent
His only begotten Son into the world, to save that
which was lost, and to seek the sheep that went astray
(John iii. 16).

23. That God never forsaketh the creature until there
be no remedy, neither doth He cast away His innocent
creature from all eternity; but casteth away men irrecoverable in sin (Isa. v. 4; Ezek. xviii. 23, 32, and xxxiii. 11;
Luke xiii. 6, 9).

24. That as there is in all creatures a natural inclination to their young ones, to do them good, so there is in
the Lord toward man; for every spark of goodness in

the creature is infinitely good in God (Rom. i. 20; Psal. xix. 4; Rom. x. 18).

25. That as no man begetteth his child to the gallows, nor no potter maketh a pot to break it; so God doth not create or predestinate any man to destruction (Ezek. xxxiii. 11; Gen. i. 27; 1 Cor. xv. 49; Gen. v. 3).

26. That God before the foundation of the world hath determined the way of life and salvation to consist in Christ, and that He hath foreseen who would follow it (Eph. i. 5; 2 Tim. i. 9), and on the contrary hath determined the way of perdition to consist in infidelity, and in impenitency, and that He hath foreseen who would follow after it (Jude, 4th verse).

27. That as God created all men according to His image, so hath He redeemed all that fall by actual sin, to the same end; and that God in His redemption hath not swerved from His mercy, which He manifested in His creation (John i. 3, 16; 2 Cor. v. 19; 1 Tim. ii. 5, 6; Ezek. xxxiii. 11).

28. That Jesus Christ came into the world to save sinners, and that God in His love to His enemies did send Him (John iii. 16); that Christ died for His enemies (Rom. v. 10); that He bought them that deny Him (2 Peter ii. 1), thereby teaching us to love our enemies (Matt. v. 44, 45).

29. That Jesus Christ after His baptism by a voice out of heaven from the Father, and by the anointing of the Holy Ghost, which appeared on His head in the form of a dove, is appointed the prophet of the church, whom all men must hear (Matt. iii.; Heb. iii. 1, 2); and that both by His doctrine and life, which He led here in the earth, by all His doings and sufferings, He hath declared and published, as the only prophet and lawgiver of His Church, the way of peace and life, the glad tidings of the gospel (Acts iii. 23, 24).

30. That Jesus Christ is the brightness of the glory and the engraven form of the Father's substance, supporting all things by His mighty power (Heb. i. 3); and that He is become the mediator of the New Testament (to wit) the King, Priest, and Prophet of the Church, and that the faithful through Him are thus made spiritual

Kings, Priests, and Prophets (Rev. i. 6; 1 John ii. 20; Rev. xix. 10).

31. That Jesus Christ is He which in the beginning did lay the foundation of the heavens and earth which shall perish (Heb. i. 10; Psalm cii. 26); that He is Alpha and Omega, the beginning and the end, the first and the last, He is the wisdom of God, which was begotten from everlasting before all creatures (Micah v. 2; Prov. viii. 24; Luke xi. 49); He was in the form of God, and thought it no robbery to be equal with God; yet He took to Him the shape of a servant, the Word became flesh (John i. 14), wonderfully by the power of God in the womb of the Virgin Mary; He was of the seed of David according to the flesh (Phil. ii. 7; Heb. 10.; Rom. i. 3); and that He made Himself of no reputation, humbled Himself, and became obedient unto the death of the cross, redeeming us from our vain conversation, not with silver or gold, but with the precious blood of Himself, as of a lamb without spot and undefiled (1 Peter i. 18, 19).

32. That although the sacrifice of Christ's body and blood offered up unto God His Father upon the cross, be a sacrifice of a sweet smelling savour, and that God in Him is well pleased, yet it doth not reconcile God unto us, which did never hate us, nor was our enemy, but reconcileth us unto God (2 Cor. v. 19), and slayeth the enmity and hatred, which is in us against God (Eph. 1. 14, 17; Rom. 1. 30).

33. That Christ was delivered to death for our sins (Rom. iv. 25), and that by His death we have the remission of our sins (Eph. ii. 7), for He cancelled the handwriting of ordinances, the hatred, the law of commandments in ordinances (Eph. ii. 15; Colos. ii. 14) which was against us (Deut. xxxi. 26); He spoiled principalities and powers, made a shew of them openly, and triumphed over them on the cross (Colos. ii. 15); by death He destroyed him that had the power of death, that is the devil (Heb. ii. 14).

34. That the enemies of our salvation, which Christ vanquished on His cross, are the gates of hell, the power of darkness, Satan, sin, death, the grave, the curse or condemnation, wicked men, and persecutors (Eph. vi. 12;

1 Cor. xv. 26, 54, 57; Matt. xvi. 18; Rev. xx. 10, 14, 15),
which enemies we must overcome no otherwise than
Christ hath done (John xxi. 22; 1 Peter ii. 21; Rev. xiv.
4).

35. That the efficacy of Christ's death is only derived to
them, which do mortify their sins, which are grafted with
Him to the similitude of His death (Rom. vi. 3-6), which
are circumcised with circumcision made without hands,
by putting off the sinful body of the flesh, through the
circumcision which Christ worketh (Colos. ii. 11) who is
the minister of the circumcision for the truth of God, to
confirm the promises made to the fathers (Rom. xv. 8
compared with Deut. xxx. 6).

36. That there are three which bear witness in the
earth, the spirit, water and blood, and these three are one
in testimony, witnessing that Christ truly died (1 John v.
8) for He gave up the ghost (John xix. 30); and out of
His side pierced with a spear came water and blood (verse
34, 35), the cover of the heart being pierced, where there
is water contained.

37. That every mortified person hath this witness in
himself (1 John v. 10), for the spirit blood, and water of
sin is gone, that is the life of sin with the nourishment
and cherishment thereof (1 Pet. iv. 1; Rom. vi. 7; 1
John iii. 6).

38. That Christ Jesus being truly dead was also buried
(John xix. 39, 42), and that he lay in the grave the whole
Sabbath of the Jews; but in the grave He saw no corrup-
tion (Psal. xvi. 10; Acts ii. 31).

39. That all mortified persons are also buried with
Christ, by the baptism, which is unto His death (Rom. vi.
4; Colos. ii. 12); keeping their Sabbath with Christ in the
grave (that is) resting from their own works as God did
from His (Heb. iv. 10), waiting there in hope for a
resurrection (Psal. xvi. 9).

40. That Christ Jesus early in the morning, the first
day of the week, rose again after His death and burial
(Matt. xxviii. 6) for our justification (Rom. iv. 25), being mightily declared to be the Son of God, by the Spirit
of sanctification, in the resurrection from the dead (Rom.
i. 4).

41. That these that are grafted with Christ to the similitude of His death and burial shall also be to the similitude of His resurrection (Rom. vi. 4, 5.) ; for He doth quicken or give life unto them, together with Himself (Colos. ii. 13; Eph. ii. 5, 6) ; for that is their salvation, and it is by grace (Eph. ii. 5; 1 John v. 11, 12, 13; Titus iii. 5, 6, 7).

42. That this quickening or reviving of Christ, this laver of regeneration, this renewing of the Holy Ghost, is our justification and salvation (Titus iii. 6, 7). This is that pure river of water of life clear as crystal, which proceedeth out of the throne of God, and of the Lamb (Rev. xxii. 1) ; which also floweth out of the belly of him that believeth in Christ (John vii. 38) ; this is those precious promises whereby we are made partakers of the divine nature, by flying the corruptions that are in the world through lust (2 Pet. i. 4) ; this is the fruit of the tree of life which is in the midst of the paradise of God; this is the white stone wherein there is a name written, which no man knoweth, save he that receiveth it. This is the morning star, this is the new name, the name of God, the name of the City of God; the new Jerusalem which descendeth from God out of heaven; this is the hidden manna, that white clothing, eye salve and gold, and that heavenly supper which Christ promises to them, that overcome (Rev. ii. 7, 17, 18, and iii. 5, 12, 18, 20).

43. That there are three which bear record in heaven, the Father, the Word, and the Holy Spirit; and that these three are one in testimony, witnessing the resurrection of Christ. The Father saith thou art my Son, this day have I begotten thee (Acts xiii. 33-35). The Son testifieth of his own resurrection being forty days with His disciples (Act. i. 3). The Holy Ghost testifieth the same whom Christ sent to His disciples upon the day of Pentecost (Acts. ii).

44. That every person that is regenerate and risen again with Christ hath these three aforesaid witnesses in himself (1 John v. 10) ; for Christ doth dwell in his heart by faith (Eph. iii. 17) ; and the Father dwelleth with the Son (Joh. xiv. 23) ; and the Holy Ghost likewise (1 Cor. iii. 16) ; and that the grace of our Lord Jesus Christ,

and the love of God, and the fellowship of the Holy
Ghost is with them (2 Cor. xiii. 13).

45. That Christ having forty days after His resurrection conversed with his disciples (Acts i. 3), ascended
locally into the heavens (Acts i. 9), which must contain
Him unto the time that all things be restored (Acts iii.
21).

That they which are risen with Christ, ascend up spiritually with Him, seeking those things which are above,
where Christ sitteth at the right hand of God, and that
they set their affections on heavenly things, and not on
earthly things (Col. iii. 1-5).

46. That Christ now being received into Heaven, sitteth
at the right hand of God (Mark xvi. 9), having led captivity captive, and given gifts unto men (Eph. iv. 8) ; that
God hath now highly exalted Him, and given Him a
name above every name; that at the name of Jesus every
knee should bow, of things in heaven, in earth and under
the earth (Phil. ii. 9, 10), that He hath obtained all power
both in heaven and in earth (Matt. xxviii. 18), and hath
made all things subject under His feet, and hath appointed
Him over all things to be the head to the church, that is
His body, the fulness of Him that filleth all in all things
(Eph. i. 2-23).

47. That the regenerate do sit together with Christ
Jesus in heavenly places (Eph. ii. 6), that they sit with
Him in His throne as He sitteth with the Father in His
throne (Rev. iii. 21), that they have power over nations
and rule them with a rod of iron, and as a potter's vessel
they are broken in pieces (Rev. ii. 26, 27) ; and that sit-
ting on twelve thrones, they do judge the twelve tribes of
Israel (Matt. xix. 28), which spiritually is to put all their
enemies in subjection under their feet, so that the evil
one doth not touch them (1 John v. 18), nor the gates of
hell prevail against them (Matt. xvi. 28), and that they
are become pillars in the house of God, and go no more
out (Rev. iii. 12).

48. That Christ Jesus being exalted at the right hand
of God the Father, far above all principalities and powers,
might, and domination, and every name that is named, not
only in this world, but in the world to come (Eph. i. 21),

hath received of His Father the promise of the Holy
Ghost, which He also shed forth upon His disciples on
the Day of Pentecost (Act ii. 33).

49. That Christ Jesus, in His resurrection, ascension,
and exaltation, is more and rather Lord and Christ, Saviour, anointed, and King, than in His humiliation, sufferings and death (Acts. ii. 36; Phil. ii. 7, 11), for the end is
more excellent than the means, and His sufferings were
the way by the which He entered into His glory (Luke
xxiv. 16), and so by consequent the efficacy of His
resurrection in the new creature, is more noble and excellent, than the efficacy of His death in the mortification
and remission of sins.

50. That the knowledge of Christ according to the
flesh is of small profit (2 Cor. v. 16, 17), and the knowledge of Christ's genealogy and history, is no other but
that which the Devil hath as well if not better than any
man living; but the knowledge of Christ according to the
spirit is effectual to salvation, which is spiritually to be
grafted to the similitude of Christ's birth, life, miracles,
doings, sufferings, death, burial, resurrection, ascension,
and exaltation (Rom. vi. 3, 6).

51. That Christ Jesus, according to the flesh and history
in His doings and suffering, is a great mystery, and divine
sacrament of Himself, and of His ministry in the spirit,
and of those spiritual things which He worketh in those
which are to be heirs of salvation (Rom. vi. 3, 6; Eph. ii.
5, 6), and that spiritually He performeth all those miracles in the regenerate which He wrought in His flesh;
He healeth their leprosy, bloody issue, blindness, dumb-
ness, deafness, lameness, palsy, fever, He casteth out the
devils and unclean spirits, He raiseth the dead, rebuketh
the winds and the sea, and it is calm; He feedeth thousands with the barley loaves and fishes (Matt. viii. 16, 17,
compared with Isaiah liii. 4, John vi. 26, 27).

52. That the Holy Ghost proceedeth from the Father
and the Son (John xiv. 26, and xvi. 7); that He is the
eternal spirit, whereby Christ offered Himself without
spot to God (Heb. ix. 14); and He is that other comforter, which Christ asketh, obtaineth, and sendeth from
the Father (John xiv. 16), which dwelleth in the regener-

ate (1 Cor. iii. 16), which leadeth them into all truth (John xvi. 13), He is that anointing which teacheth them all things, and that they have no need that any man teach them, but as the same anointing teacheth (1 John ii. 20, 27).

53. That although there be divers gifts of the Spirit yet there is but one Spirit, which distributeth to every one as He will (2 Cor. xii. 4, 11; Eph. iv. 4), that the outward gifts of the spirit which the Holy Ghost poureth forth, upon the Day of Pentecost upon the disciples, in tongues and prophesy, and gifts, and healing, and miracles, which is called the Baptism of the Holy Ghost and fire (Acts. i. 5) were only a figure of and an hand leading to better things, even the most proper gifts of the spirit of sanctification, which is the new creature; which is the one baptism (Eph. iv. 4, compared with Acts ii. 33, 38, and with Luke x. 17, 20).

54. That John Baptist and Christ are two persons, their ministries are two ministries several, and their baptisms are two baptisms, distinct the one from the other (John i. 20; Acts xiii. 25; Acts i. 4, 5; Matt. iii. 11).

55. That John taught the baptism of repentance for the remission of sins, baptizing with water to amendment of life (Matt. iii. 11), thus preparing a way for Christ and His baptism (Luke iii. 3, 6), by bringing men to repentance and faith in the Messias, whom he pointed out with the finger (saying), behold the Lamb of God that taketh away the sins of the world (John i. 31, 29; Acts xix. 4).

56. That Christ is stronger, and hath a more excellent office and ministry than John (Matt. iii. 11); that He baptiseth with the Holy Ghost and fire; that He cometh and walketh in the way which John hath prepared; and that the new creature followeth repentance (Luke iii. 6).

57. That repentance and faith in the Messias, are the conditions to be performed on our behalf, for the obtaining of the promises (Acts ii. 38; John i. 12); that the circumcision of the heart, mortification and the promise of the spirit, that is, the new creature, are the promises which are made to the aforesaid conditions (Deut. xxx. 6;

Acts ii. 38; Gal. iii. 14; 2 Pet. 1. 4, 5), which promises are all yea and Amen in Christ Jesus (2 Cor. i. 20), and that in the regenerate (Gal. iii. 16).

58. That repentance and faith are wrought in the hearts of men, by the preaching of the word, outwardly in the Scriptures, and creatures, the grace of God preventing us by the motions and instinct of the spirit, which a man hath power to receive or reject (Matt. xxiii. 37; Acts vii. 51; Acts vi. 10; Rom. x. 14, 18), that our justification before God consisteth not in the performance of the conditions which God requireth of us, but in partaking of the promises, the possessing of Christ, remission of sins, and the new creature.

59. That God, the Father, of His own good will doth beget us, by the word of truth (James i. 18), which is an immortal seed (1 Pet. i. 23), not the doctrine of repentance and faith which may be lost (Luke viii. 13); and that God the Father, in our regeneration, neither needeth nor useth the help of any creature, but that the Father, the Word, and the Holy Ghost, immediately worketh that work in the soul, where the free will of men can do nothing (John ii. 13).

60. That such as have not attained the new creature, have need of the scriptures, creatures and ordinances of the Church, to instruct them, to comfort them, to stir them up the better to perform the condition of repentance to the remission of sins (2 Pet. i. 19; 1 Cor. xi. 26; Eph. iv. 12-23).

61. That the new creature which is begotten of God, needeth not the outward scriptures, creatures, or ordinances of the Church, to support or help them (2 Cor. xiii. 10, 12; 1 Joh. ii. 27; 1 Cor. 1. 15, 16; Rev. xxi. 23), seeing he hath three witnesses in himself, the Father, the Word, and the Holy Ghost: which are better than all scriptures, or creatures whatsoever.

62. That as Christ who was above the law notwithstanding was made under the law, for our cause: so the regenerate in love to others, can and will do no other, than use the outward things of the church, for the gaining and supporting of others: and so the outward church and ordinances are always necessary, for all sorts of per-

sons whatsoever (Matt. iii. 15; xxviii. 19, 20; 1 Cor. viii. 9).

63. That the new creature although he be above the law and scriptures, yet he can do nothing against the law or scriptures, but rather all his doings shall serve to the confirming and establishing of the law (Rom. iii. 31). Therefore he cannot lie, nor steal, nor commit adultery, nor kill, nor hate any man, or do any other fleshly action, and therefore all fleshly libertinism is contrary to regeneration, detestable, and damnable (John viii. 34; Rom. vi. 15, 16, 18; 2 Pet. ii. 18, 19; 1 John v. 18).

64. That the outward church visible, consists of penitent persons only, and of such as believing in Christ, bring forth fruits worthy amendment of life (1 Tim. vi. 3, 5; 2 Tim. iii. 1, 5; Acts xix. 4).

65. That the visible church is a mystical figure outwardly, of the true, spiritual invisible church; which consisteth of the spirits of just and perfect men only, that is of the regenerate (Rev. i. 20, compared with Rev. xxi. 2, 23, 27).

66. That repentance is the change of mind from evil to that which is good (Matt. iii. 2), a sorrow for sin committed, with a humble heart for the same; and a resolution to amend for time to come; with an unfeigned endeavor therein (2 Cor. vii. 8, 11; Isaiah i. 16, 17; Jer. xxxi. 18, 19).

67. That when we have done all that we can we are unprofitable servants, and all our righteousness is as a stained cloth (Luke xvii. 20), and that we can only suppress and lop off the branches of sin, but the root of sin we cannot pluck up out of our hearts (Jer. iv. 4, compared with Deut. xxx. 6, 8).

68. That faith is a knowledge in the mind of the doctrine of the law and gospel contained in the prophetical, and apostolical scriptures of the Old and New Testament: accompanying repentance with an assurance that God, through Christ, will perform unto us His promises of remission of sins, and mortification, upon the condition of our unfeigned repentance, and amendment of life (Rom. x. 13, 14, 15; Acts v. 30-32; and Acts ii. 38, 39; Heb. xi. 1; Mark i. 15).

69. That all penitent and faithful Christians are brethren in the communion of the outward church, wheresoever they live, by what name soever they are known, which in truth and zeal, follow repentance and faith, though compassed with never so many ignorances and infirmities; and we salute them all with a holy kiss, being heartily grieved that we which follow after one faith, and one spirit, one Lord, and one God, one body, and one baptism, should be rent into so many sects and schisms: and that only for matters of less moment.

70. That the outward baptism of water, is to be administered only upon such penitent and faithful persons as are (aforesaid), and not upon innocent infants, or wicked persons (Matt. iii. 2, 3, compared with Matt. xxviii. 19, 20, and John iv. 1).

71. That in Baptism to the penitent person, and believer, there is presented, and figured, the spiritual baptism of Christ, (that is) the baptism of the Holy Ghost, and fire: the baptism into the death and resurrection of Christ: even the promise of the Spirit, which he shall assuredly be made partaker of, if he continue to the end (Gal. iii. 14; Matt. iii. 11; 1 Cor. xii. 13; Rom. vi. 3, 6; Col. ii. 10).

72. That in the outward supper which only baptised persons must partake, there is presented and figured before the eyes of the penitent and faithful, that spiritual supper, which Christ maketh of His flesh and blood: which is crucified and shed for the remission of sins (as the bread is broken and the wine poured forth), and which is eaten and drunken (as is the bread and wine bodily) only by those which are flesh, of His flesh, and bone of His bone: in the communion of the same spirit (1 Cor. xii. 13; Rev. iii. 20, compared with 1 Cor. xi. 23, 26; John vi. 53, 58).

73. That the outward baptism and supper do not confer, and convey grace and regeneration to the participants or communicants: but as the word preached, they serve only to support and stir up the repentance and faith of the communicants till Christ come, till the day dawn, and the day-star arise in their hearts (1 Cor. xi. 26; 2 Peter i. 19; 1 Cor. 1. 5-8).

74. That the sacraments have the same use that the word hath; that they are a visible word, and that they teach to the eye of them that understand as the word teacheth the ears of them that have ears to hear (Prov. x. 12), and therefore as the word pertaineth not to infants, no more do the sacraments.

75. That the preaching of the word, and the ministry of the sacraments, representeth the ministry of Christ in the spirit; who teacheth, baptiseth, and feedeth the regenerate, by the Holy Spirit inwardly and invisibly.

76. That Christ hath set in His outward church two sorts of ministers: viz., some who are called pastors, teachers or elders, who administer in the word and sacraments, and others who are called Deacons, men and women: whose ministry is, to serve tables and wash the saints' feet (Acts vi. 2-4; Phil. i. 1; 1 Tim. iii. 2, 3, 8, 11, and chap. v.).

77. That the separating of the impenitent, from the outward communion of the church, is a figure of the eternal rejection, and reprobation of them that persist impenitent in sin (Rev. xxi. 27, and xxii. 14-45; Matt. xvi. 18 and xviii. 18; John xx. 23, compared with Rev. iii. 12).

78. That none are to be separated from the outward communion of the Church but such as forsake repentance, which deny the power of Godliness (2 Tim. iii. 5), and namely that sufficient admonition go before, according to the rule (Matt. xviii. 15-18), and that none are to be rejected for ignorance or errors, or infirmities as long as they retain repentance and faith in Christ (Rom. xiv., and 1 Thess. v. 14; Rom. xvi. 17, 18), but they are to be instructed with meekness; and the strong are to bear the infirmities of the weak; and that we are to support one another through love.

79. That a man may speak a word against the Son, and be pardoned (that is), a man may err in the knowledge of Christ's history, and in matters of the outward church, and be forgiven, doing it in an ignorant zeal; but he that speaketh a word against the Holy Ghost (that is) that after illumination forsaketh repentance and faith in Christ, persecuting them, trampling under

foot the blood of the covenant: returning with the dog to
the vomit; that such shall never be pardoned, neither in
this world, nor in the world to come (Matt. xii. 31, 32,
compared with Heb. vi. 4, and chap. x. 26-29; 2 Pet.
ii. 20, 22).

80. That persons separated from the communion of the
church, are to be accounted as heathens and publicans
(Matt. xviii.), and that they are so far to be shunned, as
they may pollute: notwithstanding being ready to instruct
them, and to relieve them in their wants: seeking by all
lawful means to win them: considering that excommunication is only for the destruction of the flesh, that the
spirit may be saved in the day of the Lord (1 Cor. v. 5,
11; Matt. xi. 19; Luke xv. 1, 2).

81. That there is no succession in the outward church,
but that all succession is from heaven, and that the new
creature only, hath the thing signified, and substance,
whereof the outward church and ordinances are shadows
(Col. ii. 16, 17), and therefore he alone hath power,
and knoweth aright, how to administer in the outward
church, for the benefit of others (John. vi. 45): yet God
is not the God of confusion but of order, and therefore
we are in the outward church, to draw as near the first
institution as may be, in all things (1 Cor. xiv. 33); therefore it is not lawful for every brother to administer the
word and sacraments (Eph. iv. 11, 12, compared with 1
Cor. xii. 4, 5, 6, 28, 29).

82. That Christ hath set in his outward church the
vocation of master and servant, parents and children,
husband and wife (Eph. v. 22-25, chap. vi. 1, 4, 5, 9),
and hath commanded every soul to be subject to the
higher powers (Rom. xiii. 1), not because of wrath only,
but for conscience sake (verse 5) that we are to give
them their duty, as tribute, and custom, honour, and fear,
not speaking evil of them that are in authority (Jude,
verse 8), but praying and giving thanks for them (1 Tim.
ii. 1, 2), for that is acceptable in the sight of God, even
our Saviour.

83. That the office of the magistrate, is a disposition or
permissive ordinance of God for the good of mankind:
that one man like the brute beasts devour not another

F

(Rom. xiii.), and that justice and civility, may be preserved among men: and that a magistrate may so please God in his calling, in doing that which is righteous and just in the eyes of the Lord, that he may bring an outward blessing upon himself, his posterity and subjects (2 Kings, x. 30, 31).

84. That the magistrate is not by virtue of his office to meddle with religion, or matters of conscience, to force or compel men to this or that form of religion, or doctrine: but to leave Christian religion free, to every man's conscience, and to handle only civil transgressions (Rom. xiii), injuries and wrongs of man against man, in murder, adultery, theft, etc., for Christ only is the king, and lawgiver of the church and conscience (James iv. 12).

85. That if the magistrate will follow Christ, and be His disciple, he must deny himself, take up his cross, and follow Christ; he must love his enemies and not kill them, he must pray for them, and not punish them, he must feed them and give them drink, not imprison them, banish them, dismember them, and spoil their goods; he must suffer persecution and affliction with Christ, and be slandered, reviled, blasphemed, scourged, buffeted, spit upon, imprisoned and killed with Christ; and that by the authority of magistrates, which things he cannot possibly do, and retain the revenge of the sword.

86. That the Disciples of Christ, the members of the outward church, are to judge all their causes of difference, among themselves, and they are not to go to law, before the magistrates (1 Cor. vi. 1, 7), and that all their differences must be ended by (yea) and (nay) without an oath (Matt. v. 33-37; James v. 12).

87. That the Disciples of Christ, the members of the outward church, may not marry any of the profane, or wicked, godless people of the world, but that every one is to marry in the Lord (1 Cor. vii. 39), every man one only wife, and every woman one only husband (1 Cor. vii. 2).

88. That parents are bound to bring up their children in instruction and information of the Lord (Eph. vi. 4), and that they are to provide for their family: otherwise they deny the faith, and are worse than infidels (1 Tim. v. 8).

89. That notwithstanding if the Lord shall give a man

any special calling, as Simon, and Andrew, James, and
John, then they must leave all, father, ship, nets, wife,
children, yea, and life also to follow Christ (Luke xiv. 26;
Matt. iv. 18-20).

90. That in the necessities of the church, and poor
brethren, all things are to be common (Acts iv. 32), yea
and that one church is to administer to another in time of
need (Gal. ii. 10; Acts xi. 30; 1 Cor. iv. 8, and chap. ix.).

91. That all the bodies of all men that are dead, shall
by the power of Christ, be raised up, out of his own
proper seed, as corn out of the seed rotting in the earth
(1 Cor. xv.).

92. That these which live in the last day shall not die,
but shall be changed in a moment: in the twinkling of an
eye, at the last trumpet (1 Cor. xv. 52), for the trump
shall blow, and the dead shall be raised up incorruptible,
and we shall be changed, not in substance but in qualities;
for the bodies shall rise in honour, in power, in incorruption, and spiritual: being sown in dishonour, in weakness,
in corruption, and natural (1 Cor. xv. 42, 44).

93. That the bodies, being raised up, shall be joined
to the souls, whereto formerly they were united; which
to that time were preserved in the hands of the Lord
(Rev. vi. 9, Job xix. 25-27).

94. That it is appointed to all men that they shall once
die, and then cometh the judgment (Heb. ix. 27),
and that the change of them that live on earth at the
last day, shall be as it were a death unto them (1 Cor. xv.
52; 1 Thes. iv. 15-17).

95. That there shall be a general, and universal day of
judgment, when every one shall receive according to
the things that are done in the flesh, whether they be good
or evil (1 Cor. v. 10, Acts xvii. 31).

96. That of the day and hour knoweth no man; no,
not the Angels in heaven, neither the Son Himself, but
the Father only. (Mark xiii. 32).

97. That Christ Jesus that man, shall judge in that
day (Acts xvii. 31), that he shall come in the clouds with
glory: and all His holy angels with Him (Matt. xxv.),
with a shout, and with the voice of the Archangel, and
with the trump of God (1 Thes. iv. 16), and He shall

sit upon the throne of His glory; and all nations shall be gathered before Him, and He shall separate them one from another, as a shepherd separateth the sheep from the goats, setting the sheep on His right hand and the goats on the left (Matt. xxv.).

98. That the king shall say to the sheep, the regenerate, which are on His right hand, " Come, ye blessed of my Father, inherit the kingdom prepared for you before the foundation of the world; " and it shall be performed accordingly (Matt. xxv.).

99. That the king shall say to them on His left hand, the goats, the wicked ones, " Depart from me, ye cursed, into everlasting fire prepared for the Devil and his angels," and it shall be accomplished accordingly (Matt. xxv.).

100. That after the judgment ended and accomplished, and the last enemy that is death being put under the feet of Christ, then the Son himself shall deliver up the kingdom into the hands of the Father, and be subject unto Him, that subdued all things unto Him, that God may be all in all (1 Cor. xv. 24-28).

5. On the occasion of the split in the church Helwys and his party also submitted a set of Latin articles to their Dutch brethren. About 1612 Helwys became convinced that it was his duty to return to England and begin Baptist work there. But before leaving the Netherlands, he drew up and printed in Amsterdam, in 1611, a Confession of twenty-seven articles in English (possibly a translation of the Latin articles) which has been generally recognized as the earliest Baptist Confession.

In republishing it, in 1738, Crosby (Vol II, 389ff) accidentally combined articles twenty-four and twenty-five, thus reducing the number to twenty-six. He was followed by Underhill in his reprint, pp. 1-10. The following text is a reproduction of the only copy of the original known to be in existence, and now in the library of York Minster. The transcript was made by Dr. W. T. Whitley, of Preston, England:

A

DECLARATION OF | FAITH

of

ENGLISH | PEOPLE

REMAINING AT AM | STERDAM IN HOLLAND. |

Heb. 11 . 6.

Without Faith it is impossible to please | GOD. Heb. 11.

Rom. 14 . 23.

Whatsoever is not off Faith is sin.

Prynted . 1611.

To Al The Humble mynded | which love the truth in simplicitie Grace and | peace.

[This is followed by two pages of preface.]

A DECLARATION, ETC.

WEE BELEEVE AND | CONFESSE |

1.

That there are THREE which beare record in heaven, the FATHER, the WORD, and the SPIRIT; and these THREE are one GOD, in all equalitie, 1 Jno. 5.7; Phil. 2.5, 6. By whome all thinges are created and preserved, in Heaven and in Earth. Gen. 1 Chap.

2.

That this GOD in the begining created al things off nothinge, Gen. 1. 1. and made man off the dust off the earth, Chap. 2.7, in his owne ymage, Chap. 1.27, in righteousnes and true Holines. Ephes. 4.24: yet being tempted, fel by disobedience. Chap. 3.1-7. Through whose disobedience, all men sinned. Rom. 5.12-19. His sinn being imputed vnto all; and so death went over all men.

3.

That by the promised seed off the woman, IESVS CHRIST, [and by] his obedience, al are made righteous. Rom. 5.19. Al are made alive, 1 Cor. 15.22. His righteousness being imputed vnto all.

4.

That notwithstanding this Men are by nature the Children off wrath, Ephes. 2.3. borne in iniquitie and in sin conceived. Psal. 51.5. Wise to all evill, but to good they have no knowledg. Jer. 4.22. *The natural mā perceiveth not the thinges off the Spirit off God.* 1 Cor. 2.14. And therefore man is not restored vnto his former estate, but that as man, in his estate off innocency, haveing in himselff all disposition vnto good, & no disposition vnto evill, yet being tempted might yeild, or might resist:

even so now being fallen, and haveing all disposition
vnto evill, and no disposition or will vnto anie good, yet
GOD giveing grace, man may receave grace, or my
reject grace, according to that saying; Deut. 30.19. *I call
Heaven and Earth to record. This day against you, that
I have set before you life and death, blessing and cursing:
Therefore chuse life, that both thou and thy seed may live.*

5.

That GOD before the Foundatiō off the World hath
Predestinated that all that beleeve in him shall-be saved,
Ephes. 1.4, 12; Mark 16.16. and aỉ that beleeve not shalbee
damned. Mark 16.16. all which he knewe before. Rom.
8.29. And this is the Election and reprobacion spoken
of in the Scripturs, concerning salvacion, and condem-
nacion, and not that GOD hath Predestinated men to bee
wicked, and so to bee damned, but that men being
wicked shallbee damned, for GOD would have all men
saved, and come to the knowledg off the truth, 1 Tim.
2.4. and would have no man to perish, but would have
all men come to repentance. 2 Pet. 3.9. and willeth not
the death of him that deith. Ezec. 18.32. And therefore
GOD is the author off no mens comdemnacion, according
to the saieing off the Prophet. Osæa. 13. Thy distruction
O Israel, is off thy selfe, but thy helpe is off mee.

6.

That man is justified onely by the righteousness off
CHRIST, apprehended by faith, Roman. 3.28. Gal. 2.16.
yet faith without works is dead. Jam. 2.17.

7.

That men may fall away from the grace off GOD,
Heb. 12.15. and from the truth, which they have received
& acknowledged, Chap. 10.26. after they have taisted off
the heavēly gift, and were made pertakers off the HOLY
GHOST, and have taisted off the good word off GOD,
& off the powers off the world to come. Chap. 6.4, 5.
And after they have escaped from the filthines off the
World, may bee taugled againe therein & overcome. 2

Pet. 2.20.   That a righteous man may forsake his
righteousnes and perish Ezec. 18.24, 26.   And therefore
let no man presume to thinke that because he hath, or
had once grace, therefore he shall alwaies have grace:
But let all men have assurance, that iff they continew
vnto the end, they shalbee saved: Let no man then presume; but let all worke out their salvacion with feare and
trembling.

8.

That IESVS CHRIST, the Sonne off GOD the second Person, or subsistance in the Trinity, in the Fulnes
off time was manifested in the Flesh, being the seed off
David, and off the Isralits, according to the Flesh. Roman. 1.3 and 8.5. the Sonne off Marie the Virgine, made
of hir substance, Gal. 4.4.   By the power off the HOLIE
GHOST overshadowing hir, Luk. 1.35. and being thus
true Man was like vnto us in all thing, sin onely excepted.
Heb. 4.15. being one person in two distinct natures,
TRVE GOD, and TRVE MAN.

9.

That IESVS CHRIST is Mediator off the New Testament betweene GOD and Man, 1 Tim. 2.5, haveing all
power in Heaven and in Earth given vnto him. Mat.
28.18.   Being the onely KING, Luke 1.33, PREIST, Heb.
7.24, and PROPHET, Act. 3.22.   Off his church, he
also being the onely Law-giver, hath in his Testament set
downe an absolute, and perfect rule off direction, for all
persons, at all times, to bee observed; Which no Prince,
nor anie whosoever, may add to, or diminish from as
they will avoid the fearefull judgments denounced against
them that shal so do. Revel. 22.18, 19.

10.

That the church off CHRIST is a companie off faithful
people 1 Cor. 1.2. Eph. 1.1. seperated frō the world by
the word & Spirit off GOD. 2 Cor. 6, 17. being kint vnto
the LORD, & one vnto another, by Baptisme. 1 Cor.
12.13.   Vpon their owne confessiō of the faith. Act.
8.37. and sinnes. Mat. 3.6.

11.

That though in respect off CHRIST, the Church bee one, Ephes. 4.4. yet it consisteth off divers particuler congregacions, even so manie as there shallbee in the World, every off which congregacion, though they be but two or three, have CHRIST given them, with all the meanes off their salvacion. Mat. 18.20. Roman. 8.32. 1. Corin. 3.22. Are the Bodie off CHRIST. 1. Cor. 12.27. and a whole Church. 1. Cor. 14.23. And therefore may, and ought, when they are come together, to Pray, Prophecie, breake bread, and administer in all the holy ordinances, although as yet they have no Officers, or that their Officers should bee in Prison, sick, or by anie other meanes hindered from the Church. 1 : Pet. 4.10 & 2.5.

12.

That as one congregacion hath CHRIST, so hath all, 2. Cor. 10.7. And that the Word off GOD cometh not out from anie one, neither to anie one congregacion in particuler. 1. Cor. 14.36. But vnto everie particuler Church, as it doth vnto al the world. Coll. 1.5. 6. And therefore no church ought to challeng anie prerogative over anie other.

13.

That everie Church is to receive in all their members by Baptisme vpon the Confession off their faith and sinnes wrought by the preaching off the Gospel, according to the primitive Institucion. Mat. 28.19. And practice, Act. 2.41. And therefore Churches constituted after anie other manner, or off anie other persons are not according to CHRISTS Testament.

14.

That Baptisme or washing with Water, is the outward manifestacion off dieing vnto sinn, and walkeing in newnes off life. Roman. 6.2, 3, 4. And therefore in no wise apperteyneth to infants.

15.

That the LORDS Supper is the outward manifestacion off the Spiritual communion betwene CHRIST and the faithful mutuallie. 1. Cor. 10.16, 17. to declare his death vntil he come. 1 Cor. 11.26.

16.

That the members off everie Church or Congregacion ought to knowe one another, that so they may performe all the duties off love one towards another both to soule and bodie. Mat. 18.15. 1 Thes. 5.14. 1 Cor. 12.25. And especiallie the Elders ought to knowe the whole flock, whereoff the HOLIE GHOST hath made them overseers. Acts 20.28; 1 Pet. 5.2, 3. And therefore a Church ought not to consist off such a multitude as cannot have particuler knowledg one off another.

17.

That Brethren impenitent in one sin after the admonition off the Church, are to bee excluded the cōmunion off the Sainets. Mat. 18.17. 1 Cor. 5.4, 13. & therfore not the cōmitting off sin doth cut off anie from the Church, but refusing to heare the Church to reformacion.

18.

That Excommunicants in respect of civil societie are not to bee avoided, 2. Thess. 3.15. Mat. 18.17.

19.

That everie Church ought (according to the exāple off CHRISTS Disciples and primitive Churches) vpon everie first day off the weeke, being the LORDS day, to assemble together to pray Prophecie, praise GOD, and breake Bread, and performe all other partes off Spirituall communiō for the worship off GOD, their owne mutuall edificacion, and the preservacion off true Religion, & pietie in the church Io 20.19. Act. 2.42 and 20.7, 1. Cor. 16.2. and that ought not to labor in their callings according to the equitie off the moral law, which CHRIST came not to abolish, but to fulfill. Exod. 20.8, &c.

20.

That the Officers off everie Church or congregation are either Elders, who by their office do especially feed the flock concerning their soules, Act. 20.28,   Pet. 5.2, 3. or Deacons Men, and Women who by their office re-leave the necessities off the poore and impotent brethrē concerning their bodies, Acts. 6.1-4.

21.

That these Officers are to bee chosen when there are persons qualified according to the rules in Christs Testament, 1. Tim. 3.2-7. Tit. 1.6-9. Act. 6.3. 4. By Election and approbacion off that Church or congregacion whereoff they are members, Act. 6.3. 4 and 14.23, with Fasting, Prayer, and Laying on off hands, Act. 13.3. and 14.23. And there being but one rule for Elders, therefore but one sort off Elders.

22.

That the Officers off everie Church or congregacion are tied by Office onely to that particuler congregacion whereoff they are chosen, Act. 14.23, and 20.17. Tit. 1.5. And therefore they cannot challeng by office anie aucthoritie in anie other congregation whatsoever except they would have an Apostleship.

23.

That the scriptures off the Old and New Testament are written for our instruction, 2. Tim. 3.16 & that wee ought to search them for they testifie off CHRIST, Io. 5.39. And therefore to bee vsed withall reverence, as conteyning the Holie Word off GOD, which onelie is our direction in al thinges whatsoever.

24.

That Magistracie is a Holie ordinance off GOD, that every soule ought to bee subject to it not for feare onelie, but for conscience sake. Magistraets are the ministers off GOD for our wealth, they beare not the sword for nought. They are the ministers off GOD to take vengance on them that doe evil, Rom. 13. Chap. That it is a fearefull sin to speake evill off them that are in dignitie, and to dispise Government. 2. Pet. 2.10. Wee ought to pay tribute, custome and all other duties. That wee are to pray for thē, for GOD would have them saved and come to the knowledg off his truth. 1 Tim. 2.1. 4. And therefore they may bee members off the Church off CHRIST,

reteining their Magistracie, for no Holie Ordinance off
GOD debarreth anie from being a member off CHRISTS
Church. They beare the sword off GOD,—which sword
in all Lawful administracions is to bee defended and
supported by the servants off GOD that are vnder their
Goverment with their lyves and al that they have according as in the first Institucion off that Holie Ordinance.
And whosoever holds otherwise must hold, (iff they
vnderstãd themselves) that they are the ministers of the
devill, and therefore not to bee praied for nor approved in
anie off their administracions,—seing all things they do
(as punishing offenders and defending their countries,
state, and persons by the sword) is vnlawful.

25.

That it is Lawful in a just cause for the deciding off
strife to take an oath by the Name off the Lord. Heb.
6.16. 2. Cor. 1.23. Phil. 1.8.

26.

That the dead shall rise againe, and the liveingh being
changed in a moment,—haveing the same bodies in substance though divers in qualities. 1. Cor. 15. 52 and 38.
Job 19. 15-28. Luk 24.30.

27.

That after the resurrection all men shall appeare before
the judgment seat off CHRIST to bee judged according
to their workes, that the Godlie shall enioy life Eternall,
the wickeed being condemned shallbee tormented ever-
lastinglie in Hell. Mat. 25.46.

Finis

[The above is followed by a long controversial letter
against Smith. It contains seventeen leaves as against
only four and a half of the confession itself. It charges
Smith with the following six errors:]

1.

That CHRIST concerning the first mother off his
Flesh, he affirmed that all the | Scriptures would not

prove, that he had it off the virgin Marie, but his second mother | which he said was his nourishmeēt, that the Scriptures proved he had of Marie, thus | making CHRIST to have two mothers off his Flesh

2.

That men are justified partelie by the righteousness off Christ apprehended by faith, | partely by their owne inherent righteousness,

3.

That Adams sin was not imputed vnto anie of his posteritie, and that all men | are in the estate off Adam in his innocency before they commit actuall sin, and | therefore infants were not redeemed by Christ, but as the Angels and all other Creatures.

4.

That the Church and Ministery must come by succession contrary to his former, | profession, in words & writings, & that by a supposed succession, he cannot | show, from whome, nor when, nor where

5.

That an Elder off one Church is an Elder off all Churches in the World. |

6.

That Magistrates may not bee members off Christs Church, and retayne their | Magistracie. |

[To these charges Smith replied in a dignified and conciliatory tone in his " Last Book," reprinted in Barclay's *Inner Life,* etc.]

On his return to England Helwys began work in London, and congregations are soon found in other places as well. Through much opposition from all parties, and persecution from the State Church, these General Baptists persevered and grew slowly. For some years they kept up correspondence with the Dutch Mennonites, with whom they were in substantial agreement. (See Evans, II.) They were doubtless aided and stimulated by the rise of the Calvinistic Baptists about 1640. The confusion of the period of the Civil War and the Commonwealth afforded them as well as all other free church parties an excellent opportunity which they faithfully utilized. Beginning with this period we have a second group of Arminian Confessions, all of which fall within the latter half of the century.

1. That of 1651.

The earliest was drawn up in 1651. Thirty congregations in Leicestershire, Lincolnshire, and adjoining counties, sent two representatives each to a meeting to draw up a statement of their views. This is the first General Baptist Confession to speak for more than one church. The original is very rare, and even a facsimile reprint by John Taylor, of Northampton, is not at all common. This reprint is reproduced here. Only the Scripture references are here given, while in the original the passages are quoted in full; and the signatures of the authors are omitted. The Confession thus abridged is as follows:

THE

FAITH

AND

PRACTISE

OF THIRTY

CONGREGATIONS,

GATHERED ACCORDING TO THE

PRIMITIVE PATTERN.

Published (in love) by consent of two from
each Congregation, appointed for that purpose.
1. To inform those who have a desire to know what
Religious Duties they hold forth.
2. To undecieve those that are mis-informed thereof.
3. To the end that the said Congregations may in love,
and the spirit of Meekness, be informed by any
that conceive they walk amiss.

Rom. 12. 18. *If it be possible, as much as in you is,
have Peace with all men.*

London, Printed by *J. M. for Will. Larnar,*
at the Blackmore neer *Fleet-bridge,* 1651.

To all the Saints and Churches of God,
    who walk according to the commands
    of Jesus Christ, in *England, Wales,
    Army,* or else-where.

        Dearly Beloved, and Fellow Citizens
        of the household of God, Grace,
        Mercy, and Peace be multiplyed
        unto you from God, through Jesus
        Christ; The Lord preserve your
minds and hearts by his holy Spirit, with all
those gifts of his Free Grace which he hath
bestowed upon you, to adorn the doctrine of
the Gospel in every thing whereunto ye are
called, to live to the glory and praise of his
Grace.

    Loving Brethren, if we could have con-
veniently convayed this Copie unto your
hands before it went to the Press, doubtless
we might have gained your Christian Advice and Assistance herein, which might
have been very Beneficial to the Truth,
wherein you are with us alike concerned and
engaged; but by reason of the distance of
place, and also being unacquainted, hath
hindred our sending; but we hope our for-
wardness herein will not be any hinderance
to you for the future, to manifest your con-
currence with us, so far as we own the
Truth; for the preserving our Union with
God, and our Joy and Peace with each
other, but the rather to give you occasion to
make use of the Ability and Power God
hath betrusted you with, for our Informati-
ons in what you judge is wanting, and for
our further Confirmation and Encouragement in those things you approve of with us,
have we published this ensuing Treatise;
That so we may agree with love in peace and
truth, by the Assistance of our blessed Lord

and Saviour Jesus Christ. So with our
Prayers, we subscribe our selves
Your Servants in the Lord.
[Signatures of its sixty-one authors here.]

The Faith and Practise of
Thirty Congregations

Ezek. 43. 11.

*And if they be ashamed of all that they
have done, show them the form of the house,
and the fashion thereof, and the goings out
thereof, and the comings in thereof, and all
the forms thereof, and all the ordinances
thereof, and all the laws thereof; and write
it in their sight, that they may keep the whole
form thereof, and all the ordinances thereof,
and do them.*

M a t t h. 5. 16.

Let your light so shine before men, &c.

H e b r. 3. 6.

But Christ as a Son, over his own &c.

1. That that God whom we acknowledge, ought to be worshipped by
all, and above all that are called
Gods, and he is Infinite in power and
wisdom, universal, invisible, eternal. *Ps.* 96.
3. 4. *Ier.* 23. 24. *Col.* 1. 17. *Rom.* 1. 20.

2. That God created all creatures visible and invisible, by his own wisdome and
power, *Col.* 1. 16. *Ier.* 10. 12.

3. That God preserveth all creatures
which are in being. *Nehemiah.* 9. 6. *Rom.* 11. 36.

4. That the creation doth plainly declare the Power and Righteousness of
God; *Rom.* 1. 20. *Isa.* 40. 26.

5. That God commandeth men to take
a view of his Wise, Powerful, and Righteous workes of creation. *Isa.* 40. 26.

6. That God by his good creatures

G

called or calleth men to a serious consideration, or meditation, that they may further
understand his Wisdom and Power. *Rom.* 1. 20.

7. That God doth command men to
speak or declare that which they have
learned by the teaching of the creatures;
Psal. 145. 5.

8. That the consideration of the Lord's
handyworks in creatures, is a means to beget thoughts of God, and of our selves,
sutable to his greatness, and our inferior-
ity; *Psal.* 8. 3, 4.

9. That whatsoever good Meditations,
or serious Considerations we have of the
glorious works of Creation, ought to break
forth with admiration unto thankfulness to
God, *Psal.* 136. *from ver. 3. to ver. 9.*

10. That those who did refuse to worship or glorifie God answerably to the
teaching of the Creation, the Lord gave
them over, or forsook them so far, that they
became so desperately wicked, that they
did things contrary to nature, *Rom.* 1. 26, 27.

11. God created or made *Adam* a
living soul, and in his own Likeness in
Soveraignty or Dominion; *Gen.* 1. 26. 27.

12. That God gave unto *Adam*
Lawes or commands, that he might know
his Will; *Gen.* 2. 16. 17.

13. That God declared unto *Adam*
what penalty or punishment he would
cause to befall him, if he disobeyed his
Will, *Gen.* 2. 17.

14. That *Adam* did sin or disobey the
righteous commands of the Lord, *Gen.*
3. 6.

15. That God told *Adam* very plainly
what death it should be that he would
cause to come on him, and what sorrows
should attend him in the meanwhile; *Gen.*
3. 17, 19.

16. That all mankind are liable to partake of the same death or punishment which the Lord in his righteous judgment caused to fall on *Adam* for his transgression; *Rom.* 5. 18.

17. That *Jesus Christ,* through (or by) the grace of God, suffered death for all mankind, or every man; *Heb.* 2. 9.

18. That *Christ Jesus,* the second *Adam,* will as certainly raise all mankind from that death which fell on them, through or by the first *Adam's* sin or offence, as surely as they partake of it; *Rom.* 5. 18.

19. That *Jesus Christ,* his Lordly or Kingly preheminence over all mankind, is vindicated or maintained in the Scriptures account, by vertue of his dying or suffering for them; *Rom.* 14. 9.

20. That God's Word, Son, or Spirit, are one, 1 *Ioh.* 5. 7. *Jude* 1. *Heb.* 10. 29. *Rom.* 15. 16.

God and his Word are one; *Ioh.* 1. 1. The Word quickneth, *Psal.* 119. 50. The Son quickeneth, *Eph.* 2. 1. And the spirit quickneth Ioh. 6. 63. So they are one. God giveth Gifts, and the Son doth the same, also the holy Ghost, So they are one. *Iam.* 1. 71. *Eph.* 4. 10, 11. *Acts* 2. 38. 1. *Thes.* 1. 5. *Ioh.* 6. 44. *Io.* 14. 6. *Eph.* 1. 18. 1 *Cor.* 12. 3. *Math.* 10. 40. *Gal.* 3. 2.

21. That the Lord of all mankind, *Jesus Christ,* hath the power of giving Lawes for the governing or ruling every man in the World in spiritual worship, *Isa.* 9. 6, 7. *Math.* 28. 18. 19, 20.

22. That this Prince of Peace, *Jesus Christ,* is the only or principal high Priest, which offered up sacrifice, or made reconciliation for the Sins of the people, *Heb.* 2. 17.

23. That the high Priest *Jesus Christ,*

is not onely King or Governour, but also
the Apostle or Prophet of the Truth professed, or the true profession of Saints
Heb. 3. 1.

24. That all the riches appertaining to
a spiritual and eternal life, were treasured up
in *Jesus Christ.* *Col.* 2. 3.

25. That there is not, neither ever was
any man endued with any abilities and
power to do the revealed will of God, but
it was given him from above. *Iam.* 1. 17.

26. That the gifts of God spring from
the pleasure of his will, or of his free grace;
even the Lord *Jesus Christ* sprung from
thence, from whom commeth all spiritual
mercies: *Rom.* 8. 32. *Heb.* 2. 9.

27. That *Iesus Christ* was faithfull in
all things whereunto he was appointed,
Heb. 3. 1, 2.

28. That *Iesus Christ* was not only the
Lawmaker, but the Law giver to every
man that liveth in the world, in that he
giveth every man therein some measure of
light. *Io.* 1. 9.

29. That God of his free love giveth
several gifts unto men, dividing severally as
it pleaseth him, by one and the same spirit;
1 *Cor.* 12. 11. *Eph.* 4. 7.

30. That the gifts of God given unto
men of his own free grace, though never so
richly they may be furnished both with abilities
and power, yet those gifts of grace do not
demonstrate, or declare them to be faithfull
servants; but it doth very plainly prove,
that they are called upon thereby to be
faithfull Servants; 1 *Cor.* 4. 1. 2.

31. That those gifts which God of his
free grace gives unto men to the enabling or
impowering them to obey or believe in his
name, are called the grace of God, as they

spring from the spirit of grace; *Acts.* 18.
17.

32. That when God of his own boun-
tifulness hath given gifts unto men to be
improved by them to the praise of his grace,
as to believe or obey, then those so endued
are Stewards of the grace of God, 1 *Pet.*
4. 10.

33. That God requireth or commandeth service of men, answerable to those gifts
of grace which he of his good pleasure
hath bestowed upon them, *Col.* 2. 6.
Ioh. 12. 37.

34. That it is the gracious pleasure of
God, that *Iesus Christ* his life, death, and
resurrection, should be made known unto
men, and by men, as arguments, or motives,
to allure or provoke them to live holy and
righteous in this present world; *Eph.* 5. 1. 2.
Rom. 6. 4, to *ver.* 14.

35. That God requireth that man
should worship him in Spirit and in truth, or
with all the heart, before they outwardly
make a profession of him: *Acts* 8. 36. 37.

36. That all actions performed by
man towards God, ought to flow from a
principle of Love; 1. *Cor.* 13. 1, 2, 3.

37. That God loves man first, and de-
clareth, or maketh known his love to men,
before any man can Act from a principle of
love in obedience to him, *Io.* 15. 16.

38. That whosoever obeyeth God
with those gifts of his free grace, (as a-
bilities and power to do his will) never so
faithfully, Evangelically, or Unfainedly,
giving him the glory of those performances;
yet thus believing or obeying doth not procure salvation as eternal life, neither are they
any cause at all to move God to bestow it;
Ezek. 16. from *ver.* 3. to *ver,* 10.
Eph. 2. 9. *Rom.* 4. 2. *Jo.* 15. 15.

39. That the ground or principal end of mens believing or obeying God, ought to be for the advancing of the glory of God, or for the Praise of his free grace; 1. *Cor.* 6. 19, 20.

40. That those who serve or fear the Lord, honouring or glorifying him with his gifts bestowed on them, to the praise of his free grace, do demonstratively of openly manifest themselves to be his faithful servants, or children, 1. *Io.* 3. 10. Acts 10. 35.

41. That those which serve the Lord with integrity of mind and spirit, improving their abilities and power given unto them of God, to his glory and praise, are not only called faithful Servants, or the children of the living God, but they have the promises of God to be intrusted with more of the manifestations of himself, which is called the misterie which hath bin hid from many ages, and generations, which the disobedient shall not injoy. *Col.* 1. 26. 27.

42. That those which love the Lord Jesus Christ, so as to walke in his appointed ways with that strength of ability and power which God of his own mercy hath given unto them, they shall have peace of conscience, being freed from anguish of spirit, having their hearts comforted by the holy Ghost; *Rom.* 2. 10.

43. That all those that continue stedfastly unto the end of their lives, pressing forward to the mark (Jesus Christ) that is set before them, shall not only have the comfort and joy which is a part of their portion in this life, but they shall also have a Crown of eternal glory in the life to come; *Rev.* 22. 14. 2 *Tim.* 4. 8.

44. That God of his free grace or love, called or calleth sinners to repentance, and

afforded or affordeth them time or opportunity to repent or returne unto him; *Rom.* 4. 2.

45. That all those who refuse to improve the gifts of grace which God hath afforded them, so that they repent not, neither turne to him in obedience to his commands made manifest unto them, they do despise the goodness of God or his free grace, denying the Lord that bought them, and so are liable to destruction, 1 *Pet.* 2. 1, 2.

46. That whosoever shall preach, teach, or practise any doctrine in the worship of God, pretending it in the name of Jesus Christ, which is not to be heard or read of in the record of God, which was given by inspiration of the holy Ghost; such teachers are lyable to the curse of God, howsoever, countenanced by men, *Gal.* 1. 8, 9.

47. That the Baptisme which the Lord Jesus commanded his disciples to teach, ought to be known by every one, before they submit themselves, or obey it; *Acts.* 2. 38. 41.

48. That the way and manner of baptising, both before the death of Christ, and since his resurection and ascension, was to go into the water, and to be baptised; *Math.* 3. 6. *Math,* 1. 5. and 8. 9.

49. That when Baptisme is made known, or any other Action of obedience, then for men to refuse it, they are said to reject the counsel of God against themselves; *Luk.* 7. 30.

50. That those which received the word of God preached by the Ministrie of the Gospel, and were Baptized according to the Counsel of God, at the same time or day they were of the visible Church of God, *Acts.* 2. 41.

51. That the only foundation of the Church

of God, is the Doctrines of the Apostles or
Prophets, as they spring from Jesus Christ
the chiefe corner stone, whereon this or any-
other people are to be built together as the
house of God; *Eph.* 2. 20, 21.

52. That the chief or only ends of a people baptised according to the counsel of
God, when they meet together as the congregation or fellowship of Christ, are, or
ought to be, for to walk sutably; or to give
up themselves unto a holy conformity to all
the Laws or Ordinances of Jesus Christ,
answerable to the gifts and graces received,
improving them for the glory of God, and
the edification of each other in love, *Eph.*
4. 15, 16.

53. That Jesus Christ took Bread, and
the juice of the Vine, and brake, and gave
to his Disciples, to eat and drink with
thanksgiving; which practise is left upon
record as a memorial of his suffering, to
continue in the Church until he come a-
gain; 1 *Cor.* 11. 23, 24, 25, 26.

54. That the Church ought to call upon
God, seeking him by prayer in the name of
Jesus Christ, and to be thankful to him for
mercies received, sounding forth his praises
with understanding. *Eph.* 6. 16, 17, 18.

55. That if any one of the fellowship
neglect the watching over his own heart,
and so break out into an evill life and conversation, and all good meanes that God
hath appointed hath been used towards
such a one, and that person hath not performed, then ought not such a one to break
bread with obedient walkers, to shew forth
the death of Christ, seeing he doth deny
him in life and conversation; 1 *Cor.* 5. 12.

56. That the people of God ought to have
a tender respect towards them, as long as
there is any hope of being instrumental in the

use of that means which God hath appointed
for the recovering them out of the snare of
sin or wickedness. *2. Thes.* 3. 14, 15.

57. That there be contributions made
for the relief of those that cannot help themselves with food and rayment, that are willing to the utmost to put forth their strength
and skill in some lawful Way or Calling,
especially those that are of the household of
Faith; such as through sickness or weakness of body cannot labour. *Gal.* 6. 9. 10.

58. That it is the good pleasure of
God, which hath given gifts of his grace
to the Saints or Church of God, that some
of the gifted men should be appointed or
set apart to attend upon the preaching of
the word, for the further edifying of the
Churches, that they may be enabled to
stand against all oppositions according as
necessity requires, to the glory of God and
their comfort. *Eph.* 4. 11, 21.

59. That it is the will of God that those
Saints or members of the fellowship which
are appointed so to spend their labors in
teaching or exhorting them in the knowledge of God to their edification and consolation, ought to have maintenance of
those that receive spiritual food by them.
1 *Cor.* 9. 11.

60. That the maintenance of the Ministers which labour in the Word of God,
ought to be the free and Charitable Bene-
volence, or the chearful contribution of
those that acknowledge themselves members of the same fellowship; 2 *Cor.* 9. 13.

61. That the servants of God, or the
Ministers of the Gospel, ought to be content with necessary food and rayment,
and to labour with their hands, that they
may not be overchargeable, 1 *Cor.* 4. 12.

because they are to teach that doctrine to
every member. *Heb.* 13. 5.

62. That those servants of God which
labour in the word much, and well, ought
to be had in very good estimation; 1 *Tim.* 5. 17.

63. That the Church of Jesus Christ
ought not to think of any man above what
is meet, lest that they give that honour to
man, which properly and alone belongeth
to God; *Psal.* 115. 1.   2 *Cor.* 12. 6.

64. That the Church hath directions of
God to set apart some men that are sute-
ably qualified, to oversee, or order the affairs concerning the poor distressed members of Christ, that they may not be neglected, and so perish for want of food and
rayment, and to take off that work from ly-
ing too heavy upon the care of those which
labour in the word and doctrine; *Acts.* 6. 3, 4.

65. That if the poor fearing God, cannot conveniently have a competent maintenance, for the supply of their necessities in
that society whereunto they must commonly resort, that then those men that have
the care laid upon them, send or give in-
telligence to the other Churches or saints of
God, who have ingaged themselves by
declaring their willingness towards the relief of such a distressed people, *Rom.* 15. 26.

66. That those men which the Church
of God are to make such uses of as the setting them to minister unto the saints in
things spritual or temporall, it is required
that the Church judge those men found in
the faith, that their lives and conversations
be unblameable, that those which are
without, cannot have any just occasion to
speak reproachfully of them, that they be
not covetous of filthy lucre, neither selfwill-
ed, but loving and patient towards all men,
apt to teach, and to do good works answer-

able to their abilities. *Titus* 1. 7, 8. 9. *Acts*. 6. 3.

67. That some men amongst the brother-hood who are able to judge in causes of difference that may arise betwixt them in the Church, may be approved or appointed to put an end thereto without partiality, that there may be no unnecessary strivings in the Law to vex one another; 1 *Cor*. 6. 5, 6, 7.

68. That whosoever of the Society or Church of God which shall willfully or carelessly neglect any lawful way or calling, and to fall into hunger and nakedness, ought to be exhorted with love and meek-ness, to labour with their abilities in some honest way or calling for their relief which being done orderly, and he or they will not reform, so that sutable exhortations take no place, such an one shall be excluded or ex-communicated, as one that hath denyed the faith; 1. *Tim*. 5. 8.

69. That the offended ought to proceed according to rule, not delaying or prolonging time, but out of a tender care, that their hearts may not be hardned by a custome in sin, that thereby the reclaiming of them from sin may be done with less difficulty; *Mat*. 18. 15, 16, 17.

70. That if any controversie should so fall out, that the case cannot easily be deter-mined by that society or church where it is first presented, that then use be made of some other society which they are in fellow-ship with, for their assistance therein; *Acts* 16. 1, 2.

71. That there be an orderly improving those gifts that God of his free grace hath bestowed on the Saints, that one may not hinder another, but as occasion serveth, one by one, speaking the things that they have learned of God, that the hearers may be

profited, and so put in a capacity to judge of things concerning the glory of God, and their own peace; 1 *Cor.* 14. 30, 31.

72. That if any one which hath been of the fellowship of Christ, and hath so far subjected himself to temptations that he denyeth to live righteously, or in the fear and love of God and makes shipwrack of Faith and a good Conscience, for which he hath been excommunicated according to Order, that it be recorded, and made known to other the Churches, for prevention of evils in them; 1 *Tim.* 1. 19, 20.

73. That Fasting and Prayer ought to be used, and laying on of hands, for the Ordaining of servants or Officers to attend about the service of God; *Acts* 13. 3.

74. That we ought to behave our selves towards all men, no otherwise then we would freely and cheerfully they in the like case (if it should fall out) should do toward us, and that we ought to seek a peaceable life with all men, as far as possibly we can, keeping faith and a good conscience; *Luke* 6. 31. *Rom.* 12. 18. 1 *Tim.* 1. 19.

75. That we ought to clear our selves, not only from evil Thoughts harbouring in our hearts, or the evils in life and conversation; but as far as we can, vindicate our selves from all those scandalous aspersions that daylie fall about our ears, setting our good names on fire, to the dishonour of God, whereof many are the Instruments by their wilful contrivances, or by the mis-informations of others, which father upon us such principles and practises as we abhor, through ignorant mistakes cunningly suggested by some evil willers at least; 2 *Cor.* 2. 17.

Postscript.

THat we do own a Magistratical power
for the governing of this our English
Nation, to be determined in a just Parliamentary way; and that we ought to pray
for good Governors, and good Government; that we may live a peaceable and
godly life in all honesty; standing ready at
all times, as necessity may require, to vindicate such a Magistracy or Magistrates, not
only with arguments of sound reason, but
also with our Estates and Lives; that
Righteousness may reigne, and Vice may be
overthrown, without respect of persons.

FINIS.

2. The Standard Confession of 1660

The standard Confession of the English General Baptists was drawn up in March, 1660, in the midst of the
calumnies and persecutions of the Restoration. It is
supposed to have been composed by Thos. Grantham
(Taylor, "His. Eng. General Baptists," I, 466), and
was subscribed by certain elders, deacons, and brethren
from various parts of the kingdom, met in London and
composing the General Assembly of the General Baptists

and representing, they claim, upwards of twenty thousand members. It was formally presented to King Charles II July 26, 1660, along with an address (Crosby, II, 19f; Taylor, I, 186f). It was at once published and was often reprinted. It was also " printed on a sheet to be hung up in a frame," and in this form adorned many homes. It was reaffirmed by the General Assembly, 1663, edited by Thos. Grantham in 1678, with " a few explanatory supplements, and the testimony of many ancient writers of Christianity," " to shew, that though the composition of these articles be new, yet the doctrine contained therein is truly ancient." The changes were numerous but unimportant. In 1691 the General Assembly approved its republication " with Brother Grantham's explication of the third article "; it was again approved by the General Assembly in 1697 and 1704, and many later editions are known.

The Confession was rather freely edited and reprinted by Crosby, Vol. II, App. IV, and by Underhill, pp. 107f. It represented the entire body of General Baptists in England, and is the first of the General Baptist Confessions to prescribe dipping or immersion as the essential form of baptism. If Smyth and his immediate followers did originally practise affusion, as seems most probable, it is not known when the General Baptists began the practice of immersion. The Calvinistic Baptists (or, perhaps we should say Anabaptists) began immersion as early as 1640 or 1641, and incorporated immersion as the only acceptable form of baptism in their first Confession in 1644. This action would naturally influence the General Baptists, and it has been supposed that they gradually adopted immersion until it was made the only acceptable mode in this Confession of 1660.

The following is an exact reproduction of the original:

A BRIEF

CONFESSION

OR

DECLARATION

OF

FAITH

Set forth by many of us, who are (falsely)
called Ana-Baptists, to inform all Men
(in these days of scandal and reproach) of our
inno | cent Belief and Practise; for which we
are not on | ly resolved to suffer Persecution,
to the loss of | our Goods, but also Life it self,
rather | than to decline the same.

Subscribed to by certain Elders, Deacons, and Brethren,
met at | *London,* in the first month (called *March,*
1660.) in the be | half of themselves, and many others
unto whom they belong, in | *London,* and in several
Counties of this Nation, who are of the | same Faith
with us.

*After the Way which men call Heresie, so Worship we
the God of our | Fathers; Believing all things which are
written in the Law, and | in the Prophets,* Acts 24, 14.

LONDON
Printed by *G. D.* for *F. Smith,* at the *Elephant* and
Castle, near | *Temple-Barr,* 1660.
[page 3]

A BRIEF
CONFESSION
OR
Declaration of Faith,

Set out by many of Us, who are (falsely) called
Ana-Baptists, to inform all men (in these days of
scandal | and reproach) of our innocent Belief, and
Practise: for which | we are not only resolved to suffer
persecution, to the loss of our | Goods, but also to life
it self, rather then to decline the same.

I. We Believe and are verily confident, that | there is but
one God the Father, of | whom are all things,
from everlasting | to everlasting, glorious, and
unword | able in all his attributes, 1 *Cor.* 8, 6.
Isa. 40. 28.

II. That God in the beginning made | Man
Upright, and put him into a state | and condition
of Glory, without the | least mixture of misery,
from which he | by *transgression* fell, and so
came into a miserable and mortal estate, | subject unto the
first death, *Gen.* 1. 31. *Eccles.* 7. 29. *Gen.* 2. 17. 3.
17, 18, 19.

III. That there is one Lord Jesus Christ, by whom
are all things, | who is the only begotten Son of God, born
of the Virgin *Mary;* | yet as truly *Davids* Lord, and
Davids root, as *Davids* Son, and *Da* [page 4] *vids* Off-
spring, Luke 20. 44. *Revel.* 22. 16. whom God freely *sent*
| *into the World* (because of his great love unto the
World) who as | *freely gave himself a ransome for all,* I
Tim. 2. 5, 6. *tasting death* | *for every man, Heb.* 2. 9. *a
propitiation for our sins; and not for ours* | *only, but also
for the sins of the whole World,* I John 2. 2.

IV. That *God is not willing that any should perish, but
that all* | *should come to repentance,* 2 Pet. 3. 9. *and the
knowledge of the truth,* | *that they might be saved,* I Tim.
2. 4. For which end Christ hath | commanded, that the
Gospel (to wit, the glad tydings of remission | of sins)
should be preached to every creature, *Mark* 16. 15. So |
that no man shall eternally suffer in Hell (that is, the

second death) | for want of a Christ that dyed for them,
but as the Scripture saith, | for *denying the Lord that
bought them,* 2 *Pet.* 2. 1. or because they | *believe not in
the name of the only begotten Son of God, John* 3. | 18.
Unbelief therefore being the cause why the just and
righteous | God, will condemn the children of men; it fol-
lows against all con | tradiction, that all men at one time
or other, are put into such a | capacity, as that (through
the grace of God) they may be eternally | saved, *John*
1. 7. *Acts* 17. 30. *Mark* 6. 6. *Heb.* 3. 10, 18, 19. 1 *John*
| 5. 10. *John* 3. 17.

V. That such who first orderly comes into, and are
brought up | in the School of Christs Church, and wait-
ing there, comes to de|grees of Christianity, rightly quali-
fied and considerably gifted by | Gods Spirit; ought to
exercise their gifts not only in the Church, | but also (as
occasion serves) to preach to the World (they being | ap-
proved of by the Church so to do) *Acts* 11. 22, 23, 24.
Acts 11. | 19. 20. and that among such some are to be
chosen by the Church, | and ordained by Fasting, Prayer,
and Laying on of Hands, for the | work of the Ministry,
Acts 13. 2, 3. *Acts* 1. 23. Such so ordained, | (and abi-
ding faithful in their work) we own as Ministers of the
Gos | pel; but all such who come not first to repent of
their sins, believe | on the Lord Jesus, and so *Baptized*
in his name for the remission of | Sins, but are only
brought up in the Schools of humane learning, | to the
attaining humane arts, and variety of languages, with
ma | ny vain curiosities of speech, 1 *Cor.* 1. 19, 21. 2. 1, 4,
5. seeking | rather the gain of large revenues, then the
gain of souls to God: | such (we say) we utterly deny,
being such as have need rather to | be taught themselves,
than fit to teach others, *Rom.* 2. 21. |

VI. That the way set forth by God for men to be
justified in, is | by faith in Christ, *Rom.* 5. 1. | [page 5]

That is to say, when men shall assent to the truth of
the Gospel, | believing with all their hearts, that there is
remission of sins, and e | ternal life to be had in Christ.|

And that Christ therefore is most worthy their con-
stant affecti | ons, and subjection to all his Commande-
ments, and therefore re | solve with purpose of heart so to

H

subject unto him in all things, and | no longer unto themselves, 2 *Cor.* 5. 15. |

And so, shall (with godly sorrow for the sins past) commit | themselves to his grace, confidently depending upon him for that | which they believe is to be had in him: such so believing are justifi | ed from all their sins, their faith shall be accounted unto them for | righteousness, *Rom.* 4. 22, 23, 24. *Rom.* 3. 25, 26. |

VII. That there is one holy Spirit, the pretious gift of God, free | ly given to such as *obey him, Ephes.* 4. 4. *Acts* 5. 32. that there | by they may be throughly sanctified, and made able (without which | they are altogether unable) to abide stedfast in the faith, and to | honour the Father, and his Son Christ, the Author and finisher of | their faith; I *Cor.* 6. 11. There are three that bear record in Hea | ven, the Father, the Word, the holy Spirit, and these three are one; | which Spirit of promise such have not yet received, (though they | speak much of him) that are so far out of *Love, Peace, Long-suffe* | *ring, Gentleness, Goodness, Meekness, and Temperance,* (*the* | *fruits of the Spirit, Gal.* 5. 22, 23.) as that they breath out much | cruelty, and great envy against the Liberties, and peaceable living | of such, as are not of their judgment, though holy as to their conver | sations. |

VIII. That God hath even before *the foundation of the world* | *chosen,* (or elected) *to eternal life, such as believe,* and so are in | Christ, *John* 3. 16. *Ephes.* 1. 4, 2 *Thes.* 2. 13. yet confident we | are, that the purpose of God according to election, was not in the | least arising from fore-seen faith in, or works of righteousness done | by the creature, but only from the mercy, goodness, and com | passion dwelling in God, and so *it is of him that calleth, Rom.* 9. 11. | whose purity and unwordable holiness, cannot admit of any unclean | person (or thing) to be in his presence, therefore his decree of mer | cy reaches only the godly man, whom (saith *David*) God hath | *set apart for himself,* Psal. 4. 3. |

IX. That men not considered simply as men, but ungodly men, | *were of old ordained to condemnation,* considered as such, who turn [page 6] the grace of God

unto wantonness, and deny the only Lord God, | and our
Lord Jesus Christ, *Jude* 4. God indeed sends a strong
de | lusion to men, that they might be damned; but we
observe that they | are such (as saith the Apostle) that
received not the love of the | *truth, that they might be*
saved, 2 Thes. 2. 10, 11, 12. and so the | indignation and
wrath of God, is upon *every soul* of man that doth | *evil,*
(living and dying therein,) *for there is no respect of*
persons | *with God.* Rom. 2. 9, 10, 11. |

X. That all Children dying in Infancy, having not ac-
tually trans | gressed against the Law of God in their
own persons, are only sub | ject to the first death, which
comes upon them by the sin of the first | *Adam,* from
whence they shall be all raised by the second *Adam*; | and
not that any one of them (dying in that estate) shall suf-
fer for | *Adams* sin, eternal punishment in Hell, (which
is the second death) | *for of such belongs the Kingdome*
of Heaven, 1 Cor. 15. 22. Mat. 19. | 14. not daring
to conclude with that uncharitable opinion of others, |
who though they plead much for the bringing of children
into the | visible Church here on earth by *Baptism,* yet
nevertheless by their | Doctrine that Christ dyed but for
some, shut a great part of them out | of the Kingdome of
Heaven for ever. |

XI. That the right and only way, of gathering
Churches, (accor | ding to Christs appointment, *Mat.* 28.
19, 20.) is first to teach, or | preach the Gospel, *Mark* 16.
16. to the Sons and Daughters of | men,; and then to
Baptise (that is in English to *Dip*) in the name of | the
Father, Son, and holy Spirit, or in the name of the Lord
Jesus | Christ; such only of them, as profess *repentance*
towards God, and | *faith towards our Lord Jesus Christ,*
Acts. 2. 38. Acts 8. 12. Acts | 18. 8. And as for all
such who preach not this Doctrine, but instead | thereof,
that Scriptureless thing of Sprinkling of Infants (*falsly*
called|Baptisme) whereby the pure *word of God is made*
of no effect, and the | new Testament-way of bringing
in Members, into the Church by re | generation, cast out;
when as the bond-woman & her son, that is to | say, the
old Testament-way of bringing in Children into the
Church | by generation, is cast out, as saith the Scrip-

ture, *Gal.* 4. 30, 22, 23, 24. | *Mat.* 3. 8, 9. all such we utterly deny, forasmuch as we are com | manded to *have no fellowship with the unfruitful works of darkness,* | *but rather to reprove them,* Ephes. 5. 11. |

XII. That it is the duty of all such who are believers *Baptized,* | to draw nigh unto God in submission to that principle of Christs [page 7] Doctrine, to wit, Prayer and Laying on of Hands, that they may | receive the promise of the holy Spirit, *Heb.* 6. 1. 2. *Acts* 8. 12, 15, | 17. *Acts* 19. 6. *2 Tim.* 1. 6. whereby they may *mortifie the deeds of* | *the body,* Rom. 8. 13. and live in all things answerable to their pro | fessed intentions, and desires, even to the honour of him, *who hath* | *called them out of darkness into his marvellous light.* |

XIII. That it is the duty of such who are constituted as aforesaid, | to *continue stedfastly in Christs and the Apostles Doctrine, and assem* | *bling together, in fellowship, in breaking of Bread, and Prayer, Acts* | 2. 42. |

XIV. That although we thus declare the primitive way, and | order of constituting Churches, yet we verily believe, and also de | clare, that unless men so professing, and practising the forme and or|der of Christs Doctrine, shall also beautifie the same with a holy and | wise conversation, in all godliness and honesty; the profession of | the visible form will be rendered to them of no effect; *for without* | *holiness no man shall see the Lord,* Heb. 12. 14. Isa. 1. 11, 12, 15, | 16. |

XV. That the Elders or Pastors which God hath appointed to | oversee, and feed his Church (constituted as aforesaid) are such, | who first being of the number of Disciples, shall in time appear to *be* | *vigilent, sober, of good behavour, given to hospitality, apt to teach,* | &c. *not greedy of filthy lucre* (as too many National Ministers are) | *but patient; not a brawler, not covetuous,* &c. and as such chose, | and ordained to office (according to the order of Scripture, *Acts* 14. | 23.) who are to feed the flock with meat in due season, and in much | love to rule over them, with all care, seeking after such as go astray; | but as for all such who labour to feed themselves with the fat, more | than to feed the flock, *Ezek.* 34. 2, 3. seeking more after theirs, | than them, expresly contrary to the practise of the Ministers of | old, who said, *we seek not yours, but you*, 2 *Cor*. 12. 14. All such we | utterly deny, and hereby bear our continued Testimony against, | *Ezek*. 34.

XVI. That the Ministers of Christ, that have freely received | from God, ought freely to Minister to others, 1 *Cor*. 9. 17. and | that such who have spiritual things, freely Ministered unto them, | ought freely to communicate necessary things to the Ministers, (up|on the account of their charge) 1 *Cor*. 9. 11. *Gal*. 6. 6. And as for [page 8] Tyths, or any forced Maintenance, we utterly deny to be the Main | tenance of Gospel Ministers.

XVII. That the true Church of Christ, ought after the first and | second admonition, to reject all Hereticks, *Tit*. 3. 10, 11. and in the | name of the Lord to withdraw from all such, as profess the way of | the Lord, but walks disorderly in their conversations, 2 *Thes*. 3. 6. | or any wayes causes divisions or offences, contrary to the Doctrine | (of Christ) which they have learned, *Rom*. 16. 17. |

XVIII. That such who are true Believers, even Branches in | Christ the Vine, (and that in his account, whom he exhorts to a | bide in him, *John* 15. 1, 2, 3, 4, 5.) or such who have charity out of | a pure heart, and of a good conscience, and of Faith unfeigned, | 1 *Tim*. 1. 5. may nevertheless for want of watchfulness, swerve and | turn aside from the same, *vers*. 6, 7. and become as withered Bran | ches, cast into the fire and burned, *John*. 15. 6. But such *who add un* | *to their Faith Vertue, and unto Vertue Knowledge, and unto Know* | *ledge Temperance*, &c. 2 *Pet*. 1. 5, 6, 7. such *shall never fall, vers*. | 8, 9, 10. 'tis impossible for all the false Christs, and false Prophets, | that are, and are to come, to deceive such, for they are *kept by the po* | *wer of God, through Faith unto Salvation*, 1 *Pet*. 1. 5.

XIX. That the poor Saints belonging to the Church of Christ, | are to be sufficiently provided for by the Churches, that they neither | want food or rayment, and this by a free and voluntary contributi | on, (and not of necessity, or by the constraint or power of the Ma | gistrate) 2 *Cor*. 9. 7. 1 *Cor*. 8. 11, 12, and this through

the free and | voluntary help of the Deacons, (called
Overseers of the poor) be | ing faithful men, chosen by
the Church, and ordained by Prayer | and Laying on of
Hands, to that Work, *Acts* 6. 1, 2. 3, 4, 5, 6. So | that
there is no need in the Church of Christ, of a Magesterial
compul | sion in this case, as there is among others, who
being constituted in | a fleshly and generational way, are
necessitated to make use of a | carnal sword, to compel
even a small, mean, and short Maintenance | for their
poor; when as many other Members of their Churches,
can | and do part with great and large Sums of Money, to
maintain their | vain fashions, Gold, Pearls, and costly
Array, which is expressly con | trary to the Word of God.
1 *Tim.* 2. 9, 10.   1 *Pet.* 3. 3.   Alas, *what | will such do
when God riseth up, and when he visiteth, what will they
| answer him?* Job 31. 14. | [page 9]

XX. That there shall be (through Christ who was
dead, but is a | live again from the dead) a Resurrection
of all men from the graves | of the Earth, *Isa.* 26. 19.
both the just and the unjust, *Acts* 24. 15. | that is, the
fleshy bodies of men, sown into the graves of the earth, |
corruptable, dishonourable, weak, natural, (which so con-
sidered | cannot inherit the Kingdome of God) shall be
raised again, incor | ruptable, in glory, in power, spiritual,
and so considered, the | bodies of the Saints, (united
again to their spirits) which here suffer | for Christ, shall
inherit the *Kingdome, raigning* together with | Christ, 1
Cor. 15. 21, 22, 42, 43, 44, 49. |

XXI. That there shall be after the Resurrection from
the graves of | the Earth, *An eternal Judgement,* at
the appearing of Christ, and | his Kingdome, 2 *Tim.* 4. 1.
Heb. 9. 27. at which time of judgement | which is un-
alterable, and irrevocable, *every man shall receive ac |
cording to the things done in his body,* 2 Cor. 5. 10. |

XXII. That the same Lord Jesus who shewed himself
alive af | ter his passion, by many infallible proofs, *Acts*
1. 3. which was | taken up from the Disciples, and carried
up into Heaven, *Luke* | 24. 51. *Shall so come in like
manner as he was seen go into Heaven,* | Acts. 1. 9, 10,
11. *And when Christ who is our life shall appear, we |
shall also appear with him in glory, Col.* 3. 4.   For then

shall he be | King of Kings, and Lord of Lords, *Rev.* 19.
16. for the Kingdome | is his, and he is the Governour
among the Nations, *Psal.* 22. 28. | and King over all the
earth, *Zech.* 14. 9. *and we shall raign (with | him) on the
Earth,* Rev. 5. 10. the Kingdomes of this World, | (which
men so mightily strive after here to enjoy) shall become
the | Kingdomes of our Lord, and his Christ, *Rev.* 11. 15.
for *all is yours,* | (O ye that overcome this world) *for
ye are Christs, and Christ is* | *Gods,* 1 Cor. 3. 22, 23. *For
unto the Saints shall be given the King* | *dome, and the
greatness of the Kingdome, under* (mark that) *the* |
whole Heaven, Dan. 7. 27. Though (alas) now many
men be | scarce content that the Saints should have so
much as being a | mong them; but when Christ shall ap-
pear, then shall be their day, | then shall be given unto
them power over the Nations, to rule | them with a Rod
of Iron, *Rev.* 2. 26, 27. then shall they receive a | Crown
of life, which no man shall take from them, nor they by |
any means turned, or overturned from it, for the op-
pressor shall | be broken in pieces, *Psal.* 72. 4. and their
now vain, rejoycings | turned into mourning, and bitter
Lamentations, as 'tis written, [page 10] *Job* 20. 5, 6, 7.
The triumphing of the wicked is short, and the joy | *of
the Hypocrite but for a moment; though his excellency
mount up to* | *the Heavens, and his head reach unto the
clouds, yet shall he perish* | *for ever, like his own dung;
they which have seen him, shall say, where* | *is he?* |

XXIII. That the holy Scriptures is the rule whereby
Saints both | in matters of Faith, and conversation are to
be regulated, they being | able to make men wise unto
salvation, through Faith in Christ | Jesus, profitable for
Doctrine, for reproof, for instruction in | righteousness,
that the man of God may be perfect, throughly | furnished
unto all good works, 2 *Tim.* 3. 15, 16, 17. *John* 20. 31. |
Isa. 8. 20. |

XXIV. That it is the will, and mind of God (in these
Gospel | times) that all men should have the free liberty
of their own Consci | ences in matters of Religion, or
Worship, without the least op | pression, or persecution,
as simply upon that account; and that | for any in Au-
thority otherwise to act, we confidently believe is ex |

pressly contrary to the mind of Christ, who requires that whatsoe | ver men would that others should do unto them, they should even | so do unto others, *Mat.* 7. 12. and that the Tares, and the Wheat | should grow together in the field, (which is the world) until the | harvest (which is the end of the world,) *Mat.* 13. 29, 30, 38, | 39. |

XXV. We believe that there ought to be civil Magistrates in all | Nations, *for the punishment of evil doers, and for the praise of them* | *that do well,* 1 *Pet.* 2. 14. and that all wicked lewdness, and fleshly | filthiness, contrary to just and wholesome (Civil) Laws, ought | to be punished according to the nature of the offences; and this | without respect of any Persons, Religion, or profession whatsoe | ver; and that we and all men are obliged by Gospel rules, to be | subject to the higher Powers, to obey Magistrates, *Tit.* 3. 1. *and to* | *submit to every Ordinance of man, for the Lords sake,* as saith *Peter* 2. | 13. But in case the Civil Powers do, or shall at any time impose | things about matters of Religion, which we through conscience to | God cannot actually obey, then we with *Peter* also do say, that we | ought (in such cases) to obey God rather than men; *Acts* 5. 29. | and accordingly do hereby declare our whole, and holy intent and | purpose, that (through the help of grace) we will not yield, nor | (in such cases) in the least actually obey them; yet humbly pur [page 11] posing (in the Lords strength) patiently to suffer whatsoever shall | be inflicted upon us, for our conscionable forbearance. |

These things (O ye Sons and Daughters of Men) we verily believe | to be the Lords will and mind, and therefore cannot but speak, | and if herein we differ from many, yea from multitudes, from the | learned, the wise and prudent of this World, we (with *Peter* and | *John*) do herein make our solemne, and serious appeale, namely, | *whether it be right in the sight of God, to hearken unto men,* (of a con | trary perswasion) *more than unto God?* Oh let the judicious, | judge righteous judgement! *Acts* 4. 19, 20.

And in the beleife, and practise of these things, (it being the | good old Apostolical way) our souls have found that rest, and soul | peace, which the world knows not, and which they cannot take | from us; of whom then should we be afraid? *God is become our* | *strength, our light, our salvation; therefore,* we are resolved | (through grace) to seal the truth or these things in way of suffer | ing persecution, not only to the loss of our goods, free-domes, or | liberties, but with our lives also (if called thereunto.) |

Moreover we do utterly, and from our very hearts, in the | Lords fear, declare against all those wicked, and divillish reports, | and reproaches, falsly cast upon us, as though some of us (in & about | the City of *London*) had lately gotten **knives, booked knives,** & the | like, & great store of Arms besides what was given forth by order of | Parliament, intending to cut the throats of such as were contrary | minded to us in matters of Religion, and that many such **knives,** and | Armes, for the carrying on some secret design, hath been found in | some of our houses by search; we say, from truth of heart, in the | Lords fear, that we do utterly abhor, and abominate the thoughts | thereof, and much more the actions; and do hereby challenge both | City, and Coun-try (in our innocency herein) as being not able | to prove the things whereof they accuse us; and do for evermore | declare the Inventors of such reports, to be lyers, and wicked de | visers of mischeife, and corrupt designs: God that is above all will | justifie our innocency herein, who well knows our integrity, in what | we here declare, the Lord lay it not to their charge. |

In the time of building the decayed House of *God,* Samballet, & | Tobiah, (*wicked Counsellors*) *hired* Shemaiah *to make good* Nehemiah | *afraid;* and la-boured against him, that they might have *matter for* [page 12] *an evil report,* that they might reproach him, & hinder the building | of the house of God. Neh. 6. 12. *For I have heard (saith the Prophet)* | *the defaming of many; report, say they, and we will report it,* Jer. 20. | 10. |

Suscribed by certain Elders, Deacons, and Brathren met | at *London,* in the first Month (called *March,* 1660.) in the | behalf of themselves, and many others unto whom they be | long, in *London,* and in several

Counties of this Nation, | who are of the same Faith
with Us.

Joseph Wright,	*John Hammersly,*
William Jeffery,	*William Russel,*
Thomas Monck,	*Joseph Keeich,*
John Hartnoll,	*Nicholas Newberry,*
Benjamine Morley,	*Samuel Lover,*
Francis Stanley,	*George Wright,*
George Hammon,	*John Parsons, Junior,*
William Smart,	*John Claton,*
John Reeve,	*Thomas Seele,*
Thomas Parrot,	*Michaiel Whiticar,*
John Wood,	*Giles Browne,*
Francis Smith,	*John Wells,*
Edward Jones,	*Stephen Torie,*
Humphrey Jones,	*Thomas Lathwel,*
Matthew Caffen,	*William Chadwell,*
Samuel Loveday,	*William Raph,*
John Parsons, Senior	*Henry Browne,*
Thomas Stacy,	*William Paine,*
Edward Stanley,	*Richard Bowin,*
Jonathan Gennings,	*Thomas Smith,*

, THE END

3. The " Orthodox Creed," 1678.

Charles II had received the Baptist messengers who
presented the preceding Confession very graciously, and
promised redress. But January 6, 1661, Thomas Venner
and the Fifth Monarchy men broke into open rebellion
in London. The king at once forbade all meetings of
sectaries, and suspicion of complicity in the rebellion
fell on the Baptists. In order to clear themselves from
such an unjust imputation, they presented to the king and
then published a noble apology, setting forth their loyal
attitude toward the State (Crosby II, 35-49). As persecution continued, they published, on May 8, 1661, a
powerful plea for toleration, addressed to the king, Parliament, and people of England (Crosby II, 98-146). It

is marked by ability and learning, but accomplished little or no mitigation of the severe persecutions.

The common sufferings of all Dissenters during this period drove them nearer together, and aroused a desire for closer relations. They emphasized points of agreement, rather than differences. This tendency manifested itself in both wings of the Baptists by the production of union Confessions almost simultaneously. In 1677 the Calvinistic Baptists, in order to show their large agreement with Presbyterians and Congregationalists, formulated a new Baptist Confession by slightly revising the Westminster Confession, which had also been adopted by the Congregationalists after necessary adaptations. The next year, 1678, the General Baptists drew up their so-called " Orthodox Creed " " to unite and confirm all true protestants in the fundamental articles of the Christian religion, against the errors and heresies of Rome." It is supposed to have been written by Thos. Monk, and was signed by fifty-four " messengers, elders, and brethren " from Buckinghamshire, Oxfordshire, and adjoining counties, Jan. 30, 1678 [9]. In accordance with its unionistic design, it approaches the Calvinistic position as nearly as possible, and is of special interest as the first attempt at that compromise between the two great systems of theology which was such a marked characteristic of the work of Andrew Fuller and others in the latter part of the eighteenth century. Moreover, it seeks to meet and overthrow the Socinian views, which had been inherited by the General Baptists from the Anabaptists, and had disturbed them somewhat from the beginning of their history. Accordingly it is quite full on the Trinity and Person of Christ and related doctrines, seeking to explain all phases of these abstruse questions. It was reprinted by Crosby (III, Appendix I) and by Underhill (pp. 121f). Crosby's text is reproduced here.

AN

ORTHODOX CREED,

OR

A PROTESTANT CONFESSION OF FAITH,

BEING AN

ESSAY TO UNITE AND CONFIRM ALL TRUE PROTESTANTS

IN THE FUNDAMENTAL ARTICLES OF THE CHRISTIAN RELIGION, | AGAINST THE ERRORS AND HERESIES OF ROME.

LONDON, Printed in the year, 1679.

An orthodox CREED.

I. ARTICLE.

Of the Essence of God.

We verily believe, that there is
but one, only living and true
God; whose subsistence is in
and of himself, whose essence
cannot be comprehended by
any but himself; a most pure, spiritual,
or invisible substance; who hath an absolute, independent, unchangeable, and infinite being; without matter or form,
body, parts, or passions.
For I am the Lord, I change not; God is
a spirit. Now unto the king eternal, immortal, invisible, the only wise God, be honour and glory, for ever and ever, Amen.
Ye heard a Voice, but saw no similitude.

Deut. 6 : 4; 5 : 26.
Ps. 42 : 2.
Jer. 10 : 10.
Exod. 3 : 14.
Ps. 147 : 5.
Hab. 1 : 13.
Deut. 4 : 15, 16.
Col. 1 : 15.
Acts 17 : 28.
Luke 24 : 39.
Mal. 3 : 6.
John 4 : 24.
I Tim. 1 : 17.
Deut. 14 : 12.

II. ARTICLE.

Of the divine Attributes in God.

Every particle of being in heaven and
earth, leads us to the infinite being of
beings, namely God, who is simplicity,
viz. one mere and perfect act, without
all composition, and an immense sea of
perfections; who is the only eternal being, everlasting without time, whose immense presence, is always every where
present, having immutability without any
alteration in being, or will; in a word,
God is infinite, of universal, unlimited,
and incomprehensible perfection, most holy,
wise, just, and good; whose wisdom is
his justice, whose justice is his holiness,
and whose wisdom, justice, and holiness,
is himself. Most merciful, gracious, faithful, and true, a full fountain of love, and
who is that perfect, sovereign, divine will,
the Alpha of supreme being.
Is it true, indeed, that God will dwell on
the earth? Behold, the heaven, and heaven
of heavens, cannot contain thee: how much less
this house which I have built. Great is the
Lord, and worthy to be praised, and his
greatness is incomprehensible.

John 5 : 26.
I John 1 : 5.
Matt. 5 : 48.
Exod. 6 : 3.
Isaiah 40 : 28.
Ps. 90 : 2 : 39 : 7.
Heb. 6 : 17.
James 1 : 17.
Mal. 3 : 6.
Num. 23 : 19.
Lev. 20 : 26.
Rom. 16 : 27.
Ps. 119 : 68.
Deut. 32 : 4.
Exod. 34 : 6.
Isaiah 41 : 4.
Job 33 : 13.
I Kings 8 : 27.
Ps. 145 : 3.

III. ARTICLE.

Of the holy Trinity.

In this divine, and infinite being, or unity of the Godhead, there are three persons, or subsistences, the father, the word, or son, and the holy spirit, of one substance, power, eternity, and will, each having the whole divine essence, yet the essence undivided. The father is of none, neither begotten nor proceeding; the son is eternally begotten of the father; the holy ghost is of the father, and the son, proceeding. All infinite, without beginning, therefore but one God, who is indivisible, and not to be divided in nature, or being, but distinguished by several properties and personal relations; and we worship and adore a Trinity in Unity, and a Unity in Trinity, three persons, and but one God; which doctrine of the Trinity, is the foundation of all our communion with God, and comfortable dependance on him. And there are three that bare record in heaven, the father, the word, and the holy spirit, and these three are one. Baptizing them in the name of the father, son, and holy Ghost, &c.

I John 5 : 7.
John 15 : 26.
2 Cor. 13 : 13.
Gen. 1 : 26.
Matt. 3 : 16, 17.
John 5 : 17.
Gal. 1 : 3.
Matt. 16 : 16 ; 12 : 32.
Heb. 1 : 3.
Gen. 1 : 2, 26.
Rev. 1 : 8.
John 1 : 5.
I Cor. 12 : 6, 11.
John 14 : 11.
I John 5 : 7, 26.
Gal. 4 : 6.
I Pet. 1 : 11.
2 Cor. 13 : 14.
I John 5 : 7.
Matt. 28 : 19.

IV. ARTICLE.

Of the divine Nature, or Godhead of Christ.

We confess and believe, that the Son of God, or the eternal word, is very and true God, having his personal subsistance of the father alone, and yet for ever of himself as God; and of the father as the son, the eternal son of an eternal father; not later in beginning. There was never any time when he was not, not less in dignity, not other in substance, begotten without diminution of his father that begat, of one nature and substance with the father; begotten of the father, while the father communicated wholly to the son, which he retained wholly in himself, because both were infinite, without inequality of nature, without division of essence, neither made, nor created, nor adopted, but begotten before all time; not

John 5 : 20 ; 1 : 1, 2, 3.
Heb. 1 : 3.
I Cor. 15 : 16, 17.
Col. 1 : 2, 9.
Mic. 5 : 2.
Gnolam, or Eternity.
Matt. 2 : 6.
Prov. 8 : 22, 23, 35.
Phil. 2 : 6.

John 16 : 27, 28.
1 : 18.
Isaiah 40 : 11, 12, 22.
Rev. 1 : 8, 11.

a metaphorical, or subordinate God; not
a God by office, but a God by nature, coequal, coessential, and coeternal, with the
father and the holy ghost.

Phil. 2 : 6.
John 10 : 30.
Isaiah 9 : 6.
John 17 : 5; 8 : 58.

Jesus said unto them, Verily, verily, I say
unto you, before Abraham was, I am. Jesus
Christ the same yesterday, and to day, and
for ever. David therefore calleth him Lord,
how is he then his son?

Heb. 13 ; 8.
Luke 20 : 44.

V. ARTICLE.

Of the second Person of the holy Trinity, taking our flesh.

We believe that the only begotten son
of God, the second person in the sacred
Trinity, took to himself a true, real, and
fleshly body, and reasonable soul, being conceived in the fulness of time, by the holy
ghost, and born of the virgin Mary, and
became very and true man like unto us in
all things, even in our infirmities, sin
only excepted, as appeareth by his conception, birth, life, and death. He was
of a woman, and by the power of the holy ghost,
in a supernatural and miraculous manner,
was formed of the only seed,
or substance of the virgin Mary, in
which respect he hath the name of the
son of man, and is the true son of David
the fruit of the virgin's womb, to that
end he might die for Adam.
Gen. 26: 17.   Heb. 2. 16.

I John 5 : 7.
Isaiah 7 : 14.
John 1 : 14.
Luke 1 : 31, 32.
Heb. 2 : 16, 17.
John 19 : 34, 36.
Matt. 26 : 38.
Luke 2 : 6, 7; 1 : 35.

Matt.1 :18,20; 23 :25.
Gal. 4 : 4.

Heb. 4 :15; 2 :13, 14.
Luke 2 : 52.
Gal. 4 : 4.
Rom. 1 : 3, 4.
Luke 3 : 23, 24.
Heb. 7 : 14.

VI. ARTICLE.

Of the union of the two natures in Christ.

We believe the person of the son of
God, being a person from all eternity existing, did assume the most pure nature of
man, wanting all personal existing of its
own, into the unity of his person, or
Godhead, and made it his own; the
properties of each nature being preserved,
and this inseparable and indissolvable union
of both natures, and was made by the
holy ghost, sanctifying our nature in the
virgin's womb, without change of either
nature, or mixture of both, and of two

Heb. 2 : 14, 16.
Acts 20 : 28.

Matt. 1 : 20.
Luke 1 : 35.
Rom. 1 : 3, 4.

natures is one Christ, God-man, or Imma-   Matt. 1 : 23.
nuel, God with us. Which mystery ex-   I Tim. 3 : 16; 2 : 5.
ceeds the conception of men, and is the
wonder of angels, one only mediator,
Jesus Christ, the son of God.

VII. ARTICLE.

Of the communication of Properties.

We believe that the two natures in   John 10 : 30; 5 : 26,
Christ, continue still distinct in substance,   27, &c.
properties, and actions, and remain one   I John 4 : 9.
and the same Christ: For the properties   Matt. 9 : 6.
of the Godhead, cannot agree to the   John 7 : 42.
properties of the manhood, nor the properties of the manhood, to the properties
of the Godhead; for as the Godhead or
divine nature cannot thirst, or be hungry, no more can the manhood
be in all, or many places at once. Therefore, we believe, the Godhead was neither turned nor transfused into the manhood, nor the
manhood into the Godhead, but both, the
divine nature keepeth entire all his essential
properties to its self, so that the humanity is neither omnipotent, omniscient,
nor omnipresent: And the human also
keepeth his properties, tho' often that   Acts 20 : 28.
which is proper to the one nature, is   I Cor. 2 : 8.
spoken of the person denominated from   John 3 : 13.
the other, which must be understood by   Mark 2 : 10.
the figure synecdoche, viz. a part being
taken for the whole, by reason of the
union of both natures into one person.
Hereby perceive we the love of God, be-   I John 3 : 16.
cause he laid down his life for us.

VIII. ARTICLE.

Of the holy Spirit.

We believe that there is one holy spi-   John 5 : 7.
rit, the third person subsisting in the sa-   Matt. 28 : 19.
cred trinity, one with the father and son,   Gen. 1 : 26.
who is very and true God, of one substance   Acts 5 : 4.
or nature with the father and son, coequal,   2 Cor. 13 : 13.
coeternal, and coessential with the father   I Cor. 12 : 6, 11.
and son, to whom with the father and son,   Isaiah 6 : 8, 9.
three persons, and but one eternal and   Acts 28 : 25, 26.
almighty God, be by all the hosts of
saints and angels, ascribed eternal glory,   Isaiah 6 : 3.
and Hallelujahs. Amen.

IX. ARTICLE.

Of Predestination and Election.

The decrees of God are founded on
infinite wisdom, and situate in eternity,
and are crowned with infallibility, as to
the event. Now predestination unto life,
is the everlasting purpose of God, whereby before the foundation of the world
was laid, he hath constantly decreed in
his counsel secret to us, to deliver
from curse and damnation, those whom
he hath chosen in Christ, and bring them
to everlasting salvation, as vessels made
to honour, thro' Jesus Christ, whom he
elected before the foundation of the
world, and is called God's elect, in
whom his soul delighteth, being the
lamb foreordain'd, and so predestinated
unto the superlative glory of the hypostatical union. And this not for any foreseen holiness in his human nature, sith all
that did flow out of the hypostatical
union, being elected of mere grace, as
are all the members of his mystical body.
And God the father gave this his elected
and beloved son, for a covenant to the
people, and said, that his covenant shall
stand fast with him; and his seed shall endure for ever. And albeit God the father
be the efficient cause of all good things
he intended to us, yet Christ is the meriting cause of all those good things God
intended to us in election, viz. repentance, faith and sincere obedience to all
God's commandments. And so God the
father, that he might bring about the
eternal salvation of his elect, chose the
man Christ, with respect to his human
nature, out of the fallen lump of mankind,
which in the fulness of time, he made of
a woman, made under the law, to redeem
those that were under it, that we might
receive the adoption of sons. And tho'
Christ came from Adam, as Eve did, yet
not by Adam, as Cain did, viz. by natural propagation. Therefore without any
stain of sin, and this second Adam, being
by God's eternal decree, excepted out of
the first covenant, as being neither God

Isaiah 46 : 10.
Acts 15 : 18; 17 : 26.

Eph. 1 : 11.
Matt. 25 : 34.
I Tim. 1 : 9.
John 6 : 37; 10 : 28,29.
Eph. 1 : 4.
Rom. 11 : 33; 8 : 30;
9 : 29.
I Thess. 1 : 4.
Tit. 1 : 1.
I Pet. 1 : 19, 20.
Isaiah 42 : 1.
Matt 12 : 17, 18.

I Pet. 2 : 6.
Luke 23 : 35.
I Pet. 1 : 19.
John 1 : 14.
Heb. 2 : 16.
Col. 2 : 9.
I Tim. 1 : 9.
Ps. 89 : 23, &c.
John 3 : 16.
I John 4 : 9, 10, 19.
Rom. 3 : 24, 25.
8 : 3.
I Cor. 8 : 30.
Eph. 2 : 8, 9, 10.

Heb.7:14; 10 : 5,6,&c.
Gal. 4 : 3.
Eph. 1 : 5.
Gen. 2 : 21, &c.
4 : 1.
5 : 3.
Matt. 1 : 18, 19.
Luke 1 : 35.
2 Tim. 2 : 5.
Heb. 9 : 15.
Eph. 2 : 13, &c.

Isaiah 49 : 6, &c.
2 Thess. 2 : 13.
Eph. 1 : 17, &c.
I Cor. 2 : 13.

I

the father, who was justly offended, nor
yet sinful Adam, who had offended him
in breaking of it. Therefore Christ, the
second Adam, was a fit mediator between
God and man, to reconcile both in him
self, by the shedding and sprinkling of
his blood, according to God's eternal
purpose in electing of Christ, and of all
that do, or shall believe in him, which eternal
election or covenant transaction between the father and son, is very consistent with his revealed will in the gospel; for we ought not to oppose the grace
of God in electing of us, nor yet the
grace of the son in dying for all men, and
so for us, nor yet the grace of the holy
ghost in propounding the gospel, and
persuading us to believe it. For until we
do believe, the effects of God's displeasure
are not taken from us; for the wrath of
God abideth on all them that do not believe in Christ; for the actual declaration
in the court of conscience, is by faith as
an instrument, not for faith as a meriting
cause: for Christ is the meriting cause of
eternal life to all that believe, but not of
God's will to give eternal life to them,
nor yet of God's decree to save us, albeit
we are chosen in Christ before the foundation of the world. Now faith is necessary as the way of our salvation, as an instrumental cause: but the active and passive obedience of Christ, is necessary as
a meriting cause of our salvation; therefore God's eternal decree doth not oppose his revealed will in the gospel, it
being but one, not two diverse or contrary
wills. For his decree as king, decreeth
the event, or what shall be done infallibly;
but his command as a lawgiver, sheweth
not what shall be done, but what is the
duty of man to do, and leave undone.
Therefore God hath, we believe, decreed,
that faith as the means, and salvation as
the end, shall be joined together, that
where one is, the other must be also, for
it is written, he that believeth shall be saved;
also, believe in the Lord Jesus Christ, and
thou shalt be saved. Now here is a great
mystery indeed, for God so administereth
his absolute decree that he leaveth us

I Thess. 1 : 5.
John 3 : 18, 36.
Rom. 3 : 30.
Gal. 3 : 8, 11.
Phil. 3 : 9.
Rom. 5 : 1, 2.

I John 4 : 9, 10, 19.
Heb. 11 : 6.
John 1 : 11, 12.
Acts 13 : 39; 20 : 28.
Eph. 1 : 14.

Rom. 5 : 9, &c.
John 6 : 40.
I Tim. 2 : 3, 4.
Job 23 : 13.
Ps. 115 : 3.
Job 42 : 2.
Isaiah 33 : 22.
John 3 : 36.
Mark 16 : 16.
Acts 16 : 31.
Isaiah 14 : 24.
Ps. 115 : 3; 32 : 11, 12.

89 : 30, 31, &c.

much place for an efficacious conditional dispensation, as if the decree itself were conditional.

X. ARTICLE.

Of Preterition or Reprobation.

We do believe, that known unto God are all his works from eternity; therefore he foresaw Adam's fall, but did not decree it, yet foreseeing it in his eternal counsel and wisdom, did elect and chuse Jesus Christ, and all that do or shall believe in him, out of that fallen lump of mankind. And hath manifested his love and grace by Jesus Christ, his elect or beloved son, thro' the gospel means, to all; and hath given us his word and oath, to assure us that he desires not the death of the wicked, but rather that they repent, or return to him and live, and if any do perish, their destruction is of themselves: and hath decreed to punish all those wicked, or ungodly, disobedient, and unbelieving or impenitent sinners, that have, or shall despise his grace, love, and woings, or strivings of the holy ghost, or long-suffering, whether by a total and continued rejection of grace, or by an universal and final apostacy; and such persons, so living and dying, shall be punished with everlasting destruction in hell fire, with the fallen angels, or devils, and shall be fixed in an irrecoverable state of damnation, irrevocable under the wrath of God, they being the proper objects of it; and shall remain under his inexpressible wrath and justice, in inconceivable torment, soul and body, to all eternity.

Acts 15 : 18.

Ezek. 18 : 23, 32.
33 : 11.
Hos. 13 : 9.
Jam. 1 : 13, 14.
2 Thess. 1 : 9,
10 ; 2 : 12

Heb. 10 : 26, &c.

Isa. 30 : 33;
66 : 24.
Mark 9 : 45, 46.

Jude 4.

Matt. 25 : 41, 46.

Rev 20. : 13, 14.

XI. ARTICLE.

Of Creation.

In the beginning it pleased god the father, son, and holy ghost, according to his eternal, and immutable decree, for the manifestation of the glory of his eternal power, wisdom, and goodness, to create, or make out of nothing, the world, and all things

Gen. 1 : 1.
Rom. 11 : 36.
Rev. 4 : 11.
Heb. 11 : 3.
Col. 1 : 16.
Gen. 5 : 1, 2 ; 2 : 7.

therein, whether visible or invisible, and
created man male and female, with a
fleshly body, and a reasonable, and invisible, or spiritual, angelical, and immortal soul, made after the image of God,
in knowledge, righteousness, and true
holiness, having the law written in his
heart, and power or liberty of will to fulfil
it, yet mutable, or under a possibility
of transgressing, being left to the liberty
of their own will, which was subject to
change; and also gave them command
not to eat of the tree of knowledge of
good and evil, and while they kept this
command, they enjoyed most happy communion with God, and had dominion
over the creatures. And all this wonderful work of creation, both in heaven and
in earth, was finished in the space of six
days, and all very good, and altho' reason
cannot conceive nor comprehend it, yet
God's word hath plainly revealed it, and
faith believes it.

Matt. 10:28; 22:31,32.
Rev. 6 : 9.
Luk 23 : 46.
Acts 7 : 59.
Gen. 1 : 27; 9 : 6.
Eph. 4 : 24.
Rom. 2 : 14, 15.
Eccles. 7 : 29.

Gen. 3 : 6; 2 : 16, 17.

Gen. 1 : 1, 2, 31.

XII. ARTICLE.

Of Divine Providence.

The Almighty God, that created all
things, and gave them their being, by
his infinite power and wisdom, doth sustain and uphold, and move, direct, dispose, and govern all creatures and things,
from the greatest to the least, according
to the counsel of his own good will and
pleasure, for his own glory, and his creatures good.

Heb. 1 : 3.
Job 28 : 11.
*   26 : 7, &c.*
Ps. 135 : 5, 6.

Matt. 10 : 19, &c.
Ps. 65 : 8, &c.
Eph. 1 : 11.

XIII. ARTICLE.

Of the first Covenant.

The first covenant was made between
God and man, before man had sinned in
eating of the forbidden fruit, in which
covenant God required of man perfect
obedience to all the commands thereof,
and in case he did so obey he promised
to be his God. And on the other part,
man promised to perform entire and perfect obedience to all God's holy commands in that covenant, by that strength
wherewith God endowed him in his first

Hos. 6 : 7; 8 : 1.

Deut. 26 : 17, 18, 19.

creation; by the improvement of which
he might have attained unto eternal life
without faith, in the blood of the mediator of the new covenant of grace; but
he sinning against this covenant, which
consisted in two roots, viz. To love God a-
bove all things; and his neighbour as himself; it being the substance of that law
which was afterwards written in two
tables of stone, and delivered unto Moses
upon mount Sinai, and fell under the just
sentence of eternal death, which was the
punishment that God had appointed for
the breach of it. And under this righteous
judgment of God, Adam and his natural
posterity, had for ever remained, as
the fallen Angels do, had not God of his
infinite grace and love, provided his son,
to take unto himself our nature, and so became a fit mediator between God the father, who was offended, and man, who
had offended him in breaking his holy
law and covenant.

Matt. 22 : 37, 40.
Rom. 2 : 14, 15.

Gen. 3 : 12, 13.

Deut. 29 : 19, 20, 21.
Eph. 2 : 3.
Rom. 1 : 20, 32.

Rom. 5 : 12, 18.

Eph. 2 : 13, 14.

XIV. ARTICLE.

Of the fall of man, of his sin, and of the punishment thereof.

The first man Adam, in eating voluntarily of the forbidden fruit, incurred the
curse of God upon himself, and all his
posterity, that came of him by natural
propagation, viz. corporal and spiritual
death, in body and soul eternally; but
this covenant was not only made with
him, but with his seed also, which should
descend from his loins by natural generation; he standing as a publick person
in the stead of all mankind. And, as St.
Paul saith, by him came sin, and death by
sin, &c. and so deprived himself, and all
his posterity, of that original righteousness, which God created him in.

Rom. 5 : 12, 14.

Gen. 3 : 10, 12.
Eph. 2 : 1, 3.
Rom. 5 : 15, 16, 17.

Heb. 7 : 9, 10.
Ps. 51 : 5.
Gen. 6 : 5.
Rom. 7 : 7.
James 1 : 14.

XV. ARTICLE.

Of original, or birth, sin.

Original sin, is the fault and corruption
of the nature of every man, that naturally

Rom. 7 : 21.
Gen. 6 : 5.

descendeth from Adam by natural generation, by means of which, man has not
only lost that original righteousness, that
God created him in, but is naturally inclined to all manner of evil, being conceived in sin, and brought forth in iniquity; and, as St. Paul saith, the flesh
lusteth against the spirit. And therefore
every man justly deserveth God's wrath,
and damnation. And this concupisence,
or indwelling lust, remaineth even in the
regenerate, that they cannot love nor
obey God perfectly in this life, according
to the tenour of the first covenant.

Tit. 1 : 15.
Rom. 3 : 23.
Gen. 5 : 3.
Jer. 17 : 9.
Ps. 51 : 4, 5.
Job 14 : 4.
Gal. 5 : 16, 17.
I Cor. 15 : 22.
Rom. 6 : 23.
Gen. 2 : 17.
John 5 : 24.
Isa. 64 : 6.
Gal. 3 : 10.
Rom. 7 : 17, 21, 22.
2 : 14, 15.
Gal. 3 : 21, 22.
Matt. 12 : 33.

XVI. ARTICLE.

Of the new covenant of grace.

The first covenant being broken by
mans disobedience, and by his sin, he was
excluded from the favour of God, and
eternal life, in which deplorable condition
of his, God being pleased, out of his free
grace and love to fallen man, in order to
his recovery out of this sinful and deplorable estate, hath freely offered him a
second, or a new covenant of grace,
which new covenant of grace is Jesus
Christ, in remission of sins, thro' faith in
his blood, which God hath promised to
give to all them that do obey and submit
to the conditions of this covenant, which
covenant of grace, and eternal salvation
annexed to it, is freely and fully offered
unto all men, upon the terms of the gospel, viz. repentance and faith. And the
benefits of this covenant, by God's free
grace, thro' the redemption that is in
Jesus Christ, whom God has set forth to
be a propitiation thro' faith in his blood,
to declare his righteousness for the remission of sins that are past thro' the for-
bearance of God, that he might be just,
and the justifier of him that believeth in
Jesus. Therefore, we conclude, that a
man is justified by faith, without the deeds
of the law; for by faith we receive that
righteousness that the law, or the first
covenant, required of the first Adam;
which righteousness Christ hath fulfilled

Deut. 27 : 26.
Col. 1 : 13.
2 Cor. 4 : 4.
John 3 : 16.
Jer. 31 : 31, 32.

Rom. 3 : 23, 24.
Gal. 3 : 21, 22.
Rom. 3 : 31.
Heb. 8 : 7.
Gen. 3 : 15.
Luk. 24 : 47.
Eph. 1 : 7.
Ps. 20 : 3.
Acts 10 : 43; 3 : 19;
26 : 18; 2 : 37, 38.
Mark 1 : 15.
Gal. 3 : 11, 17.
Jer. 32 : 40.
Isa. 42 : 6.
Rom. 3 : 23, &c.

Acts 10 : 43.
Isa. 93 : 11.
Rom. 5 : 9; 3 : 20.
Gal. 3 : 8; 2 : 16.
Rom. 5 : 10, 19;
10 : 4.
Matt. 3.
2 Cor. 5 : 21.
I Cor. 1 : 30.

in our nature which he took of the virgin Mary, by his active obedience, and is, by God's free donation, made over to us by imputation; for he hath made him to us wisdom, righteousness and sanctification. For as by one man's disobedience, many were made sinners, so by the obedience of one, that is Christ, shall many be made righteous. For Christ hath not only fulfilled the sanction of the law, viz. To love God with all his heart, and his neighbour as himself, but hath also voluntarily suffered the curse of the law, being made a curse for us, that we might receive the blessing of Abraham, and the promise of the spirit thro' faith in his blood. And now, albeit the essential righteousness of Christ, as he is God equal with his father, be not imputed unto us, nor yet his personal righteousness, as he was or is man, only, yet we believe his mediatorial righteousness, as God man, is imputed, reckoned, or made over to us, upon the terms of this new covenant of grace; and so being justified by his grace, we are thereby made heirs according to the hope of eternal life: for, as St. Paul saith, If righteousness come by the law, then Christ is dead in vain.

Gal. 3 : 13.
I Pet. 2 : 24.
Isa. 53 : 6, 7, 8.
Phil. 2 : 7, 8.
Gal. 3 : 13, 14.
Heb. 7 : 26.
Matt. 3 : 15.
Rom. 5 : 18.
Gal. 4 : 6, 7.
Rom. 4 : 3, 4, 23.
    3 : 25, 28.
Tit. 3 : 7; 1 : 2.

XVII. ARTICLE.

Of Christ and his mediatorial Office.

It pleased God, in his eternal purpose, to chuse and ordain the Lord Jesus Christ, his only begotten son, according to the covenant made between them both, to be the alone mediator between God and man, viz. God the father, who was by Adam's sin justly offended, and Adam, our common parent, the person offending. Now in order to reconcile God to man, and man to God, who were at a distance, Christ Jesus, the second person in the trinity, being very God, of the same substance with his father, did, when the fulness of time was come, take unto him man's nature, with all the essential properties, and common infirmities, sin

Zech. 6 : 12, 13.
Gal. 3 : 17.
Ps. 89 : 28 ; 109 : 10.

Gal. 3 : 19, 20.
Heb. 10 : 15; 12 : 24.

I Tim. 2 : 5.
Job 9 : 33.
any days-man betwixt | us, &c.
Gal. 3 : 16.
Gen. 3 : 15.
I Chron. 17 : 11.

only excepted, being made of a woman,
of the seed of Abraham and David; and
altho' he came from Adam, and had truly the nature of man, yet not by Adam;
and the person of Christ took our nature
into union with the divine nature, but he
did not take the person of Adam which
sinned, therefore we believe he was neither
the covenantee, nor yet the coventanter,
and so, by consequence, neither the cre-
ditor nor the debtor. And being concerned by this office or appointment of the
father to make peace, it plainly appears,
that he is the only fit mediator between
God and man, who is very God, and very
man; yet one Christ, who was sanctified,
and anointed with the holy spirit above
measure, and was superlatively and ad-
mirably fitted for, and called unto this
office by his father, who put all judgment into his hand, and power to execute the same, and he willingly under-
took the same; and being made under
the law, did perfectly fulfil or keep it,
and underwent the punishment due to us,
which we should have suffered; our sin,
and the punishment of it, being reckoned
or imputed to him, he being made a curse
for us, and underwent and trod the wine-
press of his father's wrath for us, in do-
lorous pangs and agony of soul, and painful sufferings in his body, was crucified,
dead, and buried, or remained in the state
of the dead, yet saw no corruption,
and on the third day he arose from the
dead, with the same body in which he
suffered, with which he also ascended,
and there sitteth at the right hand of his
father, making intercession for his saints,
and shall return to judge men and angels
at the end of the world. And the same
Lord Jesus, by his perfect obedience to
the whole law, and sacrifice of himself,
which he, thro' the eternal spirit offered
up unto the father, hath fully satisfied the
justice of God and reconciled him
to us; and hath purchased an everlasting inheritance in the kingdom of
heaven, for all those that the father hath
given unto him, and now, by a continued act of intercession in heaven, doth

Luke 1 : 35.
Heb. 7 : 26.
Rom. 9 : 5.
Heb. 5 : 5 ; 7 : 21, &c.
Eph. 2 : 14.
Ps. 42 : 1, 6.
I Pet. 1 : 19, 20.
Heb. 9 : 15 ; 1 : 9.
Ps. 45 : 7.
Isaiah 61 : 1.
Col. 2 : 3.
Heb. 5 : 5.
John 5 : 22, 27.
Rom. 10 : 4.
2 Cor. 5 : 21.
Gal. 3 : 13.
Luke 22 : 44, 45.

Isaiah 53 : 10, 11, 12
I Pet. 2 : 24.
Matt. 27 : 46.
26 : 37, 38.
Acts 13 : 28, &c.

Luke 24 : 7.
John 20 : 25, 27.
Acts 1 : 9, 10, 11.

Mark 16 : 19.
Rom. 8 : 34.
Matt. 25 : 31, &c.
Heb. 9 : 14, 15.

Eph. 2 : 14, &c.
John 17 : 2.
I Pet. 1 : 2, &c.

apply the benefits he hath purchased
unto the elect. And in this office of
mediator, he hath the dignity of three
offices, viz. Priest, Prophet, and King:
all which offices are necessary for the benefit
of his church, and without which
we can never be saved. For, in
respect of our ignorance, we stand
in need of his prophetical office, and
in respect of our alienation from God,
and imperfect services, and God's wrath
and justice, we stand in need of his
priestly office, to reconcile God to us,
and us to God; and in respect of our
bondage to sin and Satan, and averseness to return to God, we need his
kingly office to subdue our enemies, and
deliver us captives out of the kingdom
and power of sin, and preserve us to
his heavenly kingdom. And thus, in
our nature, he living the life of the
law, and suffering the penalty due to
us, continually presents us at the
throne of grace; so is a most wonderful and compleat mediator for his
elect.

Heb. 7 : 17.
Acts 3 : 22.
Ps. 45 : 5, &c.
Acts 4 : 11, 12.

2 Tim. 4 : 18.
Col. 1 : 13, 14.
Heb. 4 : 14, &c.

XVIII. ARTICLE.

Of Christ dying for all mankind.

God the father, out of his royal bounty,
and fountain of love, when all mankind
was fallen by sin, in breaking of the first
covenant of works made with them in
Adam, did chuse Jesus Christ, and sent
him into the world to die for Adam, or
fallen man. And God's love is manifest to all mankind, in that he is not
willing, as himself hath sworn, and abundantly declared in his word, that mankind
should perish eternally, but would have all
to be saved, and come to the knowledge of
the truth. And Christ died for all men,
and there is a sufficiency in his death and
merits for the sins of the whole world,
and hath appointed the gospel to be
preached unto all, and hath sent forth
his spirit to accompany the word in
order to beget repentance and faith:
so that if any do perish, it's not for

Rom. 5 : 8.
Matt. 20 : 28.
Rom. 8 : 3.
Heb. 9 : 15.
Ezek. 18 : 23.
Heb. 2 : 9.
I John 2 : 2.
I Tim. 2 : 3, &c.
Heb. 10 : 12, &c.
Mark 16 : 16.
Tit. 2 : 11, 12.
I Thess. 1 : 5, 6, 7.

John 5 : 39, 40.
Matt. 23 : 37, 38.
24 : 12.
Acts 13 : 46, 48.

want of the means of grace manifested
by Christ to them, but for the non-
improvement of the grace of God, offered freely to them through Christ in
the gospel.

XIX. ARTICLE.

Of the agreement between the Old and New Testament.

The Gospel, or new Covenant, was
held forth, or preached to the fathers,
from Adam to Christ's coming in the flesh,
though it was revealed by sundry degrees,   Gal. 3 : 8.
and in diverse manners, in types and sha-   Gen. 12 : 3.
dows, darkly; yet it was the same gos-   Heb. 4 : 2, 3 ; 1 : 1, 2.
pel, the same Christ, the same faith for kind,   10 : 1.
and the very same covenant, that they
were justified and saved by, before Christ
took flesh of the virgin, that we have
now, and is to continue to the end of
the world. For as the church of the   Heb. 9, 10, and
Jews, in their gospel types, had a priest,   11 chapt.
and an altar, and a lamb, and a fire, and
without all these no sacrifice could, or
was accepted of God, then, nor now,
without faith in the anti-type, Christ,
whose human nature is the true lamb,
the union of natures, the high priest, the
divine nature, the altar, and the holy
ghost, the heavenly fire. And again:
The blood shed upon the brazen altar,   Heb. 9 : 14.
may be applied to our justification, and
the sprinkling of it upon the incense altar,
may be applied to the work of sanctification by Christ's spirit, sprinkling his
blood upon us. And the blood that was   Eph. 5 : 2.
carried within the vail, into the most   I Pet. 1 : 2.
holy place, is applied to our glorifica-
tion in heaven. And as they had in
their church the ark, a figure of Christ's
presence, so have we the promise of   Heb. 9 : 7, &c.
his presence to the end of the world.
And as they had the tables of the old
covenant or law, in the ark, so have
we the law fulfilled by Christ; and meet-   Matt. 18 : 20.
ing God in Christ, it's handed forth by   28 : 19, 20.
Christ now to us, as the only rule of our   Rom. 3 : 31 ; 8 : 3, 4
sanctification and obedience through his   10 : 4.
grace. And as they had the manna   I John 2 : 6, 7, 8.
to nourish them in the wilderness to

Canaan; so have we the sacraments, to nourish us in the church, and in our wilderness-condition, till we come to heaven. And as they had the rod that corrected them; so have we the church censures now to correct us, when we offend his law; and their burnt offerings may be applied to Christ, killing of original sin in us, and their sin offering may be applied to Christ, killing, or taking away our actual sins, and their peace offering may be applied to our reconciliation with God in Christ by his spirit, and so all the rest of those gospel-antitypes may be applied. And thus the Old and New Testaments, like the faces of the Cherubins, look one toward another, and hold forth the self-same gospel, salvation to them and us.

James 4 : 12.
John 16 : 14, 15.

I Cor. 4 : 19, &c.

XX. ARTICLE.

Of Free-Will in Man.

God hath endued the will of man with that natural liberty and power of acting upon choice, that it's neither forced, nor by any necessity of nature determined, to do good or evil: but man, in the state of innocency, had such power and liberty of will to chuse and perform that which was acceptable and well pleasing to God, according to the requirement of the first covenant; but he falling from his state of innocency, wholly lost all ability, or liberty of will, to any spiritual good, for his eternal salvation, his will being now in bondage under sin and Satan, and therefore not able of his own strength to convert himself nor prepare himself thereunto, without God's grace taketh away the enmity out of his will, and by his special grace, freeth him from his natural bondage under sin, enabling him to will freely and sincerely, that which is spiritually good, according to the tenure of the new covenant of grace in Christ, tho' not perfectly, according to the tenure of the first covenant, which perfection of will is only attainable in the

Matt. 17 : 12.

Eccles. 7 : 29.
Rom. 5 : 6; 8 : 7, 8
John 8 : 44.

Eph. 2 : 8, &c.
Phil. 2 : 13.
Rom. 7 : 14, &c.
    8 : 23.
Eph. 4 : 13.

state of glory, after the redemption, or resurrection of our fleshly bodies.

XXI. ARTICLE.

Of Vocation and effectual Calling.

Vocation, or calling, general, or common, is, when God by the means of his word and spirit, freely of his own grace and goodness, doth ministerially acquaint mankind with his gracious good purpose of salvation, by Jesus Christ; inviting and wooing them to come to him, and to accept of Christ revealing unto them the gospel covenant, and those that with cordial hearts do improve this common grace, he in time worketh unfeigned faith, and sincere repentance in them; and by his grace they come to accept of Christ, as their only Lord and Saviour, with their whole heart; and God becomes their father in Christ, and they being then effectually called, are by faith united to Jesus Christ by grace unto salvation.

Matt. 11 : 28.
Acts 20 : 21.
Rom. 16 : 25, 26.
Tit. 2 : 11.
Acts 5 : 31; 11 : 18.
Rom. 8 : 28, 30.
   11 : 5, 7.

Eph. 1 : 11, &c.
Rom. 5 : 1.
Eph. 2 : 8.
Rom. 4 : 16.

XXII. ARTICLE.

Of evangelical Repentance.

Unfeigned repentance, is an inward and true sorrow of heart for sin, with sincere confession of the same to God, especially that we have offended so gracious a God, and so loving a father, together with a settled purpose of heart, and a careful endeavor to leave all our sins, and to live a more holy and sanctified life, according to all God's commands. Or it is a turning, or change of the whole man to God, with endeavour, thro' his grace, to mortify the indwelling lust, or corruptions, and obtain a great reformation both in the outward and inward man, according to the will of God, and this repentance, for the nature of it, must be continued throughout the whole course of our lives, and is wrought in us by the spirit of God; by the ministry of the law and gospel, in order to our obedience to

Tit. 2 : 3, 4, 5.
Acts 2 : 37, 38.
2 Cor. 7 : 10, 11.
Acts 17 : 30.
Ps. 51 : 4.
Luke 15 : 17, &c.

Ezek. 18 : 30.
Eph. 2 : 10.
Rom. 8 : 13.
Eph. 4 : 20, &c.

John 8 : 31, &c.

Rom. 8 : 13.

Christ, or being baptized in his name, but this repentance unto life, is not wrought without faith in the soul; for by faith we receive that grace, that perfects, or carrieth on the work of repentance in the soul, from first to last.

I Thess. 1 : 5, 6.
Acts 3 : 19, 26.
2 : 38.
Heb. 11 : 6.
Gal. 3 : 26, &c.

XXIII. ARTICLE.

Of justifying, and saving Faith.

Faith is an act of the understanding, giving a firm assent to the things contained in the holy scriptures. But justifying faith is a grace, or habit, wrought in the soul, by the holy ghost, through preaching the word of God, whereby we are enabled to believe, not only that the Messias is offered to us, but also to take and receive him, as a Lord and Saviour, and wholly and only to rest upon Christ, for grace and eternal salvation.

Rom. 10 : 14, 17.
Matt. 13 : 20, 21.

Acts 24 : 14.
Ps.19 : 7,&c.; 119 : 72.
2 Pet. 1 : 1.
I John 5 : 4, 5.
2 Cor. 4 : 13.
Eph. 2 : 8.
Acts 31 : 31 ; 15 : 11.
2 Pet. 1 : 5, 11.
Phil. 3 : 8, 9.
Acts 8 : 37.

XXIV. ARTICLE.

Of Justification by Christ.

Justification is a declarative, or judicial sentence of God the father, whereby he of his infinite love, and most free grace, for the alone and mediatorial righteousness of his own son, performed in our nature and stead, which righteousness of God man, the father imputing to us, and by effectual faith, received and embraced by us, doth free us by judicial sentence from sin and death, and accept us righteous in Christ our surety, unto eternal life; the active and passive obedience of Christ being the accomplishment of all that righteousness and sufferings the law, or justice of God required, and this being perfectly performed by our mediator, in the very nature of us men, and accepted by the father in our stead, according to that eternal covenant-transaction, between the father and the son. And hereby we have deliverance from the guilt and punishment of all our sins, and are accounted righteous

Acts 13 : 38, 39.
Rom. 8 : 34, 35.
3 : 23, &c.
4 : 22, &c.
I Cor. 1 : 30, 31.

2 Thess. 1 : 3, 4.
Acts 15 : 9.
Gal. 5 : 6.
Rom. 8 : 1 ; 4 : 6, 7, 8.
Gal. 3 : 13, 14.
John 5 : 24.
Rom. 3 : 22, 30;
5 : 19.
2 Cor. 1 : 30.
Eph. 1 : 7.
Rom. 5 : 9; 10 : 4.
Gal. 3 : 13.
Heb. 2 : 9, &c.
2 Cor. 5 : 21.
Isaiah 53 : 10, &c.

before God, at the throne of grace,
by the alone righteousness of Christ the
mediator, imputed, or reckoned unto us
through faith; for we believe there are
six necessary causes of man's justification,
or salvation; viz. First, The efficient
cause of our justification, is God's free
grace. Secondly, The meritorious cause   Rom. 3 : 24.
is the blood of Christ. Thirdly, The ma-   Rom. 5 : 9.
terial cause is Christ's active obedience.   5 : 19; 4 : 6.
Fourthly, The imputation of Christ, his   5 : 1.
obedience for us, is the formal cause.   Eph. 1 : 11, 12
Fifthly, The instrumental cause is faith.
Sixthly, God's glory, and man's salvation,
is the final cause. Now we principally apply the first and last to God the
father; the second and third to Christ the
mediator; the fourth and fifth to the blessed
comforter, the holy ghost; hence it   Matt. 28 : 19.
is we are baptized in the name of the   2 Cor. 13 : 14.
father, of the son, and holy ghost, and   I John 5 : 7.
so we worship a trinity in unity, and unity
in trinity.

XXV. ARTICLE.

Of Reconciliation, and Sonship by Christ.

Two privileges flow out of our justification by faith in Christ, viz. our reconciliation, and adoption, or sonship. Reconciliation is a gracious privilege, whereby we that were enemies are made friends; or
we that were enemies, rebels, and
aliens, are received into favour, or brought
near to God through faith in Christ Jesus.
And adoption is that power and privilege   Rom. 5 : 8, &c.
to be the sons of God, through faith in   Eph. 2 : 12, &c.
Christ our surety, who being the eternal   1 : 5.
son of God, became by incarnation our   Gal. 4 : 4, 5, 6.
brother, that by him God might bring   Rom. 8 : 16, 17.
many sons unto glory, according to his
eternal decree of preserving the human   Heb. 2 : 10, &c.
nature of Christ, that it never fell in   4 : 15.
Adam. And so we are, by faith accord-   Matt. 1 : 18.
ing to God's free grace, and Christ's pur-   Heb. 7 : 26.
chase, or redemption, and the holy spi-   Rom. 8 : 16, 17.
rit's application of it to us, made heirs
and joint heirs with Christ, our elder brother,
of the same kingdom, and stupendous
and unutterable glory, for ever and ever.

XXVI. ARTICLE.

Of Sanctification, and good Works.

Those that are united unto Christ by effectual faith, are regenerated, and have a new heart and spirit created in them, through the virtue of Christ his death, resurrection, and intercession, and by the efficacy of the holy spirit, received by faith, and are sanctified by the word and spirit of truth, dwelling in them, by destroying and pulling down the strong holds, or dominion of sin and lust, and more and more quickened and strengthened in all saving graces, in the practice of holiness, without which no man shall see the lord. And this sanctification is throughout the whole man, tho' imperfect in this life, there abiding still in the best saints, some remnants of corruption, which occasions a continual war in the soul, the flesh lusting against the spirit, and the spirit against the flesh; yet through the continual supply of strength from Christ, which flows from him to believers by means of the covenant of grace or hypostatical union with our nature, the regenerate part doth overcome, pressing after a heavenly life, in evangelical obedience to all the commands that Christ, their king, and law-giver, hath commanded them in his word, or holy scriptures, which are the only rule, and square of our sanctification and obedience in all good works, and piety. And sith our only assistance to good works, such as God hath commanded, is of God, who worketh in us both to will and to do, we have no cause to boast, nor ground to conclude, we merit any thing thereby, we receiving all of free and undeserved grace, and when we have done the most, yet we are unprofitable servants, and do abundantly fall short; and the best duties that we can now perform, will not abide the judgment of God. Neither do any good works whatsoever, that are done by unregenerate men, or without faith in, and love to Christ, please God, or are accepted of him. Yet good works are of great ad-

Ezek. 36 : 26.
Eph. 4 : 24.
2 Cor. 5 : 17.
1 John 3 : 9.
Tit. 3 : 5.
1 Cor. 4 : 15.
2 Cor. 3 : 18.
1 Tim. 2 : 20.
Ps. 110 : 3.
2 Cor. 10 : 4, 5; 5 : 17.
John 17 : 17; 16:14,15.
Heb. 12 : 14.
Rom. 7 : 20.
Gal. 5 : 16, 17.
1 John 3 ; 8 ; 2 : 20.

Rom. 6 : 14.
Eph. 4 : 15.
2 Cor. 3 : 18 ; 7 : 1.
Ps. 112 : 1 ; 119 : 48.

John 15 : 4, 6.
Isaiah 43 : 13 ; 26 : 12.
Phil. 2 : 13.
2 Cor. 3 : 5.
Job 9 : 2, 3, 20.
    25 : 4.
Gal. 2 : 16.
James 2 : 9, 10; 3 : 2.
Heb. 11 : 6.
Isa. 64 : 6.
Prov. 8 : 17.
1 Cor. 16 : 22.
James 1 : 18, &c.

vantage, being done in faith, and love,
and wrought by the holy spirit, and are
to be done by us, to shew our thankfulness to God, for the grace of the new
covenant by Christ, and to fit us more and
more for glory. And in this sense the
ten commandments, as handed forth by
Christ the mediator, are a rule of life to a
believer, and shew us our duty to God
and man, as also our need of the grace
of God, and merit of Christ.

Gal. 5 : 22, 23.
John 4 : 14; 5 : 25.

Gal. 5 : 6.
I Cor. 6 : 9, &c.
Heb. 12 : 28, 29.

I Cor. 13 : 2, 3.
Ps. 50 : 14.

XXVII. ARTICLE.

Of Baptism, and the Lord's-supper.

Those two sacraments, viz. Baptism,
and the Lord's-supper, are ordinances of
positive, sovereign, and holy institution,
appointed by the Lord Jesus Christ, the
only lawgiver, to be continued in his
church, to the end of the world; and to
be administred by those only who are
rightly qualified, and thereunto called,
according to the command of Christ.

Matt. 28 : 19, 20.
I Cor. 11 : 26; 4 : 1.

XXVIII. ARTICLE.

Of the right subject and administration of holy Baptism.

Baptism is an ordinance of the new
testament, ordained by Jesus Christ, to be
unto the party baptized, or dipped, a
sign of our entrance into the covenant of
grace, and ingrafting into Christ, and into
the body of Christ, which is his church;
and of remission of sin in the blood of
Christ, and of our fellowship with Christ,
in his death and resurrection, and of our
living, or rising to newness of life. And
orderly none ought to be admitted into
the visible church of Christ, without being
first baptized; and those which do really
profess repentance towards God, and faith
in, and obedience to our Lord Jesus
Christ, are the only proper subjects of this
ordinance, according to our Lord's holy
institution, and primitive practice; and
ought by the minister, or administrator,
to be done in a solemn manner, in the

Rom. 6 : 3, 4, 5.
I Cor. 12 : 13.
Gal. 3 : 27.
Mark 16 : 16.
Matt. 3 : 11.
Acts 2 : 38.
Rom. 6 : 1, &c.
Matt. 28 : 19.

Acts 8 : 37.
Matt. 3 : 6.
Heb. 6 : 1, 2.
Acts 2 : 37, 38;
      8 : 35, 36, &c.

name of the father, son, and holy ghost,
by immersion or dipping of the person in
the element of water; this being necessary
to the due administration of this holy
sacrament, as holy scripture sheweth and
the first and best antiquity witnesseth for
some centuries of years. But the popish doctrine
which they teach and believe, that
those infants that die without baptism,
or have it not actually, or in desire,
are not, nor cannot be saved, we do not
believe. Nor yet their practice of admitting persons only upon an implicit
faith of the church, nor their superstitious
and popish ceremonies of salt, and spittle,
and breathing on the face of the party
baptized, together with their chrisoms
and hallowed lights. Neither do we
believe, that infants dying in infancy,
without baptism, go to purgatory or lim-
bus infantum, as they erroneously teach.
Nor do we believe, that the Pope of
Rome, or any other persons whomsoever,
have power to alter, or change, this ordinance of Christ, as they have done by
this superstitious, and such like idolatrous
inventions and practices of the Romish
church. All which superstitions of theirs,
are contrary to Christ's institution, or the
apostles practice of holy baptism.

Matt. 28 : 19.
John 1 : 2, 8, 31.
3 : 22, 23.

Mark 1 : 9, 10.

XXIX. ARTICLE.

Of the invisible catholick Church of Christ.

There is one holy catholick church,
consisting of, or made up of the whole
number of the elect, that have been, are,
or shall be gathered, in one body under
Christ, the only head thereof; which
church is gathered by special grace, and
the powerful and internal work of the
spirit; and are effectually united unto
Christ their head, and can never fall
away.

Heb. 12 : 22, 23.
Rev. 14 : 1, &c.
Col. 1 : 18.
Eph. 1 : 10, 22 ;
5 : 23, 26, 27.

John 10 : 16.
Gal. 3 : 28.
Ps. 72 : 17; 102 : 28.
Rev. 13 : 8.

XXX. ARTICLE.

Of the catholick Church as visible.

Nevertheless, we believe the visible
church of Christ on earth, is made up of

K

several distinct congregations, which make up that one catholick church, or mystical body of Christ. And the marks by which she is known to be the true spouse of Christ, are these, viz. Where the word of God is rightly preached, and the sacraments truly administred, according to Christ's institution, and the practice of the primitive church; having discipline and government duly executed, by ministers or pastors of God's appointing, and the church's election, that is a true constituted church; to which church, and not elsewhere, all persons that seek for eternal life, should gladly join themselves. And altho' there may be many errors in such a visible church, or congregations, they being not infallible, yet those errors being not fundamental, and the church in the major, or governing part, being not guilty, she is not thereby unchurched; nevertheless she ought to detect those errors, and to reform, according to God's holy word, and from such visible church, or congregations, no man ought, by any pretence whatever, schismatically to separate.

Gal. 3 : 26, &c.
Acts 2 : 41, &c.

Eph. 2 : 19, &c.

I Cor. 11 : 23, &c.
Gal. 3 : 1.
Eph. 3 : 21.
Acts 18 : 8.
I Cor. 12 : 13.
I John 2 : 19.
Rev. 2 : 2, 14, &c.
Tit. 3 : 10, 11.
Jude 17 : 18, 19.
Jam. 3 : 13, &c.
I Tim. 4 : 1.
2 Tim. 1 : 13, &c.

Acts 20 : 29, &c.
I Cor. 12 : 25.

XXXI. ARTICLE.

Of Officers in the Church of Christ.

The visible church of Christ, being completely gathered and organized, according to the mind of Christ, consists of officers and members; and the officers, appointed by Christ, to be chosen by his church, for the peculiar administration of ordinances, and execution of the power and duty Christ hath enjoined them to the end of the world, are these three, viz. *Bishops, or Messengers; and Elders, or Pastors; and Deacons, or Overseers of the poor; and the way appointed by Christ, for the calling of any person fitted and gifted by the holy ghost, unto the office of bishop, or messenger, in the churches, is, viz, That he be chosen thereunto by the common suffrage of the church, and solemnly set apart by fasting and prayer,

Acts 1 : 20, &c.
13 : 2, 3; 14 : 23.
20 : 17, 18.
6 : 3, 4, 5, 6.
1 : 23, 24, &c.
14 : 23.

* Or overseer, or shepherd.

with imposition of hands, by the bishops
of the same function, ordinarily, and
those bishops so ordained, have the government of those churches, that had
suffrage in their election, and no other
ordinarily; as also to preach the word,
or gospel, to the world, or unbelievers.
And the particular pastor, or elder, in
like manner is to be chosen by the common suffrage of the particular congregation, and ordained by the bishop or messenger God hath placed in the church he
hath charge of; and the elder, so ordained, is to watch over that particular
church; and he may not ministerially act
in any other church before he be sent,
neither ought his power, or office, any
way to infringe the liberty, or due power,
or office of his bishop *, God being a
God of order, having ordained things
most harmoniously, tending every way to
unity. The deacons are in like manner
to be chosen by election and ordination,
and are in their particular congregations,
to receive the charity and free benevo-
lence of the people; and the bisops and
elders so chosen, and ordained, to the
work of God, ought to be enabled and
capacitated thereunto, by a sufficient and
honourable maintenance of the people
that chose them, answerable to the dignity
of their places, and charge committed to
them, without which they cannot discharge their duty, as they ought to do,
in studying to divide the word of God
aright, as St. Paul adviseth Timothy, and
also to give themselves wholly to it; and
this maintenance is to be given out of the
labours, profits, and estates of the people,
by equality, and proportionable to their
ability, in liberality, God having reserved
a portion for all his labourers, out of all
the members worldly goods and possessions.

Col. 4 : 11, 17; 2 Cor. 8 : 12, &c.; 2 Cor. 9 : 5, 6, &c.

I Tim. 1 : 3.
Tit. 1 : 5.
Rev. 2 : 1, 2, &c.
Matt. 28 : 19.

Mark 16 : 16.
Acts 1 : 22.
2 Tim. 4 : 2.
Acts 14 : 23.
Rom. 10 : 15.
Acts 13 : 2, 3, 4.
I Cor. 16 : 16.
I Tim. 1 : 3.
Acts 20 : 28.
I Cor. 11 : 34.
Tit. 1 : 5.
Heb. 13 : 17.
I Cor. 14 : 33.
Acts 6 : 1, 2, &c.
I Tim. 3 : 8, &c.
I Cor. 3 : 9.
I Tim. 3 : 5 ; 4 : 6, 16.
2 Tim. 4 : 5.
Tit. 1 : 7.
1 Cor. 9 : 1, &c.
Phil. 4 : 15, &c.

I Tim. 5 : 17, 18.

Gal. 6 : 6, 10.
Deut. 25 : 4.
2 Cor. 11 : 7, 8.
I Tim. 3 : 5, &c.
11 : 13, &c
2 Tim. 1, 2, &c.
3 : 14, &c.
4 : 1, 2, 5.

XXXII. ARTICLE.

Of Prayer, with laying on of Hands.

Prayer, with imposition of hands by
the bishop, or elder, on baptized be-

Acts 8 : 12, &c.
19 : 6, 7.

lievers, as such, for the reception of the
holy promised spirit of Christ, we believe
is a principle of Christ's doctrine, and
ought to be practised and submitted to
by every baptized believer in order to receive the promised spirit of the father
and son.

2 Tim. 1 : 6, 7.
Heb. 6 : 2.
John 13 : 16, &c.
16 : 7.
Eph. 1 : 13, 14.
2 Tim. 1 : 6.
Acts 2 : 38, 39.

XXXIII. ARTICLE.

Of the End, and right Administration of the Lord's-supper.

The supper of the Lord Jesus, was
instituted by him the same night wherein
he was betrayed; to be observed in his
church, to the end of the world, for the
perpetual remembrance, and showing forth
the sacrifice of himself in his death; and
for the confirmation of the faithful believers in all the benefits of his death and
resurrection, and spiritual nourishment and
growth in him; sealing unto them their
continuance in the covenant of grace, and
to be a band and pledge of communion
with him, and an obligation of obedience
to Christ, both passively and actively, as
also of our communion and union each
with other, in the participation of this
holy sacrament. And the outward elements of bread and wine, after they are
set apart by the hand of the minister,
from common use, and blessed, or consecrated, by the word of God and prayer,
the bread being broken, and wine poured
forth, signify to the faithful, the body
and blood of Christ, or holdeth forth
Christ, and him crucified; and the minister distributing the bread and wine to the
communicants, who are to take, or receive, both the bread and wine at the
hands of the minister, applying it by
faith, with thanksgiving to God the
father, for so great a benefit, and no unbaptized, unbelieving, or open profane,
or wicked heretical persons, ought to be
admitted to this ordinance to profane
it.

Neither is that popish doctrine of
transubstantiation to be admitted of, nor
adoration of the unbloody sacrifice of
the mass, as they call it, together with
their denying of the cup to the laity,

Luk. 22 : 17, &c.
Matt. 26 : 26, &c.
I Cor. 11 : 23, &c.

Matt. 28 : 20.

Gal. 3 : 1.

I Cor. 10 : 16, 17.

Gal. 3 : 1.

I Cor. 11 : 27, &c.

Matt. 26 : 30.
I Cor. 5 : 7, 8, 15.

Acts 2 : 41, &c.

See the popish
catechism, p.286,&c.

and many more idolatrous and superstitious practices, decreed in the popish councils of Lateran and Trent. In opposition
to which, and such like idolatry of Rome,   Ib. p. 197, &c.
many of our worthy and famous antients,
and renowned protestants, lost their lives
by fire and faggot in England, whose   See Mr. Fox's Book
spirits we hope are now in heaven, as   of Martyrs.
worthy martyrs and witnesses of Christ,
in bearing a faithful testimony to this
holy ordinance of their Lord and master.
Neither may we admit of consubstantia-
tion, it being not consonant to God's word.
Nor are little infants, that cannot examine
themselves, nor give account of their
faith, nor understand what is signified by
the outward signs of bread and wine, to
be admitted to this sacrament. Though
St. Austin taught so from John 6:63.
and many of the Greek churches so believe
and practise to this day. And this holy
ordinance ought to be often celebrated
among the faithful, with examination of
themselves, viz. of their faith, and love,
and knowledge of these holy and divine
mysteries, lest they eat and drink their
own damnation, for prophaning of God's   I Cor. 11 : 18, &c.
holy ordinance, as many, we fear, have
done, and yet do at this day; whose hard
and blind hearts the Lord in mercy open,
if it be his blessed will.

XXXIV. ARTICLE.

Of the Discipline and Government of the Church of Christ.

We believe that the great king, and
lawgiver, Christ, the universal and only
head of his church, hath given to his
visible church, a subordinate power, or   Isaiah 9 : 6.
authority, for the well-being, ordering,   Matt. 28 : 18.
and governing of it, for his own glory,   18 : 17, 11.
and the church's profit, and good, the   Rev. 2 : 3.
executive part of which derivative   I Cor. 5 : 4.
power of discipline and government, is   Heb. 13 : 7, 17.
committed to his ministers, proportionable
to their dignities and places in the
church in a most harmonious way, for
the beauty, order, government, and e-
stablishment of the same, and consisteth

in the exercise and execution of the
censors, or rod of correction, he hath
appointed therein, for the purgation, or
pruning of the same, in order to prevent
scandals and offences, both publick and
private. And in case of personal and
private trespasses between party and party,
that the member so offended, tell his
offence to his brother, between them
alone; and if he shall not hear him, to
take one or two more; if he will not
hear him then, to tell it unto the church:
And the ministers of Christ ought to rebuke them sharply, that sin before them
in the church; and in case there be any
wicked, publick, and scandalous sinners,
or obstinate hereticks, that then the church
ought speedily to convene such her members, and labour to convict them of their
sin and heresy, schism, and prophaneness,
whatsoever it be; and after such regular
suspension, and due admonition, if such
sinners repent not; that then for the
honour of God, and preserving the credit
of religion, and in order to save the sinner's
soul, and good of the church, in
obedience to God's law, to proceed and
excommunicate the sinner, by a judicial
sentence in the name of Christ and his
church, tendring an admonition of repentance to him, with gravity, love, and authority, and all this without hypocrisy,
or partiality, praying for the sinner, that
his soul may be saved in the day of the
Lord; and under this second degree, of
withdrawing, or excommunication, to account him as a heathen, or publican, that
he may be ashamed. But upon the third
and highest act of excommunication, it
being a most dreadful thunderclap of God's
judgment, it is most difficult for any
church now to proceed in, it being difficult to know when any man hath sinned
the unpardonable sin, and so to incur a
total cutting off from the church.

2 Thess. 3 : 6.
1 Thess. 5 : 12, &c.
2 Cor. 2 : 5, 6, 7.

Lev. 19 : 17, 18.

Matt. 18 : 15, &c.
1 Tim. 5 : 20.
2 Tim. 2 : 14.
Tit. 1 : 12, 13, 14.

Lev. 13 : 1, &c.
Numb. 12 : 14, 15.

2 Thess. 3 : 6.

1 Cor. 5 : 4, &c.
Tit. 3 : 10.
Rev. 2 : 14, 20, &c.

Matt. 18 : 17.
1 Cor. 16 : 22.

XXXV. ARTICLE.

Of Communion of Saints, and giving to the Poor.

All christians that have been baptized
into one faith, and united in one true

Eph. 4 : 5.
Col. 3 : 15.

visible way of worshipping the true God, by Christ Jesus our Lord, should keep the unity of the spirit, in the bond of peace, seeing there is but one mystical body of Christ, and should have fellowship and communion in each other's sufferings, or afflictions, for if one member suffer, all are pained with it. Hence it is also they partake of each other's gifts in great variety, which make the harmony of dependency on each other, seeing a need of every member, for the publick use, and common profit of the whole, both in the private as well as more publick, and solemn worship of God's house; as also an interest in each other's goods and possessions, so far as comports with necessity and charity, according to the charter privileges, or law of their king; and tho' no equality, or property, be pleaded for; yet the works of charity and mercy, must be minded as a duty to lend to the Lord, and pity and relieve the Lord's poor, weekly laying out for them, as God hath prospered us, according to our ability in freedom, liberality, and charity, according to our brethrens necessity, whether sick, or in prison, to visit and relieve them, and not only within the church, but to all as we have opportunity, and ability to be doing good.

Acts 2 : 46.
Eph. 4 : 3, 4, &c.
I Cor. 12 : 12, 13.
Acts 4 : 32.
I Cor. 12 : 26; 12 : 4, 5, &c.

2 Cor. 8 : 9, 11, &c.
Ps. 37 : 26.
Prov. 11 : 25.
19 : 17.
22 : 22.
Deut. 15 : 10.
Eph. 4 : 28.
I Cor. 16 : 1, 2;
3 : 14, 15.
Deut. 15 : 7, &c.
Matt. 25 : 35, &c.

XXXVI. ARTICLE.

Of Perseverance.

Those that are effectually called, according to God's eternal purpose, being justified by faith do receive such a measure of the holy unction, from the holy spirit, by which they shall certainly persevere unto eternal life.

Jer. 31 : 33, 34. Rom. 8 : 30.

Rom. 8 : 28.
Gal. 3 : 14.
John 1 : 12, 13.
John 17 : 12, 21.
10 : 28, 29.
Rom. 1 : 17.

XXXVII. ARTICLE.

Of the sacred Scripture.

The authority of the holy scripture dependeth not upon the authority of any

2 Pet. 1 : 19, &c.
2 Tim. 3 : 15, &c.

man, but only upon the authority of God, who hath delivered and revealed his mind therein unto us, and containeth all things necessary for salvation; so that whatsoever is not read therein, nor may be proved thereby, is not to be required of any man, that it should be believed as an article of the christian faith, or be thought requisite to salvation. Neither ought we, since we have the scriptures delivered to us now, to depend upon, hearken to, or regard the pretended immediate inspirations, dreams, or prophetical predictions, by or from any person whatsoever, lest we be deluded by them. Nor yet do we believe, that the works of creation, nor the law written in the heart, viz. natural religion, as some call it, or the light within man, as such, is sufficient to inform man of Christ the mediator, or of the way to salvation, or eternal life by him; but the holy scriptures are necessary to instruct all men into the way of salvation, and eternal life. And we do believe, that all people ought to have them in their mother tongue, and diligently, and constantly to read them in their particular places and families, for their edification, and comfort; and endeavour to frame their lives, according to the direction of God's word, both in faith and practice, the holy scriptures being of no private interpretation, but ought to be interpreted according to the analogy of faith, and is the best interpreter of itself, and is sole judge in controversy. And no decrees of popes, or councils, or writings of any person whatsoever, are of equal authority with the sacred scriptures. And by the holy scriptures we understand, the canonical books of the old and new testament, as they are now translated into our English mother-tongue, of which there hath never been any doubt of their verity, and authority, in the protestant churches of Christ to this day.

John 20 : 30, 31.
21 : 25.
Matt. 22 : 29.
John 5 : 39, 46, 47.
10 : 35.
17 : 12.
Prov. 30 : 5, 6.

Joshua 1 : 7.
Rev. 22 : 18.
Deut. 12 : 32.
Isaiah 8 : 20.
2 Pet. 1 : 19.
2 John 7 : 8, 9, 10.
Matt. 24 : 23, &c.
2 Thess. 2 : 7, &c.

1 Cor. 1 : 20, &c.
2 : 6, 7, &c.

Rom.15:4,5; 16:25,26.
1 : 16, &c.
Gal. 5 : 22.
Rom. 11 : 31, 32.

10 : 13, &c.
1 Cor. 14 : 4, 9, &c.
Col. 3 : 16.
2 Pet. 1 : 20, 21.
Acts 15 : 15, 16.

Matt. 22 : 29, 30,

Acts 17 : 10, &c.
18 : 28.

" Then follows the names of the books of the Old and New Testament, as acknowledged in all Protestant confessions, after which follow these words " [Crosby's note] :

All which are given by the inspiration
of God, to be the Rule of faith and
life.

XXXVIII. ARTICLE.

Of the three Creeds.

The three creeds, viz. Nicene creed,
Athanasius's creed, and the Apostles creed,
as they are commonly called, ought
throughly to be received, and believed.
For we believe, they may be proved, by
most undoubted authority of holy scripture, and are necessary to be understood
of all christians; and to be instructed in
the knowledge of them, by the ministers
of Christ, according to the analogy of
faith, recorded in sacred scriptures, upon
which these creeds are grounded, and ca-
techistically opened, and expounded in all
christian families, for the edification of
young and old, which might be a means
to prevent heresy in doctrine, and practice, these creeds containing all things in
a brief manner, that are necessary to be
known, fundamentally, in order to our
salvation; to which end they may be considered, and better understood of all men,
we have here printed them under their
several titles as followeth, viz.

The Apostles Creed.

I believe in God the father almighty, &c.

The Nicene Creed.

We believe in one God, the father al-
might, &c.

Athanasius his Creed.

Whosoever will be saved, before all
things, &c.

" I have omitted inserting the creeds at length, they being to be found in every common prayer-book, and only
observe, that upon the article in the Apostles' Creed, he

descended into hell, they thus comment, Not that he, to wit, Christ, went into the place of the damned, but that he went absolutely into the state of the dead. See Doctor Usher in his body of Divinity, p. 174, and Mr. Perkins on the creed " [Crosby's note].

XXXIX. ARTICLE.

Of general Councils, or Assemblies.

General councils, or assemblies, consisting of Bishops, Elders, and Brethren, of the several churches of Christ, and being legally convened, and met together out of all the churches, and the churches appearing there by their representatives, make but one church, and have lawful right, and suffrage in this general meeting, or assembly, to act in the name of Christ; it being of divine authority, and is the best means under heaven to preserve unity, to prevent heresy, and superintendency among, or in any congregation whatsoever within its own limits, or jurisdiction. And to such a meeting, or assembly, appeals ought to be made, in case any injustice be done, or heresy, and schism countenanced, in any particular congregation of Christ, and the decisive voice in such general assemblies is the major part, and such general assemblies have lawful power to hear, and determine, as also to excommunicate.

Acts 15 : 1, &c.

Acts 15 : 11, &c.
Matt. 18 : 20.

Acts 15 : 30, 31.

Matt. 18 : 18, 19.
I Cor. 5 : 4, 5, 6.

XL. ARTICLE.

Of religious Worship, and the Sabbath-day.

The light of nature sheweth there is a God, who hath a sovereignty over all, but the holy scripture hath fully revealed it; as also that all men should worship him according to God's own institution and appointment. And hath limited us, by his own revealed will, that he may not be worshipped according to the imaginations and devices of men, or the suggestions of Satan, under any visible representations whatsoever, or any other way not pre-

Rom. 1 : 19, 20; 2 : 15.

I Chron. 16 : 29.
Ps. 95 : 6, 7, 8.

scribed in the holy scriptures; and all religious worship is to be given to the father, son, and holy ghost, and to God alone, not to angels, saints, or any other creature, and since the fall, not without a mediator, nor in the mediation of any other but Christ alone; nor is this worshipping of God now under the gospel, tied to any place, or made more acceptable by one place than another. Yet the assembly of the church, ought not to be neglected by any. And in order to his being worshipped, and served, God hath instituted one day in seven, for his sabbath to be kept holy unto him, which from the resurrection of Christ, is the first day of the week, which is called the Lord's-day, and is to be observed and continued to the end of the world, as a christian sabbath, the last day of the week being abolished. And this christian sabbath is to be kept after a due and reverent manner, in preparing of our hearts, and ordering of affairs so beforehand, that we may rest that day from worldly and carnal employments, and frequent the solemn assemblies of the church, and in all publick and private duties of religion, as hearing, meditating, and conferring, and reading in, or of the holy scriptures, together with prayer, publick and private, and in the duties of necessity, charity, and mercy, and not in any vain or worldly discourse, or idle recreations whatsoever.

97 : 7.
99 : 5.
Deut. 8 : 6.
Ps. 103 : 7; 14 : 6.

Mark 7 : 7.
Ps. 99 : 8, 9.
106 : 29, 39.
John 4 : 24.
Rev. 9 : 20.
Exod. 34 : 14.
I Cor. 8 : 4.
Matt. 28 : 19.
Deut. 5 : 26, &c.
John 14 : 6.
Gal. 3 : 9.
Heb. 9 : 15.
I Tim. 2 : 5.
Matt. 18 : 20.
John 4 : 21.
Mal. 1 : 11.
I Tim. 2 : 8.
Heb. 10 : 25.
Acts 2 : 42.
Exod. 20 : 8.
I Cor. 16 : 1, 2.
Acts 20 : 7.
Rev. 1 : 10.
Isaiah 58 : 13.
Neh. 13 : 15, &c.
Heb. 10 : 25.
Rev. 1 : 3.
James 1 : 23, 25.
Rom. 10 : 14.
Ps. 119 : 15.
Zech. 7 : 2.

Luke 21 : 36.   Acts 16 : 13, 16.   Isa. 56 : 2, 6.

XLI. ARTICLE.

Of publick and private Prayer.

Prayer is an holy, religious, and sacred ordinance of God, and the duty of all men to perform, by the law of God; and to God alone, and no other, whether saint or angel, and in the name of Christ the mediator, and in his name alone, and no other, whether saint or angel, or any other creature. And that for all men living, except they have sinned the un-

Matt. 6 : 7.
Jude 20.
Heb. 12 : 28.
Isaiah 55 : 6.
Jer. 29 : 12; 10 : 6, 25.

Ps. 32 : 6.
Matt. 26 : 41.
Isaiah 30 : 2.
Hos. 4 : 12.

pardonable sin, both high and low; especially for ministers and magistrates. And not for dead saints, nor infernal spirits. And prayer is to be made in a tongue understood by the people: And we ought to pray for all things necessary according to the will of God in Christ Jesus, in a solemn and reverent manner, every way suitable and agreeable to the platform, or manner of prayer, which Christ taught his disciples, and us, in his holy gospel, which is the only perfect rule of all prayers; and by the assistance of the holy spirit of God, without which we cannot pray aright. And this religious worship all men are bound, and required to serve God in, both public and private, at least two times a day, in all christian families, by prayers, and supplications, intercessions, and giving of thanks to God the father, in the name and mediation of Christ Jesus our Lord.

James 1 : 5.
John 14 : 13, 14.
15 : 16.
16 : 23.
I Tim. 2 : 1, 2, 3.
James 5 : 16.
I Thess. 5 : 17, 25.

2 Thess. 3 : 1, 2.
Matt. 9 : 38.
I Cor. 14 : 14, &c.

Matt. 6 : 6, &c.
Rom. 8 : 26, 27.
I Thess. 5 : 18.
Isa. 17 : 65.
Jer. 18 : 14, 15.

Hos. 5 : 4.
Ps. 69 : 6.
Dan. 6 : 10.
Ps. 5 : 2, 3.

Ps. 55 : 15, 16, 17. Zach. 8 : 21. Phil. 1 : 4, 6.
I Tim. 4 : 5. Isaiah 1 : 15. Rev. 5 : 8.

XLII. ARTICLE.

Of publick Humiliation, by Fasting and Prayer.

Publick humiliation, by fasting and prayer, is an ordinance of God, appointed for his church and people. And it being an extraordinary duty, especially as it hath respect to the church generally, or the nation as such, and therefore we must have due regard to the grounds, ends, and manner, of its being performed; confessing of, and reforming from sin, both in publick as well as private fasts. Abstaining from our pleasures, as also our common food, in a sensible and real afflicting of our souls before the Lord; or to seek to God by prayer and fasting for some spiritual, or temporal good, that God hath promised us, or that we stand in need of having due regard to God's word and glory, in this solemn or divine ordinance.

Joel 1 : 14, 15.
2 : 12, 13, &c.
2 Chron. 20 : 3.

Lev. 23 : 27, &c.
Ezra 8 : 21 ; 9 : 4.
10 : 1.
Neh. 9 : 1, 2, 3.

Isaiah 58 : 3, 4, &c.

Jonah 3 : 4, 6, &c.

Zech. 7 : 5.
Matt. 6 : 16, &c.
2 Sam. 12 : 21, 22.

Esther 4 : 16.

XLIII. ARTICLE.

Of Family, or relative Duties therein.

Parents, and masters, are a sort of subordinate governors, and rulers, in their respective jurisdictions and families; in their respective relative places, according to their capacities, and opportunities; and are engaged from God's word, to take charge of their families, and rule and govern them according to the word of God, both husbands, parents, masters, and all others concerned in any such relation; and by their godly and religious example, instruct their families; they being found carefully keeping of the sabbath-day, in the holy and religious services of hearing the word preached, with publick and private prayer. As also requiring and instructing their families and relations, to follow their godly and religious example, in the private and publick exercises of religion; and calling them to an account, how they spend the sabbath, and other times, and mercies they enjoy; especially the reading of the scriptures, and hearing the word preached, with publick prayer with them, and for them, in order to a blessing for them, and their families. The neglect of which duty, or power of godliness, and religion in families, is one main cause of that wicked atheism, and impiety in the world and families; and of the carnal lukewarmness, and ignorance in churches, to gether with contempt of government; because many professors make so little account, or conscience of performing any duty at home in their own families.

Gen. 18 : 19.
I Sam. 2 : 23, &c.
Prov. 30 : 11, &c.
I Tim. 5 : 8.
Matt. 7 : 9, 10.
Col. 4 : 1.
Eph. 4 : 25, &c.
   5 : 4.

Josh. 24 : 15.
Eph. 5 : 19, &c.
   6 : 1, 2, &c.
Prov. 1 : 1.
Acts 10 : 30, 33
I Tim. 3 : 4.
I Kings 2 : 1, 2, 3.
Gen. 49 : 28, 29.

Job 1 : 5.
I Chron. 29 : 19.
Prov. 22 : 6, 15.
2 Kings 2 : 24.

Prov. 29 : 15, 21.
2 Tim 3 : 15.

XLIV. ARTICLE.

Of Children dying in Infancy.

We do believe, that all little children, dying in their infancy, viz. before they are capable to chuse either good or evil, whether born of believing parents, or unbelieving parents, shall be saved by the grace of God, and merit of Christ their redeemer, and work of the holy ghost,

Isaiah 7 : 16; 8 : 4.

2 Sam. 12 : 19, &c.
Ezek. 18 : 4, &c.

I Kings 14 : 13.
Matt. 18 : 2, 3, 4.

and so being made members of the invisible church, shall enjoy life everlasting; for our Lord Jesus saith, of such belongs the kingdom of heaven. Ergo, we conclude, that that opinion is false, which saith, that those little infants dying before baptism, are damned.

Jer. 31 : 29, 30.
Deut. 1 : 39.
Matt. 19 : 13, 14.
Mark 10 : 13, &c.

XLV. ARTICLE.

Of the civil Magistrate.

The supreme lord and king of all the world, hath ordained civil magistrates to be under him, over the people for his own glory, and the publick good. And the office of a magistrate, may be accepted of, and executed by christians, when lawfully called thereunto; and God hath given the power of the sword, into the hands of all lawful magistrates, for the defence and encouragement of them that do well, and for the punishment of evil doers, and for the maintenance of justice, and peace, according to the wholesome laws of each kingdom, and commonwealth, and they may wage war upon just and necessary occasions. And subjection in the Lord ought to be yielded to the magistrates in all lawful things commanded by them, for conscience sake, with prayers for them, for a blessing upon them, paying all lawful and reasonable custom, and tribute to them, for the assisting of them, against foreign, domestical, and potent enemies.

Rom. 13 : 1, &c.
Prov. 8 : 15.
I Pet. 2 : 14.
Prov. 20 : 26.
2 Sam. 23 : 3.
Ps. 82 : 3, 4; 72 : 4, 7.
Eccles. 3 : 8.
Prov. 20 : 18.
Luke 3 : 15.
Acts 10 : 22.
I Chron. 5 : 22.
Prov. 24 : 6.
Tit. 3 : 1.
2 Pet. 2 : 13, 17.
Eccles. 10 : 20.
Prov. 21 : 22.
Rom. 13 : 5.
I Tim. 2 : 1, 2.
Matt. 22 : 17, 21.
        17 : 25, 27.
2 Sam. 21 : 16, 17.
        23 : 15, 16.

XLVI. ARTICLE.

Of Liberty of Conscience.

The Lord Jesus Christ, who is king of kings, and lord of all by purchase, and is judge of quick and dead, is only Lord of Conscience; having a peculiar right so to be. He having died for that end, to take away the guilt, and to destroy the filth of sin, that keeps the consciences of all men in thraldom, and bondage, till they are set free by his special grace. And therefore he would not have the consciences of men in bondage to, or im-

I Tim. 6 : 15.
Acts 10 : 36 ; 4:17,&c.
James 4 : 12.
Rom. 14 : 4.
Acts 5 : 29.
I Cor. 7 : 23.
Matt. 15 : 9; 24 : 9.
Col. 2 : 20, &c.
I Cor. 11 : 23.
I Pet. 5 : 2, 3.
Matt. 15 : 14.

posed upon, by any usurpation, tyranny,
or command whatsoever, contrary to his
revealed will in his word, which is
the only rule he hath left, for the consciences of all men to be ruled, and regulated, and guided by, through the assistance of his spirit. And therefore the
obedience to any command, or decree,
that is not revealed in, or consonant to
his word, in the holy oracles of scripture,
is a betraying of the true liberty of conscience. And the requiring of an implicit
faith, and an absolute blind obedience,
destroys liberty of conscience, and reason
also, it being repugnant to both, and that
no pretended good end whatsoever, by
any man, can make that action, obedience,
or practice, lawful and good, that is not
grounded in, or upon the authority of
holy scripture, or right reason agreeable
thereunto.

Deut. 12 : 32.
Micah 6 : 6, 7, 8.
Acts 17 : 25, &c.
Deut. 4 : 17, 19.

I Cor. 10 : 18.
I Sam. 15 : 3, &c.
Rom. 14 : 10, 12.

Gal. 1 : 14.
Phil. 3 : 6.
John 4 : 22.
2 Sam. 3 : 6, &c.

XLVII. ARTICLE.

Of Marriage.

Marriage is to be between one Man,
and one Woman; neither is it lawful for
any Man, to have more than one wife,
nor for any woman to have more than
one husband, at the same time. And it
is lawful for all sorts of people to marry,
who are able of judgment to give their
consent. But marriage must not be within the degree of consanguinity, or affinity,
forbidden in the word, nor can any such
incestuous marriages ever be made lawful
by any law of man, or consent of parties,
to live together as man and wife. And
it is the duty of christians to marry in the
Lord, and therefore those that profess
the true religion, ought not to marry
with infidels, or idolaters, nor prophane
wicked persons in their life, nor yet with
any that maintain damnable heresies.

Matt. 19 : 5, 6.
Gen. 2 : 24.
Mal. 2 : 15.
I Cor. 7 : 36.
Heb. 13 : 4.
1 Tim. 4 : 3.
Exod. 22 : 16, 17.
Gen. 29 : 23.
Lev. 18 : 6, &c.
2 Sam. 13 : 14.
Gen. 38 : 16.
Deut. 22 : 28.

Eph. 5 : 3.
I Cor. 7 : 2; 5 : 1, 4, 13.
Gen. 6 : 2.
I Cor. 7 : 39.
Numb. 25 : 1, 2;
2 Cor. 6 : 14, &c.

XLVIII. ARTICLE.

Of the Lawfulness of an Oath.

A lawful oath, is a part of religious
worship, wherein the person swearing in

Exod. 20 : 7.
Deut. 6 : 13; 10 : 20.

truth, righteousness, and judgment, solemnly calleth God to witness what he
sweareth, and to judge him according to
the truth or falseness thereof. And we
are to swear by no other name, but by
the name of God only, when we are called before a lawful magistrate, upon a lawful matter, warranted by God's holy
word; and an oath is to be taken in the
plain and common sense of the words,
without equivocation, or mental reservation, in a solemn and reverent using of
God's holy name; and such an oath, we
believe all christians, when lawfully called
thereunto by the magistrate, may take.
But the foolish monastical vows of papists,
and all idle and vain swearing, is an abominable, and wicked prophaning of the
holy name of God.

Jer. 4 : 2.
Ps. 15 : 4.
Zech. 5 : 4.
2 Chron. 6 : 22, 23.
Isa. 65 : 16.
Jer. 12 : 16.
Matt. 5 : 34.
Neh. 13 : 25.
2 Kings 11 : 4, 17.
Ps. 24 : 4.
Heb. 6 : 16.
Jer. 23 : 10.
Lev. 19 : 12.
Eph. 4 : 28.
Amos 8 : 14.
James 5 : 12.
1 Sam. 14 : 29.
2 Kings 6 : 31.
Isaiah 48 : 1.
Zeph. 1 : 5.

XLIX. ARTICLE.

Of the State of man after Death, and of the Resurrection of the Dead.

The bodies of men after death, return
to dust, and see corruption; but their
souls, or spirits, which neither die nor
sleep, having an immortal subsistence, immediately return to God who gave them;
the souls of the righteous being then
made perfect in holiness, are received
into paradise where they are with Christ,
and behold the face of God in light and
glory, waiting for the full redemption of
their bodies, and the souls of the wicked
are cast into hell, where they remain in
torment and utter darkness, reserved to
the judgment of the great day. And
besides these two places, for souls separated from their bodies, the holy scripture mentions none. And at the last day,
such of the saints as shall be found alive,
shall not sleep, but be changed, and all
the dead shall be raised up with the self
same bodies and none other, although
with different qualities, which shall be
united to their souls for ever and ever,
but the bodies of the unjust, shall by the
power of Christ, as a severe and just judge,
be raised to dishonour; and the bodies

Gen. 3 : 19.
Acts 13 : 36.
Eccles. 12 : 7.
Acts 7 : 59.
Luke 23 : 43.
2 Cor. 5 : 1, 6, 8.
Phil. 1 : 23.
Heb. 12 : 23.
Jude 6.
I Pet. 3 : 19.
Luke 16 : 23, 24.
I Cor. 15 : 51, 52.
I Thess. 4 : 17.
Job 19 : 26, 27.
I Cor. 15 : 42, &c,
John 5 : 28, 29.
Dan. 12 : 2.
I Cor. 15 : 21, &c.

Rev. 20 : 5, 6.
Acts 24 : 15.
Phil. 3 : 21.
Rev. 19 : 1, &c.
14 : 37.

of the just and righteous, by his spirit,
as he is head of the catholick church,
unto honour, and be made conformable
with his glorious body, and shall enjoy
everlasting life; in singing perpetual
praises, and hallelujahs to God for ever
and ever. Amen.

L. ARTICLE.

Of the last Judgment.

And lastly, we believe, God hath appointed a day, wherein he will judge the world in righteousness, by Jesus Christ, to whom all power, and judgment is given of the father; in which day, not only the apostate angels shall be judged, but likewise all persons that have lived upon the earth, shall appear before the tribunal of Christ, to give an account of their thoughts, words, and deeds, and shall receive a just sentence, according to what they have done in their bodies, whether good, or evil, when God, according to his purpose, will manifest the glory of his mercy, in the salvation of his elect, and of his justice in the eternal damnation of the wicked and disobedient; for then shall the righteous go into everlasting life, and receive the fullness of joy and glory, but the wicked, who know not God, nor obey the gospel offered them in Christ, shall be cast into eternal torments, and punished with everlasting destruction, from the presence of the Lord, and from the glory of his power. Amen.

Acts 17 : 31.
John 5 : 22, 27.
Rom. 2 : 16.
2 Tim. 4 : 1.
1 Cor. 6 : 3.
Jude 6.
Matt. 12 : 36.
2 Cor. 5 : 10.
Eccles. 12 : 14.
Rom. 14 : 10, 12.
Matt. 25 : 32.
Luke 21 : 28.
1 Thess. 4 : 17.
Ps. 16 : 11.
Luke 12 : 32.
Matt. 25 : 46.
Ps. 58 : 10.
2 Tim. 4 : 8.
Luke 16 : 28.
Rev. 14 : 11.
John 8 : 24.
2 Thess. 1 : 8, &c.
Rev. 20 : 10, 11, &c.
22 : 11, 15.

4. Somerset Confession

In 1691 the General Baptists, who lived in Somerset and adjacent counties, published a Confession in twenty-seven articles; but it does not seem to have circulated extensively in other parts of the kingdom (Crosby, III, 259-261; IV Appen. I; Taylor, I, 361). As it was comparatively unimportant and the text is accessible in Crosby, it is omitted.

L

5. Trinitarian Articles

The General Baptists were early troubled with doubts on the doctrine of the trinity and the divinity of Christ, having inherited them from the Dutch. The brevity and ambiguity of the Confession of 1660 on this subject was regarded as proof of uncertainty, if not heterodoxy among them. Early in the last quarter of the century, Matthew Cafin, the gifted and inquisitive pastor of the church at Horsham, in Sussex, denied both the true divinity and the true humanity of Christ. The matter was brought before the General Assembly, and after some ten years of fruitless agitation, some brethren, dissatisfied with the ambiguity and uncertainty of the position of the main body, withdrew and formed the " General Association " in 1696, on the basis of a clear, distinct statement on the doctrine of the Trinity. In June, 1704, the two bodies reunited on the basis of two brief articles, entitled, " The Unity of the Churches." These were immediately published, and are as follows (Taylor I, 47.):

First, respecting Almighty God.—We do believe, and are very confident, that there is one, and but one living and true *God,* who is from everlasting to everlasting, and changeth not; without body, parts, or imperfections: essentially present in all places; of infinite power, wisdom and goodness; the Maker of all things in heaven and earth, visible and invisible: and, that in this divine and infinite Being, or Unity of the Godhead, there are Three Persons, the *Father, Word,* and *Holy Ghost,* of one substance, power, and eternity. Secondly, respecting the Lord Jesus Christ—We do believe, that there is but one Lord Jesus Christ, the second Person in the Trinity, and the only begotten Son of God; and that he did, in the fulness of time, take to himself our nature, in the womb of the blessed Virgin Mary, of whom, in respect of the flesh, he was made; and so is true God, and true Man, our Immanuel.

The union, however, lasted but a short time, and the General Baptists became deeply leavened with Socinian views. Religion in England was suffering a sad and general decline during the first half of the eighteenth century, and the General Baptists suffered like other denominations. Lack of preachers, coldness, strife, division, afflicted all their churches, many of which became Socinian or ceased to exist altogether. By the middle of the century the cause lay in almost complete ruins.

6. Present Doctrinal Position

This body still preserves its corporate existence under the title, " The General Assembly of the General Baptist Churches in England." The Confession of 1660 has never been repudiated, but the Assembly has welcomed Unitarian churches into its fellowship, and probably a majority of its members are now Unitarian in sentiment. For some years the following summary of faith has been authoritatively prefixed to the Proceedings of the Assembly as its only statement of doctrine:

The Assembly has borne from its foundation, in 1653, the designation, " General Baptist."

It consists of Churches which believe that the way of salvation is open to all, and which also regard it as the duty and privilege of all disciples of Christ to avow their faith in their common Lord by observing the Christian ordinance of baptism by immersion, whereby they signify their death to sin and resurrection to newness of life. They mostly, however, believe that the gates of any sectional part of Christ's Church should be as wide open as the gate of His Universal Church, and therefore, that all His Churches may gladly receive into membership any persons who shall confess their personal faith in Christ, and avow their determination to obey Him according to their light. Considerable difference on various doctrinal points also exists in the Churches belonging to the Assembly, and some of those Churches may desire to add some other designation, besides General Baptist, to the name of their Chapel, but these are questions that must be determined by each Church for itself, as the Assembly has no power to interfere in the matter " (Minutes of the General Assembly).

7. *The New Connection*

In the year 1755, a body of people, who had been converted to evangelical, experimental religion under the impulse of the Methodist revival, and had set up independent societies, adopted scriptural views of the mode and subjects of baptism, and proceeded to institute the ordinance anew by baptizing one another (Taylor, II, 31). In 1770 these churches united with some of the old General Baptist churches, which had either preserved their orthodoxy during the general decline or had been revived by contact with Methodism, to form " The New Connection of General Baptists, formed in 1770, with a design to revive Experimental Religion or Primitive Christianity in Faith and Practice." In order to set forth their views and guard against the introduction of the prevalent Socinianism they drew up six " Articles of Religion," which the preachers were all required to sign. For five years subscription was rigidly enforced on every preacher entering the connection, but in 1775 the Association decided " that subscription to a creed was not needful." Instead, the candidate for ordination was allowed to relate his experience before the Association, and was admitted or rejected, according as his experience was approved or disapproved. These articles were composed by the celebrated Dan Taylor, the chief factor in the organization of " The New Connection," and are given by Taylor, II, 139-142, as follows:

ARTICLE 1. *On the Fall of Man.* We believe, that man was made upright in the image of God, free from all disorder natural and moral; capable of obeying perfectly the will and command of God his Maker; yet capable also of sinning: which he unhappily did, and thereby laid himself under the divine curse; which, we think, could include nothing less than the mortality of the body and the eternal punishment of the soul. His nature also became depraved; his mind was defiled; and the powers of his soul weakened—that both he was, and his posterity are, captives of Satan till set at liberty by Christ.

ARTICLE 2. *On the Nature and Perpetual Obligation of the Moral Law.* We believe, that the moral law not only extends to the outward actions of the life, but to all the powers and faculties of the mind, to every desire, temper and thought; that it demands the entire devotion of all the powers and faculties of both body and soul to God: or, in our Lord's words, to love the Lord with all our heart, mind, soul and strength:—that this law is of perpetual duration and obligation, to all men, at all times, and in all places or parts of the world. And, we suppose that this law was obligatory to Adam in his perfect state —was more clearly revealed in the ten commandments— and more fully explained in many other parts of the bible.

ARTICLE 3. *On the Person and Work of Christ.* We believe, that our Lord Jesus Christ is God and man, united in one person: or possessed of divine perfection united to human nature, in a way which we pretend not to explain, but think ourselves bound by the word of God firmly to believe:—that he suffered to make a full atonement for all the sins of all men—and that hereby he has wrought out for us a compleat salvation; which is received by, and as a free gift communicated to, all that believe in him; without the consideration of any works done by us, in order to entitle us to his salvation.— Though we firmly believe, that no faith is the means of justification, but that which produces good works.

ARTICLE 4. *On Salvation by Faith.* We believe, that as this salvation is held forth to all to whom the gospel revelation comes without exception, we ought in the course of our ministry, to propose or offer this salvation to all those who attend our ministry: and, having opened to them their ruined wretched state by nature and practice, to invite all without exception, to look to Christ by faith, without any regard to any thing in, or done by, themselves; that they may, in this way alone, that is, by faith be possessed of this salvation.

ARTICLE 5. *On Regeneration by the Holy Spirit.* We believe, that, as the scriptures assure us, we are justified, made the children of God, purified and sanctified by fáith:—that when a person comes to believe in Jesus (and not before) he is regenerated or renewed in his soul, by the spirit of God, through the instrumentality of the word, now believed and embraced; which renewal of his soul naturally produces holiness in heart and life:—that this holiness is the means of preparing us for the enjoyments and employments of the heavenly world; and of preserving in our souls a comfortable sense of our interest in the Lord, and of our title to glory; as well as to set a good example before men, and to recommend our blessed Redeemer's cause to the world.

ARTICLE 6. *On Baptism.* We believe, that it is the indispensible duty of all who repent and believe the gospel, to be baptized, by immersion in water, in order to be initiated into a church state; and that no person ought to be received into the church without submission to that ordinance. Signed

Dan Taylor	William Smith	Geo. Hickling.
David Wilkin	Samuel Deacon	John Tarrott
W. Thompson	James Fenn	Robert French
John Knott	Francis Smith	N. Pickering
John Stouger	Thomas Perkins	Charles Parman
John Brittain	John Grimley	W. Summers
Henry Poole		

These " Articles " long continued to be the recognized statement of doctrines among the Baptists of the " New Connection." They are not a complete system, but comprise a very clear statement of the views of these Baptists where they differed from the Calvinistic and from other General Baptists. In 1813 it was declared that " the design of the Association, by the maintenance of this institution [for educating ministers] was to promote and cherish the sentiments contained in the articles, drawn up and signed in the year 1770, at the formation of the New Connection" (Taylor, II, 456); in 1815 the articles were reprinted in the minutes in lieu of a circular letter, and the next year the Association reaffirm these principles and determine " that all churches which may hereafter be admitted into it, satisfy it that they maintain the same; and if any church in the connection depart from these principles either in doctrine or practice, and by proper steps cannot be reclaimed, it shall be excluded from the connection" (Taylor, II, 459). These views were also incorporated by Dan Taylor in a catechism for children and young people, which was widely used and was reprinted again and again. A fuller statement of their views may be seen in a Confession which was laid before his church by Dan Taylor when he became pastor in London in 1785, but which was never published (Taylor, II, 470-477).

Prior to 1800 a General Baptist preacher, or church, had now and then gone over to the Calvinistic Baptists. The latter had, by that time, forged ahead into a place of influence and power. Moreover, their high and rigid Calvinism had been materially modified by the Methodist revival, the rise of the modern missionary movement, and the theological labors of Andrew Fuller. As the nineteenth century advanced, these two wings of English Baptists gradually approached each other until the majority of the two parties united in a common statement of beliefs in 1891. Divisive names were dropped, and their work united. (See statement under Calvinistic Baptists.)

II. THE CALVINISTIC OR PARTICULAR BAPTISTS

1. FIRST LONDON CONFESSION

The Calvinistic wing of the English Baptists, unlike the General Baptists, rose in England, and so far as known, apart from Mennonite influences. In 1616 Henry Jacob and some of the exiled Independents returned to England from the Netherlands and began work in London. In 1633, John Spilsbery and a few others left this church, apparently because they had come to oppose infant baptism. In 1638, others withdrew, and soon afterward a new church was formed on the basis of believers' baptism. There was division of sentiment as to the best means of beginning scriptural baptism again. A part sent Richard Blount to Holland where, as they had heard, there were some who baptized believers by immersion. Having obtained baptism in this way from the Rhynsburger Collegiants, he returned and baptized those who sent him. "But the greatest number of the English Baptists, and the more judicious, looked upon all this as needless trouble, and what proceeded from the old Popish Doctrine of right to administer sacraments by an uninterrupted succession, which neither the Church of Rome, nor the Church of England, much less the modern dissenters, could prove to be with them. They affirmed, therefore, and practised accordingly, that after a general corruption of baptism, an unbaptized person might warrantably baptize, and so begin a reformation." And so it was done (Crosby, I, 101-103; Kiffin MS). This was not later than 1641. The members of this first English Calvinistic Baptist church had all been, as far as known,

168

Independents. In becoming Baptists they needed only to change their views of the subjects and mode of baptism. They preserved Calvinistic theology, the independence, democracy, and officials of the local churches as they were in the Congregational church. To the controversy over the proper "subject" of baptism which had been agitated on the continent for a century and had been raging in England for twenty-five years, is now added one on the mode of baptism, which begins in 1641 and soon becomes violent. The distractions of the time somewhat lightened persecution and gave the Baptists a rare opportunity. Many of the best minds of England were attracted to their views, and they gained important converts from all the religious parties of the time. England was at this time almost solidly Calvinistic, and their Calvinistic theology secured for these a much more favorable reception than was accorded the General Baptists, as soon as the difference was recognized. By 1644 there were seven churches in London. They were called Anabaptists and accused of all the errors and enormities which that sect had ever been guilty of or charged ith. The General Baptists were becoming somewhat known, and were Arminian if not Pelagian in theology. In order to distinguish themselves from both the Anabaptists and the General Baptists, refute the slanders and remove the misunderstandings of which they were the innocent victims, they determined to draw up and publish a statement of their views. Accordingly, the seven congregations united in publishing the following Confession, the first Baptist Confession of the Calvinistic type. The Confession, as will be seen on examination, was not very carefully drawn, and is moderately Calvinistic. It is the first Confession of history to prescribe a single immersion as the form of baptism. ("The Orthodox Confession of the Eastern Church," drawn up in 1643, prescribes a threefold immersion.)

It is perhaps the most independent of the Baptist Confessions, and is one of the noblest productions ever put forth by them. It probably still represents the views of the Baptists of the world more nearly than any other single Confession. The following is an attempt to reproduce exactly the original edition.

* The

CONFESSION

OF FAITH,

Of those CHURCHES which are
commonly (though falsly) cal
led ANABAPTISTS;

Presented to the view of all that feare
GOD, to examine by the touchstone of the Word
of Truth: As likewise for the taking off those
aspersions which are frequently both in Pulpit and
Print, (although unjustly) cast upon them.

Acts 4. 20.

*Wee can not but speake the things which wee have seene
and heard.*

Isai. 8. 20.

*To the Law and to the testimony, if they speake not
according to | this Rule, it is because there is no light
in them.*

2 Cor. 1. 9, 10.

*But wee had the sentence of death in our selves, that
wee should not | trust in our selves, but in the living
God, which raiseth the dead; | who delivered us from so
great a death, and doth deliver, in whom | wee trust that
he will yet deliver.*

LONDON

Printed by *Matthew Simmons* in *Aldersgate-street.*
1644.

---

* Title page of edition of 1646 reads, "A Confession of Faith of † seven Congregations or Churches of Christ in London, which are commonly (but unjustly) called
Anabaptists. Published for the vindication of the Truth, and Information of the
ignorant; likewise for the taking off of those Aspersions which are frequently both
in Pulpit and Print unjustly cast upon them. The second Impression corrected and
enlarged. Published according to Order, 1646."

† For "seven," subsequent editions have "the severall."

To

ALL THAT DESIRE

The lifting up of the Name of the | LORD JESUS in
sinceritie, the poore despi- | sed Churches of God in
London send greeting, | with prayers for their farther
increase in the | knowledge of CHRIST JESUS.

*Wee question not but that it will seeme strange to
many men, | that such as wee are frequently termed to
be, lying under that | calumny and black brand of Here-
tickes, and sowers of di | vision as wee doo, should pre-
sume to appear so publickly as | now wee have done: But
yet notwithstanding wee may well | say, to give answer
to such, what* David *said to his brother,|when the* Lords
battell was a fighting, 1 Sam. 29. 30. *Is there not a cause?
| Surely, if ever people had cause to speake for the
vindication of the truth of |* Christ *in their hands, wee
have, that being indeed the maine wheele at this | time
that sets us aworke; for had any thing by men been trans-
acted against | our persons onely, wee could quietly have
sitten still, and committed our Cause to | him who is a
righteous Judge, who will in the great day judge the
secrets of | all mens hearts by Jesus Christ: But being it
is not only us, but the truth pro | fessed by us, wee
cannot, wee dare not but speake; it is no strange thing
to any | observing man, what sad charges are laid, not
onely by the world, that know | not God, but also by
those that thinke themselves much wronged, if they be
not | looked upon as the chiefe Worthies of the Church
of God, and Watchmen of the | Citie: But it hath fared
with us from them, as from the poor Spouse seeking |
her Beloved,* Cant. 5. 6, 7. *They finding us out of that
common road-way | themselves walke, have smote us
and taken away our vaile, that so wee may by | them be
recommended odious in the eyes of all that behold us,
and in the hearts | of all that thinke upon us, which they
have done both in Pulpit and Print, | charging us with*

holding Free-will, Falling away from grace, denying
Origi | nall sinne, disclaiming of Magistracy, denying to
assist them either in persons | or purse in any of their
lawfull Commands, doing acts unseemly in the dispen |
sing the Ordinance of Baptism, not to be named amongst
Christians: All | which Charges wee disclaime as notor-
iously untrue, though by reason of these | calumnies cast
upon us, many that feare God are discouraged and fore-
stalled | in harbouring a good thought, either of us or
what wee professe; and many that | know not God
incouraged, if they can finde the place of our meeting, to
get | together in Clusters to stone us, as looking upon us
as a people holding such | things, as that wee are not
worthy to live: Wee have therefore for the cleering | of
the truth we professe, that it may be at libertie, though
wee be in bonds, | briefly published a Confession of our
Faith, as desiring all that feare God, seri | ously to con-
sider whether (if they compare what wee here say and
confesse in the | presence of the Lord Jesus and his
Saints) men have not with their tongues in | Pulpit, and
pens in Print, both spoken and written things that are
contrary to | truth; but wee know our God in his owne
time will cleere our Cause, and lift | up his Sonne to
make him the chiefe cornerstone, though he has been (or
now | should be) rejected of Master Builders. And be-
cause it may be conceived, that | what is here published,
may be but the Judgement of some one particular Con |
gregation, more refined then the rest; We doe therefore
here subscribe it, some | of each body in the name, and
by the appointment of seven Congregations, | who though
wee be distinct in respect of our particular bodies, for con-
veniency | sake, being as many as can well meete together
in one place, yet are all one in | Communion, holding
Jesus Christ to be our head and Lord; under whose go ǁ
vernment wee desire alone to walke, in following the
Lambe wheresoever he | goeth; and wee beleeve the
Lord will daily cause truth more to appeare in the |
hearts of his Saints, and make them ashamed of their
folly in the Land of | their Nativitie, that so they may
with one shoulder, more studie to lift up the | Name of
the Lord Jesus, and stand for his appointments and

*Lawes; which | is the desires and prayers of the con-
temned Churches of Christ in* London *| for all Saints.*
Subscribed in the Names of seven Churches in *London.*

William Kiffin.
Thomas Patience.

John Spilsbery.
George Tipping.
Samuel Richardson.

Thomas Skippard.
Thomas Munday.

Thomas Gunne.

John Mabbatt.

John Webb.
Thomas Killcop.

Paul Hobson.
Thomas Goare.

Joseph Phelpes.
Edward Heath.

The
CONFESSION
Of FAITH, of those Churches
which are commonly (though falsly)
called ANABAPTISTS.

I.

THat GOD as he is in himselfe, cannot |
be comprehended of any but himselfe,
[1] dwelling in that inaccessible light, that
no eye can attaine unto, whom never man
saw, nor can see; that there is but [2] one
God, one Christ, one Spirit, one Faith,| one
Baptisme; [3] one Rule of holinesse and obedience
for | all Saints, at all times, in all places to be
observed.

[1] 1 Tim. 6 . 16.
[2] 1 Tim. 2 . 5.
Eph. 4 . 4, 5, 6.
1 Cor. 12 . 4, 5,
6, 13.
John 14. chap.
[3] 1 Tim. 6 . 3.
13, 14.
Gal. 1 . 8, 9.
2 Tim. 3 . 15.

II.

That God is [1] of himselfe, that is, neither from
ano- | ther, nor of another, nor by another, nor
for another: | [2] But is a Spirit, who as his being is
of himselfe, so he | gives [3] being, moving, and
preservation to all other | things, being in him-
selfe eternall, most holy, every way | infinite in
[4] greatnesse, wisdome, power, justice, goodnesse, |
truth, &c. In this God-head, there is the Father,
the | Sonne, and the Spirit; being every one of
them one and | the same God; and therefore not

[1] Esa. 44 . 67
& 43 . 11.
& 46 . 9.
[2] John 4 . 24.
[3] Exod. 3 . 14.

[4] Rom. 11 . 36.
Act. 17 . 28

divided, but distingui- | shed one from another
by their severall properties; the | ⁵ Father being
from himselfe, the ⁶ Sonne of the Father | from
everlasting, the holy ⁷ Spirit proceeding from the |
Father and the Sonne.

⁵ ₁ Cor. 8 . 6.
⁶ Pro. 8 . 22, 23
Heb. 1 . 3
John 1 . 18
⁷ Joh. 15 . 16.
Gal. 4 . 6.

[Page 2]

III.

¹ Esa. 46 . 10
Rom. 11 . 34,
35, 36
Mat. 10 . 29, 30
² Eph. 1 , 11.

³ Col. 2 . 3.
⁴ Num. 23 . 19,
20.
⁵ Jere. 10 . 10.
Rom. 3 . 4.

That God hath ¹ decreed in himselfe from ever-
lasting | touching all things, effectually to work
and dispose them | ² according to the counsell of
his owne will, to the glory | of his Name; in
which decree appeareth his wisdome, con- |
stancy, truth, and faithfulnesse; ³ Wisdome is that
where- | by he contrives all things; ⁴ Constancy is
that whereby | the decree of God remaines al-
wayes immutable; ⁵ Truth | is that whereby he
declares that alone which he hath de- | creed,
and though his sayings may seeme to sound
some- | times another thing, yet the sense of
them doth alwayes | agree with the decree;
⁶ Faithfulnesse is that whereby he | effects that he
hath decreed, as he hath decreed. And | touching
his creature man, ⁷ God had in Christ before | the
foundation of the world, according to the good
plea- | sure of his will, foreordained some men
to eternall life | through Jesus Christ, to the praise
and glory of his | grace, ⁸ leaving the rest in their
sinne to their just con- | demnation, to the praise
of his Justice.

⁶ Esa. 44 . 10.
⁷ Eph. 1, 3, 4, 5,
6, 7.
2 Tim. 1 . 9.
Acts 13 . 48.
Rom. 8 . 29, 30.
⁸ Jude ver. 4.
& 6.
Rom. 9 . 11,
12, 13.
Prov. 16 . 4.

IV.

¹ Gen. 1, chap.
Col. 1 . 16.
Heb. 11 . 3.
Esa. 45 . 12.
² Gen. 1 . 26.
1 Cor. 15 . 45,
46
Eccles. 7 . 31.
³ Psal. 49 . 20.
⁴ Gen. 3 . 1 4, 5.
2 Cor. 11 . 3.
⁵ 2 Pet. 2 . 4.
Jude ver. 6.
Joh. 8 . 44
⁶ Gen. 3 . 1, 2, 6.
1 Tim. 2 . 14.
Eccles. 7 . 31.
Gal. 3 . 22.

¹ In the beginning God made all things very
good, | created man after his own ² Image and
likenesse, filling | him with all perfection of all
naturall excellency and up- | rightnesse, free from
all sinne. ³ But long he abode not in | this hon-
our, but by the ⁴ subtiltie of the Serpent, which |
Satan used as his instrument, himselfe with his
Angels | having sinned before, and not ⁵ kept
their first estate, but | left their owne habitation;
first ⁶ *Eve*, then *Adam* being | seduced did wit-
tingly and willingly fall into disobedience | and
transgression of the Commandement of their
great | Creator, for the which death came upon
all, and reigned | over all, so that all since the
Fall are conceived in sinne, | and brought forth
in iniquitie, and so by nature children | of wrath,
and servants of sinne, subjects of ⁷ death, and all
[Page 3] other calamities due to sinne in this
world and for ever, | being considered in the
state of nature, without relation | to Christ.

⁷ Rom. 5 . 12,
18, 19
& 6 . 23.
Eph. 2 . 3.
Rom. 5 . 12.

V.

All mankind being thus fallen, and become altogether | dead in sinnes and trespasses, and subject to the eternall | wrath of the great God by transgression; yet the elect, | which God hath [1] loved with an everlasting love, are [2] re- | deemed, quickened, and saved, not by themselves, neither | by their own workes, | lest any man should boast himselfe, | but wholly and onely by God of [3] his free grace and mer- | cie through Jesus Christ, who of God is made unto us | wisdome, righteousnesse, sanctification and re- | dempti | on, that as it is written, Hee that re- | joyceth, let him re- | joyce in the Lord.

[1] Jer. 31 . 2
[2] Gen. 3 . 15.
Eph. 1 . 3, 7.
& 2 . 4, 9.
1 Thess. 5 . 9.
Acts 13 . 38
[3] 1 Cor. 1 . 30, 31.
2 Cor. 5 . 21.
Jer. 9 . 23, 24.

VI.

[1] This therefore is life eternall, to know the onely true | God, and whom he hath sent Jesus Christ. [2] And on the | contrary, the Lord will render vengeance in flaming fire | to them that know not God, and obey not the Gospel of | our Lord Jesus Christ.

[1] Joh. 17 . 3.
Heb. 5 . 9.
Jer. 23 . 5, 6.
[2] 2 Thess. 1 . 8.
Joh. 3 . 36.

VII.

The Rule of this Knowledge, Faith, and Obedi- | ence, | concerning the worship and service of God, and all other | Christian duties, is not mans inventions, opinions, devi- | ces, lawes, constitu- | tions, or traditions unwritten whatso- | ever, but onely the word of God contained in the Cano- | nicall Scriptures.

Joh. 5 . 39
2 Tim. 3 . 15.
16, 17.
Col. 21 . 18, 23.
Matth. 15 . 9.

VIII.

In this written Word God hath plainly re- | vealed | whatsoever he hath thought needfull for us to know, be- | leeve, and acknowledge, touch- | ing the Nature and Office | of Christ, in whom all the promises are Yea and Amen | to the praise of God.

Acts 3 . 22, 23
Heb. 1 . 1, 2
2 Tim. 3 , 15,
16, 17.
2 Cor. 1 . 20.

[Page 4]

IX.

[1] Gen. 3 . 15
& 22 . 18 &
49 . 10
Dan. 7 . 13 &
9 . 24, 25, 26
[2] Prov. 8 . 23
Joh. 1 . 1, 2, 3.
Col. 1 . 1, 15,
16, 17.
[3] Gal. 4 . 4
[4] Heb. 7 . 14
Rev. 5 . 5 with
Gen. 49 . 9, 10.

Touching the Lord Jesus, of whom [1] *Moses* and the | Prophets wrote, and whom the Apostles preached, is the | [2] Sonne of God the Father, the brightnesse of his glory, | the ingraven forme of his being, God with him and with | his holy Spirit, by whom he made the world, by whom | he upholds and governes all the workes hee hath made, | who also [3] when the fulnesse of time was come, was made | man of a [4] woman, of the Tribe of [5] *Judah,* of the seed of | *Abraham* and David,

Rom. 1 . 3. &
9 . 5
Mat. 1 . 16 with
Luke 3 . 23, 26.
Heb. 2 . 16
6 Esa. 53 . 3, 4, 5.
Phil. 2 . 8.

to wit, of *Mary* that blessed Vir- | gin, by the holy Spirit comming upon her, and the power | of the most High overshadowing her, and was also in 6 all | things like unto us, sinne only excepted.

X.

1 2 Tim. 2 . 15
Heb. 9 . 15.
Joh. 14 . 6

2 Heb. 1. 2. & 3.
1, 2 & 7 . 24.
Esa. 9 . 6, 7.
Acts 5 . 31.

Touching his Office, 1 Jesus Christ onely is made the | Mediator of the new Covenant, even the everlasting Co- | venant of grace between God and Man, to 2 be perfectly | and fully the Prophet, Priest and King of the Church of | God for evermore.

XI.

1 Prov. 8 . 23
Esa. 42 . 6 &
49 . 1, 5
2 Esa. 11 . 2, 3,
4, 5, & 61 . 1, 2,
3 with Luk. 4.
17, 22.
Joh. 1 . 14, 16.
& 3 . 34.

Unto this Office hee was fore-ordained from everla- | sting, by the 1 authority of the Father, and in respect of | his Manhood, from the womb called and separated, and | 2 anointed also most fully and abundantly with all gifts | necessary, God having without measure poured the Spi- | rit upon him.

XII.

In this Call the Scripture holds forth two speciall | things considerable; first, the call to the Office; secondly, | the Office it self. First,

1 Heb. 5 . 4, 5, 6.

that 1 none takes this honour but | he that is called of God, as was *Aaron*, so also Christ, it | being an action especially of God the Father, whereby a | speciall covenant being made, hee ordaines his Sonne to | this office: which Cove-

2 Esa. 53 . 10.

nant is, that 2 Christ should be [Page 5] made a Sacrifice for sinne, that hee shall see his seed, and | prolong his dayes, and the pleasure of the Lord shall | prosper in his hand; which calling there- | fore contains in | it selfe 3 chusing, 4 fore-ordain- | ing, 5 sending. Chusing re- | spects the end, fore- | ordaining the means, sending the ex- | ecution it self, 6 all of meere grace, without any condi- | tion | fore-seen either in men, or in Christ him- | selfe.

3 Esa. 42 . 13
4 1 Pet. 1 . 20
5 Joh. 3 . 17 &
9 . 27 & 10 . 36
Esa. 61 . 1.
6 Joh. 3 . 16
Rom. 8 . 32.

XIII.

So that this Office to be Mediator, that is, to be Pro- | phet, Priest, and King of the Church of God, is so proper | to Christ, as neither in the whole, nor in any part there- | of, it can be trans- ferred from him to any other.

1 Tim. 2 . 5.
Heb. 7 . 24
Dan. 5 . 14
Act. 4 . 12.
Luke 1 . 33.
Joh. 14 . 6.

M

XIV.

This Office it self to which Christ was called, is three- | fold, of [1] a Prophet, of [2] Priest, & of [3] a King: this num- | ber and order of Offices is shewed; first, by mens necessi- | ties grievously labouring [4] under ignorance, by reason | whereof they stand in infinit necessity of the Prophetical | office of Christ to relieve them. Secondly, alien- ation from | God, wherein they stand in need of the Priestly Office to | reconcile them: Thirdly, our [6] utter disability to return | to him, by which they stand in need of the power of Christ | in his Kingly Office to assist and govern them.

[1] Deut. 18 . 15 with Acts 3 . 22, 23.
[2] Psal. 110 . 3.
Heb. 3 . 1. & 4 . 14. 15. & 5 . 6.
[3] Psal. 2 . 6.
[4] Acts 26 . 18.
[5] Col. 1 . 3. Col. 1 . 21.
Eph. 2 . 12.
[6] Cant. 1 . 3.
Joh. 6 . 44.

XV.

Touching the Prophesie of Christ, it is that whereby | he hath [1] perfectly revealed the whole will of God out of | the bosome of the Father,

[1] Joh. 1 . 18 & 12 . 49, 50 & 15 & 17 . 8.
Deut. 18 . 15.

that is needful for his servants [Page 6] to know, beleeve, and obey; and therefore is called not | onely a Prophet and [2] a Doctor, and the [3] Apostle of our profession, and the [4] Angel of the Cove-nant; but also the | very [5] wisdome of God, and [6] the treasures of wisdome | and understanding.

[2] Matth. 23 . 10.
[3] Heb. 3 . 1.
[4] Mal. 3 . 1.
[5] 1 Cor. 1 . 24.
[6] Col. 2 . 3.

XVI.

That he might be such a Prophet as thereby to be every | way compleat, it was necessary that he should bee [1] God, | and withall also that he should be man; for unlesse hee | had been God, he could never have perfectly understood | the will of God, [2] neither had he been able to reveale it | throughout all ages; and unlesse hee had been man, hee | could not fitly have unfolded it in his [3] own person to | man.*

[1] Joh. 1 . 18 & 3 . 13.
[2] 1 Cor. 2 . 11, 16.
[3] Acts 3 . 22 with Deut. 18 . 15. Heb. 1 . 1.

XVII.

Touching his Priesthood, Christ [1] being conse-crated, | hath appeared once to put away sinne by the offering and | sacrifice of himself, and to this end hath fully performed | and suffered all those things by which God, through the | blood of that his Crosse in an acceptable sacrifice, might | reconcile his elect onely; [2] and having broken downe the | partition wall, and therewith finished & removed all those | Rites, Shadowes, and Ceremonies, is now entred within | the Vaile,

[1] Joh. 17 . 19.
Heb. 5 . 7, 8, 9 & 9 . 26.
Rom. 5 . 19.
Eph. 5 . 12.
Col. 1 . 20.
[2] Eph. 2 . 14, 15, 16.
Rom. 8 . 34.

* Many additional Scriptural proofs of Christ's deity and his humanity were added to this article in subsequent editions.

into the Holy of Holiest, that is, to the very |
Heavens. and presence of God, where he for ever
liveth | and sitteth at the right hand of Majesty,
appearing before | the face of his Father to make
intercession for such as | come to the Throne of
Grace by that new and living way; | and not that
onely, but [3] makes his people a spirituall | House,
an holy Priesthood, to offer up spirituall sacri-
[Page 7] fice acceptable to God through him;
neither doth the | Father accept, or Christ offer
to the Father any other | worship or worship-
pers.

[3] 1 Pet. 2 . 5.
Joh. 4 . 23, 24.

XVIII.

This Priesthood was not legall, or temporary,
but ac- | cording to the order [1] of *Melchi-*
sedec; [2] not by a carnall | commandement, but by
the power of an endlesse life; | [3] not by an order
that is weak and lame, but stable and per- | fect,
not for a [4] time, but for ever, admitting no suc- |
cessor, | but perpetuall and proper to Christ, and
of him that ever | liveth. Christ himselfe was
the Priest, Sacrifice and Al- | tar: he was [5] Priest,
according to both natures, hee was a | sacrifice
most properly according to his humane nature: |
[6] whence in the Scripture it is wont to be at- |
tributed to his | body, to his blood; yet the
chiefe force whereby this sa- | crifice was made
effectuall, did depend upon his [7] divine | nature,
namely, that the Sonne of God did offer him- |
selfe | for us: he was the [8] Altar properly ac- |
cording to his di- | vine nature, it belonging to
the Altar to sanctifie that | which is offered upon
it, and so it ought to be of greater | dignity then
the Sacrifice it selfe.

[1] Heb. 7 . 17.
[2] Heb. 7 . 16.
[3] Heb. 7 . 18, 19,
20, 21.
[4] Heb. 7 . 24, 25
[5] Heb. 5 . 6.
[6] Heb. 10 . 10.
1 Pet. 1 . 18, 19
Col. 1 . 20, 22.
Esa. 53 . 10.
Matth. 20 . 28.
[7] Act. 20 . 28.
Rom. 8 . 3.
[8] Heb. 9 . 14 &
13 . 10, 12, 15.
Matth. 23 . 17
Joh. 17 . 19.

XIX.

Touching his Kingdome, [1] Christ being risen
from the | dead, ascended into heaven, sat on the
right hand of God | the Father, having all power
in heaven and earth, given | unto him, he doth
spiritually govern his Church, exerci- | sing his
power [2] over all Angels and Men, good and bad, |
to the preservation and salvation of the elect,
to the over- | ruling and destruction of his ene-
mies, which are Re- [Page 8] probates, [3] commu-
nicating and applying the benefits, | vertue, and
fruit of his Prophesie and Priesthood to his |
elect, namely, to the subduing and taking away of
their | sinnes, to their justification and adoption
of Sonnes, re- | generation, sanctification, preser-

[1] 1 Cor. 15 . 4.
1 Pet. 3 . 21, 22.
Matth. 28 . 18, 19,
20.
Luke 24 . 51.
Acts 1 . 11 & 5 .
30, 31.
John 19 . 36.
Rom. 14 . 17.
[2] Mark 1 . 27.
Heb. 1 . 14.
Joh. 16 . 7, 15.
[3] John 5 . 26, 27.
Rom. 5 . 6, 7, 8 &
14 . 17.
Gal. 5 . 22, 23.
John 1 . 4, 13.

vation and strengthe- | ning in all their conflicts against Satan, the World, the | Flesh, and the temptations of them, continually dwelling | in, governing and keeping their hearts in faith and filiall | feare by his Spirit, which having [4] given it, he never takes | away from them, but by it still begets and nourisheth in | them faith, repentance, love, joy, hope, and all heaven- | ly light in the soule unto immortality, notwithstanding | through our own unbeliefe, and the temptations of Satan, | the sensible sight of this light and love be clouded and | overwhelmed for the time. [5] And on the contrary, ruling | in the world over his enemies, Satan, and all the vessels of | wrath, limiting, using, restraining them by his mighty po- | wer, as seems good in his divine wisdome & justice to the | execution of his determinate counsell, delivering them | up to a reprobate mind, to be kept through their own de- | serts, in darknesse and sensuality unto judgement.*

[4] John 13 . 1 &
10. 28, 29 & 14.
16, 17.
Rom. 11 . 29.
Psal. 51 . 10, 11.
Job 33 . 29, 30.
2 Cor. 12 . 7, 9.

[5] Job 1. and 2.
chap.
Rom. 1 . 21 &
2 . 4, 5, 6 & 9.
17, 18.
Eph. 4 . 17, 18.
2 Pet. 2. chap.

XX.

1 Cor. 15 . 24, 28.
Heb. 9 . 28
2 Thess. 1 . 9, 10.
1 Thess. 4 . 15, 16,
17.
John 17 . 21, 26.

This Kingdome shall be then fully perfected when hee | shall the second time come in glory to reigne amongst | his Saints, and to be admired of all them which doe be- | leeve, when he shall put downe all rule and authority un- | der his feet, that the glory of the Father may be full and | perfectly manifested in his Sonne, and the glory of the | Father and the Sonne in all his members.

[Page 9]

XXI.

That Christ Jesus by his death did bring forth salva- | tion and reconciliation onely for the [1] elect, which were | those which [2] God the Father gave him; & that the Gospel | which is to be preached to all men as the ground of faith, | is, that [3] Jesus is the Christ, the Sonne of the everblessed | God, filled with the perfection of all heavenly and spi- | rituall excellencies, and that salvation is onely and alone | to be had through the beleeving in his Name.

[1] John 15 . 13.
Rom. 8 . 32, 33,
34.
Rom. 5 . 11 &
3 . 25.
[2] Job 17 . 2 with
6, 37.
[3] Matth. 16 . 16.
Luke 2 . 26.
Joh. 6 . 9 & 7,
3. & 20 . 31.
1 John 5 . 11.

XXII.

That Faith is the [1] gift of God wrought in the hearts | of the elect by the Spirit of God, whereby they come to | see, know, and beleeve the truth

[1] Eph. 2 . 8.
Joh. 6 . 29 & 4.
10.
Phil. 1 . 29.
Gal. 5 . 22.

* This article was considerably shortened in subsequent editions.

of [2]the Scriptures, & not | onely so, but the
excellencie of them above all other wri- | tings
and things in the world, as they hold forth the
glory | of God in his attributes, the excellency
of Christ in his | nature and offices, and the
power of the fulnesse of the | Spirit in its work-
ings and operations; and thereupon | are inabled
to cast the weight of their soules upon this |
truth thus beleeved.

[2] Joh. 17 . 17.
Heb. 4 . 11, 12.
Joh. 6 . 63.

XXIII.

Those that have this pretious faith wrought
in them | by the Spirit, can never finally nor
totally fall away; and | though many stormes
and floods do arise and beat against | them, yet
they shall never be able to take them off that |
foundation and rock which by faith they are
fastened up- | on, but shall be kept by the power
of God to salvation, [Page 10] where they shall
enjoy their purchased possession, they | being
formerly engraven upon the palms of Gods hands.

Matth. 7 . 24, 25
John 13 . 1.
1 Pet. 1 . 4, 5, 6.
Esa. 49 . 13, 14,
15, 16.

XXIV.

That faith is ordinarily [1]begot by the preaching
of the | Gospel, or word of Christ, without re-
spect to [2]any | power or capacitie in the creature,
but it is wholly [3]pas- | sive, being dead in sinnes
and trespasses, doth beleeve, and | is converted
by no lesse power, [4]then that which raised |
Christ from the dead.

[1] Rom. 10 . 17.
1 Cor. 1 . 21.
[2] Rom. 9 . 16.
[3] Rom. 2 . 1, 2.
Ezek. 16 . 6.
Rom. 3 . 12.
[4] Rom. 1 . 16.
Eph. 1 . 19.
Col. 2 . 12.

XXV.

That the tenders of the Gospel to the conver-
sion of | sinners, [1]is absolutely free, no way
requiring, as absolute- | ly necessary, any quali-
fications, preparations, terrors of | the Law, or
preceding Ministry of the Law, but onely | and
alone the naked soule, as a [2]sinner and ungodly
to re- | ceive Christ, as crucified, dead, and
buried, and risen a- | gaine, being made [3]a Prince
and a Saviour for such sin- | ners.

[1] Joh. 3 . 14, 15
& 1 . 12.
Esa. 55 . 1.
Joh. 7 . 37.
[2] 1 Tim. 1 . 15.
Rom. 4 . 5.
& 5 . 8.
[3] Act. 5 . 30, 31
& 2 . 36.
1 Cor. 1 . 22,
23, 24.

XXVI.

That the same power that converts to faith in
Christ, | the same power carries on the [1]soule
still through all du- | ties, temptations, conflicts,
sufferings, and continually | what ever a Chris-
tian is, he is by [2]grace, and by a con- | stant
renewed [3]operation from God, without which he |
cannot performe any dutie to God, or undergoe
any | temptations from Satan, the world, or men.

[1] 1 Pet. 1 . 5.
2 Cor. 12 . 9.

[2] 1 Cor. 15 . 10.
[3] Phil. 2 . 12, 13.
Joh. 15 . 5.
Gal. 19, 20.

XXVII.

That God the Father, and Sonne, and Spirit, is one [Page 11] with [1] all beleevers, in their [2] full-nesse, in [3] relations, [4] as | head and members, [5] as house and inhabitants, as [6] hus- | band and wife, one with him, as [7] light and love, and one | with him in his inheritance, and in all his [8] glory; and | that all beleevers by vertue of this union and one-nesse | with God, are the adopted sonnes of God, and heires | with Christ, co-heires and joynt heires with him of the | inheritance of all the promises of this life, and that which | is to come.*

[1] 1 Thess. 1 . 1.
Joh. 14 . 10, 20.
   & 17 . 21.
[2] Col. 2 . 9, 10.
   & 1 . 19.
Joh. 1 . 17.
[3] Joh. 20 . 17.
Heb. 2 . 11.
[4] Col. 1 . 18
Eph. 5 . 30.
[5] Eph. 2 . 22
1 Cor. 3 . 16, 17.
[6] Esa. 16 . 5.
2 Cor. 11 . 3.
[7] Gal. 3 . 26.
[8] Joh. 17 . 24

XXVIII.

That those which have union with Christ, are justified | from all their sinnes, past, [1] present, and to come, by the | bloud of Christ; which justification wee conceive to be | a gracious and free [2] acquittance of a guiltie, sinfull crea- | ture, from all sin by God, through the satisfaction that | Christ hath made by his death; and this applyed in the | manifestation of it through faith.

[1] Joh. 1 . 7.
Heb. 10 . 14
   & 9 . 26.
[2] Cor. 5 . 19.
Rom. 3 . 23.
[2] Acts 13 . 38, 39.
Rom. 5 . 1
   & 3 . 25, 30.

XXIX.

That all beleevers are a holy and [1] sanctified people, | and that sanctification is a spirituall grace of the [2] new | Covenant, and effect of the [3] love of God, manifested | to the soule, whereby the beleever is in [4] truth and rea- | litie sepa-rated, both in soule and body, from all sinne and | dead workes, through the [5] bloud of the everlasting Co- | venant, whereby he also presseth after a heavenly and | Evangelicall perfection, in obedience to all the Com- | mands, [6] which Christ as head and King in this new Co- | venant has prescribed to him.

[1] 1 Cor. 1 . 1
1 Pet. 2 . 9
[2] Eph. 1 . 4
[3] 1 Joh. 4 . 16.
[4] Eph. 4 . 24
[5] Phil. 3 . 15.
[6] Mat. 28 . 20.

XXX.

All beleevers through the knowledge of [1] that Justi- [Page 12] tification of life given by the Father, and brought forth | by the bloud of Christ, have this as their great privi- | ledge of that new [2] Covenant, peace with God, and re- | conciliation, whereby they that were afarre off, were | brought nigh by [3] that bloud, and have (as the Scripture | speaks) peace [4] passing all under-

[1] 2 Cor. 5 . 19.
Rom. 5 . 9, 10.
[2] Esa. 54 . 10
   & 26 . 12.
[3] Eph. 2 . 13, 14.
[4] Phil. 4 . 7.

---

* Considerably shortened in subsequent editions.

standing, yea, joy in God, | through our Lord
Jesus Christ, by [6] whom wee have re- | ceived the
Atonement.

[5] Rom. 5 . 10,
11.

XXXI.

That all beleevers in the time of this life, are
in a con- | tinuall warfare, combate, and oppo-
sition against sinne, | selfe, the world, and the
Devill, and liable to all manner | of afflictions,
tribulations, and persecutions, and so | shall con-
tinue untill Christ comes in his Kingdome, | be-
ing predestinated and appointed thereunto; and
what- | soever the Saints, any of them doe
possesse or enjoy of | God in this life, is onely by
faith.*

Eph. 6 . 10, 11,
12, 13,
2 Cor. 10 . 3.
Rev. 2 . 9, 10.

XXXII.

That the onely strength by which the Saints
are ina- | bled to incounter with all opposition,
and to overcome | all afflictions, temptations, per-
secutions, and tryalls, is | onely by Jesus Christ,
who is the Captain of their salva- | tion, being
made perfect through sufferings, who hath | in-
gaged his strength to assist them in all their
afflictions, | and to uphold them under all their
temptations, and to | preserve them by his power
to his ever- | lasting Kingdome.

Joh. 16 . 33.

Heb. 2 . 9, 10.

John 15 . 5.

XXXIII.

That Christ hath here on earth a spirituall
Kingdome, [Page 13] which is the Church, which
he hath purchased and re- | deemed to himselfe,
as a peculiar inheritance: which | Church, as
it is visible to us, is a company of visible |
[1] Saints, [2] called & separated from the world, by
the word | and [3] Spirit of God, to the visible pro-
fession of the faith | of the Gospel, being bap-
tized into that faith, and joyned | to the Lord, and
each other, by mutuall agreement, in | the prac-
tical injoyment of the [4] Ordinances, commanded |
by Christ their head and King.

[1] 1 Cor. 1 . 1.
Eph. 1 . 1.
[2] Rom. 1 . 7.
Act. 26 . 18
1 Thes. 1 . 9.
2 Cor. 6 . 17.
Rev. 18 . 18.
[3] Acts 2 . 37 with
Acts 10 . 37.
[4] Rom. 10 . 10.
Act. 20 . 21.
Mat. 18 . 19,
20.
Act. 2 . 42.
1 Pet. 2 . 5.

XXXIV.

To this Church he hath [1] made his promises,
and gi- | ven the signes of his Covenant, pres-
ence, love, blessing, | and protection: here are the
fountains and springs of his | heavenly grace

[1] Mat. 28 . 18,
19, 20.
[2] Cor. 6 . 18.

---

* Featley criticised this article as denying real ownership to any but
believers. The criticism was recognized in subsequent editions by adding
these words: " Outward and temporall things are lawfully enjoyed by a
civill right by them who have no faith."

continually flowing forth; ²thither ought | all men
to come, of all estates, that acknowledge him to |
be their Prophet, Priest, and King, to be in-
rolled amongst | his houshold servants, to be
under his heavenly conduct | and government,
to lead their lives in his walled sheep- | fold,
and watered garden, to have communion here
with | the Saints, that they may be made to be
partakers of their | inheritance in the Kingdome
of God.

² Esa. 8 . 16.
1 Tim. 3 . 15.
&4 . 16.
&6 . 3, 5.
Acts 2 . 41, 47
Song, 4 . 12.
Gal. 6 . 10.
Eph. 2 . 19.

XXXV.

And all his servants are called thither, to
present their | bodies and soules, and to bring
their gifts God hath gi- | ven them; so being
come, they are here by himselfe be- | stowed in
their severall order, peculiar place, due use, be- |
ing fitly compact and knit together, according to
the ef- | fectuall working of every part, to the
edification of it | selfe in love.

1 Cor. 12 . 6, 7,
12, 18.
Rom. 12 . 4, 5, 6.
1 Pet. 4 . 10.
Eph. 4 . 16.
Col. 2 . 5, 6, 19.
1 Cor. 12 . 12
to the end.

[Page 14]

XXXVI.

1 Acts 1 . 2.
&6 . 3.
with 15. 22,25
1 Cor. 16 . 3.
² Rom. 12 . 7, 8
& 16 . 1.
1 Cor. 12 . 8, 28
1 Tim. 3. chap.
Heb. 13 . 7.
1 Pet. 5 . 1, 2, 3.

That being thus joyned, every Church has
¹power gi- | ven them from Christ for their
better well-being, to | choose to themselves meet
persons into the office of | ² Pastors, Teachers(a),
Elders, Deacons, being qualified ac- | cording to
the Word, as those which Christ has appoin- |
ted in his Testament, for the feeding, governing,
serving, | and building up of his Church, and that
none other have | power to impose them, either
these or any other.

XXXVII.

Heb. 5 . 4.
Acts 4 . 23.
1 Tim. 4 . 14.
Joh. 10 . 3, 4.
Acts 20 . 28.
Rom. 12 . 7, 8.
Heb. 13 . 7, 17.

That the Ministers aforesaid, lawfully called
by the | Church, where they are to administer,
ought to conti- | nue in their calling, according
to Gods Ordinance, and | carefully to feed the
flock of Christ committed to them, | not for
filthy lucre, but of a ready mind.

(b) XXXVIII.

1 Cor. 9 . 7, 14.
Gal. 6 . 6.
1 Thes. 5 . 13.
1 Tim. 5 . 17,
18.

That the due maintenance of the Officers afore-
said, | should be the free and voluntary com-
munication of the | Church, that according to
Christs Ordinance, they that | preach the Gospel,
should live on the Gospel and not by | con-

(a) " Pastors " and " teachers " are omitted in later editions.

(b) The final clause, beginning " and not by constraint," was criticised
by Featley and consequently omitted in the edition of 1646. The entire
article was omitted from the editions of 1651 and 1652, probably owing to
Quaker influence.

Phil. 4 . 15, 16.   straint to be compelled from the people by a forced | Law.

XXXIX.

Mat. 28 . 18, 19.   That Baptisme is an Ordinance of the new
Mark 16 . 16.   Testament, | given by Christ, to be dispensed (*a*) onely upon persons pro- [Page 15] fessing faith,   Acts 2 . 37, 38 or that are Disciples, or taught, who upon | a   & 8 . 36, 37, 38 [1] profession of faith, ought to be baptized. (*b*)   & 18 . 8.

XL.

The way and manner of the [1] dispensing of this Ordi- | nance (*c*) the Scripture holds out to be dipping or plung- | ing the whole body under water : it being a signe, must an- | swer the thing signified, which are these : first, the [2] wash- | ing the whole soule in the bloud of Christ : Second- ly, | that interest the Saints have in the [3] death, buriall, and re- | surrection ; thirdly, together with a [4] confirmation of our | faith, that as cer- tainly as the body is buried under water, | and riseth againe, so certainly shall the bodies of the | Saints be raised by the power of Christ, in the day of the | resurrection, to reigne with Christ.

The word *Baptizo*, signi- fying to dip under water, yet so as with convenient garments both upon the ad- ministrator and subject, with all mo- destie. (*d*)
[1] Mat. 3 . 16.
Joh. 3 . 23.
Acts 8 . 38.
[2] Rev. 1 . 5
& 7 . 14.
with Heb. 10, 22.
[3] Rom. 6 . 3, 4, 5, [4] 1 Cor. 15 . 28, 29.

XLI.

The persons designed by Christ, to dispense this Or- | dinance, the [1] Scriptures hold forth to be a (*e*) preaching | Disciple, it being no where tyed to a particular Church, | Officer, or person extraordinarily sent, the Commission | injoyning the administration, being given to them under | no other consideration, but as considered Dis- ciples.

[1] Esa. 8 . 16.
Mat. 28 . 16, 17, 18, 19.
John 4 . 1, 2.
Acts 20 . 7.
Mat. 26 . 26.

(*a*) Featley declared this article would not be objectionable if the word *only* were omitted, and again strangely enough it was omitted in subse- quent editions.

(*b*) Later editions added, " and after to partake of the Lord's Supper."

(*c*) In criticising this article, Doctor Featley denied that the Scripture de- fines baptism as an immersion, and in subsequent editions the phrase, " the Scripture holds out to be," is omitted, as well as the words " first, the washing the whole soule in the bloud of Christ." To the words " death, buriall, and resurrection " are added " of Christ " in later editions.

(*d*) Editions 1651 and 1652 add " which is also our practice, as many eye witnesses can testifie."

(*e*) Doctor Featley ridiculed the expression " preaching Disciple," and in later editions " preaching " is omitted, and the words " being men able to preach the Gospel " are added at the end of the article. " Church, Officer " is changed into " Church-officer " in later editions, as it appears in Doctor Featley.

XLII.

Christ has likewise given power to his whole Church | to receive in and cast out, by way of Excommunication, | any member; and this power is given to every particular | Congregation, and not one particular person, either | member or Officer, but the whole.

Acts 2 . 47.
Rom. 16 . 2.
Math. 18 . 17.
1 Cor. 5 . 4
2 Cor. 2 . 6, 7, 8.

[Page 16]

XLIII.

Mat. 18 . 16, 17, 18.
Act. 11 . 2, 3.
1 Tim. 5 . 19, 20, 21.

And every particular member of each Church, how | excellent, great, or learned soever, ought to be subject to | this censure and judgement of Christ; and the Church | ought with great care and tendernesse, with due advice | to proceed against her members.

XLIV.

1 Acts 20 . 27, 28.
Heb. 13 . 17, 24.
Mat. 24 . 25.
1 Thes. 5 . 14.
2 Mark 13 . 34, 37.
Gal. 6 . 1.
1 Thes. 5 . 11.
Jude ver. 3, 20.
Heb. 10 . 34, 35.
& 12 . 15.

And as Christ for the [1] keeping of this Church in holy | and orderly Communion, placeth some speciall men | over the Church, who by their office are to governe, o- | versee, visit, watch; so likewise for the better keeping | thereof in all places, by the members, he hath given [2] au- | thoritie, and laid dutie upon all, to watch over one ano | ther.

XLV.

1 Cor. 14. cha.
Rom. 12 . 6.
1 Pet. 4 . 10, 11.
1 Cor. 12 . 7.
1 Thes. 5 . 17, 18, 19.

That also such to whom God hath given gifts, being | tryed in the Church, may and ought by the appointment | of the Congregation, to pro-phesie, according to the pro- | portion of faith, and so teach publickly the Word of | God, for the edification, exhortation, and comfort of | the Church.

XLVI.

Rev. 2. & 3, Chapters
Acts 15 . 12.
1 Cor. 1 . 10.
Ephef. 2 . 16.
& 3 . 15, 16.
Heb. 10 . 25.
Jude ver. 15.
Matth. 18 . 17.
1 Cor. 5 . 4, 5.

Thus being rightly gathered, established, and still pro- | ceeding in Christian communion, and obedience of the | Gospel of Christ, none ought to separate for faults and | corruptions, which may, and as long as the Church con- | sists of men subject to failings, will fall out and arise a- | mongst them, even in true constituted Churches, untill | they have in due order sought redresse thereof.

[Page 17]

XLVII.

And although the particular Congregations be distinct | and severall Bodies, every one a compact and knit Ci- | tie in it selfe; yet are they

1 Cor. 4 . 17, & 14 . 33, 36. & 16 . 1.
Matth. 28 . 20.

all to walk by one and the same | Rule, and by all meanes convenient to have the counsell | and help one of another in all needfull affaires of the | Church, as members of one body in the common faith | under Christ their onely head.

1 Tim. 3 . 15.
& 6 . 13, 14.
Rev. 22 . 18, 19.
Col. 2 . 6, 19,
& 4 . 16.

XLVIII.

That a civill Magistracie is an ordinance of God set up | by God for the punishment of evill doers, and for the | praise of them that doe well; and that in all lawfull things | commanded by them, subjection ought to be given by us | in the Lord: and that we are to make supplication and | prayer for Kings, and all that are in authority, that under | them we may live a peaceable and quiet life in all godliness | and honesty.

Rom. 13. 1, 2, 3, 4.
1 Pet. 2 . 13, 14.
1 Tim. 2 . 2.

*XLIX.

The supreme Magistracie of this Kingdome we beleeve | to be the King and Parliament freely chosen by the King- | dome, and that in all those civill Lawes which have been | acted by them, or for the present is or shall be ordained, | we are bound to yeeld subjection and obedience unto in | the Lord, as conceiving our selves bound to defend both | the persons of those thus chosen, and all civill Lawes | made by them, with our persons, liberties, and estates, with | all that is called ours, although we should suffer never so | much from them in not actively submitting to some Ec- | clesiasticall Lawes, which might be conceived by them to [Page 18] be their duties to establish which we for the present could | not see, nor our consciences could submit unto; yet are | we bound to yeeld our persons to their pleasures.

L.

1 Tim. 1 . 2, 3, 4.
Psal. 126 . 1.
Acts 9 . 31.

And if God should provide such a mercie for us, as to | incline the Magistrates hearts so far to tender our con- | sciences, as that we might bee protected by them from | wrong, injury, oppression and molestation, which long we | formerly have groaned under by the tyranny and op-

---

* Articles XLIX and L, somewhat modified, are in the second edition added as a note to Art. XLVIII. Art. LI then becomes XLIX. An Art. L is added, expressing the lawfulness of oaths and of a Christian's holding civil office; Art. LII becomes LI, and a final Art. LII on the resurrection is added. All references to the king and Parliament are omitted from editions of 1651 and 1652 when Cromwell was in control of affairs.

pres- | sion of the Prelaticall Hierarchy, which
God through | mercy hath made this present
King and Parliament won- | derfull honourable,
as an instrument in his hand, to throw | downe;
and we thereby have had some breathing time, |
we shall, we hope, look at it as a mercy beyond
our expe- | ctation, and conceive our selves fur-
ther engaged for ever | to blesse God for it.

LI.

[1] Acts 2 . 40, 41.
& 4 . 19, & 5 . 28,
29, 41. & 20 . 23.
1 Thess. 3 . 3.
Phil. 1 . 27, 28, 29.
Dan. 3 . 16, 17. &
6 . 7, 10, 22, 23.

[2] Matth. 28 . 18,
19, 20.
1 Tim. 6 . 13, 14,
15.
Rom. 12 . 1, 8.
1 Cor. 14 . 37.
2 Tim. 4 . 7, 8.
Rev. 2 . 10.
Gal. 2 . 4, 5.

But if God with-hold the Magistrates allow-
ance and | furtherance herein; [1]yet we must not-
withstanding pro- | ceed together in Christian
communion, not daring to give | place to suspend
our practice, but to walk in obedience to | Christ
in the profession and holding forth this faith be- |
fore mentioned, even in the midst of all trialls
and affli- | ctions, not accounting our goods,
lands, wives, children,|fathers, mothers, brethren,
sisters, yea, and our own lives | dear unto us,
so we mag finish our course with joy: re- |
membering alwayes we ought to [2]obey God
rather then | men, and grounding upon the com-
mandement, commissi- | on and promise of our
Lord and master Jesus Christ, who [Page 19] as
he hath all power in heaven and earth, so also
hath pro- |mised, if we keep his commandements
which he hath gi- | ven us, to be with us to the
end of the world: and when we | have finished
our course, and kept the faith, to give us the |
crowne of righteousnesse, which is laid up for all
that | love his appearing, and to whom we must
give an account | of all our actions, no man being
able to discharge us of | the same.

LII.

And likewise unto all men is to be given what-
soever is | their due; tributes, customes, and all
such lawful duties, | ought willingly to bee by
us paid and performed, our | lands, goods, and
bodies, to submit to the Magistrate in | the Lord,
and the Magistrate every way to bee acknow- |
ledged, reverenced, and obeyed, according to |
godlinesse; | not because of wrath onely but for
conscience sake. And | finally, all men so to be
esteemed and regarded, as is due | and meet
for their place, age, estate and condition.

Rom. 13 . 5, 6. 7.
Matth. 22 . 21.
Titus 3.
1 Pet. 2 . 13.
Ephes. 5 . 21, 22.
& 6 . 1, 9.
1 Pet. 5 . 5.

LII [sic].

And thus wee desire to give unto God that
which is | Gods, and unto *Cesar* that which is

Matth. 22 . 21.
Acts 24 . 14, 15,
16.

Cesars, and unto all | men that which belongeth
unto them, endevouring our | selves to have al-
wayes a cleare conscience void of offence |
towards God, and towards man. And if any take
this that | we have said, to be heresie, then doe
wee with the Apostle | freely confesse, that after
the way which they call heresie, | worship we the
God of our Fathers, beleeving all things | which
are written in the Law and in the Prophets and
A- | postles, desiring from our soules to dis-
claime all heresies [Page 20] and opinions which
are not after Christ, and to be sted- | fast, unmo-
veable, always abounding in the worke of the |
Lord, as knowing our labour shall not be in vain
in the | Lord.

John 5 . 28.
2 Cor. 4 . 17.
1 Tim. 6 . 3, 4, 5.
1 Cor. 15 . 58, 59.

1 Cor. 1. 24.

*Not that we have dominion over your faith, but
are helpers of | your joy: for by faith we stand.*

FINIS

Second Edition, 1646

The Confession, which appeared in print in 1644,
created great surprise by its orthodoxy, sanity, and
moderation. So favorable was the impression made that
opponents of the Baptists could scarcely believe that these
articles fairly represented their views. They elicited
much favorable comment, but of course occasioned criticism also.

In 1645 Dr. Daniel Featley wrote a scurrilous book
against the Baptists, entitled, " The Dippers dipt. or, The
Anabaptists duck'd and plunged Over Head and Eares,
at a Disputation in Southwark." He was a famous
scholar and controversialist, and a preacher in the State
church in London. He had been a member of the Westminster Assembly, but having fallen under suspicion of
disloyalty, he was imprisoned by the Parliamentary authorities. In prison he furbished up the notes of a disputation he had had with the General Baptists in 1642,
added several chapters against the errors, extravagancies,

and doctrines of the continental Anabaptists of the sixteenth century, which he ascribed to the English Baptists
whom he called Anabaptists, dedicated the whole to'
Parliament, and published it in 1645. The last chapter
was a criticism of the Confession of 1644, in which, however, he could find only six articles out of fifty-three
which he regarded as erroneous. Such an attack from a
man of such prominence and fame demanded some reply
from the Baptists, especially since it was dedicated to
Parliament, at that time not only the lawmaking, but also
the ruling body of the kingdom. It seemed best to reply
by issuing a new and improved edition of the very Confession which Featley had criticized. Accordingly it was
subjected to a careful revision, removing obscurities and
infelicities of language, reclassifying the material and re-
arranging the articles, and removing as far as possible the
language objected to by Featley in the six articles criticized by him. Indeed, they went so far in this latter respect as seriously to weaken the distinctive Baptist character of some of the articles. (See "Review and Ex-
positor" for October, 1909.) This revised edition was
then dedicated to Parliament, as Featley's attack had
been, in a brief but vigorous epistle. They begin:

To the Right Honorable the Lords,
Knights, Citizens and Burgesses in
Parliament Assembled.

Right Honorable and Most Noble Patriots,

In as much as there hath been a Book [Featley's]
lately presented unto you, in whose Dedicatory Epistle
there are many hainous accusations unjustly and falsely
laid against us, we conceived it necessary to make some
declaration of our innocency, and (to that end) humbly
to present unto your view this our Confession of Faith.

Here wee unfainedly declare, what in our hearts wee judge, and what wee teach, and according to this Rule wee desire and endeavour, through the grace of God, to lead our lives. This Confession of our Faith we send forth to speak the truth for us, and so to make our innocency to appeare; desiring that the same light may guide others also to the same way of truth and of obedience both to God and to the Magistrate, who is the Minister of God to us for good, etc.*

In lieu of the brief preface of the original edition, there was a lengthy address " To the judicious and impartiall Reader," in which it is pointed out that all the accusations made against them were made against Christ and the apostles, such as stirring up sedition, introducing novelties, preaching in private houses, perverting the people, sectarianism, etc. It then continues:

Not fearing to charge us, with holding freewill, falling from grace, denying election, originall sin, children's salvation, the Old Testament, and men's proprietie in their estates, and censuring all to be damned that are not of our judgement and practice; all which we disclaime, because they are untrue. And as for the other things whereof wee are accused, wee referre those who desire further satisfaction, to the answers of them†; yet by reason of the many accusations that are cast upon us, although they cannot prove the things whereof we are accused, yet the generalitie of the people are incensed against us, and are incouraged, and set on by such, to seek out the place of our meetings, which are the more private, not because they are private, but because wee have not any more publicke places; but if any shall please to procure us more larger places to meet in, wee are willing to embrace them with thankfulness and joy, although no man should speak for us to those in authoritie, from whom one word were enough to protect us, from the

* The whole, with this edition of the Confession, in Underhill, p. 13f.
† *Briefe Considerations on* Dr. Featly, *his Book,* intituled *The Dippers Dippt,* by *Samuel Richardson.*

violence wee should be subject unto; but as it was then, Acts 17. 5, 6, 7, so it is now; yet must we beare all the blame; but our God will in his time cleare our innocency, although now many stand looking upon us as a people (holding such things) not worthy to live, and are in danger by the rude multitude gathering together to stone us: and had it been against our persons onely, we would have held our peace, and committed our cause to God; but considering it is the truth that we profess that suffers, we may not, nor dare not be neuters in matters of so high a nature, but come in and speak to the help of the Lord against the mighty.

Therefore to free ourselves, and the truth we profess, from such unjust aspersions, that it may be at liberty, though we are in bonds, wee have published a brief confession of our Faith, (which wee conceive most void of contention in these sad and troublesome times), the thoughts of our hearts as in the presence of God wee here declare, that it may appeare to the consciences of them that feare God, what wrong we suffer from some who have ability to (Jude 14, 15) cast mists, and dark clouds, which overshadow the glory of the truth, and them that profess it. And although they acknowledge with us, that the truth is not fully discovered, yet they will tie all future discovery to a former light, and conceive they doe well in so doing. But God will by his truth shew their error, and exalt Jesus Christ the chiefe corner stone, which the builders so much reject. And lest this should be thought to be the judgement of some particular persons, this is done by the consent and appointment of seven Congregations or Churches in London, with the names of some of each of them subscribed in behalf of the whole. And although wee bee distinct in our meetings, for conveniency; yet wee are one in faith, fellowship, and communion, holding Jesus Christ for our Head and Law-giver, under whose rule and government we desire to walke, and to follow the Lamb wheresoever he goeth, that when our Lord and King shall call us to account, we may be found ready and worthy to be received into our Master's joy. Untill which time we desire to spend these few dayes we have here to remain, to the glory of God, the honour of the Gospel, the Saints comfort, and our Countries good, to our own account at (2 Thess. 1. 8) the great day when Christ shall come in flaming fire, taking vengeance on them that know not God, and that obey not the Gospel of our Lord Jesus Christ.

Subscribed by us in behalf of seven Congregations or Churches of Christ in London. As also by a French Congregation of the same judgement.

Thomas Gunne	John Spilsbery	Paul Hobson
John Mabbit	Samuel Richardson	Thomas Goare
Benjamin Cockes	Thomas Munden	William Kiffen
Thomas Kilikop	George Tipping	Thomas Patient
Hanserd Knollys	Denis le Barbier	
Thomas Holms	Christophle Duret	

The sense was in no wise changed in this second edition, contrary to the opinion of Underhill.* The articles on magistracy were somewhat condensed and also altered to suit the changed condition of the kingdom. The two following articles were added:

Article L † reads:

It is lawfull for a Christian to be a Magistrate or Civill Officer; and also it is lawfull to take an Oath, so it be in truth, and in judgement, and in righteousnesse, for confirmation of truth, and ending of all strife; and that by rash and vaine Oaths the Lord is provoked, and this Land mournes. Acts 8. 38. & 10. 1, 2, 35, 44. Rom. 16. 23. Deut. 6. 13. Rom. 1. 9. 2 Cor. 10. 11. Jer. 4. 2. Heb. 6. 16.

Art. LII, also added in this edition, is as follows: "There shall be a resurrection of the dead, both of the just and unjust, and every one shall give an account of

---

* Complete in Underhill, pp. 18–23.

† Featley had argued that Anabaptists opposed Christians taking the oath and holding office. This article is the answer.

N

himselfe to God, that every one may receive the things done in his body, according to that he hath done, whether it be good or bad." Acts 24. 15. Rom. 14. 12.

The edition is completed by the addition of this noble and touching conclusion following the Confession:

The Conclusion.

Thus we desire to give unto Christ that which is his, and unto all lawfull Authority that which is their due, and to owe nothing to any man but love, to live quietly and peaceably, as it becometh Saints, endeavouring in all things to keep a good conscience, and to doe unto every man (of what judgement soever) as we would they should doe unto us, that as our practice is, so it may prove us to be a conscionable, quiet, and harmless people, (no ways dangerous or troublesome to human Society) and to labour and work with our hands, that we may not be chargeable to any, but to give to him that needeth both friends and enemies, accounting it more excellent to give than to receive. Also we confesse that we know but in part, and that we are ignorant of many things which we desire and seek to know: and if any shall doe us that friendly part to shew us from the word of God that we see not, we shall have cause to be thankfull to God and them. But if any man shall impose upon us any thing that we see not to be commanded by our Lord Jesus Christ, we should in his strength, rather embrace all reproaches and tortures of men, to be stript of all outward comforts, and if it were possible, to die a thousand deaths, rather than to doe any thing against the least tittle of the truth of God, or against the light of our own consciences. And if any shall call what we have said Heresie, then doe we with the Apostle acknowledge, that after the way they call heresie, worship we the God of our Fathers, disclaiming all Heresie (rightly so called) because they are against Christ, and to be stedfast and immoveable, always abounding in obedience to Christ, as knowing our labour shall not be in vain in the Lord.

Psalm 74. 21, 22.

Arise, O God, plead thine own cause.   Remember how the foolish man blasphemeth thee daily.

O let not the oppressed returne ashamed, but let the poore and needy praise thy Name.

Come, Lord Jesus, come quickly.

Finis.

Nov. 30, 1646, shortly after the publication of this edition, Benjamin Cox, an Oxford graduate of some culture, who was one of the signers of this edition, and probably assisted in the revision, published twenty-two articles,* which he says were " occasioned by the inquiry of some well-affected and godly persons in the country," and which he entitles, " An Appendix to a Confession of Faith," " published for the further clearing the Truth." They stiffen the Calvinism, declare belief in eternal punishment, define the Christian's relation to the law and to good works more clearly, and express some other points a little more fully than the Confession.   They were never published with the Confession so far as known.

Later Editions

A third edition appeared in London in 1651, and a fourth the following year.   These were substantially reprints of the edition of 1646.   The more important changes from this edition are indicated in the notes to the Confession.   In addition to those there indicated, a few minor verbal changes occur; there is a slight softening of the Calvinism in Articles III and XXI, and Article XXXVIII, enjoining the support of the ministry, is omitted altogether.   This last important change was probably due to the criticism of the Quakers who sharply op-

* Underhill, pp. 49–60.

posed all ministerial support. It marks the beginning of
that opposition to ministerial support among the Baptists
which has been so hurtful to them. These two editions
were termed " The third Impression corrected," and
" The fourth Impression corrected."

In lieu of the " Epistle Dedicatory " and the " Preface "
to the edition of 1646, these two editions are introduced
with an " Epistle to the Reader," which is of sufficient
interest to reproduce entire. (Reproduced from 1652
edition.)

Courteous Reader,

T*Here is nothing wherein Saints should be
more conversant than in promoting the honour of the Lord and his Christ, striving
and studying to walk before him agreeable to the truth recorded in his word, the
consideration of which, is a strong inducement
unto us to ingage (to the utmost of our
abilities) in this work, that when other men content themselves by living below the rule, we may strive to walk
close thereunto, (suitable to the pattern left us by God in
his word) and when many account it their glory to turn
their backs upon what they professed to have received
from Christ, we may strive to honour God, by a steadfast
continuance in what we have received, and in a diligent
speaking the things which we have seen and heard from
him; the weight of which at first prevailed upon us to
declare unto the world this our* Confession of faith, and
faithful Epistle, *which we have again reprinted, and
made publique for the reasons following.*

*First, the invitations and earnest solicitations of several
of our Brethren, from all parts of the Nation, whose
hearts long to behold (in publique) our stability and
perseverance in the way and truth of our God, that by it
they may have wherewith to put to silence those who have
lately taken liberty to reproach and undervalue the truth
professed by us.*

Secondly, that the world may behold that through

grace, (by which alone we stand) we are preserved from back-sliding or revolting from the way and truth, we for some years have followed God in: In which (through the faith and obedience) we trust to be continued, unto the coming of our Lord and Saviour Jesus Christ.

Thirdly, that we might prevent Satan and his accomplices in their enterprizes, who have of late abounded more than ordinary, with stratagems and inventions to circumvent poor Saints, in their stability and love unto the truth, amongst which this was no small one (in several remote parts) that we had cast off all our former profession and practise, so that none remained together, worshipping God in his way, owning themselves the Churches of Christ, but were grown up to a further attainment and light (as they say) to live more immediately with God and Christ, than in so low, mean, and contemptible a way as Ordinances, thinking thereby to stumble and dishearten many, whose hearts were approved to God.

Fourthly, That we might take off prejudice from the hearts of those (many of which we have comfortable hopes) who are or may be prejudiced against us, from these many invectives, and bitter unjust reproaches, we are or may be (for worshipping our God according to our consciences and rule of truth) exposed unto, and they (if it be the good pleasure of our God) come to understand our practise, and subject themselves to the Lord in his commands.

Lastly, The remembrance of what good this our undertaking hath formerly done in the Countries, where it hath been spread (of which we have had particular notice from several, whose hearts have been refreshed therewith) is no small inducement to us to bring this forth again in print.

Courteous Friend, we desire thee soberly to weigh and consider what we have professed before men and Angels, out of the simplicity of our hearts, and let not prejudice prevent thy profiting, but make it thy great care and study to give up thy understanding to love and receive the truth, as it is in Jesus, delighting thy self in that Government, which is by his own hand established in his house;

*be not disheartened although thou shouldst hear of the
miscarriage of some, knowing that in many things we
sinne all, and come short of the grace of our God, or if
thou shouldst be advertised of the falling away of any one,
do but consider we live in the last ages of the world,*
Wherein many shall bepart [sic] from the truth, (*neither
is it a new thing for men to relinquish their profession.*)

*But strive thou to follow God fully, and to stand fast
in the simplicity of the truth; and God our Father, and
our Lord Jesus Christ be with thee, and be thy guide and
Counsellour.*

Signed in the name, and by the appointment of the
aforesaid several Churches, meeting in *London.*

William Kiffin,	Edward Harrison,
John Spilsbery,	Richard Graves,
Joseph Sanson,	Edward Roberts,
Hugh Gosnell,	Thomas Waters,
Thomas Pault,	Henry Forty,
Joseph Patshall,	Thomas Young,
William Conset,	John Watson.

In the kaleidoscopic changes of these years in England,
both king and Parliament had, by 1651, ceased to be
except in name. Moreover, the Baptists who had at
first suffered as sectaries were themselves suffering from
sectaries, especially the Quakers. In the way of a re-
action against the years of tyranny and oppression, freedom was running into license. George Fox began his
work in 1646, emphasizing the authority of the inner light,
depreciating if not denying the authority of revelation
in Scripture, the atoning work of Christ, the ordinances;
in short, historical and institutional Christianity. This
was particularly hurtful to the Baptists who, in some respects, had already traveled a long distance on the road
Fox was going. Many of their members fell away and
made shipwreck of the faith. Rumor, in remote parts of
the kingdom, exaggerated the defection in London into

the report that all the churches had fallen away. To correct this impression among the Baptists outside London, as well as to state to the world again their views, the Baptist churches of London, of which there were now several, united in publishing these editions of 1651 and 1652. The two former editions constituted the answer of the Baptists to the slanders and misrepresentations of their enemies; these last two editions were the answer of the London Baptists to the rumor spreading in the country that they had given up their former views and "were grown up to a further attainment and light." It was hoped also that it might steady and confirm any who might be confused and wavering on account of Quakerism.

To fit the Confession for more effective service in this direction, there was appended an address of eight closely printed pages, "To all the Churches of God sanctified in Christ Jesus, called to be saints, with all that in every place profess the name of Jesus Christ our Lord, both theirs and ours." It was entitled "Heart-bleedings for Professors' Abominations." The title sufficiently indicates the spirit and earnestness of its authors. It is in fact a burning and powerful plea for biblical Christianity against the views of the Quakers and Ranters as well as an earnest denial of the charge made by some that Baptist views naturally run into these extremes. It is maintained that those who had left the Baptists went out from them because they were not of them rather than as a logical result of the Baptist doctrines they had once held. It closes with a strong plea for steadfastness and faithfulness to the truth in the midst of all discouragements.*

What is called "The Fourth Impression, corrected"

---

* This address had been published by the churches of London in 1650 as a "general epistle" of warning; it was now and henceforth attached to this confession.

was issued in March, 1653, at Leith, Scotland. A brief letter " To the impartiall Reader " is prefixed, setting forth, as the reason for the publication, the errors and prejudices of the time. Apparently Quaker teachings are chiefly in mind. It is " signed in the name and by the Appointment of the Church of Christ, usually meeting at Leith and Edinburgh " by

> Tho. Spenser,
> Abra. Holmes,
> Tho. Powell,
> John Brady.

A " Fifth Impression Corrected " was issued by Henry Hills, London, in 1653. It is a reproduction of the third and fourth editions.

The " Assembly," in 1689, speak of " divers impressions " of the Confession, but declare that it was then difficult to obtain. It was printed in Crosby's " His. of the Baptists, Vol. I, Appendix." It was reprinted in 1809, and in 1847 appeared as No. 86 in the series of publications issued by the Baptist Tract Society. There may have been other editions.

2. SOMERSET CONFESSION

The first Confession, as we have seen, was a London Confession, drawn up and published by the seven churches of the city. As is too frequently the case, there was some jealousy and fear of the London churches on the part of those in the country. Accordingly the churches in the west of England, in Somerset and adjacent counties which had formed an Association in 1653, composed and published a Confession of their faith in 1656. It is signed by representatives from sixteen churches in the counties of Somerset, Wilts, Devon, Gloucester, and Dorset, and in a special manner by Thomas Collier who, in the year 1655, had been ordained to the office of "General Superintendent and Messenger to all the Associated Churches," and who probably composed the Confession. In "The Epistle Dedicatory," they disclaim any dislike to "the former Confession of our beloved brethren, whom we own, and with whom we are one both in faith and practice, neither is there anything in ours contradictory to our brethren that we know of." The reasons given for publishing this Confession are: to show their agreement with the London churches, especially in the matter of Calvinism; to bear "a public testimony before all men that (through grace) we do with one soul desire to cleave to the Lord, contending earnestly for the faith that was once given to the saints" (this in opposition to the Quakers, against whose dangerous errors there is a long and earnest warning and exhortation); there is exhortation also against formality, hypocrisy, and especially "pride in apparel and covetousness"; Underhill, pp. 61 to 106. Crosby's text is reproduced here, except that the Scripture quotations are omitted. (See also Crosby I, Appendix III, for the text.)

A

CONFESSION

OF THE

FAITH

OF SEVERAL

CHURCHES OF CHRIST

In the County of Somerset, and of
some Churches in the Counties neer adjacent.

I Peter iii. 15.

Sanctifie the Lord God in your hearts, and be ready
alwaies to give an answer to every man that asketh
you a reason of the hope that is in you with meekness
and fear.

Mattew x. 32.

Whosoever therefore shall confess me before men, him
will I confess also before my Father, which is in
heaven.

Isaiah viii. 20.

To the Law and to the Testimony, if they speak not
according to this rule it is because there is no light in
them.

Acts xvii. 11.

These were more noble than those in Thessalonica, in
that they received the word with all readiness of minde,
and searched the Scriptures daily, whether those things
were so.

London, Printed by Henry Hills, and are to be
sold by Thomas Brewster, at the three Bibles
at the West end of Pauls, 1656.
August 10.

A CONFESSION of the FAITH of several congregations of Christ in the county of Somerset, and some
churches in the counties near adjacent. Printed at
London, Anno 1656.

I.

WE believe that there is but one God (1 Cor. 8:6.),
who is immortal, eternal, invisible, only wise (I Tim.
1:17.), holy (Lev. 11:44.), almighty (Gen. 17:1.), infinite (I Kings 8:27; Isa. 40:28; Ps. 147:5); a Spirit
(John 4:24.), glorious in holiness (Ex. 15:11), just,
merciful, gracious, long-suffering, abundant in mercy and
truth (Ex. 34:6, 7.), faithful in all things (Deut. 7:9.).

II.

THAT this God, who is so in himself, did according
to his own will in time, create all things, by, and for
Jesus Christ (Heb. 1:2; Col. 1:16; John 2:3); who
is the word of God (John 1:1) and upholds all things
by the word of his power (Heb. 1:3.).

III.

THAT God made man after his own image (Gen.
1:27), in an estate of uprightness and human perfection
(Eccles. 7:29.).

IV.

THAT God gave Adam a just law, requiring obedience
under the penalty of death (Gen. 2:17), which law he
brake, and brought himself and his posterity under the
guilt and judgment denounced (Gen. 3:6; Rom. 5:12,
17, 18, 19.).

V.

MAN being in this undone estate, God did in the riches
of his mercy hold forth Christ in a promise (Gen. 3:15.).

VI.

THAT in process of time God gave forth his laws by
the hand of Moses (Exod. 20; John 1:17), to fallen man
(Gal. 3:19), not for justification to eternal life (Gal.

3 : 17; Rom. 3 : 20.), but that all might appear guilty before the Lord by it (Rom. 3 : 19; 5 : 20).

VII.

THAT out of this condition none of the sons of Adam were able to deliver themselves (Rom. 8 : 3; Eph. 2 : 1, 5; Rom. 5 : 6.).

VIII.

THAT God continued and renewed the manifestation of his grace and mercy in Christ after the first promise made (Gen. 3), in other promises (Gen. 22 : 18 with Gen. 12 : 3; Gal. 3 : 16.); and in types, as the passover (Exod. 12 : 8 and ver. 13 with I Cor. 5 : 7.), and the brazen serpent (Numb. 21 : 9 compared with John 3 : 14); with the ministry and ministration of Moses and Aaron, the sacrifices, &c. being all figures of Christ (Heb. 7 : 8 and Chap. 9.); and in prophesies (as Isa. 9 : 6; 11 : 1, 2; 53 : 6 compared with I Pet. 2 : 24; I Cor. 15 : 3.).

IX.

THAT God in his son did freely, without respect to any work done, or to be done by them as a moving cause, elect and choose some to himself before the foundation of the world (Eph. 1 : 3, 4; 2 Tim. 1 : 9.), whom he in time hath, doth, and will call, justify, sanctify and glorify (Rom. 8 : 29, 30).

X.

THAT those that were thus elected and chosen in Christ were by nature (before conversion) children of wrath even as others (Eph. 2 : 3; Rom. 3 : 9.).

XI.

THAT those that are chosen of God, called and justified, shall never finally fall from him, but being born from above are kept by the power of God through faith unto salvation (John 6 : 39; 10 : 28; 11 : 26; I Pet. 1 : 5; Ps. 89 : 30, 31, 32, 33, 34; I John 3 : 9; John 14 : 19; Heb. 12 : 2; Jer. 31 : 3; John 10 : 29; Ps. 37 : 28; Jer. 32 : 40; Rom. 8 : 39; I Cor. 1 : 8, 9; Rom. 8 : 30; Ps. 48 : 14.).

XII.

THAT when the fulness of time was come, God sent forth his Son, made of a woman (Gal. 4:4, 5.) according to the promises and prophesies of the scriptures; who was conceived in the womb of Mary the virgin by the power of the Holy Spirit of God, (Luke 1:35; Matt. 1:20.), and by her born in Bethlehem (Matt. 2:11; Luke 2:6, 7.).

XIII.

WE believe that Jesus Christ is truly God (Isa. 9:6; Heb. 1:8; Rom. 9:5.) and truly man, of the seed of David (I Tim. 2:5; Acts 13:23; Rom. 1:3.).

XIV.

THAT after he came to be about thirty years of age, being baptized, he manifested himself to be the Son of God (Luke 3:21, 23 with John 2:7, 11.), the promised Messiah, by doing such works both in his life and in his death which were proper unto, and could be done by none but the Son of God, the true Messiah (John 1:49; 6:9, &c.).

XV.

THAT this man Christ Jesus suffered death under Pilate, at the request of the Jews (Luke 23:24.), bearing the sins of his people on his own body on the cross (I Pet. 2:24), according to the will of God (Isa. 53:6), being made sin for us, (2 Cor. 5:11) and so was also made a curse for us (Gal. 3:13, 14; I Pet. 3:18.), that we might be made the righteousness of God in him (2 Cor. 5:11.), and by his death upon the cross, he hath obtained eternal redemption and deliverance for his church. (Col 1:14; Eph. 1:7; Acts 20:28; Heb. 9:12; I Pet. 1:18, 19.).

XVI.

THAT this same Jesus having thus suffered death for our sins, was buried (Matt. 27:59, 60.), and was also raised by the power of God (Eph. 1:19.) the third day according to the scriptures (I Cor. 15:3, 4.), for our justification (Rom. 4:25.).

XVII.

THAT after he had been seen forty days upon the earth, manifesting himself to his disciples (Acts 1:3.), he ascended into the heavens (Acts 1:9, 10, 11; Heb. 4:14.), and is set on the right hand of the throne of God (Heb. 8:1; Heb. 1:3.), whom the heavens must receive until the time of the Restitution of all things. (Acts 3:21.).

XVIII.

THAT the Father having thus exalted him, and given him a name above every name (Phil. 2:9.), and hath made him who is mediator (I Tim. 2:5), priest (Heb. 10:21; 8:1), prophet (Acts 3:22.), and king to his people (Ps. 2:6; Rev. 15:3.). As he is our priest, so is he our peace and reconciliation (Eph. 2:14, 15; Rom. 5:9, 10.), and being enter'd into the holy place, even heaven itself, there to appear in the presence of God (Heb. 9:24.), making continual intercession for us (Heb. 7:24, 25.), he is become our advocate (I John 2:1.) by whom we have boldness and access unto the throne of grace with acceptance (Heb. 10:19; Eph. 3:12; Heb. 4:16.). As he is our prophet, so he hath given us the scriptures, the Old and New Testament, as a rule and direction unto us both for faith and practice (John 5:39; I Pet. 1:10, 11, 12; 2 Tim. 3:16; I Pet. 10:20, 21; Eph. 2:20; I Cor. 14:37; Tit. 1:2, 3.); and that he hath sent, doth and will (according to his promise) send his Holy Spirit the Comforter, by whom he leadeth us into all truth (John 14:26; 16:13.); and by his continual presence with us, and in us (John 14:16, 17.), teaching, opening and revealing the mysteries of the kingdom, and will of God unto us (I Cor. 2:10, 11, 12, 13; Rev. 2:29; 5:5.), giving gifts in his church for the work of the ministry, and edifying the body of Christ (Eph. 4:8, 12; I Cor. 12:4, 5, 6.), that through the powerful teachings of the Lord, by his Spirit in his church, they might grow up in him (Eph. 4:15.), be conformed to his will (Ezek. 36:27; I Pet. 1:2.), and sing praises unto his name (Heb. 2:12; I Cor. 14:15.). And as he is our prophet, and king, lord, and law-giver (Isa. 33:22; 55:4.), Prince of life (Acts 3:15.), Prince of peace (Isa. 9:6.), Master of his people (Matt. 23:8.), Head of his church (Col. 1:18.), the Almighty (Rev. 1:8.), so he hath given rules unto us, by the which he ruleth over us (Luke 6:46; John 10:16; I John 2:4; John 14:15; Matt. 28:20.), and ruleth over all things for his church (Eph. 1:22; Rev. 19:16.) and by the power of love ruleth by his Spirit in us (2 Cor. 5:14; I John 2:5.), making us (in a measure) both able and willing to honour him (Phil. 4:13; Heb. 13:21; Eph. 6:10; Phil. 2:13), and bow before him (Ps. 95:6; 110:3; Rev. 4:10, 11.), submitting ourselves to him alone in all his commands with joy (John 15:14; Rev. 14:4; 7:15; Ps. 119:2, 47; Rev. 15:3, 4.).

XIX.

THAT the Spirit is administred by or through the word of faith preached (Gal. 3:2.), which word was first declared by the Lord himself, and was confirm'd by them that heard him (Heb. 2:3.), which word is called the gospel of God's grace (Acts 20:24.), the word of reconciliation (2 Cor. 5:19.), the sword of the Spirit (Eph. 6:17.), the weapon of a Christian (2 Cor. 10:4.); a faithful (Rev. 22:6.), quick, powerful (Heb. 4:12.), plain (Prov. 8:9.), comfortable (Rom. 15:4.), pure (Ps. 12:6.), right, true (Ps. 33:4.), sound (Tit. 2:8.), and wholesome word (I Tim. 6:3.).

XX.

THAT this spirit of Christ, being administer'd by the word of faith, worketh in us faith in Christ (John 3:5; I Pet. 1:22; Acts 16:14; Gal. 5:22.) by virtue of which we come to receive our sonship (John 1:12; Gal. 3:26.), and is further administer'd unto us through faith in the promises of God (Eph. 1:13; Acts 2:38, 39; Acts 1:4.), waiting on him in those ways and means that he hath appointed in his word (John 14:15, 16, 17; Luke 11:9, 13.), this faith being the ground of things hoped for, and the evidence of things not seen (Heb. 11:1.).

XXI.

THAT justification is God's accounting and declaring that man justified from the guilt and condemnation of all his sin, who hath received Jesus Christ and doth believe in him (in truth and power) according to the record given of him by God in scripture (Rom. 4:5; I John 5:10, 11; Joh. 3:36.).

XXII.

THAT justification from the guilt and condemnation of sin is only obtained through faith in that man Jesus Christ, crucified at Jerusalem, and by God raised from the dead (Rom. 5:1, 9; Acts 13:38, 39; Rom. 4:25; 10:9.). And that those who bring in any other way of justification, do therein make void, and acquit themselves of having any interest in the gospel and grace of Christ (Gal. 2:21; 5:4.).

XXIII.

THAT this faith being wrought in truth and power, it doth not only interest us in our justification, sonship, and glory, but it produceth as effects and fruits, a conformity, in a measure, to the Lord Jesus, in his will, graces and virtues (Rom. 5:3, 4; I John 3:23, 24; 2 Pet. 1:5, 6, 7; Gal. 5:6; Acts 26:18; I Thess 1:3.).

XXIV.

THAT it is the duty of every man and woman, that have repented from dead works, and have faith towards God, to be baptized (Acts 2:38; 8:12, 37, 38.), that is, dipped or buried under the water (Rom. 6:3, 4; Col. 2:12.), in the name of our Lord Jesus (Acts 8:16.), or in the name of the Father, Son, and Holy Spirit (Matt. 28:19.), therein to signify and represent a washing away of sin (Acts 22:16.), and their death, burial, and resurrection with Christ (Rom. 6:5; Col. 2:12.), and being thus planted in the visible church or body of Christ (I Cor. 12:3.), who are a company of men and women separated out of the world by the preaching of the gospel (Acts 2:41; 2 Cor. 6:17.), do walk together in communion in all the commandments of Jesus (Acts 2:42.), wherein God is glorified and their souls comforted (2 Thes. 1:11, 12; 2 Cor. 1:4.).

XXV.

THAT we believe some of those commandments further to be as followeth.

1. CONSTANCY in prayer (Col. 2:23, 24.).
2. BREAKING of bread (I Cor. 11:23, 24.).
3. GIVING of thanks (Eph. 5:20.).
4. WATCHING over one another (Heb. 12:15.).
5. CARING one for another (I Cor. 12:25) by visiting one another, especially in sickness and temptations (Matt. 25:36.).
6. EXHORTING one another (Heb. 3:13.).
7. DISCOVERING to each other, and bearing one another's burdens (Gal. 6:2.).
8. LOVING one another (Heb. 13:1.).
9. REPROVING when need is one another (Matt. 18:15.).
10. SUBMITTING one to another in the Lord (I Pet. 5:5.).
11. ADMINISTERING one to another according to the gift received, whether it be in spirituals, or temporals (I Pet. 4:10.).
12. THE offender to seek reconciliation, as well as the offended (Matt. 5:23, 24.).
13. LOVE our enemies and persecutors, and pray for them (Matt. 5:44).
14. EVERY one to work if he be able, and none to be idle (2 Thes. 3:10, 11, 12.
15. THE women in the church to learn in silence, and in all subjection (I Tim. 2:11; I Cor. 14:37.).
16. PRIVATE admonition to a brother offending another; and if not prevailing, to take one or two more; if he hear not them, then to tell it to the church; and if he hear not them, to be accounted as an heathen and publican (Matt. 18:15.).
17. PUBLICK rebuke to publick offenders (I Tim. 5:20.).
18. THE brethren in ministring forth their gifts, ought to do it decently and in order, one by one, that all

o

may learn, and all may be comforted (I Cor. 14:31, 40.).

19. A SPECIAL care to assemble together, that their duty to God, and the church, may not be neglected (Heb. 10:24, 25.).

20. AND all things in the church, done in the name and power of the head, the Lord Christ Jesus (Col. 3:17.).

21. THAT in admitting of members into the church of Christ, it is the duty of the church, and ministers whom it concerns, in faithfulness to God, that they be careful they receive none but such as do make forth evident demonstration of the new birth, and the work of faith with power (John 3:3; Matt. 3:8, 9; Acts 8:37; Ezek. 44:6, 7; Acts 2:38; 2 Cor. 9:14; Ps. 26:4, 5; 101:7.).

XXVI.

THAT those that truly repent, and believe, and are baptized in the name of the Lord Jesus, are in a fit capacity to exercise faith, in full assurance to receive a greater measure of the gifts and graces of the Holy Spirit (Acts 2:38, 39; Eph. 1:13.).

XXVIII. [Sic Original]

THAT it is the duty of the members of Christ in the order of the gospel, tho' in several congregations and assemblies (being one in the head) if occasion be, to communicate each to other, in things spiritual, and things temporal (Rom. 15:26; Acts 11:29; 15:22; 11:22.).

XXIX.

THAT the Lord Christ Jesus being the foundation and corner stone of the gospel church whereon his apostles built (Eph. 2:20; Heb. 2:3), He gave them power and abilities to propagate, to plant, to rule and order (Matt. 28:19, 20; Luke 10:16), for the benefit of that his body, by which ministry he did shew forth the exceeding riches of his grace, by his kindness towards it in the ages to come (Eph. 2:7), which is according to his promise (Matt. 28:20.).

XXX.

THAT this foundation and ministration aforesaid, is a sure guide, rule and direction, in the darkest time of the anti-christian apostacy, or spiritual Babylonish captivity, to direct, inform, and restore us in our just freedom and liberty, to the right worship and order belonging to the church of Jesus Christ (I Tim. 3:14, 15; 2 Tim. 3:15, 16, 17; John 17:20; Isa. 59:21; Rev. 2:24; Isa. 40:21; Rev. 2:5; I Cor. 14:37; Rev. 1:3; 2 Thes. 3:14; Rev. 2:11; I Pet. 1:25; I John 4:6; 2 Pet. 1:15, 16; Isa. 58:11, 12; 2 Pet. 3:2; Isa. 8:20.).

XXXI.

THAT the church of Jesus Christ with its ministry may from among themselves, make choice of such members, as are fitly gifted and qualified by Christ, and approve and ordain such by fasting, prayer, and laying on of hands (Acts 13:3; 14:23.), for the performance of the several duties, whereunto they are called (Acts 20:28; Rom. 12:6, 7, 8; 2 Tim. 4:2; Acts 6:3.).

XXXII.

THAT such a ministry labouring in the word and doctrine, have a power to receive a livelihood of their brethren, whose duty it is to provide a comfortable subsistance for them, if they be able, to whom for Christ's sake they are servants (I Cor. 9:4, 7; I Tim. 5:17, 18.). Yet it is commendable in cases of necessity, for them, for example sake, and that they may be able to support the weak, to labour and work with their hands (Acts 20:24, 25.).

XXXIII.

THAT the authority of Christ in an orderly ministry in his church, is to be submitted unto (Heb. 13:17; 2 Thes. 3:14.).

XXXIV.

THAT as it is an ordinance of Christ, so it is the duty of his church in his authority, to send forth such brethren

as are fitly gifted and qualified through the Spirit of
Christ to preach the gospel to the world (Acts 13: 1, 2,
3; 11: 22; 8: 14.).

XXXV.

THAT it is the duty of us believing Gentiles, not to
be ignorant of that blindness that yet lieth on Israel,
that none of us may boast (Rom. 11: 25.), but to have
bowels of love and compassion to them, praying for them
(Rom. 10: 1.), expecting their calling, and so much the
rather, because their conversion will be to us life from
the dead (Rom. 11: 15.).

XXXVI.

THAT it is the will of the Lord, and it is given to the
saints not only to believe in him, but to suffer for his
name (John 16: 13; Phil. 1: 26.) and so to pass through
many tribulations into the kingdom of God (Acts 14: 22;
2 Tim. 3: 12; 2: 12.).

XXXVII.

THAT the angels of the Lord are ministring spirits,
sent forth for the good of those that shall be the heirs
of salvation (Heb. 1: 14; Ps. 91: 11, 12; Acts 27: 23;
Luke 22: 43.).

XXXVIII.

THAT the wicked angels (Ps. 78: 49.) kept not their
first estate in which they were created (Jude 6.), the
prince of whom is called the devil (Matt. 8: 28.), and
the great dragon, and the old serpent, and satan (Rev.
12: 9.), and the accuser of our brethren (Rev. 12: 10.),
and the prince of this world (John 14: 30.), and a prince
that ruleth in the air; a spirit working in the children of
disobedience (Eph. 2: 2.), and our adversary (I Pet.
5: 8.), whose children the wicked are (Matt. 13: 39;
John 8: 44.) To him we ought not to give place (Eph.
4: 27.), whose power Christ hath overcome for us (Heb.
2: 14.), and for him and his angels everlasting fire is
prepared (Matt. 25: 41.).

XXXIX.

THAT it is our assured expectation, grounded upon promises, that the Lord Jesus Christ shall the second time appear without sin unto salvation, unto his people, to raise and change the vile bodies of all his saints, to fashion them like unto his glorious body, and so to reign with him, and judge over all nations on the earth in power and glory (Phil. 3:20, 21; Heb. 9:28; Acts 3:19, 20, 21; Matt. 19:28; Rev. 2:26, 27; I Cor. 6:2; Ps. 72:8, 11; Dan. 7:27; Zech. 14:9; Ps. 2:8, 9; Jer. 23:5, 6; Ezek. 21:26, 27; Isa. 32:1; Rev. 11:15; Ps. 82:8; Rev. 5:9, 10; 20:6.).

XL.

THAT there is a day appointed, when the Lord shall raise the unjust as well as the righteous, and judge them all in righteousness (John 5:28, 29; Acts 24:15,), but every man in his own order (I Cor. 15:23; I Thes. 4:16.), taking vengeance on them that know not God, and obey not the gospel of our Lord Jesus Christ, whose punishment will be everlasting destruction from the presence of the Lord (2 Thes. 1:7, 8, 9, 10; Jude 14, 15; Rev. 20:11, 12, 13, 14.).

XLI.

THAT there is a place into which the Lord will gather all his elect, to enjoy him for ever, usually in scripture called heaven (2 Cor. 5:1; John 14:2, 3.).

XLII.

THAT there is a place into which the Lord will cast the devil, his angels and wicked men, to be tormented for ever, from his presence and the glory of his power, usually in scripture called hell (Mark 9:43, 44, 45; Ps. 9:17; Matt. 25:41; 10:28; 23:33; Luke 10:15; 16:23.).

XLIII.

THAT it is both the duty and privilege of the church of Christ (till his coming again) in their fellowship together in the ordinances of Christ, to enjoy, prize, and press after, fellowship through and in the Spirit with the Lord, and each with other (Acts 2:42; I Cor. 11:26; Eph. 2:21, 22; Eph. 4:3, 4, 5, 6; I Cor. 12:13; Eph. 3:9; Col. 2:2), which we believe to be attained through the exercise of faith in the death, resurrection, and life of Christ (2 Cor. 5:14, 15, 16; Col. 2:12; Phil. 3:9, 10, 11; I Pet. 2:5.).

XLIV.

THAT the ministry of civil justice (being for the praise of them that do well, and punishment of evil-doers) is an ordinance of God, and that it is the duty of the saints to be subject thereunto not only for fear, but for conscience sake (Rom. 13:1, 2, 3, 4, 5; I Pet. 2:13, 14.) and that for such, prayers and supplications are to be made by the saints (I Tim. 2:1, 2.).

XLV.

THAT nothing doth come to pass by fortune or chance, but all things are disposed by the hand of God, and all for good to his people (Gen. 45:5; 50:20; Rom. 8:28; Eph. 1:11; Job 14:5; Isa. 4:5, 7.).

XLVI.

AND that a church so believing, and so walking, though despised, and of low esteem, is no less in the account of her Lord and King, than though

BLACK, yet comely, Cant. 1:5.
FAIREST, without spot, Cant. 4:7.
PRECIOUS, Isa. 43:4.
BEAUTIFUL, Cant. 7:1.
HOLY, without blemish, Eph. 5:27.
PLEASANT, Cant. 1:15.
WHOSE soul loveth Christ, Cant. 1:7.
RUNNERS after Christ, Cant. 1:4.
HONOURABLE, Isa. 43:4.
THE desire of Christ, Cant. 7:10.
COMPLEAT in Christ, Col. 2:10.
LOVERS of the Father, John 16:27.

THE blessed of the Father, Matt. 25 : 34.

KEPT by the Lord, I Pet. 1 : 5 ; Isa. 27 : 3.

GRAVEN on the palms of his hands, Isa. 49 : 16.

TENDER to the Lord as the apple of his eye, Zech. 2 : 8.

TAUGHT of the Lord, Isa. 54 : 13.

ONE that hath obtained mercy, I Pet. 2 : 10.

ONE that hath a redemption, Eph. 1 : 7.

THE gates of hell shall not prevail against it, Matt. 16 : 18.

IN that church be glory unto God by Jesus Christ, throughout all ages, world without end. Amen. Eph. 2 : 21.

3. ASSEMBLY OR SECOND LONDON CONFESSION

The Restoration, in 1660, greatly altered the position of the Baptists in England. During the Civil War and the Commonwealth, the Presbyterians and Quakers and to some extent other parties had bitterly assailed the Baptists, charging them with all the errors and all the calumnies that had once been heaped upon the Anabaptists. But by 1660 Baptist writings and Confessions had largely corrected the misapprehensions and fears of their opponents. Moreover, the Restoration put the Episcopal Church in power again with a Parliament determined to enforce uniformity. Presbyterians, Independents, Baptists, and Quakers became alike Dissenters. Common hardships and sufferings as well as common needs and a better mutual understanding begot a kindlier feeling. The Baptists now gave a signal proof of their desire for as much harmony and fellowship as possible by the preparation of this new Confession.

The Westminster Confession had been published in 1648. It was the product of much labor, and is certainly one of the noblest of all the Protestant Confessions, if indeed it has a peer. It had been at once adopted by the

Scottish Kirk and Parliament, displacing Knox's Confession; slightly altered, it had been adopted by the English Parliament, and was held as authoritative by all English-speaking Presbyterians. In addition to this, it had been adapted to their view of the church and its relation to the State by the Independents or Congregationalists, and adopted as their Confession at the Savoy in 1658. The Baptists of London and the surrounding country now determined to show their agreement with these two great Christian bodies by making this Confession the basis of a new statement of doctrine by themselves. In 1675 the political situation seemed to promise some relief to Dissenters. Quick to seize every opportunity to advance the interests of the denomination, the London Baptist ministers sent out a circular letter to all the churches of England and Wales, inviting them to meet in London the following May to devise some means for providing an adequate ministry for the churches. The letter was dated October 2, 1675, and was signed by most of the London ministers, including William Collins and William Kiffin. It is not known that the meeting was held, but in 1677 such a meeting seems to have been held, and this Westminster Confession, altered to suit Baptist views of the church and its ordinances, was adopted. The work of adaptation was done, it is said, by Elder William Collins, pastor of Petty France in London. It was published anonymously, but is said to have been "put forth by the elders and brethren of many congregations of Christians (baptized upon Profession of their Faith) in London and the country." They affirm the agreement of this Confession in substance with that of 1644; but, as a matter of fact, there are differences of considerable scope and importance. After a careful reading of the former, one feels himself almost in a new world in this. There are striking phrases and other reminiscences of the former Confession, but in the main all is changed. To begin with, this is much more complete and finished in form. New subjects are treated, *e. g.*, the Scriptures, the Sabbath, marriage, etc., the Calvinism is much more pronounced in some respects, the view of the church is clearer and is more Calvinistic, the administration of the ordinances is more rigidly the function of officials, the view of the Supper is almost purely Calvinistic, and there is no restriction of it to those scripturally baptized. The controlling influence in these great changes was undoubtedly the Westminster Confession, the increasing stability and regularity of the Baptist churches, and the increasing desire for harmony with other Protestants. It is the first Confession in which the Baptists of London and the country were united. Subsequent editions were, as far as collated, exact reprints of this original edition except in minor details of capitalization, punctuation, etc.

After the Act of Toleration, in 1689, the Calvinistic Baptists of England and Wales held their first General Assembly in London. William and Mary were proclaimed king and queen of England February 13, 1689, and the Act of Toleration became the law of the land May 24. On July 22, 1689, William Kiffin, Hanserd Knollys, John Harris, George Barrett, Benjamin Keach, Edward Man, and Richard Adams united in a circular letter to all the Calvinistic Baptist churches of England and Wales, inviting them to send from each church two messengers, one of whom should be the minister, to a meeting to be held in London beginning September 3, to consider the low estate of the churches, and especially to devise means for raising up a more numerous and better equipped ministry. The response was gratifying. Messengers from one hundred and seven churches in England and

Wales met in London, September 3, and continued in session until September 12. Among the many important things done by this first Assembly was the approval of this Confession, a second edition of which had appeared in 1688, and the recommending of its perusal both by other Christians and by their own members. It was published without the appendix of the original edition, and with the following, extracted from their minutes, prefixed:

" We the Ministers and Messengers of, and concerned for, upwards of one hundred baptized congregations in England and Wales (denying Arminianism) being met together in London, from the third of the seventh month to the eleventh of the same, 1689, to consider of some things that might be for the glory of God, and the good of these congregations; have thought meet (for the satisfaction of all other Christians that differ from us in the point of Baptism) to recommend to their perusal the confession of our faith, which confession we own, as containing the doctrine of our faith and practice, and do desire that the members of our churches respectively do furnish themselves therewith."

Hanserd Knollys	Pastor	Broken Wharf	London
William Kiffin	Do.	Devonshire-Sq.	Do.
John Harris	Do.	Joiners' Hall	Do.
William Collins	Do.	Petty France	Do.
Hercules Collins	Do.	Wapping	Do.
Robert Steed	Do.	Broken Wharf	Do.
Leonard Harrison	Do.	Limehouse	Do.
George Barret	Do.	Mile End Green	Do.
Isaac Lamb	Do.	Pennington-St.	Do.
Richard Adams	Minister	Shad Thames	Southwark
Benjamin Keach	Pastor	Horse-lie-down	Do.
Andrew Gifford	Do.	Bristol, Fryars	Som. & Glouc.
Thomas Vaux	Do.	*Broadmead*	Do.
Thomas Winnel	Do.	Taunton	Do.
James Hitt	Preacher	Dalwood	Dorset
Richd. Tidmarsh	Minister	Oxford City	Oxon
William Facey	Pastor	Reading	Berks
Samuel Buttall	Minister	Plymouth	Devon
Christopher Price	Do.	Abergavenny	Monmouth
Daniel Finch	Do.	Kingsworth	Herts
John Ball		Tiverton	Devon

Edmond White	Pastor	Evershall	Bedford
William Prichard	Do.	Blaenau	Monmouth
Paul Fruin	Minister	Warwick	Warwick
Richard Ring	Pastor	Southampton	Hants
John Tomkins	Minister	Abingdon	Berks
Toby Willis	Pastor	Bridgewater	Somset
John Carter		Steventon	Bedford
James Web		Devizes	Wilts
Richard Sutton	Pastor	Tring	Herts
Robert Knight	Do.	Stukely	Bucks
Edward Price	Do.	Hereford City	Hereford
William Phips	Do.	Exon	Devon
William Hawkins	Do.	Dimmock	Gloucester
Samuel Ewer	Do.	Hempstead	Herts
Edward Man	Do.	Houndsditch	London
Charles Archer	Do.	Nook-Norton	Oxon.

In the name and behalf of the whole Assembly."

In this form this production became the most in-fluential and important of all Baptist Confessions. New editions appeared in 1693, 1699, 1719, 1720, 1791, 1809, and there were numerous other editions. In 1693 the As-sembly ordered it "translated into Latin with all conve-nient speed," but it is not known that this was ever done. Crosby says, in 1738, that it was at that time "still gen-erally received by all those congregations that hold the doctrine of personal election, and the certainty of the saints' final perseverance" (Crosby II, 317). (For its influence in America, see below.) But for a century and more it has been losing ground in England. In 1888 the Union distinctly declined to reaffirm it, and now, so far as known, only two small bodies, which have no dealings with the great body of British Baptists and little with each other, hold it.

[The following is a reproduction of the original edition of 1677.]

CONFESSION

OF

FAITH

Put forth by the

ELDERS and BRETHREN

Of many

CONGREGATIONS

OF

Christians (baptized upon Profession of their Faith) in *London* and the Country.

With the Heart man believeth unto Righteousness, and with the Mouth Confession is made unto Salvation, Rom. 10. 10.
Search the Scriptures, John 5. 39.

Printed in the Year, 1677.

THE

CONTENTS.

Chap. 1. Of the Holy Scriptures. page 1.

2. Of God and the Holy Trinity.   9

3. Of Gods decrees.   13

4. Of Creation.   17

5. Of Divine Providence.   19

6. Of the Fall of Man, of Sin, and of the
   Punishment thereof: 23

7. Of Gods Covenant.   26

8. Of Christ the Mediator.   28

9. Of Free-will.   35

10. Of Effectual Calling.   37

11. Of Justification.   40

12. Of Adoption.   43

13. Of Sanctification.   44

14. Of Saving Faith.   46

15. Of Repentance unto Life and Salvati-
    on.   49

16. Of Good works.   51

17. Of Perseverance of Saints.   56

18. Of the Assurance of Grace and Salvati-
    on.   59

[Page]

19. Of the Law of God.   62

20. Of the Gospel, and of the extent of the Grace thereof.   67

21. Of Christian Liberty, and Liberty of Conscience.   70

22. Of Religious Worship, and the Sabbath day.   73

23. Of Lawful Oaths and Vows.   78

24. Of the Civil Magistrate.   81

25. Of Marriage.   83

26. Of the Church.   85

27. Of The Communion of Saints.   94

28. Of Baptism and the Lords Supper.   96

29. Of Baptism.   97

30. Of The Lords Supper.   98

31. Of the state of Man after death, and of the Resurrection of the dead.   103

32. Of The Last Judgment.   105

'An Appendix concerning Baptism.   109

[Page]

TO THE
JUDICIOUS AND IMPARTIAL
READER.

Courteous Reader,—It is now many years since divers of
us (with other sober Christians then
living and walking in the way of
the Lord that we professe) did conceive
our selves to be under a necessity of Publishing a *Confession of our Faith,* for the
information, and satisfaction of those,
that did not thoroughly understand what
our principles were, or had entertained
prejudices against our Profession, by
reason of the strange representation of
them, by some men of note, who had
taken very wrong measures, and accord [page]
ingly led others into misapprehensions, of
us, and them: and this was first put forth
about the year, 1643, in the name of
seven Congregations then gathered in
London; since which time, diverse impressions thereof have been dispersed
abroad, and our end proposed, in good
measure answered, inasmuch as many
(and some of those men eminent, both
for piety and learning) were thereby satisfied, that we were no way guilty of
those Heterodoxies and fundamental errors, which had too frequently been
charged upon us without ground, or occasion given on our part. And forasmuch as that *Confession* is not now commonly to be had; and also that many
others have since embraced the same
truth which is owned therein; it was
judged necessary by us to joyn together
in giving a testimony to the world; of
our firm adhering to those wholesome
Principles, by the publication of this
which is now in your hand.

And forasmuch as our method, and [page]
manner of expressing our sentiments in
this doth vary from the former (although the
substance of the matter is the same)
we shall freely impart to you the reason and
occasion thereof. One thing that greatly prevailed
with us to undertake this work, was (not only to
give a full account of ourselves to those Christians that differ from us about the subject

of baptism, but also) the profit that might
from thence arise unto those that have any
account of our labours, in their instruction
and establishment in the great truths of the
gospel; in the clear understanding and steady
belief of which our comfortable walking with
God, and fruitfulness before him in all our ways
is most nearly concerned. And therefore
we did conclude it necessary to express ourselves the more fully and distinctly, and also to fix
on such a method as might be most comprehensive of those things which we designed to explain our sense and belief of; and finding no
defect in this regard in that fixed on by the
Assembly, and after them by those of the Congregational way, we did readily conclude it
best to retain the same order in our present
Confession. And also when we observed [page]
that those last mentioned did, in their Confession
(for reasons which seemed of weight both to
themselves and others), choose not only to express their mind in words concurrent with
the former in sense, concerning all those articles wherein they were agreed, but also for
the most part without any variation of
the terms, we did in like manner conclude
it best to follow their example, in making
use of the very same words with them both, in
those articles (which are very many) wherein
our faith and doctrine is the same with theirs.
And this we did, the more abundantly to
manifest our consent with both, in all the
fundamental articles of the Christian religion, as also with many others whose
orthodox confessions have been published
to the World, on the behalf of the protestants
in diverse nations and cities; and also to
convince all that we have no itch to clog religion with new words, but to readily ac-
quiesce in that form of sound words which
hath been, in consent with the holy scriptures,
used by others before us; hereby declaring
before God, angels, and men, our hearty
agreement with them, in that wholesome [page]
protestant doctrine, which, with so clear
evidence of scriptures they have asserted.
Some things, indeed, are in some places
added, some terms omitted, and some
few changed; but these alterations are of
that nature, as that we need not doubt any
charge or suspicion of unsoundness in

the faith, from any of our brethren upon the account of them.

In those things wherein we differ from others,
we have expressed ourselves with all candour
and plainness, that none might entertain
Jealousy of aught secretly lodged in our breasts,
that we would not the world should be
acquainted with; yet we hope we have also
observed those rules of modesty and humility
as will render our freedom in this respect
inoffensive, even to those whose sentiments
are different from ours.

We have also taken care to affix texts of
scripture in the margin, for the confirmation of each article in our Confession; in
which work we have studiously endea-
vored to select such as are most clear
and pertinent for the proof of what is
asserted by us; and our earnest desire [page]
is, that all into whose hands this may
come would follow that (never
enough commended) example of the
noble Bereans, who searched the scriptures daily that they might find out
whether the things preached to them were
so or not.

There is one thing more which we
sincerely profess, and earnestly desire credence in, viz., that contention
is most remote from our design in
all that we have done in this matter;
and we hope the liberty of an inge-
nuous unfolding our principles and
opening our hearts unto our brethren,
with the scripture-grounds on which
our faith and practice leans, will
by none of them be either denied to
us, or taken ill from us. Our
whole design is accomplished if we
may obtain that justice, as to be measured
in our principles and practice and the [page]
judgement of both by others, according
to what we have now published; which
the Lord (whose eyes are as a flame of
fire) knoweth to be the doctrine, which
with our hearts we most firmly believe,
and sincerely indeavour to conform our
lives to. And oh that other contentions
being laid asleep, the only care and contention of all upon whom the name of
our blessed Redeemer is called, might

P

for the future be, to walk humbly with
their God, and in the exercise of all
Love and Meekness towards each other,
to perfect holyness in the fear of the Lord,
each one endeavouring to have his conversation such as becometh the Gospel;
and also, suitable to his place and capacity, vigorously to promote in others the
practice of true Religion and undefiled in
the sight of God and our Father. And that
in this backsliding day, we might not
spend our breath in fruitless complaints of
the evils of others; but may every one
begin at home, to reform in the first place
our own hearts, and wayes; and then
to quicken all that we may have influence [page]
upon, to the same work; that if the will
of God were so, none might deceive
themselves, by resting in, and trusting
to, a form of Godliness, without the power of it, and inward experience of the
efficacy of those truths that are professed
by them.

And verily there is one spring and
cause of the decay of Religion in our
day, which we cannot but touch upon, and earnestly urge a redress of;
and that is the neglect of the worship of God
in Families, by those to whom the charge
and conduct of them is committed. May
not the grosse ignorance, and instability
of many; with the prophaneness of others,
be justly charged upon their Parents
and Masters, who have not trained them
up in the way wherein they ought to
walk when they were young; but have
neglected those frequent and solemn commands which the Lord hath laid upon
them so to catechise, and instruct them,
that their tender years might be seasoned
with the knowledge of the truth of God
as revealed in the Scriptures; and also by [page]
their own omission of Prayer, and other
duties of Religion in their families, together with the ill example of their loose
conversation, have inured them first to a
neglect, and then contempt of all Piety
and Religion? we know this will not excuse the blindness, or wickedness of any; **but**
certainly it will fall heavy upon those
that have been thus the occasion thereof;

they indeed dye in their sins; but will not
their blood be required of those under
whose care they were, who yet permitted them to go on without *warning,* yea
led them into the paths of destruction?
and will not the diligence of Christians
with respect to the discharge of these
duties, in ages past, rise up in judgment
against, and condemn many of those who
would be esteemed such now?

We shall conclude with our earnest prayer,
that the God of all grace, will pour out those measures of his holy Spirit upon us, that the profession of truth may be accompanyed with the sound
belief, and diligent practise of it by us; that his
name may in all things be glorified, through Jesus Christ our Lord, *Amen.*

A

CONFESSION OF

FAITH.

Chap. I.

Of the Holy Scriptures.

1. THe Holy Scripture is the only sufficient, certain, and
infallible [1] rule of all saving
Knowledge, Faith, and Obedience; Although the [2] light of
Nature, and the works of Creation and Providence do so far manifest the goodness, wisdom and
power of God, as to leave men
unexcusable; yet are they not sufficient to
give that knowledge [page]
of God and His will, which is necessary unto Salvation.[3] Therefore it pleased the Lord at sundry
times, and in divers manners, to
reveal himself, and to declare that
His will unto his Church; and
afterward for the better preserving, and propagating of the
Truth, and for the more sure Establishment and Comfort of the

[1] 2 Tim. 3.
15, 16, 17.
Isa. 8. 20.
Luk. 16.
29, 31.
Eph. 2. 20.
[2] Rom. 1.
19, 20, 21
etc. ch. 2.
14, 15.
Psal. 19. 1,
2, 3.

[3] Heb. 1. 1.

Church against the corruption of the flesh, and the malice of Satan, and of the World, to commit the same wholly unto [4] writing; which maketh the Holy Scriptures to be most necessary, those former ways of Gods revealing his will unto his people being now ceased.

[4] Pro. 22. 19, 20, 21. Rom. 15. 4. 2 Pet. 1. 19, 20.

2. Under the Name of Holy Scripture, or the Word of God written; are now contained all the Books of the Old and New Testament, which are these, [page]

Of the Old Testament.

Genesis, Exodus, Leviticus, Numbers, Deauteronomy, Joshua, Judges, Ruth, 1 Samuel, 2 Samuel, 1 Kings, 2 Kings, 1 Chronicles, 2 Chronicles, Ezra, Nehemiah, Esther, Job, Psalms, Proverbs, Ecclesiastes, The Song of Songs, Isaiah, Jeremiah, Lamentations, Ezekiel, Daniel, Hosea, Joel, Amos, Obadiah, Jonah, Micah, Nahum, Habakkuk, Zephaniah, Haggai, Zechariah, Malachi.

Of the New Testament.

Matthew, Mark, Luke, John, The Acts of the Apostles, Pauls Epistle to the Romans, 1 Corinthians, 2 Corinthians, Galatians, Ephesians, Philippians, Colossians, [page] 1 Thessalonians, 2 Thessalonians, 1 Timothy, 2 Timothy, to Titus, to Philemon, the Epistle to the Hebrews, the Epistle of James, The first and second Epistles of Peter, The first, second, and third Epistles of John, the Epistle of Jude, the Revelation. All which are given by the [5] inspiration of God, to be the rule of Faith and Life.

[5] 2 Tim. 3. 16.

3. The Books commonly called Apochypha not being of [6] Divine inspiration, are no part of the Canon (or rule) of the Scripture, and

[6] Luk. 24. 27, 44. Rom. 3. 2.

therefore are of no authority to
the Church of God, nor to be any
otherwise approved or made use
of, then other humane writings.

4. The Authority of the Holy
Scripture for which it ought to be
believed dependeth not upon the
testimony of any man, or Church;
but wholly upon[7] God (who [page]
is truth it self) the Author thereof; therefore it is to be received,
because it is the Word of God.

5. We may be moved and in-
duced by the testimony of the
Church of God, to an high and
reverent esteem of the Holy Scriptures; and the heavenliness of the
matter, the efficacy of the Doctrine, and the Majesty of the stile,
the consent of all the parts, the
scope of the whole (which is to
give all glory to God) the full discovery it makes of the only way
of mans salvation, and many o-
ther incomparable Excellencies,
and intire perfections thereof, are
arguments whereby it doth abundantly evidence it self to be the
Word of God; yet, notwithstanding; our[8] full perswasion, and
assurance of the infallible truth,
and divine authority thereof, is
from the inward work of the Holy
Spirit, bearing witness by and [page]
with the Word in our Hearts.

6. The whole Councel of God
concerning all things[9] necessary
for his own Glory, Mans Salvation,
Faith and Life, is either expressely set down or necessarily contained in the *Holy Scripture;* unto
which nothing at any time is to be
added, whether by new Revelation of the
Spirit, or traditions of
men.

Nevertheless we acknowledge
the[11] inward illumination of
the Spirit of God, to be necessary for the saving understanding of
such things as are revealed in the
Word, and that there are some

[7] 2 Pet. 1.
19, 20, 21.
2 Tim. 3.
16.
2 Thes. 2.
13. 1 Joh.
5. 19.

[8] Joh. 16.
13, 14.
1 Cor. 2.
10, 11, 12.
1 Joh. 2.
2, 20, 27.

[9] 2 Tim.
3. 15, 16.
17. Gal. 1.
8, 9.

[11] John 6.
45. 1 Cor.
2. 9, 10,
11, 12,

circumstances concerning the worship of God, and government of the Church common to humane actions and societies; which are to be[12] ordered by the light of nature, and Christian prudence according to the general rules of the Word, which are always to be observed. [page]

7. All things in Scripture are not alike [13] plain in themselves, nor alike clear unto all; yet those things which are necessary to be known, believed, and observed for Salvation, are so [14] clearly propounded, and opened in some place of Scripture or other, that not only the learned, but the unlearned, in a due use of ordinary means, may attain to a sufficient understanding of them.

8. The Old Testament in [15] *Hebrew*, (which was the Native language of the people of God of old) and the New Testament in *Greek*, (which at the time of the writing of it was most generally known to the Nations being immediately inspired by God, and by his singular care and Providence kept pure in all Ages, are therefore [16] authentical; so as in all controversies of Religion, the Church is finally to appeal unto them [17]. But be- [page] cause these original tongues are not known to all the people of God, who have a right unto, and interest in the scriptures, and are commanded in the fear of God to read [18] and search them, therefore they are to be translated into the vulgar language of every Nation, unto which they [19] come, that the Word of God dwelling [20] plentifully in all, they may worship him in an acceptable manner, and through patience and comfort of the Scriptures may have hope.

9. The infallible rule of interpretation of Scripture is the [21]

12 1 Cor.
11. 13, 14.
& ch. 14.
26 & 40.

13 2 Pet.
3. 16.

14 Ps. 19. 7.
and 119.

15 Rom.
3. 2.

16 Isa. 8. 20.

17 Act. 15. 15.

18 John 5.
39.

19 1 Cor.
14. 6, 9, 11,
12, 24, 28.
20 Col. 3. 16.

21 2 Pet. 1.
20, 21.
Act. 15.
15, 16.

Scripture it self: And therefore
when there is a question about the
true and full sense of any Scripture
(which is not manifold but one)
it must be searched by other
places that speak more clearly. [page]
10. The supream judge by
which all controversies of Religion are to be determined, and all
Decrees of Councels, opinions of
antient Writers, Doctrines of men,
and private Spirits, are to be exa-
mined, and in whose sentence we
are to rest, can be no other but
the Holy Scripture delivered by
the Spirit, into which [24] Scripture so delivered, our faith is finally resolved.

[21] Mat. 22.
29, 31.
Eph. 2. 20.
Acts 28. 23.

CHAP. II.

Of God and of the Ho-
ly Trinity.

1. THE Lord our God is but [1]
one only living, and
true God; whose [2] subsistence
is in and of himself, [3] infinite in
being, and perfection, whose Es- [page]
sence cannot be comprehended by
any but himself; [4] a most pure
spirit, [5] invisible, without body, parts, or passions, who only
hath immortality, dwelling in the
light, which no man can ap-
proach unto, who is [6] immutable, [7] immense, [8] eternal, incomprehensible, [9] Almighty,
every way infinite, [11] most holy,
most wise, most free, most absolute, [12]
working all things according
to the councel of his own immutable, and most righteous will, [13]
for his own glory, most loving, gracious, merciful, long-suffering, abundant in goodness and
truth, forgiving iniquity, transgression and sin, [14] the reward-
er of them that diligently seek
him, and withal most just, [15]
and terrible in his judgments, [16]
hating all sin, and who will

[1] 1 Cor. 8.
4, 6. Deut.
6. 4.
[2] Jer. 10.
10. Isaiah
48. 12.
[3] Exod. 3.
14.
[4] Joh. 4.
24.
[5] 1 Tim.
1. 17.
Deut. 4.
15, 16.
[6] Mal. 3. 6.
[7] 1 King.
8. 27. Jer.
23. 23.
[8] Psal. 90. 2.
[9] Gen. 17. 1.
[11] Isa. 6. 3.
[12] Psal. 16.
3. Isa. 46.
10.
[13] Pro. 16.
4. Rom. 11.
36.

[14] Exod.
34. 6, 7.
Heb. 11. 6.
[15] Neh. 9.
32, 33.
[16] Ps. 5. 5, 6.

[17] Exod. 34. 7.
Nahum. 1. 2, 3.
[18] Joh. 5.
26.
[19] Ps. 148.
13.
[20] Ps. 119.
68.
[21] Job 22.
2, 3.

by no means clear the [17] guilty. [page]
2. God having all [18] life,[19]
glory,[20] goodness, blessedness,
in and of himself: is alone in,
and unto himself all-sufficient, not [21]
standing in need of any Crea-
ture which he hath made, nor de-
riving any glory from them, but
onely manifesting his own glory
in, by, unto, and upon them, he

[24] Rom.
11. 34, 35,
36.

is the alone fountain of all Being,[24]
of whom, through whom, and
to whom are all things, and he

[25] Dan. 4.
25 & 5. 34, 35.

hath most soveraign [25] dominion
over all creatures, to do by them,
for them, and upon them, whatsoe-

[26] Heb. 4.
13.

ver himself pleaseth; in his sight [26]

[1] Ezek. 11.
5. Act. 15.
18.

all things are open and manifest, his knowledge is [1] infinite,
infallible, and independant upon
the Creature, so as nothing is to
him contingent, or uncertain; he is

[2] Ps. 145.
17.

most holy in all his Councels, in [2]
all his Works, and in all his

[3] Rev. 5.
12, 13, 14.

Commands; to him is due [3] from
Angels and men, whatsoever
worship, service, or obedience as [page]
Creatures they owe unto the
Creator, and whatever he is further pleased to require of them.
3. In this divine and infinite

[4] 1 Joh.
5. 7. Mat.
28. 19.
2 Cor. 13.
14.
[5] Exod. 3.
14. Joh.
14. 11.
1 Cor. 8. 6.
[6] Joh. 1.
14, 18.

Joh. 15.
26.
Gal. 4. 6.

Being there are three subsistences,[4]
the Father the Word (or Son)
and Holy Spirit, of one substance,
power, and Eternity, each having
the whole Divine Essence,[5] yet
the Essence undivided, the Father
is of none neither begotten nor
proceeding, the Son is [6] Eternally begotten of the Father, the
holy Spirit [7] proceeding from
the Father and the Son, all infinite, without beginning, therefore
but one God, who is not to be divided in nature and Being; but
distinguished by several peculiar,
relative properties, and personal
relations; which doctrine of the
Trinity is the foundation of all
our Communion with God, and
comfortable dependence on him. [page]

CHAP. III.

Of Gods Decree.

1. GOD hath [1] *Decreed* in himself from all Eternity, by the most wise and holy Councel of his own will, freely and unchangeably, all things whatsoever comes to passe; yet so as thereby is God neither the author of sin,[2] nor hath fellowship with any therin, nor is violence offered to the will of the Creature, nor yet is the liberty, or contingency of second causes taken away, but rather [3] established, in which appears his wisdom in disposing all things, and power, and faithfulness [4] in accomplishing his *Decree*.

[1] Is. 46. 10. Eph. 1. 11. Heb. 6. 17. Rom. 9. 15, 18.

[2] Jam. 1. 15, 17. 1 Joh. 1. 5.

[3] Act. 4. 27, 28, Joh. 19. 11.
[4] Numb. 23. 19. Eph. 1. 3, 4, 5.

2. Although God knoweth whatsoever may, or can come to passe upon all [5] supposed conditions; yet hath he not *Decreed* anything,[6] because he foresaw it as future, or as that which would come to pass upon such conditions.

[5] Act. 15. 18.

[6] Rom. 9. 11, 13, 16, 18.

3. By the *decree* of God, for the manifestation of his glory [7] some men and Angels are predestinated, or fore-ordained to Eternal Life, through Jesus Christ, to the [8] praise of his glorious grace; others being left to act in their sin to their [9] just condemnation, to the praise of his glorious justice.

[7] 1 Tim. 5. 21. Mat. 25. 41.
[8] Eph. 1. 5, 6.

[9] Rom. 9. 22, 23. Jud. 4.

4. These Angels and Men thus predestinated, and fore-ordained, are particularly, and unchangeably designed, and their [11] number so certain, and definite, that it cannot be either increased, or diminished.

[11] 2 Tim. 2. 19. Joh. 13. 18.

5. Those of mankind that are predestinated to life, God, before the foundation of the world was laid, according to his eternal and immutable purpose, and the secret Councel and good pleasure of his will, hath chosen in Christ unto everlasting glory, out of his meer free grace and love; [13] without any other thing in the

[12] Eph. 1. 4, 9, 11. Rom. 8. 30. 2 Tim. 1. 9. 1 Thes. 5. 9.

[13] Rom. 9. 13, 16. Eph. 1. 6, 12.

creature as a condition or cause
moving him thereunto.

6. As God hath appointed the
Elect unto glory, so he hath by
the eternal and most free purpose
of his will, fore-ordained [15] all
the means thereunto, wherefore
they who are elected, being faln
in Adam,[16] are redeemed by
Christ, are effectually [17] called
unto faith in Christ, by his spirit
working in due season, are justify-
ed, adopted, sanctified, and kept by
his power through faith [18] unto
salvation; neither are any other
redeemed by Christ, or effectually
called, justified, adopted, sancti- [page]
ed, and saved, but the Elect [19]
only.

7. The Doctrine of this high
mystery of predestination, is to
be handled with special prudence,
and care; that men attending the
will of God revealed in his word,
and yielding obedience thereunto, may from the certainty of their
effectual vocation, be assured of
their [20] eternal election; so shall
this doctrine afford matter [21] of
praise, reverence, and admiration
of God, and [24] of humility, diligence, and abundant [25] consolation, to all that sincerely obey
the Gospel. [page]

CHAP. IV.

Of Creation.

1. IN the beginning it pleased *God*
the Father,[1] Son, and Holy
Spirit, for the manifestation of
the glory of [2] his eternal power,
wisdom, and goodness, to *Create* or
make the world, and all things
therein,[3] whether visible or invisible, in the space of six days,
and all very good.

2. After God had made all o-
ther Creatures, he *Created* [4]
man, male and female, with [5]
reasonable and immortal souls, ren-

[15] 1 Pet. 1.
2.
2 Thes. 2.
13.
[16] 1 Thes.
5. 9, 10.
[17] Rom. 8.
30.
2 Thes. 2.
13.
[18] 1 Pet.
1. 5.

[19] Joh. 10.
26.
Joh. 17. 9.
Joh. 6. 64.

[20] 1 Thes.
1. 4, 5.
2 Pet. 1.
10.
[21] Eph. 1.
6. Rom.
11. 33.
[24] Rom.
11. 5, 6.
[25] Luk. 10.
20.

[1] John 1.
2, 3.
Heb. 1. 2.
Job 26. 13.
[2] Rom. 1.
20.

[3] Col. 1.
16.
Gen. 2. 1,
2.

[4] Gen. 1.
27.
[5] Gen. 2.
7.

dring them fit unto that life to
God, for which they were *Created;*
being [6] made after the image
of God, in knowledge, righteousness, and true holyness; having the [page]
Law of God [7] written in their
hearts, and power to fulfill it;
and yet under a possibility of
transgressing, being left to the liberty of their own will, which
was [8] subject to change.

  3. Besides the Law written in
their hearts, they received [9] a
command not to eat of the tree of
knowledge of good and evil;
which whilst they kept, they were
happy in their Communion with
God, and had dominion [11] over
the Creatures. [page]

[6] Eccles.
7. 29.

[7] Rom. 2.
14, 15.

[8] Gen. 3.
6.

[9] Gen. 6.
17. & ch.
3. 8, 9, 10.

[11] Gen. 1.
26, 28.

CHAP. V.

Of Divine Providence.

  1. GOD, the good *Creator* of all
things, in *his* infinite power,
and wisdom, doth [1] uphold, direct, dispose, and govern all Creatures, and things, from the greatest even to the [2] least, by *his*
most wise and holy providence, to
the end for the which they were
Created; according unto his infallible foreknowledge, and the free
and immutable Councel of *his* [3]
own will; to the praise of the
glory of *his* wisdom, power, justice, infinite goodness and mercy.

  2. Although in relation to the
foreknowledge and *Decree* of *God,*
the first cause, all things come to [page]
pass [4] immutably and infallibly;
so that there is not any thing, befalls any [5] by chance, or without
his Providence; yet by the same
Providence he ordereth them to
fall out, according to the nature
of second causes, either [6] necessarily, freely, or contingent-
ly.

  3. God in *his* ordinary *Prov-*

[1] Heb. 1.
3. Job 38.
11. Isa. 46.
10, 11. Ps.
135. 6.
[2] Mat. 10.
29, 30, 31.

[3] Eph. 1.
11.

Act. 2. 23.

[5] Prov. 16.
33.

[6] Gen. 8.
22.

idence[7] maketh use of means;
yet is free[8] to work, without,[9]
above, and[11] against them
at *his* pleasure.

4. The Almighty power, unsearchable wisdom, and *infinite*
goodness of *God,* so far manifest
themselves in *his Providence,* that
his determinate Councel[12] ex-
tendeth it self even to the first
fall, and all other sinful actions
both of Angels, and Men; (and
that not by a bare permission) which
also he most wisely and [page]
powerfully[13] boundeth, and
otherwise ordereth, and governeth, in a manifold dispensation to
his most holy[14] ends: yet so, as
the sinfulness of their acts proceedeth only from the Creatures, and
not from *God;* who being most
holy and righteous, neither is nor
can be, the author or[15] appro-
ver of sin.

5. The most wise, righteous,
and gracious *God,* doth oftentimes, leave
for a season *his* own children
to manifold temptations, and the
corruptions of their own heart, to
chastise them for their former sins,
or to discover unto them the hidden strength of corruption, and
deceitfulness of their hearts,[16]
that they may be humbled; and
to raise them to a more close, and
constant dependence for their support, upon himself; and to make
them more watchful against all
future occasions of sin, and for [page]
other just and holy ends.

So that whatsoever befalls any
of his elect is by his appointment,
for his glory,[17] and their good.

6. As for those wicked and ungodly men, whom God as a righteous judge, for former sin doth[18]
blind and harden; from them
he not only withholdeth his[19]
Grace, whereby they might have
been inlightened in their understanding, and wrought upon in

---

[7] Act. 27.
31, 44.
Isa. 55. 10,
11.
[8] Hos. 1. 7.
[9] Rom. 4.
19, 20, 21.
[11] Dan. 3.
27.
[12] Rom. 11.
32, 33, 34.
2 Sam. 24.
1. 1 Chro.
21. 1.

[13] 2 Kings
19. 28.
Ps. 76. 10.

[14] Gen. 50.
20. Isa. 10.
6, 7, 12.

[15] Ps. 50. 21.
1 Joh. 2.
16.

[16] 2 Chro.
32. 25, 26,
31.
2 Sam. 24.
1. 2 Cor.
12. 7, 8, 9.

[17] Rom. 8.
28.

[18] Rom. 1.
24, 26, 28,
ch. 11. 7, 8.
[19] Deut.
29. 4.

their hearts: But sometimes also
withdraweth[20] the gifts which
they had, and exposeth them to
such[21] objects as their *corruptions* makes occasion of sin; and
withal[24] gives them over to
their own lusts, the temptations of
the world, and the power of Satan,
whereby it comes to pass, that
they[25] harden themselves, even
under those means which God
useth for the softening of others. [page]

7. As the *Providence* of *God*
doth in general reach to all *Creatures,* so after a most special manner it taketh care of his[26]
Church, and disposeth of all things
to the good thereof.

[20] Mat. 13.
12.

[21] Deut. 2.
30.
2 King. 8.
12, 13.

[24] Psal. 81.
11, 12.
2 Thes. 2.
10, 11, 12.

[25] Exod. 8.
15, 32.
Is. 6. 9, 10.
1 Pet. 2.
7, 8.

[26] 1 Tim.
4. 10.
Amos 9.
8, 9.
Isa. 43. 3,
4, 5.

CHAP. VI.

Of the fall of Man, of Sin, and of the Punishment thereof.

1. Although *God created Man*
upright, and perfect, and
gave him a righteous law, which
had been unto life had he kept it,[1]
and threatened death upon
the breach thereof; yet he
did not long abide in this honour;[2]
Satan using the subtilty of the
serpent to seduce *Eve,* then by her [page]
seducing *Adam,* who without any
compulsion, did wilfully transgress
the Law of their *Creation,* and
the command given unto them, in
eating the forbidden fruit; which
God was pleased according to *his*
wise and holy *Councel* to permit,
having purposed to order it, to
his own glory.

[1] Gen. 2.
16, 17.

[2] Gen. 3.
12, 13.
2 Cor. 11.
3.

2. Our first *Parents* by this *Sin,*
fell from their[3] original righteousness and communion with *God,*
and we in them, whereby death
came upon all;[4] all becoming
dead in *Sin,* and wholly defiled,[5]
in all the faculties, and parts,
of soul, and body.

3. They being the[6] root,
and by *Gods* appointment, stand-

[3] Rom. 3.
23.
[4] Rom. 5.
12 etc.
[5] Tit. 1. 15.
Gen. 6. 5.
Jer. 17. 9.
Rom. 3.
10-19.
[6] Rom. 5.
12-19.
1 Cor. 15.
21, 22, 45,
49.

ing in the room, and stead of all mankind; the guilt of the *Sin* was imputed, and *corrupted* nature conveyed, to all their posterity descending from them by ordina- [page] ry generation, being now[7] conceived in *Sin,* and by nature children[8] of wrath, the servants of *Sin,* the subjects[9] of *death* and all other miseries, spiritual, temporal and eternal, unless the *Lord Jesus*[11] set them free.

4. From this original *corruption,* whereby we are[12] utterly indisposed, disabled, and made oppo..ite to all good, and wholly inclined to all evil, do[13] proceed all actual transgressions.

5. This *corruption* of nature, during this Life, doth[14] remain in those that are regenerated: and although it be through *Christ* pardoned, and mortified, yet both it self, and the first motions thereof, are truely and properly[15] *Sin.* [page]

[7] Ps. 51. 5.
Job 14. 4.
[8] Eph. 2. 3.
[9] Rom. 6. 20 & ch. 5. 12.
[11] Heb. 2. 14.
1 Thes. 1. 10.
[12] Rom. 8. 7. Col. 1. 21.
[13] Jam. 1. 14, 15.
Mat. 15. 19.
[14] Rom. 7. 18, 23.
Eccles. 7. 20.
1 Joh. 1. 8.
[15] Rom. 7. 24, 25.
Gal. 5. 17.

CHAP. VII.

Of Gods Covenant.

1. THE distance between *God* and the *Creature* is so great, that although reasonable *Creatures* do owe obedience unto him as their *Creator,* yet they could never have attained the reward of Life, but by some[1] voluntary condescension on *Gods part,* which he hath been pleased to express, by way of *Covenant.*

2. Moreover *Man* having brought himself[2] under the *curse* of the Law by his fall, it pleased the *Lord* to make a *Covenant* of *Grace* wherein he freely offereth unto *Sinners,*[3] Life and Salvation by *Jesus Christ,* requiring of them Faith in him, that they may be saved; and[4] promising to [page] give unto all those that are ordained unto eternal Life, his Holy *Spi-*

[1] Luk. 17. 10.
Job 35. 7, 8.
[2] Gen. 2. 17.
Gal. 3. 10,
Rom. 3. 20, 21.
[3] Rom. 8. 3.
Mark 16. 15, 16.
Joh. 3. 16.
[4] Ezek. 36. 26, 27.
Joh. 6. 44, 45.
Ps. 110. 3.

rit, to make them willing, and
able to believe.

3. This *Covenant* is revealed in
the Gospel; first of all to *Adam*
in the promise of Salvation by the[5]
seed of the woman, and afterwards by farther steps, until the
full[6] discovery thereof was
compleated in the new Testament;
and it is founded in that * Eternal
Covenant transaction, that was between the *Father* and the *Son,*
about the Redemption of the
Elect; and it is alone by the
Grace of this *Covenant,* that all
of the posterity of fallen *Adam,*
that ever were[7] saved, did obtain life and a blessed immortality; *Man* being now utterly uncapable of acceptance with *God* upon those terms, on which *Adam*
stood in his state of innocency. [page]

[5] Gen. 3.
15.

[6] Heb. 1.
1.

* 2 Tim.
1. 9.
Tit. 1. 2.

[7] Heb. 11.
6, 13.
Rom. 4. 1,
2, etc.
Act. 4. 12.
Joh. 8. 56.

CHAP. VIII.
Of Christ the Media-
tor.

1. IT pleased *God* in his eternal
purpose, to chuse and ordain
the *Lord Jesus* his only begotten
Son, according to the *Covenant*
made between them both,[1]
to be the *Mediator* between
God and *Man;* the[2] Prophet,[3]
Priest and[4] King; Head
and Saviour of his Church, the
heir of all things, and judge of
the world: Unto whom he did
from all Eternity[5] give a people
to be his seed, and to be by him
in time redeemed, called, justified,
sanctified, and glorified.

2. The *Son* of *God,* the second
Person in the *Holy Trinity,* being [page]
very and eternal *God,* the brightness of the Fathers glory, of one
substance and equal with *him:*
who made the World, who up-
holdeth and governeth all things
he hath made: did when the fullness of time was come take upon
him[6] mans nature, with all

[1] Is. 42. 1.
1 Pet. 1.
19, 20.
[2] Act. 3.
22.
[3] Heb. 5.
5, 6.
[4] Ps. 2. 6.
Luk. 1. 33.
Eph. 1. 23.
Heb. 1. 2.
[5] Is. 53. 10.
Joh. 17. 6.
Rom. 8.
30.

[6] Joh. 1. 1,
14.
Gal. 4. 4.

the Essential properties, and common infirmities thereof,[7] yet without sin: being conceived by the *Holy Spirit* in the *Womb* of the *Virgin Mary,* the *Holy Spirit* coming down upon her, and the power of the most *High* overshadowing her,[8] and so was made of a *Woman,* of the Tribe of *Judah,* of the Seed of *Abraham,* and *David* according to the *Scriptures*: So that two whole, perfect, and distinct natures, were inseparably joined together in one *Person:* without *conversion, composition,* or *confusion:* which *Person* is very *God,* and very *Man; yet one*[9] *Christ,* the only *Mediator* between *God* and *Man.* [page]

3. The *Lord Jesus* in his human nature thus united to the divine, in the Person of the *Son,* was sanctified, anointed [11] with the *Holy Spirit,* above measure; having in him [12] all the treasures of wisdom and knowledge; in whom it pleased the *Father* that [13] all fullness should dwell: To the end that being [14] holy, harmless, undefiled, and full [15] of *Grace,* and *Truth,* he might be thoroughly furnished to execute the office of a *Mediator,* and [16] *Surety;* which office he took not upon himself, but was thereunto [17] called by his *Father;* who also put [18] all power and judgement in his hand, and gave him Commandement to execute the same.

4. This office the *Lord Jesus* did most [19] willingly undertake, which that he might discharge he was made under the Law,[20] and did perfectly fulfill it, and under- [page] went the [21] punishment due to us, which we should have born and suffered, being made [24] *Sin* and a *Curse* for us: enduring most grievous sorrows [25] in his Soul; and most painful sufferings in his body; was crucified, and died,

---

Marginal references:

[7] Rom. 8. 3. Heb. 2. 14, 16, 17. ch. 4. 15.

[8] Luk. 1. 27, 31, 35.

[9] Rom. 9. 5. 1 Tim. 2. 5.

[11] Ps. 45. 7. Act. 10. 38. Joh. 3. 34.
[12] Col. 2. 3.

[13] Col. 1. 19.

[14] Heb. 7. 26.
[15] Joh. 1. 14.
[16] Heb. 7. 22.
[17] Heb. 5. 5.
[18] Joh. 5. 22, 27. Mat. 28. 18. Act. 2. 36.
[19] Ps. 40. 7, 8. Heb. 10. 5-11. Joh. 10. 18.
[20] Gal. 4. 4. Mat. 3. 15.
[21] Gal. 3. 13. Isa. 53. 6. 1 Pet. 3. 18.
[24] 2 Cor. 5. 21.
[25] Mat. 26. 37, 38. Luk. 22. 44. Mat. 27. 46.

and remained in the state of the
dead; yet saw no [26] *corruption*:
on the [1] third day he arose from
the dead, with the same [2] body in
which he suffered; with which he
also [3] ascended into heaven:
and there sitteth at the right hand
of *his Father*,[4] making intercession; and shall [5] return to judge
Men and *Angels,* at the end of the World.

5. The *Lord Jesus* by his perfect obedience and sacrifice of himself, which he through the Eternal *Spirit* once offered up unto
God,[6] hath fully satisfied the
Justice of *God,* procured reconciliation, and purchased an Everlast- [page]
ing inheritance in the Kingdom of
Heaven,[7] for all those whom
the *Father* hath given unto him.

6. Although the price of Redemption was not actually paid by
Christ, till after his *Incarnation*,*
yet the vertue, efficacy, and benefit
thereof were communicated to the
Elect in all ages successively, from
the beginning of the World, in
and by those Promises, Types, and
Sacrifices, wherein he was revealed, and signified to be the Seed of
the *Woman,* which should bruise
the Serpents head; [8] and the
Lamb slain from the foundation of
the World: [9] Being *the same
yesterday, and to-day, and for ever.*

7. Christ in the work of *Mediation* acteth according to both natures, by each nature doing that
which is proper to it self; yet by
reason of the Unity of the Person,
that which is proper to one na- [page]
ture, is sometimes in *Scripture* attributed to the Person [11] denominated by the other nature.

8. To all those for whom Christ
hath obtained eternal redemption, he doth certainly, and effectually [12] apply, and communicate the same; making intercession for them, uniting them to himself by his spirit,[13] revealing

Q

[26] Act. 13.
37.
[1] 1 Cor. 15. 3, 4.
[2] Joh. 20.
25, 27.
[3] Mark 16.
19.
Act. 1. 9,
10, 11.
[4] Rom. 8.
34.
Heb. 9. 24.
[5] Act. 10.
42. Rom.
14. 9, 10.
Act. 1. 10.

[6] Heb. 9.
14. Ch. 10.
14. Rom.
3. 25, 26.

[7] Joh. 17.
2. Heb. 9.
15.

* 1 Cor. 4.
10.
Heb. 4. 2.
1 Pet. 1.
10, 11.

[8] Rev. 13.
8.
[9] Heb. 13.
8.

[11] Joh. 3.
13.
Act. 20.
28.
[12] Joh. 6.
37. ch. 10.
15, 16.
& ch. 17.
9.
[13] Joh. 17.
6. Eph. 1.
9. 1 Joh.
5. 20.

[14] Rom. 8.
9, 14.

[15] Ps. 110.
1. 1 Cor.
15. 25, 26.

unto them, in and by the word, the mystery of salvation; perswading them to believe, and obey;[14] governing their hearts by his word and spirit, and[15] overcoming all their enemies by his Almighty power, and wisdom; in such manner, and wayes as are most consonant to his wonderful,

[16] Joh. 3. 8.
Eph. 1. 8.

and[16] unsearchable dispensation; and all of free, and absolute Grace, without any condition foreseen in them, to procure it. [page]

[17] 1 Tim.
2. 5.

9. This office of Mediator between God and man, is proper[17] onely to Christ, who is the Prophet, Priest, and King of the Church of God; and may not be either in whole, or any part thereof transfer'ed from him to any other.

[18] Joh. 1.
18.

10. This number and order of Offices is necessary; for in respect of our[18] ignorance, we stand in need of his prophetical Office; and in respect of our alie-

[19] Col. 1.
21.
Gal. 5. 17.

nation from God,[19] and imperfection of the best of our services, we need his Priestly office, to reconcile us, and present us acceptable unto God: and in respect of our averseness, and utter inability to return to God, and for our rescue, and security from our spiritual adversaries, we need his Kingly

[20] Joh. 16.
8. Ps. 110.
3. Luk. 1.
74, 75.

office,[20] to convince, subdue, draw, uphold, deliver, and preserve us to his Heavenly Kingdome.

CHAP. IX.

Of Free Will.

1. GOD hath indued the Will of Man, with that natural liberty, and power of acting upon choice; that it is[1] neither

[1] Mat. 17.
12. Jam. 1.
14. Deut.
30. 19.

forced, nor by any necessity of nature determined to do good or evil.

2. Man in his state of innocency, had freedom, and power, to

will, and to do that [2] which was
good, and well-pleasing to God;
but yet [3] was mutable, so that he
might fall from it.

3. Man by his fall into a state
of sin hath wholly lost [4] all ability of Will, to any spiritual good
accompanying salvation; so as a [page]
natural man, being altogether a-
verse from that good, [5] and dead
in *Sin,* is not able, by his own
strength, to [6] convert himself;
or to prepare himself thereunto.

4. When God converts a sinner, and translates him into the
state of Grace, [7] he freeth him
from his natural bondage under
sin, and by his grace alone, ena-
bles him [8] freely to will, and to
do that which is spiritually good;
yet so as that by reason of his [9]
remaining corruptions he doth not
perfectly nor only will that which
is good; but doth also will that
which is evil.

5. The Will of Man is made [11]
perfectly, and immutably free
to good alone, in the state of Glory only. [page]

[2] Eccl. 7. 29.

[3] Gen. 3. 6.

[4] Rom. 5. 6. ch. 8. 7.

[5] Eph. 2. 1, 5.

[6] Tit. 3. 3, 4, 5. Joh. 6. 44.

[7] Col. 1. 13. Joh. 8. 36.

[8] Phil. 2. 13.

[9] Rom. 7. 15, 18, 19, 21, 23.

[11] Eph. 4. 13.

CHAP. X.

Of Effectual Calling.

1. THose whom God hath predestinated unto Life, he is
pleased, in his appointed, and accepted time, [1] effectually to call
by his word, and Spirit, out of that
state of sin, and death, in which
they are by nature, to grace and
Salvation [2] by Jesus Christ; in-
lightning their minds, spiritually,
and savingly to [3] understand the
things of God; taking away their [4]
heart of stone, and giving unto them an heart of flesh; renewing their wills, and by his Almighty power determining them [5] to
that which is good, and effectually drawing them to Jesus Christ;
yet so as they come [6] most free- [page]

[1] Rom. 8. 30. Rom. 11. 7. Eph. 1. 10, 11. 2 Thes. 3. 13, 14.

[2] Eph. 2. 1-6.

[3] Act. 26. 18. Eph. 1. 17, 18.

[4] Ezek. 36. 26.

[5] Deut. 30. 6. Ezek. 36. 27, Eph. 1. 19.

[6] Ps. 110. 3. Cant. 1. 4.

ly, being made willing by his Grace.

2. This Effectual Call is of God's free, and special grace alone[7] not from anything at all foreseen in man, nor from any power, or agency in the Creature, coworking with his special Grace,[8] the Creature being wholly passive therein, being dead in sins and trespasses, until being quickened & renewed by the holy Spirit, he is thereby enabled to answer this call, and to embrace the Grace offered and conveyed in it; and that by no less[9] power, then that which raised up Christ from the dead.

3. Elect Infants dying in infancy, are[11] regenerated and saved by Christ through the Spirit; who worketh when, and where, and[12] how he pleaseth: so also are [page] all other elect persons, who are uncapable of being outwardly called by the Ministry of the Word.

4. Others not elected, although they may be called by the Ministry of the word,[13] and may have some common operations of the Spirit, yet not being effectually drawn by the Father, they neither will nor can truly[14] come to Christ; and therefore cannot be saved: much less can men that receive not the Christian Religion[15] be saved; be they never so diligent to frame their lives according to the light of nature, and the Law of that Religion they do profess. [page]

Chap. XI.

Of Justification.

1. THose whom God Effectually calleth, he also freely[1] justifieth, not by infusing Righteousness into them, but by[2] pardoning their sins, and by accounting, and accepting their

[7] 2 Tim. 1. 9. Eph. 2. 8.

[8] 1 Cor. 2. 14. Eph. 2. 5. Joh. 5. 25.

[9] Eph. 1. 19, 20.

[11] Joh. 3. 3, 5, 6.
[12] Joh. 3. 8.

[13] Mat. 22. 14. ch. 13. 20, 21. Heb. 6. 4, 5.
[14] Joh. 6. 44, 45, 65. 1 Joh. 2. 24, 25.

[15] Act. 4. 12. Joh. 4. 22. ch. 17. 3.

[1] Rom. 3, 24. ch. 8. 30.
[2] Rom. 4, 5, 6, 7, 8. Eph. 1. 7.

Persons as [3] Righteous; not for
any thing wrought in them, or
done by them, but for Christ's
sake alone, not by imputing faith
it self, the act of believing, or any
other [4] evangelical obedience
to them, as their Righteousness;
but by imputing Christs active obedience unto the whole Law, and
passive obedience in his death, for
their whole and sole Righteousness, they [5] receiving, and resting on him, and his Righteousness, [page]
by Faith; which faith they have
not of themselves, it is the gift of
God.

2. Faith thus receiving and
resting on Christ, and his Righteousness, is the [6] alone instrument
of Justification: yet it is not alone
in the person justified, but is ever
accompanied with all other saving
Graces, and is no dead faith,[7]
but worketh by love.

3. Christ by his obedience, and
death, did fully discharge the debt
of all those that are justified; and
did by the sacrifice of himself, in
the blood of his cross, undergoing
in their stead, the penalty due unto them: make a proper, real, and
full satisfaction [8] to *Gods* justice
in their behalf: yet in asmuch as
he was given by the Father for
them, and his Obedience and Satisfaction accepted in their stead,
and both [9] freely, not for any- [page]
thing in them; their Justification
is only of Free Grace, that both
the exact justice and rich Grace of
God, might be [11] glorified in the
Justification of sinners.

4. God did from all eternity decree to [12] justifie all the Elect, and
Christ did in the fulness of time
die for their sins, and rise [13] a-
gain for their Justification; Nevertheless they are not justified personally, untill the *Holy Spirit,*
doth in due time [14] actually apply
Christ unto them.

[3] 1 Cor. 1.
30, 31.
Rom. 5. 17,
18, 19.

[4] Phil. 3.
8, 9.
Eph. 2. 8,
9, 10.

[5] Joh. 1.
12.
Rom. 5.
17.

[6] Rom. 3.
28.

[7] Gal. 5. 6.
Jam. 2. 17,
22, 26.

[8] Heb. 10.
14. 1 Pet.
1. 18, 19.
Isa. 53. 5,
6.

[9] Rom. 8.
32. 2 Cor.
5. 21.

[11] Rom. 3.
26. Eph. 1.
6, 7. ch. 2.
7.

[12] Gal. 3. 8.
1 Pet. 1. 2.
1 Tim. 2.
6.

[13] Rom. 4.
25.

[14] Col. 1.
21, 22.
Tit. 3. 4, 5,
6, 7.

15 Mat. 6. 12.
1 John 1. 7, 9.
16 Joh. 10. 28.
17 Ps. 89. 31, 32, 33.

5. God doth continue to [15] Forgive the sins of those that are justified, and although they can never fall from the state of [16] justification; yet they may by their sins fall under Gods [17] Fatherly displeasure; and in that condition, they have not usually the light of his Countenance restored

18 Psal. 32. 5. & 51.
Mat. 26. 75.

unto them, until they [18] hum- [page] ble themselves, confess their sins, beg pardon, and renew their faith, and repentance.

19 Gal. 3. 9.
Rom. 4. 22, 23, 24.

6. The Justification of Believers under the Old Testament was in all these respects,[19] one and the same with the justification of Believers under the New Testament.

CHAP. XII.
Of Adoption.

1 Eph. 1. 5. Gal. 4. 4, 5.
2 Joh. 1. 12. Rom. 8. 17.
3 2 Cor. 6. 18. Rev. 3. 12.
4 Rom. 8. 15.
5 Gal. 4. 6. Eph. 2. 18.
6 Ps. 103. 13.
7 Prov. 14. 26.
9 1 Pet. 5. 7.
11 Heb. 12. 6.
12 Is. 54. 8, 9. Lam. 3. 31.
13 Eph. 4. 30.
14 Heb. 1. 14. ch. 6. 12.

ALL those that are justified, *God* vouchsafed, in, and for the sake of his only *Son Jesus Christ,* to make partakers of the Grace [1] of *Adoption;* by which they are taken into the number, and enjoy the Liberties, and [2] Privileges of Children of *God;* have his [3] name put upon them,[4] receive [page] the *Spirit of Adoption,*[5] have access to the throne of Grace with boldness, are enabled to cry *Abba Father,* are [6] pitied,[7] protected,[9] provided for, and [11] chastned by him, as by a *Father;* yet never [12] cast off; but sealed [13] to the day of Redemption, and inherit the promises,[14] as heirs, of everlasting Salvation.

CHAP. XIII.
Of Sanctification.

1 Act. 20. 32.
Rom. 6. 5, 6.

1. THey who are united to *Christ,* Effectually called, and regenerated, having a new heart, and a new *Spirit created* in them, through the vertue of *Christ's* death, and Resurrection; are also [1] farther sanctified, real-

ly, and personally, through the
same vertue,[2] by his word and [page]
Spirit dwelling in them; [3] the
dominion of the whole body of
sin is destroyed,[4] and the several lusts thereof, are more and
more weakened, and mortified; and
they more and more quickened,
and [5] strengthened in all saving
graces, to the [6] practice of all
true holyness, without which no
man shall see the Lord.

2. This Sanctification is [7]
throughout, in the whole man,
yet imperfect [8] in this life; there
abideth still some remnants of *corruption* in every part, whence a-
riseth a [9] continual, and irre-
concilable war; the Flesh lusting
against the Spirit, and the Spirit
against the Flesh.

3. In which war, although the
remaining *corruption* for a time may
much [11] prevail; yet through
the continual supply of strength
from the sanctifying *Spirit* of *Christ* [page]
the [12] regenerate part doth over-
come; and so the Saints grow in
Grace, perfecting holiness in the
fear of God,[13] pressing after an
heavenly life, in Evangelical Obedience to all the commands which
Christ as *Head* and *King,* in his
Word hath prescribed to them.

CHAP. XIV.
Of Saving Faith.

1. THE Grace of *Faith,* whereby the Elect are enabled to
believe to the saving of their souls,
is the work of the *Spirit* of *Christ* [1]
in their hearts; and is ordina-
rily wrought by the Ministry of
the [2] Word; by which also,
and by the administration of *Baptisme,* and the *Lords Supper, Prayer* [page]
and other *Means* appointed of
God, it is increased,[3] and strengthened.

2. By this *Faith* a Christian believeth to be true,* whatsoever is

[2] Joh. 17.
17. Eph.
3. 16, 17,
18, 19.
1 Thes. 5.
21, 22, 23.
[3] Rom. 6.
14.
[4] Gal. 5.
24.
[5] Col. 1. 11.
[6] 2 Cor. 7.
1.
Heb. 12.
14.
[7] 1 Thes.
5. 23.
[8] Rom. 7.
18, 23.
[9] Gal. 5.
17.
1 Pet. 2.
11.

[11] Rom. 7.
23.

[12] Rom. 6.
14.

[13] Eph. 4.
15, 16.
2 Cor. 3.
18. ch. 7. 1.

[1] 2 Cor.
4. 13.
Eph. 2. 8.

[2] Rom. 10.
14, 17.

[3] Luk. 17.
5.
1 Pet. 2. 2.
Act. 20.
32.
* Act. 24.
14.

⁴ Ps. 19.
7, 8, 9, 10.
Ps. 119. 72.

revealed in the *Word,* for the Authority of *God* himself; and also apprehendeth an excellency therein,⁴ above all other *Writings;* and all things in the *world:* as it bears forth the glory of *God* in his *Attributes,* the excellency of *Christ* in his Nature and Offices; and the Power and Fullness of the *Holy Spirit* in his Workings, and Operations; and so is enabled

⁵ 2 Tim.
1. 12.

to ⁵ cast his Soul upon the truth thus believed; and also acteth differently, upon that which each particular, passage thereof containeth; yielding obedience to

⁶ Joh. 15.
14.
⁷ Is. 66. 2.
⁸ Heb. 11.
13.

the ⁶ commands, trembling at the ⁷ threatenings, and embracing the ⁸ promises of *God,* for this life, and that which is to come: [page] But the principal acts of Saving Faith, have immediate relation to *Christ,* accepting, receiving, and

⁹ Joh. 1.
12. Act. 16.
31. Gal. 2.
20. Act.
15. 11.

resting upon ⁹ him alone, for Justification, Sanctification, and Eternal Life, by vertue of the Covenant of Grace.

3. This *Faith* although it be different in degrees, and may be

¹¹ Heb. 5.
13, 14.
Matt. 6. 30.
Rom. 4. 19,
20.
¹² 2 Pet. 1.
1.
¹³ Eph. 6.
16.
1 Joh. 5.
4, 5.
¹⁴ Heb. 6.
11, 12.
Col. 2. 2.
¹⁵ Heb. 12.
2.

weak,¹¹ or strong; yet it is in the least degree of it, different in the kind, or nature of it (as is all other saving Grace) from the Faith,¹² and common grace of temporary believers; and therefore though it may be many times assailed, and weakened; yet it gets ¹³ the victory; growing up in many, to the attainment of a full ¹⁴ assurance through *Christ,* who is both the Author ¹⁵ and finisher of our *Faith.* [page]

CHAP. XV.

Of Repentence unto
Life and Salvation.

¹ Tit. 3. 2,
3, 4, 5.

1. SUch of the Elect as are converted at riper years, having ¹ sometimes lived in the state of nature, and therein served divers lusts and pleasures, *God* in their

Effectual Calling giveth them Repentence unto Life.

2. Whereas there is none that
doth good, and sinneth[2] not;
and the best of men may, through
the power, and deceitfulness of
their corruption dwelling in
them, with the prevalency of
temptation, fall into great sins,
and provocations; God hath in
the Covenant of Grace, merciful- [page]
ly provided that Believers so sinning, and falling,[3] be renewed
through Repentance unto Salvation.

3. This saving Repentance is
an[4] evangelical Grace, whereby a person, being by the *Holy Spirit* made sensible of the manifold
evils of his sin, doth, by Faith in
Christ, humble himself for it, with
godly sorrow, detestation of it,
and self-abhorrency;[6] praying
for pardon, and strength of grace,
with a purpose and endeavour by
supplies of the *Spirit,* to[6] walk
before God unto all well pleasing
in all things.

4. As Repentance is to be continued through the whole course
of our lives, upon the account of
the body of death, and the motions thereof; so it is every mans
duty, to repent of his[7] particular known sins, particularly. [page]

5. Such is the provision which
God hath made through Christ in
the Covenant of Grace, for the
preservation of Believers unto
Salvation, that although there is
no sin so small, but it deserves[8]
damnation; yet there is no sin so
great, that it shall bring damnation on them that[9] repent;
which makes the constant preaching of Repentance necessary.

CHAP. XVI.
Of Good Works.

1. GOod Works are only such as
God hath[1] commanded

[2] Eccl. 7. 20.

[3] Luk. 22. 31, 32.

[4] Zech. 12. 10. Act. 11. 18.

[5] Ezek. 36. 31. 2 Cor. 7. 11.
[6] Ps. 119. 6. Ps. 119. 128.

[7] Luk 19. 8. 1 Tim. 1. 13, 15.

[8] Rom. 6. 23.

[9] Is. 1. 16, 18. Is. 55. 7.

[1] Mic. 6. 8. Heb. 13. 21.

in his Holy word; and not such as without the warrant thereof, are

[2] Mat. 15. 9. Isa. 29. 13.

devised by men, out of blind zeal,[2] or upon any pretence of good intentions. [page]

2. These good works, done in obedience to Gods commandments, are the fruits, and evidences[3] of a true, and lively faith; and by them Believers manifest their[4] thankfullness, strengthen their[5] assurance, edifie their[6] brethren, adorn the profession of the Gospel, stop the mouths of the adversaries, and glorifie[7] God, whose workmanship they are, created in Christ Jesus[8] thereunto, that having their fruit unto holiness, they may have the end[9] eternal life.

[3] Jam. 2. 18, 22.
[4] Ps. 116. 12, 13.
[5] 1 Joh. 2. 3, 5. 2 Pet. 1. 5-11.
[6] Mat. 5. 16.
[7] 1 Tim. 6. 1. 1 Pet. 2. 15. Phil. 1. 11.
[8] Eph. 2. 10.
[9] Rom. 6. 22.

3. Their ability to do good works, is not at all of themselves; but wholly from the *Spirit*[11] of Christ; and that they may be enabled thereunto, besides the graces they have already received, there is necessary an[12] actual influence of the same *Holy Spirit,* to work in them to will, and to do, of his good pleasure; yet are they not [page] hereupon to grow negligent, as if they were not bound to perform any duty, unless upon a special motion of the Spirit; but they ought to be diligent in[13] stirring up the Grace of God that is in them.

[11] Joh. 15. 4, 6.

[12] 2 Cor. 3. 5. Phil. 2. 13.

[13] Phil. 2. 12. Heb. 6. 11, 12. Isa. 64. 7.

4. They who in their obedience attain to the greatest height which is possible in this life, are so far from being able to superrogate, and to do more than God requires, as that[14] they fall short of much which in duty they are bound to do.

[14] Job 9. 2, 3. Gal. 5. 17. Luk. 17. 10.

5. We cannot by our best works merit pardon of Sin or Eternal Life at the hand of God, by reason of the great disproportion that is between them and the glory to come; and the infinite di-

stance that is between us and God,
whom by them we can neither
profit, nor satisfie for the debt of
our [15] former sins; but when we [page]
have done all we can, we have
done but our duty, and are unprofitable servants; and because
as they are good they proceed
from his [16] Spirit, and as they
are wrought by us they are defiled [17] and mixed with so much
weakness and imperfection that
they cannot endure the severity of
Gods judgment.

6. Yet notwithstanding the
persons of Believers being accepted through Christ their good
works also are accepted in [18]
him; not as though they were in
this life wholly unblameable and
unreprovable in Gods sight; but
that he looking upon them in his
Son is pleased to accept and reward that which is [19] sincere although accomplished with many
weaknesses and imperfections.

7. Works done by unregene-
rate men, although for the matter [page]
of them they may be things which
God commands, and of good use,
both to themselves and [20] others;
yet because they proceed not from
a heart purified by [21] faith, nor
are done in a right manner according to the [23] word, nor to a
right end the [24] glory of God; they
are therefore sinful and cannot please God; nor make a man
meet to receive grace from [25]
God; and yet their neglect of
them is more sinful and [26] displeasing to God. [page]

[15] Rom. 3.
20. Eph.
2. 8, 9.
Rom. 4. 6.

[16] Gal. 5.
22, 23.

[17] Isa. 64.
6. Ps. 143.
2.

[18] Eph. 1.
6. 1 Pet.
2. 5.

[19] Mat. 25.
21, 23.
Heb. 6. 10.

[20] 2 King.
10. 30.
1 King.
21. 27, 29.
[21] Gen. 4.
5. Heb. 11.
4, 6.
[23] 1 Cor.
13. 1.
[24] Mat. 6.
2, 5.
[25] Amos 5.
21, 22.
Rom. 9. 16.
Tit. 3. 5.
[26] Job 21.
14, 15.
Mat. 25.
41, 42, 43.

CHAP. XVII.
Of Perseverence of the Saints.

1. THose whom God hath accepted in the beloved, effectually called and Sanctified by
his *Spirit,* and given the precious
faith of his Elect unto, can neither

totally nor finally fall from the
state of grace;[1] but shall certainly persevere therein to the
end and be eternally saved, seeing the gifts and callings of God
are without Repentance, (whence
he still begets and nourisheth in
them Faith, Repentance, Love,
Joy, Hope, and all the graces of the
Spirit unto immortality) and
though many storms and floods
arise and beat against them, yet
they shall never be able to take
them off that foundation and rock [page]
which by faith they are fastned
upon: notwithstanding through
unbelief and the temptations of
Satan the sensible sight of the light
and love of God, may for a time
be clouded, and obscured from[2]
them, yet he is still the same,[3]
and they shall be sure to be
kept by the power of God unto
Salvation, where they shall enjoy
their purchased possession, they
being engraven upon the palms of
his hands, and their names having
been written in the book of life
from all Eternity.

2. This perseverance of the
Saints depends not upon their own
free will; but upon the immutability of the decree of[4] Election, flowing from the free and unchangeable love of God the Father; upon the efficacy of the merit and intercession of Jesus Christ[5]
and Union with him, the[6]
oath of God, the abiding of his [page]
Spirit & the[7] seed of God within them, and the nature of the[8]
Covenant of Grace from all which
ariseth also the certainty and infallibility thereof.

3. And though they may,
through the temptation of Satan
and of the world, the prevalency
of corruption remaining in them,
and the neglect of the means of their
preservation fall into grievous[9]
sins, and for a time continue there-

[1] Joh. 10.
28, 29.
Phil. 1. 6.
2 Tim. 2.
19. 1 Joh.
2. 19.

[2] Psal. 89.
31, 32.
1 Cor. 11.
32.
[3] Mal. 3. 6.

[4] Rom. 8.
30. ch. 9.
11, 16.
[5] Rom. 5.
9, 10.
John 14.
19.
[6] Heb. 6.
17, 18.
[7] 1 Joh. 3.
9.
[8] Jer. 32.
40.

[9] Mat. 26.
70, 72, 74.

in; whereby they incur [11] Gods
displeasure, and grieve his holy
Spirit, come to have their graces
and [12] comforts impaired have
their hearts hardened, and their
Consciences wounded, [13] hurt,
and scandalize others, and bring
temporal judgements [14] upon
themselves: yet they shall renew
their [15] repentance and be preserved through faith in Christ Jesus to the end. [page]

CHAP. XVIII.
Of the Assurance of Grace and Salvati-on.

1. ALthough temporary Believers, and other unregenerate
men, may vainly deceive themselves with false hopes, and carnal
presumptions, of being in the favour of God, and in a state of salvation,[1] which hope of theirs shall
perish; yet such as truly believe
in the Lord Jesus, and love him
in sincerity, endeavouring to walk
in all good Conscience before him,
may in this life be certainly assured [2] that they are in the state
of Grace; and may rejoice in the
hope of the glory of God which [page]
hope shall never make them [3]
ashamed.

2. This certainty is not a bare
conjectural and probable perswasion, grounded upon [4] a fallible
hope; but an infallible assurance
of faith, founded on the Blood and
Righteousness of Christ [5] revealed in the Gospel; and also
upon the inward [6] evidence of
those graces of the Spirit unto
which promises are made, and on
the testimony of the [7] Spirit of
adoption, witnessing with our Spirits that we are the children of
God; and as a fruit thereof keeping the heart both [11] humble and
holy.

3. This infallible assurance doth

[11] Is. 64. 5. 9.
Eph. 4. 30.

[12] Psal. 51. 10, 12.

[13] Psa. 32. 3, 4.

[14] 2 Sam. 12. 14.

[15] Luk. 22. 32 & 5. 61, 62.

[1] Job 8. 13, 14.
Mat. 7. 22, 23.

[2] 1 Joh. 2. 3. ch. 3. 14, 18, 19, 21, 24. ch. 5. 13.
[3] Rom. 5. 2, 5.

[4] Heb. 6. 11, 19.

[5] Heb. 6. 17, 18.
[6] 2 Pet. 1. 4, 5, 10, 11.

[7] Rom. 8. 15, 16.

[8] 1 Joh. 3. 1, 2, 3.

not so belong to the essence of faith, but that a true Believer, may wait long and conflict with many difficulties before he be [9] partaker of it; yet being enabled by the Spirit to know the things [page] which are freely given him of God, he may without extraordinary revelation in the right use of means [11] attain thereunto: and therefore it is the duty of every one, to give all diligence to make their Calling and Election sure, that thereby his heart may be enlarged in peace and joy in the holy Spirit, in love and thankfulness to God, and in strength and chearfulness in the duties of obedience, the proper [12] fruits of this Assurance; so far is it [13] from inclining men to looseness.

4. True Believers may have the assurance of their Salvation divers ways shaken, diminished, and intermitted; as [14] by negligence in preserving of it, by [15] falling into some special Sin, which woundeth the Conscience, and grieveth the *Spirit*, by some sudden or [16] vehement temptation, by Gods withdrawing the [17] light of his coun- [page] tenance and suffering even such as fear him to walk in darkness and to have no light; yet are they never destitute of the [18] seed of God, and Life [19] of Faith, that Love of Christ, and the brethren, that sincerity of Heart, and Conscience of duty, out of which by the operation of the Spirit, this Assurance may in due time be [20] revived: and by the which in the mean time they are [21] preserved from utter despair.

[9] Isa. 50. 10. Ps. 88. & Ps. 77. 1-12.

[11] 1 Joh. 4. 13. Heb. 6. 11, 12.

[12] Rom. 5. 1, 2, 5. ch. 14. 17. Ps. 119. 32.

[13] Rom. 6. 1, 2. Tit. 2. 11, 12, 14.

[14] Cant. 5. 2, 3, 6.

[15] Ps. 51. 8, 12, 14.

[16] Psa. 116. 11. Ps. 77. 7, 8. Ps. 31. 22.

[17] Ps. 30. 7.

[18] 1 Joh. 3. 9.

[19] Luk. 22. 32.

[20] Ps. 42. 5, 11.

[21] Lam. 3. 26. 27-31.

CHAP. XIX.
Of the Law of God.

[1] Gen. 1. Eccl. 7. 29.

1. GOd gave to *Adam* a Law of universal obedience,[1] written in his Heart, and a particular precept of not eating the

Fruit of the tree of knowledge of [page]
good and evil; by which he
bound him, and all his posterity to
personal entire exact and perpetual [2] obedience; promised life
upon the filfilling, and [3] threatened death upon the breach of it,
and indued him with power and
ability to keep it.

2. The same Law that was first
written in the heart of man, [4]
continued to be a perfect rule of
Righteousness after the fall; & was
delivered by God upon Mount *Sinai,* in [5] Ten Commandments and
written in two Tables; the four
first containing our duty towards
God, and the other six our duty
to man.

3. Besides this law commonly
called moral, God was pleased to
give to the people *Israel* Ceremonial Laws, containing several
typical ordinances, partly of worship, [6] prefiguring Christ, his [page]
graces, actions, sufferings, and benefits; and partly holding forth
divers instructions [7] of moral
duties, all which Ceremonial Laws
being appointed only to the time
of reformation, are by Jesus Christ
the true *Messiah* and only Law-
giver, who was furnished with power from the Father, for that end, [8]
abrogate and taken away.

4. To them also he gave sundry
judicial Laws, which expired together with the state of that people, not obliging and now by vertue of that institution; their general [9] equity onely, being of
moral use.

5. The moral Law doth for e-
ver bind all, [11] as well justified
persons as others, to the obedience thereof, and that not only in
regard of the matter contained in
it, but also in respect of the [12]
authority of God the Creator, [page]
who gave it: Neither doth *Christ*
in the Gospel any way dissolve, [13]

[2] Rom. 10.
5.
[3] Gal. 3.
10, 12.

[4] Rom. 2.
14, 15.

[5] Deut. 10.
4.

[6] Heb. 10.
1. Col. 2.
17.

[7] 1 Cor. 5.
7.

[8] Col. 2.
14, 16, 17.
Eph. 2.
14, 16.

[9] 1 Cor. 9.
8, 9, 10.

[11] Rom. 13.
8, 9, 10.
Jam. 2. 8,
10, 11, 12.

[12] Jam. 2.
10, 11.
[13] Mat. 5.
17, 18, 19,
Rom. 3.
31.

but much strengthen this obligation.

[14] Rom. 6.
14.
Gal. 2. 16.
Rom. 8. 1.
cha. 10. 4.

6. Although true *Believers* be not under the Law, as a Covenant of *Works*,[14] to be thereby Justified or condemned; yet it is of great use to them as well as to others: in that, as a Rule of *Life,* informing them of the Will of *God,* and their Duty, it directs and binds them, to walk accordingly[15] discovering also the

[15] Rom. 3.
20.
chap. 7. 7,
etc.

sinfull pollutions of their Natures, Hearts and Lives; so as Examining themselves thereby, they may come to further Conviction of, Humiliation for, and Hatred against Sin; together with a clearer sight of the need they have of *Christ* and the perfection of his Obedience: It is likewise of use to the Regenerate to restrain their Corruptions, in that it for- [page] bids Sin; and the Threatnings of it serve to shew what even their Sins deserve; and what afflictions in this Life they may expect for them, although free'd from the Curse and unallayed Rigor thereof. The Promises of it likewise shew them Gods approbation of Obedience, and what blessings they may expect upon the performance thereof, though not as due to them by the Law as a Covenant of Works; so as mans doing Good and refraining from Evil, because the Law incourageth to the one and deterreth from the o-

[16] Rom. 6.
12, 13, 14.
1 Pet. 3. 8
-13.

ther, is no Evidence of his being[16] under the Law and not under Grace.

[17] Gal. 3.
21.

7. Neither are the forementioned uses of the Law[17] contrary to the Grace of the Gospel; but do sweetly comply with it; the *Spirit* of *Christ* subduing[18] and

[18] Eze. 36.
27.

inabling the Will of man, to do [page] that freely and chearfully, which the will of God revealed in the Law, requireth to be done.

CHAP. 20.

Of the Gospel, and of the extent of the Grace thereof.

1. THE Covenant of Works being broken by Sin, and made unprofitable unto Life; God was pleased to give forth the promise of *Christ*,[1] the Seed of the Woman, as the means of calling the Elect, and begetting in them Faith and Repentance; in this Promise, the [2] Gospel, as to the substance of it, was revealed, and therein Effectual, for the Conversion and Salvation of Sinners. [page]

2. This Promise of *Christ,* and Salvation by him, is revealed only by [3] the Word of God; neither do the Works of Creation, or Providence, with the light of Nature,[4] make discovery of *Christ,* or of *Grace* by him; so much as in a general, or obscure way; much less that men destitute of the Revelation of him by the Promise, or Gospel; [5] should be enabled thereby, to attain saving Faith, or Repentance.

3. The Revelation of the Gospel unto Sinners, made in divers times, and by sundry parts; with the addition of Promises, and Precepts for the Obedience required therein, as to the Nations, and Persons, to whom it is granted, is meerly of the [6] Soveraign Will and good Pleasure of God; not being annexed by vertue of any Promise, to the due improvement of mens natural abilities, by vertue of Common light received with- [page] out it; which none ever did [7] make, or can so do: And therefore in all Ages the preaching of the Gospel hath been granted unto persons and Nations, as to the extent, or streightning of it, in great variety, according to the Councell of the Will of God.

4. Although the Gospel be the

[1] Gen. 3. 15.

[2] Rev. 13. 8.

[3] Rom. 1. 17.

[4] Ro. 10. 14, 15, 17.

[5] Pro. 29. 18. Isa. 25. 7, with ch. 60. 2, 3.

[6] Ps. 147. 20. Act. 16. 7.

[7] Rom. 1. 18 etc.

R

only outward means, of revealing
Christ, and saving Grace; and is,
as such, abundantly sufficient thereunto; yet that men who are dead
in Trespasses, may be born again,
Quickened or Regenerated; there
is morover necessary, an effectual, insuperable [8] work of the Holy
Spirit, upon the whole Soul, for
the producing in them a new spiritual Life; without which no o-
ther means will effect [9] their Conversion unto God. [page]

[8] Ps. 110.
3.
1 Cor. 2.
14.
Eph. 1. 19,
20.
[9] Joh. 6.
44.
2 Cor. 4.
4, 6.

CHAP. XXI.
Of Christian Liberty and Liberty of Conscience.

1. THE Liberty which *Christ* hath
purchased for Believers under the Gospel, consists in their
freedom from the guilt of Sin, the
condemning wrath of God, the
Rigour and [1] Curse of the Law;
and in their being delivered from
this present evil [2] World, bondage to [3] Satan, and Dominion [4]
of Sin; from the [5] Evil of
Afflictions; the Fear, and Sting [6]
of Death, the Victory of the
Grave, and [7] Everlasting Damnation; as also in their [8] free access to God; and their yielding
Obedience unto 'im not out of a
slavish fear,[9] but a Child-like [page]
love, and willing mind.

[1] Gal. 3.
13.
[2] Gal. 1. 4.
[3] Act. 26.
18.
[4] Rom. 8.
3.
[5] Rom. 8.
28.
[6] 1 Cor.
15. 54, 55,
56, 57.
[7] 2 Thes.
1. 10.
[8] Rom. 8.
15.
[9] Luk. 1.
74, 75.
1 Joh. 4.
18.
[11] Gal. 3.
9, 14.

All which were common also to
Believers under the Law [11] for
the substance of them; but under
the new Testament, the Liberty
of Christians is further enlarged
in their freedom from the yoke
of the Ceremonial Law, to which
the *Jewish* Church was subjected;
and in greater boldness of access
to the Throne of Grace; and in
fuller Communications of the [12]
Free *Spirit* of God, then Believers under the Law did ordinarily
partake of.

[12] Joh. 7.
38, 39.
Heb. 10.
19, 20, 21.

2. God alone is [13] Lord of the

[13] Jam. 4.
12.
Rom. 14.
4.

Conscience, and hath left it free
from the Doctrines and Commandments of men [14] which are in
any thing contrary to his Word, or
not contained in it. So that to
Believe such Doctrines, or obey
such Commands out of Consci-
ence,[15] is to betray true liberty [page]
of Conscience; and the requiring of
an [16] implicit Faith, and absolute
and blind Obedience, is to destroy
Liberty of Conscience, and Reason also.

3. They who upon pretence of
Christian Liberty do practice any
sin, or cherish any sinfull lust; as
they do thereby pervert the main
design of the Grace of the Gospel [17]
to their own Destruction; so
they wholly destroy [18] the end
of *Christian* Liberty, which is,
that being delivered out of the
hands of all our Enemies we might
serve the Lord without fear in
Holiness, and Righteousness before him, all the days of our Life. [page]

[14] Act. 4. 19.
& 5. 29.
1 Cor. 7.
23.
Mat. 15. 9.

[15] Col. 2. 20,
22, 23.

[16] 1 Cor. 3.
5.
2 Cor. 1.
24.

[17] Rom. 6.
1, 2.

[18] Gal. 5.
13.
2 Pet. 2.
18-21.

CHAP. XXII.
Of Religious Wor-
ship, and the Sabbath
Day.

1. THE light of Nature shews
that there is a God, who
hath Lordship, and Soveraigntye
over all; is just, good, and doth
good unto all; and is therefore
to be feared, loved, praised, called upon, trusted in, and served,
with all the Heart, and all the
Soul,[1] and with all the Might.
But the acceptable way of Worshipping the the true God, is [2] instituted by himself; and so limited by his own revealed will, that
he may not be worshipped according to the imaginations, and [page]
devices of Men, or the suggestions
of Satan, under any visible representations, or [3] any other way,
not prescribed in the Holy Scriptures.

2. *Religious Worship* is to be gi-

[1] Jer. 10.
7. Mar.
12. 33.
[2] Deut. 12.
32.

[3] Exo. 20.
4, 5, 6.

⁴ Mat. 4.
9, 10.
Joh. 6. 23.
Mat. 28.
19.
⁵ Rom. 1.
25.
Col. 2. 18.
Revel. 19.
10.
⁶ Joh. 14.
6.
⁷ 1 Tim. 2. 5.
⁸ Psal. 95.
1-7.
Psal. 65. 2.
⁹ Joh. 14.
13, 14.
¹¹ Rom. 8.
26.
¹² 1 Joh. 5.
14.
¹³ 1 Cor.
14. 16, 17.
¹⁴ 1 Tim.
2. 1, 2.
2 Sam. 7.
29.
¹⁵ 2 Sam.
12. 21, 22,
23.
¹⁶ 1 Joh. 5.
16.
¹⁷ 1 Tim.
4. 13.
¹⁸ 2 Tim.
4. 2.
Luk. 8. 18.

¹⁹ Col. 3.
16.
Eph. 5. 19.
²⁰ Mat. 28.
19, 20.
²¹ 1 Cor. 11.
26.

²⁴ Esth. 4.
16.
Joel. 2. 12.
²⁵ Exo. 15.
1 etc. Ps.
107.

²⁶ Joh. 4.
21. Mal. 1.
11. 1 Tim.
2. 8.

ven to *God* the *Father, Son* and
Holy Spirit, and to him⁴ alone;
not to *Angels, Saints,* or any other⁵
Creatures; and since the fall,
not without a⁶ *Mediator,* nor
in the *Mediation* of any other but⁷
Christ alone.

3. Prayer with thanksgiving,
being one special part of natural
worship, is by *God* required of⁸
all men. But that it may be
accepted, it is to be made in the⁹
Name of the Son, by the help¹¹
of the Spirit, according to¹²
his Will; with understanding,
reverence, humility, fervency,
faith, love, and perseverance; [page]
and when with others, in a¹³ known tongue.

4. Prayer is to be made for
things lawful, and for all sorts of
men living,¹⁴ or that shall live
hereafter; but not¹⁵ for the
dead, nor for those of whom it
may be known that they have sin-
ned¹⁶ the sin unto death.

5. The¹⁷ reading of the
Scriptures, Preaching, and¹⁸
hearing the word of God, teaching and admonishing one another
in Psalms, Hymns and Spiritual
songs, singing with grace in our
Hearts to¹⁹ the Lord; as also
the Administration²⁰ of Baptism, and²¹
the Lords Supper are all
parts of Religious worship of *God,*
to be performed in obedience to
him, with understanding, faith,
reverence, and godly fear; more-
over solemn humiliation,²⁴ with [page]
fastings; and thanksgiving upon²⁵
special occasions, ought to be
used in an holy and religious manner.

6. Neither *Prayer,* nor any o-
ther part of Religious worship, is
now under the Gospel tied unto,
or made more acceptable by, any
place in which it is²⁶ performed,
or towards which it is directed;
but God is to be worshipped every where in *Spirit,* and in truth;

as in[1] private families[2] daily,
and[3] in secret each one by himself, so more solemnly in the public Assemblies, which are not
carelessly, nor willfully, to be[4]
neglected, or forsaken, when
God by his word, or providence
calleth thereunto.

7. As it is of the Law of nature,
that in general a proportion of
time by Gods appointment, be set
apart for the Worship of God; so [page]
by his Word, in a positive moral,
and perpetual commande-
ment, binding all men, in all Ages, he
hath particularly appointed one
day in seven for a[5] *Sabbath* to be
kept holy unto him, which from
the beginning of the World to
the Resurrection of Christ, was
the last day of the week; and
from the resurrection of Christ,
was changed into the first day of
the week[6] which is called the
Lords day; and is to be continued to the end of the World, as
the *Christian sabbath;* the obser-
vation of the last day of the week
being abolished.

8. The *Sabbath* is then kept
holy unto the Lord, when men after a due preparing of their hearts,
and ordering their common affairs
aforehand, do not only observe an
holy[7] rest all the day, from their
own works, words, and thoughts,
about their worldly employment, [page]
and recreations, but also are tak-
en up the whole time in the publick and private exercises of his
worship, and in the duties[8] of
necessity and mercy.

CHAP XXIII.
Of Lawful Oaths and
Vows.

1. A lawful Oath is a part of religious worship,[1] wherein
the person swearing in Truth,
Righteousness, and Judgment,
solemnly calleth God to witness
what he sweareth;[2] and to

[1] Act. 10.
2.
[2] Mat. 6.
11. Ps. 55.
17.
[3] Mat. 6. 6.
[4] Heb. 10.
25.
Act. 2. 42.

[5] Exo. 20.
8.

[6] 1 Cor.
16. 1, 2.
Act. 20. 7.
Rev. 1. 10.

[7] Isa. 58.
13.
Neh. 13.
15-23.

[8] Mat. 12.
1-13.

[1] Exo. 20.
7. Deut. 10.
20. Jer. 4.
2.

[2] 2 Cro. 6.
22, 23.

judge him according to the Truth or falseness thereof.

2. The Name of God only is [page] that by which men ought to swear; and therein it is to be used, with all Holy Fear and reverence, therefore to swear vainly or rashly by that glorious, and dreadful name; or to *swear* at all by any other thing, is sinful and to be [3] abhorred; yet as in matter of weight and moment for confirmation of truth,[4] and ending all strife, an Oath is warranted by the word of God; so a *lawful Oath* being imposed,[5] by lawful Authority, in such matters, ought to be taken.

3. Whosoever taketh an *Oath* warranted by the word of God, ought duely to consider the weightiness of so solemn an act; and therein to avouch nothing, but what he knoweth to be the truth; for that by rash, false, and vain *Oaths* the [6] Lord is provoked, and for them this Land mournes. [page]

4. An *Oath* is to be taken in the plain, and [7] common sense of the words; without equivocation, or mental reservation.

5. A Vow, which is not to be made to any *Creature,* but to God alone,[8] is to be made and performed with all Religious care, and faithfulness; but Popish *Monastical Vows,*[9] of perpetual single life, professed [11] poverty, and regular obedience, are so far from being decrees of higher perfection, that they are superstitious,[12] and sinful snares, in which no *Christian* may intangle himself.

[3] Mat. 5. 34, 37. Jam. 5. 12.
[4] Heb. 6. 16. 2 Cor. 1. 23.

[5] Neh. 13. 25.

[6] Levit. 19. 12. Jer. 23. 10.

[7] Ps. 24. 4.

[8] Psal. 76. 11. Gen. 28. 20, 21, 22.
[9] 1 Cor. 7. 2, 9.
[11] Eph. 4. 28.

[12] Mat. 19. 11.

CHAP. XXIV.

Of the Civil Magistrate.

1. God the supream Lord, and King of all the World,

hath ordained *Civil*[1] *Magistrates* to be under him, over the
people, for his own glory, and the publick good; and to this end hath armed them with the power of the Sword, for defence and encouragement of them that do good, and for the punishment of evil doers.

2. It is lawful for Christians to Accept, and Execute the Office of a *Magistrate,* when called thereunto; in the management whereof, as they ought especially to maintain[2] Justice, and Peace, [page] according to the wholesome Laws of each Kingdome, and Commonwealth: so for that end they may lawfully now under the New Testament[3] wage war upon just and necessary occasions.

3. *Civil Magistrates* being set up by God, for the ends aforesaid; subjection in all lawful things commanded by them, ought to be yielded by us, in the Lord; not only for wrath[4] but for Conscience sake; and we ought to make supplications and prayers for Kings, and all that are in Authority,[5] that under them we may live a quiet and peaceable life, in all godliness and honesty.

[1] Rom. 13.
1, 2, 3, 4.

[2] 2 Sam.
23. 3.
Ps. 82.
3, 4.

[3] Luk. 3.
14.

[4] Rom.
13. 5, 6, 7.
1 Pet. 2.
17.

[5] 1 Tim.
2. 1, 2.

CHAP. XXV.

Of Marriage.

1. MArriage is to be between one *Man and one Woman;*[1] neither is it lawful for any man to have more then one *Wife,* nor for any *Woman* to have more then one *Husband* at the same time.

2. Marriage was ordained for the mutual help[2] of *Husband* and *Wife,*[3] for the increase of Man-kind, with a legitimate issue, and for[4] preventing of uncleanness.

3. It is lawful for[5] all sorts of people to *Marry,* who are able with judgment to give their con-

[1] Gen. 2.
24. Mal. 2.
15. Mat.
19. 5, 6.

[2] Gen. 2.
18.
[3] Gen. 1. 28.

[4] 1 Cor. 7.
2, 9.

[5] Heb. 13.
4. 1 Tim.
4. 3.

6 1 Cor. 7.
39.

sent; yet it is the duty of *Christians*[6] to *marry* in the Lord,
and therefore such as profess the [page]
true Religion, should not *Marry* with

7 Neh. 13.
25, 26,
27.

infidels,[7] or Idolators;
neither should such as are godly be
unequally yoked, by *marrying* with
such as are wicked, in their
life, or maintain damnable Heresie.

4. *Marriage* ought not to be
within the degrees of consanquini-

8 Levit.
18.

ty,[8] or Affinity forbidden in
the word; nor can such incestuous *Marriage* ever be made lawful, by any law of *Man* or consent

9 Mat. 6.
18. 1 Cor.
5. 1.

of parties,[9] so as those persons
may live together as *Man* and
Wife. [page]

CHAP. XXVI.

Of the Church.

1. The Catholick or universal
Church, which (with re-
spect to internal work of the
Spirit, and truth of grace) may be
called invisible, consists of the

1 Heb. 12.
23. Col. 1.
18. Eph.
1. 10, 22,
23, & ch.
5. 23, 27,
32.

whole[1] number of the Elect,
that have been, are, or shall be gathered into one, under Christ the
head thereof; and is the spouse, the
body, the fulness of him that filleth all in all.

2. All persons throughout the
world, professing the faith of the
Gospel, and obedience unto God
by Christ, according unto it; not
destroying their own profession by
any Errors everting the foundati- [page]

2 1 Cor. 1.
2. Act. 11.
26.
3 Rom. 1.
7. Eph. 1.
20, 21, 22.

on, or unholyness of conversation,[2]
are and may be called visible
Saints;[3] and of such ought all
particular Congregations to be
constituted.

3. The purest Churches under
heaven are subject[4] to mixture,
and error; and som have so de-

4 1 Cor.
15. Rev.
2 & ch. 3.
5 Rev. 18.
2. 2 Thes.
2. 11, 12.

generated as to become[5] no
Churches of Christ, but Synago-
gues of Satan; nevertheless Christ

always hath had, and ever shall
have a [6] Kingdome, in this world,
to the end thereof, of such as believe in him, and make profession
of his Name.

4. The Lord Jesus Christ is the
Head of the Church, in whom by
the appointment of the Father,[7]
all power for the calling, institution, order, or Government of the
Church, is invested in a supream &
soveraigne manner, neither can the
Pope of *Rome* in any sense be head [page]
thereof, but is [8] that Antichrist,
that Man of sin, and Son of perdition, that exalteth himself in
the Church against Christ, and all
that is called God; whom the
Lord shall destroy with the brightness of his coming.

5. In the execution of this power wherewith he is so intrusted,
the Lord Jesus calleth out of the
World unto himself, through the
Ministry of his word, by his Spirit,[9]
those that are given unto him
by his Father; that they may
walk before him in all the [11]
ways of obedience, which he pre-
scribeth to them in his Word.
Those thus called he commandeth
to walk together in particular societies, or [12] Churches, for their
mutual edification; and the due
performance of that publick worship, which he requireth of them
in the World. [page]

6. The Members of these
Churches are [13] Saints by calling, visibly manifesting and evi-
dencing (in and by their profession and walking) their obedience
unto that call of Christ; and do
willingly consent to walk together
according to the appointment of
Christ, giving up themselves, to the
Lord & one to another by the will
of God,[14] in professed subjection
to the Ordinances of the Gospel.

7. To each of these Churches

[6] Mat. 16.
18. Ps. 72.
17 & Ps.
102. 28.
Rev. 12.
17.

[7] Col. 1.
18. Mat.
28. 18, 19,
20.
Eph. 4.
11, 12.

[8] 2 Thes.
2. 3-9.

[9] Joh. 10.
16. chap.
12. 32.

[11] Mat. 28.
20.

[12] Mat. 18.
15-20.

[13] Rom. 1.
9. 1 Cor.
1. 2.

[14] Act. 2.
41, 42.
ch. 5. 13,
14. 2 Cor.
9. 13.

thus gathered, according to his mind, declared in his word, he hath given all that [15] power and authority, which is any way needfull, for their carrying on that order in worship, and discipline, which he hath instituted for them to observe; with commands, and rules for the due and right exerting, and executing of that power.

[15] Mat. 18. 17, 18. 1 Cor. 5. 4, 5, with 5. 13.

8. A particular Church gathered, and compleatly Organized, according to the mind of Christ, consists of Officers, and Members; And the Officers appointed by *Christ* to be chosen and set apart by the Church (so called and gathered) for the peculiar Administration of Ordinances, and Execution of Power, or Duty, which he intrusts them with, or calls them to, to be continued to the end of the World, are [16] Bishops or Elders and Deacons.

[16] Act. 20. 17, with v. 28. Phil. 1. 1.

9. The way appointed by *Christ* for the Calling of any person, fitted, and gifted by the Holy *Spirit,* unto the Office of Bishop, or Elder, in a Church, is, that he be chosen thereunto by the common [17] suffrage of the Church it self; and Solemnly set apart by Fasting and Prayer, with imposition of hands of the [18] Eldership of the Church, if there be any before [page] Constituted therein; And of a Deacon [19] that he be chosen by the like suffrage, and set apart by Prayer, and the like Imposition of hands.

[17] Act. 14. 23. See the original. [18] 1 Tim. 4. 14.

[19] Act. 6. 3, 5, 6.

10. The work of Pastors being constantly to attend the Service of *Christ,* in his Churches, in the Ministry of the Word, and Prayer,[20] with watching for their Souls, as they that must give an account to him; it is incumbent on the Churches to whom they Minister, not only to give them all due respect,[21] but also to communicate to them of all

[20] Act. 6. 4. Heb. 13. 17.

[21] 1 Tim. 5. 17, 18. Gal. 6.

their good things according to
their ability, so as they may have
a comfortable supply, without
being themselves [24] entangled in
Secular Affairs; and may also be
capable of exercising [25] Hospitality towards others; and this is required by the [26] Law of Nature,
and by the Express order of our [page]
Lord Jesus, who hath ordained
that they that preach the Gospel,
should live of the Gospel.

[24] 2 Tim.
2. 4.

[25] 1 Tim.
3. 2.

[26] 1 Cor.
9.
6-14.

11. Although it be incumbent
on the Bishops or Pastors of the
Churches to be instant in Preaching the Word, by way of Office;
yet the work of Preaching the
Word, is not so peculiarly confin-
ed to them; but that others also [1]
gifted, and fitted by the Holy *Spirit* for it, and approved, and
called by the *Church,* may and
ought to perform it.

[1] Act. 11.
19, 20, 21.
1 Pet. 4.
10, 11.

12. As all Believers are bound
to joyn themselves to particular
Churches, when and where they
have opportunity so to do; So all
that are admitted unto the priviledges of a *Church,* are also [2]
under the Censures and Government thereof, according to the
Rule of *Christ.* [page]

[2] 1 Thes.
5. 14.
2 Thes. 3.
6, 14, 15.

13. No Church-members upon
any offence taken by them, having performed their Duty required
of them towards the person they
are offended at, ought to disturb
any *Church* order, or absent themselves from the Assemblies of the
Church, or Administration of any
Ordinances, upon the account of
such offence at any of their fellow-
members; but to wait upon *Christ,* [3]
in the further proceeding of the
Church.

[3] Mat. 18.
15, 16, 17.
Eph. 4. 2,
3.

14. As each *Church,* and all the
Members of it, are bound to [4]
pray continually, for the good
and prosperity of all the *Churches* of
Christ, in all places; and upon
all occasions to further it (every

[4] Eph. 6.
18. Ps.
122. 6.

one within the bounds of their places, and callings, in the Exercise of their Gifts and Graces) so the *Churches* (when planted by the providence of God so as they may injoy opportunity and advantage for it) ought to hold [page] [5] communion amongst themselves for their peace, increase of love, and mutual edification.

[5] Rom. 16. 1, 2. 3 Joh. 8, 9, 10.

15. In cases of difficulties or differences, either in point of Doctrine, or Administration; wherein either the Churches in general are concerned, or any one Church in their peace, union, and edification; or any member, or members, of any Church are injured, in or by any proceedings in censures not agreeable to truth, and order: it is according to the mind of Christ, that many Churches holding communion together, do by their messengers meet to consider,[6] and give their advice in, or about that matter in difference, to be reported to all the Churches concerned; howbeit these messengers assembled, are not entrusted with any Church-power properly so called; or with any jurisdiction over the Churches themselves, to exercise any censures either over any [page] Churches, or Persons: or [7] to impose their determination on the Churches, or Officers.

[6] Act. 15. 2, 4, 6. & 22, 23, 25.

[7] 2 Cor. 1. 24. 1 Joh. 4. 1.

CHAP. XXVII.
On the Communion of Saints.

1. All *Saints* that are united to Jesus Christ their *Head*, by his Spirit, and Faith; although they are not made thereby one person with him, have [1] fellowship in his Graces, sufferings, death, resurrection, and glory; and being united to one another in love, they [2] have communion in each others gifts, and graces; and obliged to the perfor-

[1] 1 Joh. 1. 3. Joh. 1. 16. Phil. 3. 10. Rom. 6. 5, 6.
[2] Eph. 4. 15, 16. 1 Cor. 12. 7. 1 Cor. 3. 21, 22, 23.

mance of such duties, publick and
private, in an orderly way,[3] as
do conduce to their mutual good,
both in the inward and outward
man. [page]

2. *Saints* by profession are
bound to maintain an holy fellowship and communion in the
worship of God, and in performing such other spiritual services,[4]
as tend to their mutual edification; as also in relieving each
other in[5] outward things according to their several abilities,
and necessities; which communion, according to the rule of the
Gospel, though especially to be exercised by them, in the relations
wherein they stand, whether in[6]
families, or[7] Churches;
yet as God offereth opportunity
is to be extended to all the houshold of faith, even all those who
in every place call upon the name
of the Lord Jesus; nevertheless
their communion one with another as *Saints,* doth not take away
or[8] infringe the title or propriety, which each man hath in his
goods and possessions. [page]

[3] 1 Thes.
5. 11, 14.
Rom. 1.
12. 1 Joh.
2. 17, 18.
Gal. 6. 10.

[4] Heb. 10.
24, 25
with ch.
3. 12, 13.

[5] Act. 12.
29, 30.

[6] Eph. 6.
4.
[7] 1 Cor.
12. 14
-27.

[8] Act. 5. 4
Eph. 4. 28

CHAP. XXVIII.
Of Baptism and the
Lords Supper.

1. BAptism and the Lords Supper
are ordinances of positive, and
soveraign institution; appointed by the Lord Jesus the only Law-giver, to be continued in
his Church[1] to the end of the
world.

2. These holy appointments are
to be administered by those only,
who are qualified and thereunto
called according[2] to the com-
mission of Christ. [page]

[1] Mat. 28.
19, 20.
1 Cor.
11. 26.

[2] Mat. 28.
19. 1 Cor.
4. 1.

CHAP. XXIX.
Of Baptism.

1. BAptism is an Ordinance of
the New Testament, ordain-

³ Rom. 6.
3, 4, 5.
Col. 2. 12.
Gal. 3. 27.
⁴ Mar. 1.
4. Act.
26. 16.
⁵ Rom. 6.
2, 4.

ed by Jesus Christ, to be unto the party Baptized, a sign of his fellowship with him, in his death,³ and resurrection; of his being engrafted into him; of⁴ remission of sins; and of his⁵ giving up unto God through Jesus Christ, to live and walk in newness of Life.

⁶ Mar. 16.
16. Act.
8. 36, 37.

2. Those who do actually profess⁶ repentance towards *God,* faith in, and obedience, to our Lord Jesus, are the only proper subjects of this ordinance. [page]

⁷ Mat. 28.
19, 20,
with Act.
8. 38.

3. The outward element to be used in this ordinance⁷ is water, wherein the party is to be baptized, in the name of the Father, and of the Son, and of the Holy Spirit.

⁸ Mat. 3.
16. Joh. 3.
23.

4. Immersion, or dipping of the person⁸ in water, is necessary to the due administration of this ordinance.

CHAP. XXX.

Of the Lords Supper.

1. THE Supper of the Lord Jesus, was instituted by him, the same night wherein he was betrayed, to be observed in his Churches unto the end of the [page] world, for the perpetual remembrance, and shewing forth the sacrifice in his death¹

¹ 1 Cor.
11. 23, 24,
25, 26.

confirmation of the faith of believers in all the benefits thereof, their spiritual nourishment, and growth in him, their further ingagement in, and to, all duties which they owe unto him;²

² 1 Cor.
10. 16, 17,
21.

and to be a bond and pledge of their communion with him, and with each other.

2. In this ordinance Christ is not offered up to his Father, nor any real sacrifice made at all, for remission of sin of the quick or dead; but only a memorial of that³ one offering up of himself, by

³ Heb 9.
25, 26, 28.

himself, upon the crosse, once for
all; and a spiritual oblation of all[4]
possible praise unto God for
the same; so that the Popish sacrifice of the Mass (as they call it)
is most abominable, injurious to
Christs own only sacrifice, the [page]
alone propitiation for all the sins
of the Elect.

4 1 Cor.
11. 24.
Mat. 26.
26, 27.

3. The Lord Jesus hath in this
Ordinance, appointed his Ministers
to Pray, and bless the Elements of
Bread and Wine, and thereby to
set them apart from a common to
an holy use, and to take and break
the Bread; to take the Cup,[5]
and (they communicating also
themselves) to give both to the
Communicants.

5 1 Cor.
11. 23, 24,
25, 26, etc.

4. The denial of the Cup to
the people, worshiping the Elements, the lifting them up, or carrying them about for adoration,
and reserving them for any pretended religious use,[6] are all
contrary to the nature of this Ordinance, and to the institution of
Christ.

6 Mat. 26.
26, 27, 28.
Mat. 15. 9.
Exod. 20.
4, 5.

5. The outward Elements in
this Ordinance, duely set apart to [page]
the uses ordained by Christ, have
such relation to him crucified, as
that truely, although in terms used
figuratively, they are sometimes
called by the name of the things
they represent, to wit[7] body and Blood of
Christ; albeit in substance, and nature,
they still remain truly, and only[8]
Bread, and Wine, as they were
before.

7 1 Cor.
11. 27.

8 1 Cor.
11. 26 &
5. 28.

6. That doctrine which main-
tains a change of the substance of
Bread and Wine, into the substance
of Christs body and blood (commonly called Transubstantiation)
by consecration of a Priest, or by
any other way, is repugnant not to
Scripture[9] alone, but even to
common sense and reason; overthroweth
the[11] nature of the or-
dinance, and hath been and is the

9 Act. 3.
21. Luk.
24. 6 & 5.
39.
11 1 Cor.
11. 24, 25.

cause of manifold superstitions, yea, of gross Idolatries. [page]

7. Worthy receivers, outwardly partaking of the visible Elements in this Ordinance, do then also inwardly by faith, really and indeed, yet not carnally, and corporally, but spiritually receive, and feed upon Christ crucified [12] & all the benefits of his death: the Body and Blood of *Christ,* being then not corporally, or carnally, but spiritually present to the faith of Believers, in that Ordinance, as the Elements themselves are to their outward senses.

8. All ignorant and ungodly persons, as they are unfit to enjoy communion [13] with *Christ;* so are they unworthy of the Lords Table; and cannot without great sin against him, while they remain such, partake of these holy mysteries, [14] or be admitted thereunto: yea whosoever shall receive unworthily are guilty of the Body and Blood of the Lord, eating and drinking judgment to themselves. [page]

CHAP. XXXI.

Of the State of Man after Death and of the Resurrection of the Dead.

1. THE Bodies of Men after Death return to dust,[1] and see corruption; but their Souls (which neither die nor sleep) having an immortal subsistence, immediately [2] return to God who gave them; the Souls of the Righteous being then made perfect in holiness, are received into paradise where they are with *Christ,* and behold the face of *God,* in light [3] and glory; waiting for the full Redemption of their Bodies; and the souls of the wick- [page] ed, are cast into hell; where they remain in torment and utter dark-

[12] 1 Cor. 10. 16. ch. 11. 23. 26.

[13] 2 Cor. 6. 14, 15.

[14] 1 Cor. 11. 29. Mat. 7. 6.

[1] Gen. 3. 19. Act. 13. 36.

[2] Eccl. 12. 7.

[3] Luk. 23. 43. 2 Cor. 5. 1, 6, 8. Phil. 1. 23. Heb. 12. 23.

ness, reserved to [4] the judgement of the great day; besides
these two places for Souls separated from their bodies, the Scripture acknowledgeth none.

2. At the last day such of the
Saints as are found alive shall not
sleep but be [5] changed; and all
the dead shall be raised up with
the self same bodies, and [6] none
other; although with different [7]
qualities, which shall be united again to their Souls for ever.

3. The bodies of the unjust
shall by the power of *Christ,* be
raised to dishonour; the bodies of
the just by his spirit unto honour, [8]
and be made conformable to
his own glorious Body. [page]

[4] Jud. 6.
7. 1 Pet.
3. 19.
Luk. 16.
23, 24.

[5] 1 Cor.
15. 51, 52.
1 Thes. 4.
17.
[6] Job 19.
26, 27.
[7] 1 Cor.
15. 42, 43.

[8] Act. 24.
15. Joh. 5.
28, 29.
Phil. 3. 21.

CHAP. XXXII.

Of the Last Judge-
ment.

1. GOD hath appointed a Day
wherein he will judge the
world in Righteousness, by [1] Jesus Christ; to whom all power
and judgement is given of the Father; in which Day not only the [2]
Apostate Angels shall be judged; but likewise all persons that
have lived upon the Earth, shall
appear before the Tribunal of
Christ; [3] to give an account of
their thoughts, Words, and
Deeds, and to receive according
to what they have done in the
body, whether good or evil. [page]

2. The end of Gods appointing this Day, is for the manifestation of the glory of his Mercy, in
the Eternal Salvation of the Elect; [4]
and of his Justice in the Eternal damnation of the Reprobate,
who are wicked and disobedient; for then shall the Righteous
go into Everlasting Life, and receive that fulness of Joy, and Glory, with everlasting reward, in
the presence [5] of the Lord:

[1] Act. 17.
31.
Joh. 5. 22,
27.
[2] 1 Cor. 6.
3. Jud. 6.

[3] 2 Cor.
5. 10.
Eccles. 12.
14. Mat.
12. 36.
Rom. 14.
10, 12.
Mat. 25.
32 etc.

[4] Rom. 9.
22, 23.

[5] Mat. 25.
21, 34.
2 Tim.
4. 8.

S

but the wicked who know not
God, and obey not the Gospel of
Jesus Christ, shall be cast into E-
ternal torments, and [6] punished
with everlasting destruction, from
the presence of the Lord, and
from the glory of his power.

[6] Mat. 25.
46.   Mar. 9.
48.
2 Thes. 1.
7, 8, 9, 10.

3. As Christ would have us to
be certainly perswaded that there
shall be a Day of judgement, both [7]
to deter all men from sin, and
for the greater [8] consolation of
the godly, in their adversity; so [page]
will he have that day unknown to
Men, that they may shake off all
carnal security, and be always
watchful, because they know not
at what hour, the [9] Lord will
come; and may ever be prepared
to say, [11] *Come Lord Jesus, Come quickly,*
Amen.

[7] 2 Cor.
5. 10, 11.

[8] 2 Thes.
1. 5, 6, 7.

[9] Mar. 13.
35, 36, 37.
Luk. 13.
35, 36.
[11] Rev. 22.
20.

AN
APPENDIX.

WHosoever reads, and impartially
considers what we have in our
foregoing confession declared, may readily perceive, That we do not only con-
center with all other true Christians on
the Word of God (revealed in the Scriptures of truth) as the foundation and
rule of our faith and worship. But that
we have also industriously endeavoured
to manifest, That in the fundamental
Articles of Christianity we mind the same
things, and have therefore expressed our
belief in the same words, that have on
the like occasion been spoken by other
societies of Christians before us.

This we have done, That those who
are desirous to know the principles of
Religion which we hold and practise [page]
may take an estimate from our selves
(who jointly concur in this work) and
may not be misguided, either by undue
reports; or by the ignorance or errors
of particular persons, who going under
the same name with our selves, may give

an occasion of scandalizing the truth we
profess.

And although we do differ from our brethren who are Pædobaptists; in the subject and administration of Baptisme, and
such other circumstances as have a necessary dependence on our observance of
that Ordinance, and do frequent our
own assemblies for our mutual edification, and discharge of those duties, and
services which we owe unto God, and
in his fear, to each other: yet we would
not be from hence misconstrued, as if the
discharge of our own consciences herein,
did any wayes disoblige or alienate our
affections, or conversations from any o-
thers that fear the Lord; but that we
may and do as we have opportunity participate of the labours of those, whom
God hath indued with abilities above [page]
our selves, and qualified, and called to
the Ministry of the Word, earnestly desiring to approve ourselves to be such, as
follow after peace with holyness, and
therefore we alwaies keep that blessed
Irenicum, or healing *Word* of the Apostle
before our eyes; if in any thing ye be o-
therwise minded, God shall reveal even
this unto you; nevertheless whereto we
have already attained; let us walk by
the same rule, let us mind the same thing.   Phil. 3. v. 15, 16.

Let it not therefore be judged of us
(because much hath been written on this
subjedt, and yet we continue this our
practise different from others) that it is
out of obstinacy, but rather as the truth
is, that we do herein according to the
best of our understandings worship God,
out of a pure mind yielding obedience to
his precept, in that method which we
take to be most agreeable to the Scriptures of truth, and primitive practise.

It would not become us to give any
such intimation, as should carry a sem-
blance that what we do in the service of [page]
God is with a doubting conscience, or
with any such temper of mind that we do
thus for the present, with a reservation
that we will do otherwise hereafter upon
more mature deliberation; nor have we
any cause so to do, being fully perswad-

ed, that what we do is agreeable to the
will of God. Yet we do heartily propose this, that if any of the Servants of
our Lord Jesus shall, in the Spirit of meekness, attempt to convince us of any mi-
stake, either in judgement or practise, we
shall diligently ponder his arguments;
and accompt him our chiefest friend that
shall be an instrument to convert us
from any error that is in our ways, for we cannot wittingly do any thing against the
truth, but all things for the truth.

And therefore we have indeavoured
seriously to consider, what hath been already offered for our satisfaction in this
point; and are loth to say any more lest
we should be esteemed desirous of renewed contests hereabout: yet forasmuch as it may justly be expected that we
shew some reason, why we cannot ac- [page]
quiesce in what hath been urged against
us; we shall with as much brevity as
may consist with plainness, endeavour to
satisfie the expectation of those that shall
peruse what we now publish in this matter also.

1. As to those Christians who consent
with us, *That Repentance from dead works, and
Faith towards God, and our Lord Jesus Christ, is required in persons to be Baptised;* and do therefore supply the defect
of the (infant being uncapable of making
confession of either) by others who do
undertake these things for it. Although
we do find by Church history that this
hath been a very antient practise; yet considering, that
the same Scripture (Rom. xiv. 4, 10, 12, 23) which
does caution us against censuring our
brother, with whom we shall all stand
before the judgment seat of Christ, does
also instruct us, *That every one of us shall
give an account of himself to God,* and *whatsoever is not of Faith is sin.* Therefore we
cannot for our own parts be perswaded
in our own minds, to build such a pra- [page]
ctise as this, upon an unwritten tradition:
But do rather choose in all points of Faith
and Worship, to have recourse to the
holy Scriptures, for the information of
our judgment, and regulation of our

practise; being well assured that a conscientious attending thereto, is the best
way to prevent, and rectifie our defects
and errors. *2 Tim.* 3. 16, 17. And if any
such case happen to be debated between
Christians, which is not plainly determinable by the Scriptures, we think it safest
to leave such things undecided until the
second coming of our Lord Jesus; as they
did in the Church of old, until there
should arise a Priest with *Urim* and *Thum-*
mim, that might certainly inform them
of the mind of God thereabout, *Ezra,* 2. 62, 63.

2. As for those our Christian brethren
who do ground their arguments for Infants baptism, upon a presumed foederal
holiness, or Church-Membership, we
conceive they are deficient in this, that
albeit this Covenant-Holiness and Membership should be as is supposed, in refe- [page]
rence unto the Infants of Believers; yet
no command for Infant baptism does immediately and directly result from such a
quality, or relation.

All instituted Worship receives its sanction from the precept, and is to be
thereby governed in all the necessary circumstances thereof.

So it was in the Covenant that God
made with *Abraham* and his Seed. The
sign whereof was appropriated only to
the Male, notwithstanding that the female seed as well as the Male were comprehended in the Covenant and part of
the Church of God; neither was this
sign to be affixed to any Male Infant till
he was eight dayes old, albeit he was
within the Covenant from the first moment of his life; nor could the danger
of death, or any other supposed necessity, warrant the circumcising of him before the set time, nor was there any cause
for it; the commination of being cut off
from his people, being only upon the
neglect, or contempt of the precept. [page]

Righteous *Lot* was nearly related to
Abraham in the flesh, and contemporary
with him, when this Covenant was
made; yet inasmuch as he did not descend from his loynes, nor was of his
household family (although he was of the

same houshold of faith with Abraham) yet
neither *Lot* himself nor any of his posterity (because of their descent from him)
were signed with the signature of this
Covenant that was made with *Abraham*
and his seed.

This may suffice to shew, that where
there was both an express Covenant, and
a sign thereof (such a Covenant as did
separate the persons with whom it was
made, and all their off-spring from all the
rest of the world, as a people holy unto
the Lord, and did constitute them the
visible Church of God, (though not
comprehensive of all the faithful in the
world) yet the sign of this Covenant was
not affixed to all the persons that were
within this Covenant, nor to any of them
till the prefixt season; nor to other faithful servants of God, that were not of de- [page]
scent from Abraham. And consequently
that it depends purely upon the will of
the Law-giver, to determine what shall
be the sign of his Covenant, unto whom,
at what season, and upon what terms, it
shall be affixed.

If our brethren do suppose baptism to
be the seal of the Covenant which God
makes with every believer (of which the
Scriptures are altogether silent) it is not
our concern to contend with them herein; yet we conceive the seal of that Covenant is the indwelling of the Spirit of
Christ in the particular and individual
persons in whom he resides, and nothing
else, neither do they or we suppose that
baptism is in any such manner substituted
in the place of circumcision, as to have
the same (and no other) latitude, extent,
or terms, then circumcision had; for that
was suited only for the Male children,
baptism is an ordinance suited for every
believer, whether male, or female. That
extended to all the males that were born
in *Abrahams* house, or bought with his
money, equally with the males that pro- [page]
ceeded from his own loynes; but baptisme is not so far extended in any true
Christian Church that we know of, as to
be administered to all the poor infidel servants, that the members thereof purchase

for their service, and introduce into their
families; nor to the children born of
them in their house.

But we conceive the same parity of
reasoning may hold for the ordinance of
baptism as for that of circumcision;
Exodus 12. 49. viz. one law for the stranger, as for the homeborn: If any desire
to be admitted to all the ordinances, and
priviledges of Gods house, the door is
open; upon the same terms that any one
person was ever admitted to all, or any
of those priviledges, that belong to the
Christian Church; may all persons of
right challenge the like admission.

As for that text of Scripture, Rom 4.
11., *He received circumcision a seal of the
righteousness of the faith which he had yet
being uncircumcised;* we conceive if the
Apostles scope in that place be duly at-
tended to, it will appear that no argument [page]
can be taken from thence to inforce Infant baptism; and forasmuch as we find
a full and fair account of those words given by the learned Dr. *Lightfoot* (a
man not to be suspected of partiality in
this controversie) in his *Hor. Hebrai,* on
the 1 *Cor.* 7. 19. p. 42, 43. we shall trans-
cribe his words at large, without any
comment of our own upon them.

(Latin and English here in parallel columns. Latin
omitted and no attempt made to follow the lining of the
English.)

Circumcision is nothing, if we respect the time, for now it was
without use, that end of it being especially fulfilled; for which it
had been instituted: this end the Apostle declares in these words,
Rom. 4. 11, σφραγιδα, &c. But I fear that by most translations
they are not sufficiently suited to the end of circumcision, and the
scope of the Apostle whilst something of their own is by them
inserted.

And after the Doctor hath represented diverse versions of the
words agreeing for the most part in sense with that which we
have in our bibles he thus proceeds.

(Latin and English.)

Other versions are to the same purpose; as if circumcision was
given to *Abraham* for a Seal of that Righteousness which he had

being yet uncircumcised, which we will not deny to be in some sense true, but we believe that circumcision had chiefly a far different respect.

Give me leave thus to render the words; *And he received the sign of circumcision, a seal of the Righteousness of Faith, which was to be in the uncircumcision, Which was to be* (I say), not which had *been,* not that which *Abraham* had whilst he was yet uncircumcised; but that which his uncircumcised seed should have, that is the Gentiles, who in time to come should imitate the faith of *Abraham.*

Now consider well on what occasion circumcision was instituted unto *Abraham,* setting before thine eyes the history thereof, Gen. 17.

This promise is first made unto him, *Thou shalt be the father of many nations* (in what sense the Apostle explaineth in that chapter) and then there is subjoined a double seal for the confirmation of the thing, to wit, the change of the name *Abram* to *Abraham,* and the institution of circumcision v. 4, *Behold as for me, my Covenant is with thee, and thou shalt be the Father of many nations.* Wherefore was his name called *Abraham?* for the sealing of his promise. *Thou shalt be the father of many nations.* And wherefore was circumcision instituted to him? For the sealing of the same promise. *Thou shalt be the father of many nations.* So that this is the sense of the Apostle, most agreeable to the institution of circumcision; he received the sign of circumcision, a seal of the Righteousness of Faith which in time to come the uncircumcision (or the Gentiles) should have and obtain.

Abraham had a twofold seed, *natural,* or the Jews; and *faithful,* of the believing Gentiles: his natural seed was signed with the sign of circumcision, first indeed for the distinguishing of them from all other Nations whilst they as yet were not the seed of *Abraham,* but especially for the memorial of the justification of the Gentiles by faith, when at length they should become his seed. Therefore circumcision was of right to cease, when the Gentiles were brought into the faith, forasmuch as then it had obtained its last and chief end, and thenceforth *circumcision is nothing.* [page]

Thus far he, which we earnestly desire may be seriously weighed, for we plead not his authority, but the evidence of truth in his words.

3. Of whatsoever nature the holiness of the children mentioned, 1 *Cor.* 7. 12. be, yet they who do conclude that all such children (whether Infants or of riper years) have from hence an immediate right to baptism, do as we conceive put more into the conclusion, than will be found in the premises.

For although we do not determine positively concerning the Apostles scope in the holiness here mentioned, so as to say it is this, or that, and no other thing; Yet it is evident that the Apostle does by it determine not only the lawfulness but the expedience also of a believers cohabition with an unbeliever, in the state of marriage.

And we do think that although the Apostles asserting of the unbelieving [page] yoke-fellow to be sanctified by the believer, should carry in it somewhat more then is in the bare marriage of two infidels, because although the marriage covenant have a divine sanction so as to make the wedlock of two unbelievers a lawful action, and their conjunction and cohabitation in that respect undefiled, yet there might be no ground to suppose from thence, that both or either of their persons are thereby sanctified; and the Apostle urges the cohabition of a believer with an infidel in the state of wedlock from this ground, that the unbelieving husband is *sanctified* by the believing wife; nevertheless here you have the influence of a believers faith *ascending from an inferior to a superior relation;* from the wife to the husband who is her head, *before it can descend to their off-spring.* And therefore we say, whatever be the nature or extent of the holiness here intended, we conceive it cannot convey to the children an immediate right to baptism; because it would then be of another nature, and of a larger extent, then the root, [page] and original from whence it is derived, for it is clear by the Apostles argument that holiness cannot be derived to the child from the sanctity of one parent only, if either father or mother be (in the sense intended by the Apostle) unholy or unclean, so will the child be also, therefore for the production of a holy seed it is necessary that both the Parents be sanctified; and this the Apostle positively asserts in the first place to be done by the believing parent, although the other be an unbeliever, and then consequentially from thence argues, the holiness of their children. Hence it follows, that as

the children have no other holiness then
what they derive from their Parents; so neither can they have any right
by this holiness to any spiritual priviledge, but such as both their Parents did
also partake of: and therefore if the unbelieving Parent (though sanctified by
the believing Parent) have not thereby a
right to baptism, neither can we conceive, that there is any such priviledge, derived
to the children by their birth ho-
liness. [page]

Besides if it had been the usual practise
in the Apostles dayes for the father or
mother, that did believe, to bring all their
children with them to be baptised; then
the holiness of the believing *Corinthians'*
children, would not at all have been in
question when this Epistle was written;
but might have been argued from their
passing under that ordinance, which represented their new birth, although they
had derived no holiness from their Parents, by their first birth; and would have
layen as an exception against the Apostles
inference, *else were your Children unclean,*
&c. But of the sanctification of all the
children of every believer by this ordinance, or any other way, then what is before-
mentioned, the Scripture is altogether silent.

This may be also added; that if this
birth holiness do qualifie all the children
of every believer, for the ordinance of
baptism; why not for all other ordinances? for the Lords Supper as was practised for a long time together? for if recourse be had to what the Scriptures [page]
speak generally of this subject; it will be
found, that the same qualities which do
intitle any person to baptism, do so also
for the participation of all the Ordinances, and priviledges of the house of
God, that are common to all believers.

Whosoever can and does interrogate
his good Conscience towards God when
he is baptized (as every one must do that
makes it to himself a sign of Salvation) is
capable of doing the same thing, in every other act of worship that he performs.

4. The arguments and inferences that

are usually brought for, or against Infant baptism from those few instances
which the Scriptures afford us of whole
families being baptized; are only conjectural; and therefore cannot of themselves, be conclusive on either hand: yet
in regard most that treat on this subject
of Infant baptism, do (as they conceive)
improve these instances to the advantage
of their present argument: we think it meet (in
like manner as in the cases before mentioned so in this) to shew the invalidity
of such inferences. [page]

Cornelius worshipped God with all his
house, the *Jailor,* and *Crispus* the chief
ruler of the Synagogue, *believed God with*
each of their houses. The household of Ste-
phanus *addicted themselves to the Ministry of the*
Saints: so that thus far *Worship-*
ping, and *Believing* runs parallel with
Baptism. And if *Lydia,* had been a married person, when she believed, it is probable her husband would also have been
named by the Apostle, as in like cases, inasmuch as he would have been not only
a part, but the head of that baptized
household.

Who can assign any probable reason,
why the Apostle should make mention of
four or five households being baptized and
no more? or why he does so often vary.
in the method of his salutations, *Rom.* i. 6.
sometimes mentioning only particular
persons of great note, other times such,
and the Church in their house? the Saints
that were with them; and them belonging
to *Narcissus,* who were in the Lord; thus
saluting either whole families, or part of
families, or only particular persons in fa- [page]
milies, considered as they were in the
Lord, for if it had been a usual practise
to baptize all children, with their parents; there were then many thousands
of the Jews which believed, and a great
number of the Gentiles, in most of the
principal Cities in the World, and among
so many thousands, it is more than probable there would have been some thousands of housholds baptised; why then
should the Apostle in this respect signa-
lize one family of the Jews and three or

four of the Gentiles, as particular instances
in a case that was common? whoever
supposes that we do wilfully debar our
children, from the benefits of any promise, or priviledge, that of right belongs
to the children of believing parents; they
do entertain over-severe thoughts of us:
to be without natural affections is one of
the characters of the worst of persons,
in the worst of times. Wee do freely
confesse our selves guilty before the Lord,
in that we have not with more circumspection and diligence train'd up those
that relate to us in the fear of the Lord; [page]
and do humbly and earnestly pray, that
our omissions herein may be remitted,
and that they may not redound to the
prejudice of our selves, or any of ours:
but with respect to that duty that is incumbent on us, we acknowledge our
selves obliged by the precepts of God,
to bring up our children in the nurture
and admonition of the Lord, to teach
them his fear. both by instruction and example; and should we set light by this
precept, it would demonstrate that we
are more vile then the unnatural Heathen,
that like not to retain God in their knowledge, our baptism might then be justly
accompted, as no baptism to us.

There are many special promises that
do incourage us as well as precepts, that do
oblige us to the close pursuit of our duty herein: that God whom we serve,
being jealous of his Worship, threatens
the visiting of the Fathers transgression
upon the children to the third and fourth
generation of them that hate him: yet
does more abundantly extend his mercy,
even to thousands (respecting the off- [page]
spring and succeeding generations) of
them that love him, and keep his commandments.

When our Lord rebuked his disciples
for prohibiting the access of little children that were brought to him, that he
might pray over them, lay his hands upon them, and blesse them, does declare,
that of such is the Kingdom of God. And the
Apostle *Peter* in answer to their inquiry,
that desired to know what they must do

to be saved, does not only instruct them
in the necessary duty of repentance and
baptism; but does also thereto encourage
them, by that promise which had reference both to them, and their children; if
our Lord Jesus in the forementioned
place, do not respect the qualities of
children (as elsewhere) as to their meekness, humility, and sincerity, and the like;
but intend also that those very persons
and such like, appertain to the Kingdom
of God, and if the Apostle *Peter* in mentioning the aforesaid promise, do respect
not only the present and succeeding generations of those Jews, that heard him [page]
(in which sense the same phrase doth oc-
curre in Scripture) but also the immediate off-spring of his auditors; whether
the promise relate to the gift of the Holy
Spirit, or of eternal life, or any grace,
or priviledge tending to the obtaining
thereof; it is neither our concerne nor
our interest to confine the mercies, and
promises of God, to a more narrow, or
lesse compasse then he is pleased grati-
ously to offer and intend them; nor to
have a light esteem of them; but are o-
bliged in duty to God, and affection to
our children; to plead earnestly with
God and use our utmost endeavours that
both our selves, and our off-spring may
be partakers of his Mercies and gracious
Promises: yet we cannot from either of
these texts collect a sufficient warrant for
us to baptize our children before they
are instructed in the principles of the
Christian Religion.

For as to the instance in little children,
it seems by the disciples forbidding them,
that they were brought upon some other
account, not so frequent as Baptism must
be supposed to have been, if from the beginning believers children had been admitted thereto: and no account is given
whether their parents were baptised believers or not; and as to the instance of
the Apostle; if the following words and
practise, may be taken as an interpretation of the scope of that promise we
cannot conceive it does refer to infant
baptism, because the text does presently

subjoyn; *Then they that gladly received
the word were baptised.*

That there were some believing children of believing parents in the Apostles
dayes is evident from the Scriptures, even
such as were then in their fathers family,
and under their parents tuition, and edu-
cation; to whom the Apostle in several
of his Epistles to the Churches, giveth
commands to obey their parents in the
Lord; and does allure their tender years
to hearken to this precept, by reminding
them that it is the first command with
promise.

And it is recorded by him for the praise
of *Timothy,* and encouragement of pa- [page]
rents betimes to instruct, and children
early to attend to godly instruction, that
'απὸ βρεφως from a child, he had known the
holy Scriptures.

The Apostle *John* rejoyced greatly
when he found the children of the E-
lect Lady walking in the truth; and the
children of her Elect Sister joyn with the
Apostle in his salutation.

But that this was not generally so, that
all the children of believers were accounted for believers (as they would have
been if they had been all baptised) may
be collected from the character which the
Apostle gives of persons fit to be chosen
to Eldership in the Church which was
not common to all believers; among o-
thers this is expressely one, *viz. If there
be any having believing, or faithful children,* not accused of Riot or unruly; and
we may, from the Apostles writings on
the same subject collect the reason of this
qualification, *viz.* That in case the person
designed for this office to teach and rule
in the house of God, had children capable of it; there must be first a proof of [page]
his ability, industry, and successe in this
work in his own family; and private capacity, before he was ordained to the
exercise of this authority in the Church,
in a publick capacity, as a Bishop in the house of God.

These things we have mentioned as
having a direct reference unto the controversie between our brethren and us;
other things that are more abstruse and

prolix, which are frequently introduced
into this controversie, but do not necessarily concern it, we have purposely a-
voided; that the distance between us
and our brethren may not be by us made
more wide; for it is our duty, and concern so far as is possible for us (retaining
a good conscience towards God) to seek
a more entire agreement and reconciliation with them.

We are not insensible that as to the order of God's house, and entire communion
therein there are some things wherein we
(as well as others) are not at a full accord
among our selves, as for instance; the [page]
known principle, and state of the consciences of diverse of us, that have agreed
in this Confession is such; that we cannot hold Church-communion, with any
other than Baptised-believers, and
Churches constituted of such; yet some
others of us have a greater liberty and
freedom in our spirits that way; and
therefore we have purposely omitted the
mention of things of that nature, that we
might concurre, in giving this evidence
of our agreement, both among our selves,
and with other good Christians, in those
important articles of the Christian Religion, mainly insisted on by us: and this
notwithstanding we all esteem it our chief
concern, both among our selves, and all
others that in every place call upon the
name of the Lord Jesus Christ our Lord,
both theirs and ours, and love him in sincerity, to endeavour to keep the unity
of the Spirit, in the bond of peace; and
in order thereunto, to exercise all lowli-
ness and meekness, with longsuffering,
forbearing one another in love.

And we are purswaded if the same me- [page]
thod were introduced into frequent practise between us and our Christian friends
who agree with us in all the fundamental
articles of the Christian faith (though
they do not so in the subject and administration of baptism) it would soon beget
a better understanding, and brotherly
affection between us.

In the beginning of the Christian
Church, when the doctrine of the baptism

of *Christ* was not universally understood,
yet those that knew only the baptism of
John, were the Disciples of the Lord Jesus; and *Apollos* an eminent Minister of
the Gospel of Jesus.

In the beginning of the reformation of
the Christian Church, and recovery from
that *Egyptian* darkness wherein our fore-
fathers for many generations were held
in bondage; upon recourse had to the
Scriptures of truth, different apprehen-
sions were conceived, which are to this
time continued, concerning the practise
of this Ordinance.

Let not our zeal herein be misinterpre-
ted: that God whom we serve is jealous [page]
of his worship. By his gracious providence the Law thereof, is continued a-
mongst us; and we are forewarned by
what hapned in the Church of the Jews,
that it is necessary for every generation,
and that frequently in every generation
to consult the divine oracle, compare
our worship with the rule, and take heed
to what doctrines we receive and practise.

If the ten commandments exhibited in the
popish Idolatrous service books had
been received as the entire law of God,
because they agree in number with his
ten commands, and also in the substance
of nine of them; the second Commandment forbidding Idolatry had been utterly lost.

If *Ezra* and *Nehemiah* had not made a
diligent search into the particular parts of
Gods law, and his worship; the Feast of
Tabernacles (which for many centuries of
years, had not been duly observed, according to the institution, though it was
retained in the general notion) would
not have been kept in due order. [page]

So may it be now as to many things re-
lating to the service of God, which do
retain the names proper to them in their
first institution, but yet through inadver-
tency (where there is no sinister design)
may vary in their circumstances, from
their first institution. And if by means
of any antient defection, or of that general corruption of the service of God,

and interruption of his true worship, and
persecution of his servants by the Anti-christian
Bishop of *Rome,* for many gene-
rations; those who do consult the Word
of God, cannot yet arrive at a full and
mutual satisfaction among themselves, what
was the practise of the primitive
Christian Church, in some points rela-
ting to the *Worship* of God: yet inasmuch
as these things are not of the essence of
Christianity, but that we agree in the
fundamental doctrines thereof, we do
apprehend, there is sufficient ground to
lay aside all bitterness and prejudice, and
in the spirit of love and meekness to im- [page]
brace and own each other therein; leaving each other at liberty to perform such
other services, wherein we cannot concur apart unto God, according to the
best of our understanding.

FINIS.

4. PRIVATE CONFESSIONS

Other Confessions were published by private individuals in this period, and attained some circulation.
One was by John Bunyan, another by the famous Welsh
preacher, Vavasor Powell. In 1697 Benjamin Keach
and his son, Elias Keach, the former pastor at Horsley-
down and the latter at Tallow Chandler's Hall, London,
united in a Confession of faith for their congregations.
The body of the Confession and the appendix on discipline were identical in both, but each had a preface,
dedication, and signatures appropriate to itself. That of
Benjamin Keach was signed by members of his church,
August 10; that of his son, five days later. The
reasons given by Elias Keach in the letter "To the
Reader" for publishing this Confession were the general
ignorance of Baptist doctrines and usages on the part of
the Baptists themselves, as well as others, the bulkiness,
expensiveness, and scarcity of the former Confession, its

T

omission of some matters of importance, and the need of a treatise on discipline, as well as to distinguish themselves from some who bear the same name; and, finally, to arm the members against error and show " that the Baptists are not such Scare-Crows as some would make the unwary believe." It professes to be a condensation of the last Confession, with the addition of articles on the imposition of hands and the singing of psalms in public worship. But there are several more or less important differences in doctrine. It was provided with an appendix on discipline, entitled, " The Glory and Ornament of a True Gospel-constituted Church," written by Benjamin Keach and drawn largely from Doctor Chauncey. Only one English edition is known, but it exerted a great influence on the Philadelphia Confession and the Baptists of the middle colonies of America.

During the eighteenth century the English Calvinistic Baptists published no Confessions of note. They suffered with the general decline in religion, and for three-quarters of the century manifested little life in any direction. In 1764 Dr. John Gill's church, in London, published their Confession in twelve articles.

It is rigidly Calvinistic.

5. PRESENT DOCTRINAL POSITION OF THE ENGLISH BAPTISTS

With the rise of the Methodist movement and the work of Andrew Fuller, a great change was wrought in the theology of English Calvinistic Baptists. It was nothing less than the grafting of the Arminian doctrine of a universal atonement upon the old Calvinistic stock and the consequent serious and earnest offer of salvation to all men. Simultaneously with this change in Baptist theology came the work of Carey and the beginnings of foreign missions, with the rise of the practical tasks of the Sunday-school, Bible societies, tract societies, and similar organizations. Men's minds were turned to the practical side of Christianity, and their horizon was suddenly enlarged to include the whole world in the vision of their obligation and opportunity. They turned away from theological controversies and formulas. The old Confessions gradually fell into disuse, but no others took their places. The Union repeatedly declined to draw up any new Confession or prescribe one. The Arminian and Calvinistic wings by degrees approached each other. The rancors and contentions of former years were gradually forgotten in the presence of the great thrilling tasks of the nineteenth century. Finally, in 1888, the great majority of both parties dropped party names and united in a working compact for the furtherance of the King's business. The brief statement which forms the doctrinal basis of The Baptist Union of Great Britain and Ireland was formulated by the council and adopted by the Union April 23, 1888. It was because of dissatisfaction with this statement that Spurgeon withdrew from the Union in 1888, remaining aloof until his death in 1892. The statement was published in regular order in the proceedings of the Union for that year, and has never been reprinted. The statement, which was adopted with only seven dissenting voices in a meeting of seventeen or eighteen hundred messengers, is as follows:

Whilst expressly disavowing and disallowing any powers to control belief, or to restrict enquiry, yet, in view of the uneasiness produced in the churches by recent discussions, and to show our agreement with one another, and with our fellow-Christians on the great truths of the Gospel, the Council deem it right to say that:

A. Baptized into the name of the Father, and the Son, and the Holy Ghost, we have avowed repentance towards God and faith in the Lord Jesus Christ—the very elements of a new life; as in the Supper we avow our union with one another, while partaking of the symbol of the body of our Lord, broken for us, and of the blood shed for the remission of sins. The Union, therefore, is an association of Churches and Ministers professing not only to believe the facts and doctrines of the Gospel, but to have undergone the spiritual change expressed or implied in them. This change is the fundamental principle of our church life.

B. The following facts and doctrines are commonly believed by the churches of the Union:—

(1), The Divine Inspiration and Authority of the Holy Scripture as the supreme and sufficient rule of our faith and practice; and the right and duty of individual judgment in the interpretation of it.

(2), The fallen and sinful state of man.

(3), The Deity, the Incarnation, the Resurrection of the Lord Jesus Christ, and His Sacrificial and Mediatorial work.

(4), Justification by faith—a faith that works by love and produces holiness.

(5), The work of the Holy Spirit in the conversion of sinners and in the sanctification of all who believe.

(6), The Resurrection; the Judgment at the last day, according to the words of our Lord in Matt. 25. 46.*

Upon this statement the great majority of the Baptists of Great Britain still stand. There are still small bodies, remnants of former parties, who stand aloof; but the great majority of British Baptists stand and work together upon the basis of this brief statement of facts and doctrines.

---

* "It should be stated, as a historical fact, that there have been brethren in the Union, working cordially with it, who while reverently bowing to the authority of Holy Scripture, and rejecting the dogmas of Purgatory and Universalism, have not held the common interpretation of these words of our Lord."

Part Four

AMERICAN BAPTISTS

A. *Calvinistic Baptists*

1. The Philadelphia Confession

In England the Arminian, but in America the Calvinistic Baptists were the earlier party. Roger Williams and his associates came to America as Independents, holding the type of Calvinism which prevailed among that party at the time in England. When he became a Baptist he carried his theology with him into the organization of the First Church of Providence, the earliest Baptist church in America. At that date there was no Calvinistic Baptist Confession in existence. The church drew up none, and has continued to this day without any statement of doctrine. A few other Calvinistic Baptist churches were organized in New England, in the Middle Atlantic and Southern colonies within the seventeenth century, but no Confession of faith was published, and none adopted, as far as known. The earliest Association, the Philadelphia, was organized in 1707. The Calvinistic Baptists in this region showed more vigor, harmony, and aggressiveness than elsewhere. Moreover, they seem to have been in more constant and intimate relations with their English brethren than those of other sections. Elias Keach had been converted in this region, and had then been very active in preaching and establishing churches in Pennsylvania and New Jersey. He returned to England about 1692, and became pastor in London.

As we have seen, he and his father united in publishing a Confession of Faith in London in 1697. This Confession is the first one we hear of in America. The church at Middletown, N. J., fell into doctrinal confusion early in the eighteenth century, and being unable to restore harmony again, called a council to assist them in 1712. Among other things, this council recommended that the members " should subscribe to Elias Keach's Confession of Faith, at the least the covenant annexed to it," and that such as subscribed should be regarded as the Baptist church. Accordingly, this was done; forty-two of the sixty-eight members agreed to the proposition and subscribed, and in this way the church was reconstituted on the basis of Keach's Confession.

The first notice of the Confession of 1689 occurs in 1716, in connection with the interesting Welsh Tract Church, in New Jersey. According to the records of this church (I, 18f) the Confession was " translated to Welsh by Abel Morgan (minister of the gospel in Philadelphia), to which was added, An article relative to Laying on of hands; Singing Psalms; and Church-Covenants. This Confession (after being read and thoroughly considered at our quarterly meeting, February 4, 1716) was signed." It is not known that this Welsh edition was ever published.

The first reference to any Confession of faith by an Association in America was by the Philadelphia Association, in 1724. In reply to a query concerning the Sabbath, the Association refers " to the Confession of Faith, set forth by the elders and brethren met in London, 1689, and owned by us." It is not known that the Confession had been adopted by the Association in any formal way; nevertheless, it was evidently already regarded as their standard of doctrine. References to " our Confession of faith," " the Confession of Faith," etc., in 1727 and 1729, almost certainly refer to the same Confession. Finally, the Association assembled at Philadelphia, September 25, 1742, ordered the printing of a new edition of this Confession, the first of this or any other Baptist Confession to be printed in America. It was to have two additional articles, " concerning singing of psalms in the worship of God," and " laying of hands upon baptized believers." Jenkin Jones and Benjamin Griffith were also requested to " prepare a short treatise of discipline, to be annexed to the Confession of faith " (Minutes Philadelphia Association, 1742).

There had been tremendous controversy among English Baptists over singing in public worship and the imposition of hands upon the newly baptized, and articles in favor of both practices had found place in Keach's Confession. Imposition of hands was not general among Calvinistic Baptists in England, or in America in the earliest times; but the influence of Keach's Confession and of the Welsh Baptists (Minutes of Welsh Tract Church) had been decisive, and the Philadelphia Baptists now incorporate the practice in their doctrinal statement. The two articles, which are numbers XXIII and XXXI, are reprints of Articles XXVII and XXIII of Keach's Confession. The next year the Association adopted the Discipline, prepared and presented by Benjamin Griffith. Mr. Jones had been unable to give attention to the matter, and Mr. Griffith had used a " Tract published by Mr. Elias Keach," a manuscript by Abel Morgan, some writings of Doctors Owen and Goodwin, and previous actions of the Association on matters of discipline. His compilation was now added as an appendix to the Confession, and the whole was published 1743 by Benjamin Franklin, with the title:

A

CONFESSION

OF

FAITH,

Put forth by the
Elders and *Brethren*
Of many

CONGREGATIONS

OF

CHRISTIANS

(Baptized upon Profession of their Faith)
In *London* and the *Country*.

Adopted by the Baptist ASSOCIATION
met at Philadelphia,
Sept. 25, 1742.

The SIXTH EDITION.

To which are added,
TWO Articles *viz.* Of Imposition of Hands,
and Singing of Psalms in Public Worship.

ALSO

A Short Treatise of Church Discipline.

*With the Heart Man believeth unto Righteous-
ness, and with the Mouth Confession is
made unto Salvation,* Rom. 10.20.
Search the Scriptures, John 5.39.

PHILADELPHIA: Printed by B. FRANKLIN.
M,DCC,XLIII.

It is an exact reprint of the Assembly Confession of 1689, with the addition of the following articles, taken verbatim from Keach's Confession:

CHAPTER XXIII.
OF SINGING PSALMS, &C.

We believe that ' acts 16 25 eph 5 19 col 3 16 ' singing the praises of God, is a holy Ordinance of Christ, and not a part of natural religion, or a moral duty only; but that it is brought under divine institution, it being injoined on the churches of Christ to sing psalms, hymns, and spiritual songs; and that the whole church in their public assemblies, as well as private christians, ought to ' heb 2 12 jam 5 13 ' sing God's praises according to the best light they have received. Moreover, it was practiced in the great representative church, by ' matt 26 30 mat 14 26 ' our Lord Jesus Christ with his disciples, after he had instituted and celebrated the sacred ordinance of his Holy Supper, as a commemorative token of redeeming love.

CHAPTER XXXI.
OF LAYING ON OF HANDS.

We believe that (Heb 5 12 and 6 1 2 Acts 8 17 18 and 19 6) laying on of hands (with prayer) upon baptized believers, as such, is an ordinance of Christ, and ought to be submitted unto by all such persons that are admitted to partake of the Lord's Supper; and that the end of this ordinance is not for the extraordinary gifts of the Spirit, but for (Eph 1 13 14) a farther reception of the Holy Spirit of promise, or for the addition of the graces of the Spirit, and the influences thereof; to confirm, strengthen, and comfort them in Christ Jesus; it being ratified and established by the (Acts 8 and 19 6) extraordinary gifts of the Spirit in the primitive times, to abide in the Church, as meeting together on the first Day of the week was, Acts 2 1 that being the day of worship, or Christian Sabbath, under the gospel; and as preaching the word was, Acts 10 44 and as Baptism

was, Mat 3 16 and prayer was, Acts 4 31 and singing
Psalms, &c was Acts 16 25 26 so this of laying on of
hands was, Acts 8 & ch 19 for as the whole gospel was
confirmed by (Heb 2 3 4) signs and wonders, and divers
miracles and gifts of the Holy Ghost in general, so was
every ordinance in like manner confirmed in particular.

The Philadelphia Association published many editions
of the Confession in this form. From this Association
it went into the churches, and into other Associations, so
that it is justly called in America " The Philadelphia Confession of Faith."

The Charleston Association adopted it in 1767. The
article on the laying on of hands was omitted from all
the editions published by this Association, though the one
on singing is retained. The second edition, published at
Charleston, 1813, has, in addition to the Confession, a
" Summary of Church Discipline " and " The Baptist
Catechism," bound in leather, and making a neat volume.
In 1831 Rev. Daniel Sheppard issued an edition in which
the Scripture references were quoted in full at the bottom
of the page; the summary of discipline was retained, and
an "appendix," supposed to have been drawn up by
Oliver Hart and others, and treating various questions of
Baptist polity and practice, was added. The whole makes
a leather-bound volume of three hundred and three pages.
A fourth edition appeared in 1850, and there may have
been others.

Many churches and other Associations, both North and
South, adopted this Confession. In recent years it has
been losing ground, especially in the North, but it is
still widely used, and in the South is probably the most
influential of all Confessions.

The larger Baptist bodies in America have, as a rule,
abstained from making doctrinal statements or formally

adopting existing Confessions. Indeed, the Southern Baptist Convention, in its address "to the Brethren in the United States," at its organization in 1845, says: " We have constructed for our basis no new creed, acting in this matter upon a Baptist aversion for all creeds but the Bible."

2. THE NEW HAMPSHIRE CONFESSION

The only Confession of any note produced by American Calvinistic Baptists is the so-called " New Hampshire Confession of Faith." Indeed, it is doubtful if it ought to be called Calvinistic, since it is non-committal on every point of difference between the Calvinistic and Arminian systems. It is brief and very moderately Calvinistic. It emanated from the region where Arminian influences among American Baptists have always been strongest, and it faithfully reflects the modifying tendency of their presence. It is perhaps the most widely used and influential statement of doctrine among American Baptists at the present time. Its origin explains its name.

On June 24, 1830, the Baptist Convention of New Hampshire appointed a committee " to prepare and present at our next annual session, such a Declaration of Faith and Practice, together with a Covenant, as may be thought agreeable and consistent with the views of all our churches in this State." Next year the committee reported that it had made some progress, but had been unable to finish its task. At the request of the members they were discharged, and Rev. I. Person was " appointed to finish the work and report to the Board of this Convention as soon as convenient." June 26, 1832, he submitted to the Board the draft of a Confession, which was received and referred to " a select committee consisting of [Baron] Stow, [J. Newton] Brown, and [Jonathan] Going, with the author. Two days later this committee reported to the convention in favor of adopting the articles "with some slight alterations; but after some discussion it was resolved to refer them to the disposal of the Board." The matter never came before the convention again. The next day, however, it came before the Board anew. The articles were presented, and after discussion, referred to "brethren Stow and Brown to be revised and presented at the next meeting of the Board." October 10 and 11, 1832, the Board heard the report of the committee, discussed it at length, received it, and discharged the committee. Brown was then appointed to prepare a complete copy for the next meeting of the Board, incorporating the alterations which had been decided on in this discussion. January 15, 1833, Mr. Brown presented the work. The Board ordered the words "article" or "articles" stricken out wherever they occurred, and the word "Declaration" substituted. It was then voted "that the Declaration of Faith and Covenant prepared by Bren. Stow and Brown, and now read before the Board of this Convention, are entitled to their unanimous approbation, and are by them cordially recommended to the adoption of the churches." [1] It contained sixteen articles, and was published with the authority of the Board of the Baptist State Convention of New Hampshire.

In 1853 Rev. J. Newton Brown, who was then editorial secretary of the American Baptist Publication Society, on his own authority revised this Confession, adding two articles, one on "Repentance and Faith," and one on "Sanctification," making eighteen in all. In this form he incorporated it in "The Baptist Church Manual," and circulated it widely. It was copied in other church manuals and thus further popularized until it has become al-

[1] Minutes N. H. Bap. His. Soc. 1891.

most the sole Confession used in the North, East, and West, where Calvinism has been most modified by Arminianism.

In 1867 Rev. J. M. Pendleton, who was then pastor at Upland, Pa., incorporated this Confession in his " Church Manual." This manual was widely circulated among the " Landmark " Baptists, of whom Doctor Pendleton was a leader. It thus came to be adopted as the doctrinal statement of most of the newer churches and Associations of this type. It was recently adopted by the Landmark Convention, and is said to be the statement recognized by most of the Associations. It was adopted as the " Articles of Faith " of the Southwestern Baptist Theological Seminary after Article XIII had been changed by striking out the word " visible " and inserting " particular," making it read, " particular church," instead of " visible church."

In 1890 Rev. E. T. Hiscox, in his " Standard Manual," divided the article on " Baptism and the Lord's Supper " into two, making nineteen articles in all. In his " New Directory " he has further enlarged it, so that it now contains, as published by him, twenty articles.

All efforts to discover a copy of the original edition have proved unavailing. The following is reproduced from William Crowell's " Church Members Hand-Book," and may not be the exact original text, though it is certainly substantially so. Additions made in 1853 are enclosed in brackets, while other changes are indicated in the notes.

Declaration of Faith.

i. *Of the Scriptures.*

We believe [that] the Holy Bible was written by men divinely inspired, and is a perfect treasure of heavenly instruction; that it has God for its author, salvation for its end, and truth, without any mixture of error, for its matter; that it reveals the principles by which God will judge us; and therefore is, and shall remain to the end of the world, the true centre of Christian union, and the supreme standard by which all human conduct, creeds, and opinions should be tried.

ii. *Of the True God.*

[We believe] That there is one, and only one, living and true [1] God, [an infinite, intelligent Spirit,] whose name is JEHOVAH, the Maker and Supreme Ruler of heaven and earth; inexpressibly glorious in holiness; [and] worthy of all possible honor, confidence, and love; revealed under the personal and relative distinctions of [2] the Father, the Son, and the Holy Spirit; [3] equal in every divine perfection, and executing distinct but harmonious offices in the great work of redemption.

iii. *Of the Fall of Man.*

[We believe] That man was created in a state of [4] holiness, under the law of his Maker; but by voluntary transgression fell from that holy and happy state; in consequence of which all mankind are now sinners, not by constraint but choice, being by nature utterly void of that holiness required by the law of God, wholly given to the gratification of the world, of Satan, and of their own sinful passions, [5] therefore under just condemnation to eternal ruin, without defense or excuse.

iv. *Of the Way of Salvation.*

[We believe] That the salvation of sinners is wholly of grace; through the Mediatorial Offices of the Son of God, who [by the appointment of the Father, freely] took upon him our nature, yet without sin; honored the [divine] law by his personal obedience, and made atone-

---

[1] " true and living " in ed. 1853.
[2] " revealed . . . of the Father," is as follows in ed. 1853, " that in the unity of the Godhead there are three persons, the Father," etc.
[3] " Ghost " in ed. 1853.
[4] " a state of," omitted in ed. 1853.
[5] " wholly given . . . sinful passions " is changed to " positively inclined to evil " in ed. 1853.

ment for our sins by his death [6]; being [7]risen from the
dead he is now enthroned in heaven; and uniting in his
wonderful person the tenderest sympathies with divine
perfections, [he] is every way qualified to be a suitable,
a compassionate, and an all-sufficient Saviour.

v. *Of Justification*

[We believe] That the great Gospel blessing which
Christ of his fulness bestows on such [a] as believe in
Him, is Justification; that Justification consists in [b] the
pardon of sin and the promise of eternal life, on principles
of righteousness; that it is bestowed not in consideration
of any works of righteousness which we have done,
but solely through His own redemption and righteousness,[8] [by virtue of which faith his perfect righteousness
is freely imputed to us of God;] that it brings us into
a state of most blessed peace and favor with God, and
secures every other blessing needful for time and
eternity.

vi. *Of the Freeness of Salvation.*

[We believe] That the blessings of salvation are made
free to all by the Gospel; that it is the immediate duty of
all to accept them by a cordial, [penitent,] and obedient
faith; and that nothing prevents the salvation of the
greatest sinner on earth except [9] his own [inherent de-
pravity and] voluntary refusal to submit to the Lord
Jesus Christ,[10] which refusal will subject him to [11] an
aggravated condemnation.

vii. *Of grace in Regeneration.*

[We believe] That in order to be saved, we [12] must
be regenerated or born again; that regeneration consists

[6] Ed. 1853 reads, " and by his death made a full atonement for our sins "
for " and made . . . death."
[7] " that having risen " in ed. 1853.
[a] For " of his . . . such " ed. 1853 has " secures to such."
[b] For " consists in " ed. 1853 has " includes."
[8] For " His own redemption and righteousness " ed. 1853 has " faith
in the Redeemer's blood."
[9] " But " in ed. 1853.
[10] For " refusal to . . . Jesus Christ " ed. 1853 has " rejection of the
gospel."
[11] " which refusal . . . to " changed to " which rejection involves him in."
[12] " Sinners " in ed. 1853.

in giving a holy disposition to the mind; and [13] is effected in a manner above our comprehension or calculation,[14] by the power of the Holy Spirit, [in connection with divine truth,] so as to secure our voluntary obedience to the Gospel; and that its proper evidence is [15] found in the holy fruit which we bring forth to the glory of God.

viii. *Of Repentance and Faith.*
[This article added in 1853.]

We believe that Repentance and Faith are sacred duties, and also inseparable graces, wrought in our souls by the regenerating Spirit of God; whereby being deeply convinced of our guilt, danger, and helplessness, and of the way of salvation by Christ, we turn to God with unfeigned contrition, confession, and supplication for mercy; at the same time heartily receiving the Lord Jesus Christ as our Prophet, Priest, and King, and relying on him alone as the only and all-sufficient Saviour.

ix. *Of God's Purpose of Grace.*

[We believe] That Election is the gracious [16] purpose of God, according to which he [graciously] regenerates, sanctifies, and saves sinners; that being perfectly consistent with the free agency of man, it comprehends all the means in connection with the end; that it is a most glorious display of God's sovereign goodness, being infinitely [free,] wise, holy, and unchangeable; that it utterly excludes boasting, and promotes humility, [love,] prayer, praise, trust in God, and active imitation of his free mercy; that it encourages the use of means in the highest degree; that it is [17] ascertained by its effects in all who [truly] believe the gospel; [that it] is the foundation of Christian assurance; and that to ascertain it with regard to ourselves, demands and deserves our [18] utmost diligence.

[13] For "and" ed. 1853 has "that it."
[14] "Or calculation" omitted in ed. 1853.
[15] "Is found . . . God" appears in ed. 1853 as follows: "appears in the holy fruits of repentance, and faith, and newness of life."
[16] "eternal" in ed. 1853.
[17] "may be" in ed. 1853.
[18] "The." in ed. 1853.

x. *Of Sanctification.*
[Added in 1853.]

We believe that Sanctification is the process by which, according to the will of God, we are made partakers of his holiness; that it is a progressive work; that it is begun in regeneration; and that it is carried on in the hearts of believers by the presence and power of the Holy Spirit, the Sealer and Comforter, in the continual use of the appointed means—especially the Word of God, self-examination, self-denial, watchfulness and prayer.

xi. *Of the Perseverance of Saints.*

[We believe] That such only are real believers as endure unto the end; that their persevering attachment to Christ is the grand mark which distinguishes them from mere [19] professors; that a special Providence watches over their welfare; and [that] they are kept by the power of God through faith unto salvation.

xii. [Of the] *Harmony of the Law and the Gospel.*

[We believe] That the Law of God is the eternal and unchangeable rule of his moral government; that it is holy, just, and good; and that the inability which the Scriptures ascribe to fallen men to fulfill its precepts, arises entirely from their love of sin; to deliver them from which, and to restore them through a Mediator to unfeigned obedience to the holy law, is one great end of the Gospel, and of the means of grace connected with the establishment of the visible Church.

xiii. *Of a Gospel Church.*

[We believe] That a visible Church of Christ is a congregation of baptized believers, associated by covenant in the faith and fellowship of the Gospel; observing the ordinances of Christ; governed by his laws; and exercising the gifts, rights, and privileges invested in them by his word; that its only proper [20] officers are Bishops or

---

[19] " Superficial " in ed. 1853.
[20] " Scriptural " in ed. 1853.

U

Pastors, and Deacons, whose qualifications, claims, and duties are defined in the Epistles to Timothy and Titus.

xiv. *Of Baptism and the Lord's Supper.*

[We believe] That Christian Baptism is the immersion of a believer in water,[21] in the name of the Father [and] Son, and Spirit,[22] to show forth in a solemn and beautiful emblem, our faith in a [23] crucified, buried, and risen Saviour, with its purifying power [24]; that it is prerequisite to the privileges of a church relation; and to the Lord's Supper, in which the members of the church, by the [sacred] use of bread and wine, are to commemorate together the dying love of Christ; preceded always by solemn self-examination.

xv. *Of the Christian Sabbath.*

[We believe] That the first day of the week is the Lord's-Day, or Christian Sabbath; and is to be kept sacred to religious purposes, by abstaining from all secular labor and [sinful] recreations; by the devout observance of all the means of grace, both private and public; and by preparation for that rest which remaineth for the people of God.

xvi. *Of Civil Government.*

[We believe] That civil government is of divine appointment, for the interests and good order of human society; and that magistrates are to be prayed for, conscientiously honored, and obeyed, except [only] in things opposed to the will of our Lord Jesus Christ, who is the only Lord of the conscience, and the Prince of the kings of the earth.

xvii. *Of the Righteous and the Wicked.*

[We believe] That there is a radical and essential difference between the righteous and the wicked; that such

---

[21] " Immersion . . . in " reads " immersion in water of a believer, into."
[22] " Holy Ghost " in ed. 1853.
[23] " The " in ed. 1853.
[24] For " with its purifying power " is substituted the following: " with its effect in our death to sin and resurrection to a new life " in ed. 1853.

only as through faith are justified in the name of the Lord Jesus, and sanctified by the Spirit of our God, are truly righteous in his esteem; while all such as continue in impenitence and unbelief are in his sight wicked, and under the curse; and this distinction holds among men both in and after death.

xviii. *Of the World to Come.*

[We believe] That the end of this [25] world is approaching: that at the last day, Christ will descend from heaven, and raise the dead from the grave to final retribution; that a solemn separation will then take place; that the wicked will be adjudged to endless punishment, and the righteous to endless joy; and that this judgment will fix forever the final state of men in heaven or hell, on principles of righteousness.

3. CATECHISMS

American Baptists, especially in the earlier period, were diligent in training their children and servants in Baptist doctrines. For this purpose they have used various catechisms. The earliest and most widely used was " The Baptist Catechism," issued under the authority of the English Baptist Assembly about 1694, and adopted by the Philadelphia Association in 1742. Many editions appeared, sometimes erroneously called Keach's Catechism, sometimes with and sometimes without Scripture proofs, and it held its place until catechisms ceased to be used.

Many others were issued by individuals; by Basil Manly, by Henry D. Brown, by Jas. P. Boyce, by W. J. E. Cox, by John A. Broadus, and by others. More recently the catechism has fallen almost wholly into disuse, and efforts to introduce it into Sunday-school literature have not been very successful.

[25] " The " in ed. 1853.

B. *Arminian Baptists*

As we have seen, the earliest Baptists on American soil were Calvinistic. However, the earliest Baptist settlers in North Carolina and Virginia were Arminian, and very early, Arminian sentiments began to leaven and divide the churches of New England. They were chiefly emigrants from the English General Baptists, and in North Carolina acknowledged the General Baptist Confession of 1660.* For a century it seemed as if they might become the dominant Baptist type in America. Whitefield's revival, with its mild evangelical Calvinism, turned the tide. The old Calvinistic Baptists in New England and the middle colonies were awakened to new life and energy, and a new type, the "Separate Baptists," arose to do a wonderful work in New England and the South. The growth of the Arminian Baptists was thus checked, and the Calvinistic Baptists took the leadership.

But out of the same Whitefield revival arose another and larger Arminian body, known as "The Free-will," and more recently as "The Free Baptists." Benjamin Randall, a member of a Congregational church in New Hampshire, was converted under the preaching of Whitefield in 1770. He joined the Baptists at Berwick, Maine, in 1776, and began a remarkable career of itinerant evangelism in Maine, New Hampshire, and Vermont. He was soon excluded from the Baptists as an Arminian, and in 1780 organized an Arminian Baptist church at New Durham, N. H. The new denomination grew rapidly. For a time they opposed the use of Confessions, but in 1834 found it advisable to alter their policy.

Their General Conference, organized in 1827, took up the matter in 1832, and "agreed that the exigency of

---

* Burkitt & Read, His. Kehukee Assc., p. 28.

the times renders it necessary that we publish a Treatise, embracing all the leading points of the doctrine and practice of the Free-will Baptists, giving our scriptural reasons therefor, also our reasons for taking the Holy Scriptures as our only rule of faith and practice." After nearly two years consideration, the work was finished, April, 1834, and published the same year. It was provided with an introduction, giving an account of the rise of the body, of its attitude toward the Bible, and its reasons for publishing this " Treatise." Scripture references, often quoted in full, and extended remarks, occupy much of the page at the bottom; finally, there is an appendix on the discipline and usages of the denomination. In this form several editions appeared. In 1848 the treatise on discipline was revised and much enlarged. It was now entitled, " Usages of the Free-will Baptist Connexion, Revised by order of the Thirteenth General Conference, assembled in October, 1847." But the Confession of faith remained unchanged, and in this form several editions appeared.

Gradually the sentiments, as well as the usages of the connection, changed until it was out of harmony with its own statement of doctrine and practice. Accordingly, the General Conferences of 1865 and 1868 took up the question of a revision of the " Confession " as well as the " Usages." A committee was appointed, which finally completed its work January 1, 1869. The same year the results of their labors were published as the ninth edition of the " Free-will Baptist Faith."

The text of the original edition is reproduced here, while the important variations of the ninth edition are indicated in footnotes. This Confession has especial interest in view of the recent movement looking toward the union of Free Baptists with the larger body.

A

TREATISE

ON THE

FAITH

OF THE

FREEWILL BAPTISTS:

WITH AN

APPENDIX,

CONTAINING A SUMMARY OF THEIR USAGES
IN | CHURCH GOVERNMENT.

Written under the directions of their General Conference.

DOVER:
PUBLISHED BY DAVID MARKS,
For the Freewill Baptist Connexion.

: : : : : : :

1834.

TREATISE.

CHAPTER I.[1]
Being and Attributes of God.

The Scriptures teach that there is only one true and living God, (a) who is a Spirit, (b) self-existent, (c) eternal, (d) immutable, (e) omnipresent, (f) omniscient, (g) omnipotent, (h) independent, (i) good, (j) wise, (k) holy, (l) just, (m) and merciful; (n) the Creator, (o) Preserver, (p) and Governor, (q) of the universe; the Redeemer, (r) Saviour, (s) Sanctifier, (t) and Judge (u) of men; and the only proper object of Divine worship. (v)

The mode of his existence, however, is a subject far above the understanding of man. (w) Finite beings cannot comprehend him. (x) There is nothing in the universe that can justly represent him, for there is none like him. (y) Such is the character of God![2] He is the fountain of all perfection and happiness. He is glorified by the whole inanimate creation, and is worthy to be loved and served by all intelligences. (z)

(a) 1 Cor. 8:4; Jer. 10:10; 1 John 7:28; 2 Cor. 1:18; 1 John 5:20; Num. 13:19. (b) John 4:24; 2 Cor. 3:17. (c) Ex. 3:14; Ps. 83:18; John 5:26; Ex. 6:3; Rev. 1:4. (d) Ps. 90:2; Deut. 33:27; 1 Tim. 1:17; Rom. 1:20; Isa. 57:15; Jer. 10:10. (e) Mal. 3:6; James 1:17; Num. 23:19. (f) 1 Kgs. 8:27; Jer. 23:24; 2 Chr. 2:6; Acts 17:14; Isa. 57:15; Ps. 139:7-12. (g) Acts 15:18; 1 Tim. 1:17; Ps. 94:9, 10; 1 Chr. 28:9; Job 42:2; Acts 1:24; 1 John 3:26. (h) Rev. 19:6; Mt. 19:26; Mk. 10:27; 14:36; Lu. 18:27; Job 42:2; Ps. 135:6. (i) Eph. 4:6; Isa. 40:13-15; Rom. 1:33-36; Job. 9:12; 41:11; Dan. 4:35. (j) Ps. 119:68; 25:8; 86:5; 100:5; Ex. 9:27. (k) Rom. 16:27; 1 Tim. 1:17; Jude 25; Dan. 2:20. (l) Lev. 19:2; 21:8; 11:44, 45; Job 6:10; Ps. 71:22; Isa. 1:4; 43:3. (m) Ps. 119:137; Deut. 32:4; Ps. 92:15; Zeph. 3:5. (n) Eph. 2:4, 5; Ps. 100:5; 103:8; Ex. 34:6; Neh. 9:17. (o) Gen. 1:1; 2:5, 7; Col. 1:16; Heb. 11:3; Ps. 33:6, 9; Ex. 20:11. (p) Neh. 9:6; Heb. 1:3; Col. 1:17; Job 7:20. (q) Ps. 47:7; 2 Chr. 20:6;

---

[1] Ninth Ed. inserts as " Chapter I. *The Holy Scriptures.* These are the Old and New Testaments: they were written by holy men, inspired by the Holy Spirit, and contain God's revealed will to man. They are a sufficient and infallible guide in religious faith and practice." Chap. I of this edition then becomes Chap. II in the revised.
[2] This sentence omitted in 9th ed.

Ps. 95:3. (r) Isa. 47:4; 41:14; 59:20; Prov. 23:11; Ps. 78:35; Jer. 50:34. (s) Isa. 45:21; 43:3, 11; 45:15, 21; 49:26; 60:16; Hos. 13:4; John 4:42. (t) Ex. 31:13; 1 Thes. 5:23; Ezra 37:28; Heb. 13:12; Jude 1. (u) Heb. 12:22, 23; Gen. 18:25; Ps. 50:6; 2 Tim. 4:8. (v) Ex. 34:14; Mt. 4:10; Rev. 19:10; 22:8, 9. (w) Job 11:7; Isa. 40:28. (x) Isa. 40:25; Rom. 11:33. (y) Ex. 9:14; 3:14; 1 Chr. 17:20. (z) Ps. 19:1, 2; 150:6; 145:10.

CHAPTER II.[1]
Creation, Primitive State of Man, and his Fall.

SECTION I.—CREATION.

1. *Of the world.* God created the world and all things that it contains, for his own pleasure and glory, and the enjoyment of his creatures. (a)

2. *Of the angels.* The angels were created by God (b) to glorify him, (c) and obey his commandments. (d) Those who have kept their first estate, he employs in ministering blessings to the heirs of salvation, (e) and in executing his judgments upon the world. (f)

3. *Of man.* God created man, consisting of a corporeal [2] body and a thinking, rational soul. (g) He was made in the similitude [3] of God to glorify his Maker. (h)

(a) Rev. 4:11; Isa. 43:7; 1 Tim. 6:17. (b) Col. 1:16. (c) Rev. 7:11. (d) Ps. 103:20. (e) Jude 6; Heb. 1:14; Dan. 6:22. (f) 2 Sam. 24:16; Rev. 16:1. (g) Gen. 2:7; Mt. 2:11. (h) Gen. 1:27; 1 Cor. 11:7.

SECTION II.—PRIMITIVE STATE OF MAN AND HIS FALL.

Our first parents, in their original state of probation, were perfectly righteous: [4] they naturally preferred and

---

[1] Ninth ed. numbers this Chap. IV and inserts before it the following as "Chapter III. *Divine Government and Providence.* 1. God exercises a providential care and superintendence over all his creatures and governs the world in wisdom and mercy, according to the testimony of his word. 2. God has endowed man with power of free choice, and governs him by moral laws and motives; and this power of free choice is the exact measure of his responsibility. 3. All events are present with God from everlasting to everlasting; but his knowledge of them does not in any sense cause them, nor does he decree all events which he knows will occur"; with Scripture references.

[2] Ninth ed. has "material body."

[3] 9th ed. has "image" for "similitude."

[4] "Upright" for "righteous" in 9th ed.

desired to obey their Creator, and had no preference or desire to transgress his will, (a) till they were deceived,[5] inclined, and influenced by the tempter, to disobey God's commands. Previously to this, the only tendency of their nature was to do righteousness. In consequence of the first transgression, the state of trial,[6] under which the posterity of Adam come into the world, is so far different from that of Adam, that they have not that righteousness and purity which Adam had by creation;[7] are not naturally willing to obey God, but[8] prefer to disobey him, and are naturally inclined to evil rather than good. (b) Hence, none, by virtue of any natural goodness,[9] can become the holy children of God: (c) but they are all dependent for salvation upon the redemption effected through the blood of Christ, and upon being created anew unto holiness[10] through the operation of the Spirit; (d) both of which are freely provided for every descendant of Adam. (e)

(a) Gen. 2:7; Mt. 2:11. (b) Ps. 51:5; Job 14:4; 15:14; John 3:6; Ps. 58:3; Gen. 8:21; Rom. 5:12-19; Eccl. 7:20; Prov. 22:15; Isa. 48:8; Rom. 8:7; Gen. 6:5. (c) John 6:44; 1 Cor. 2:14; Jer. 17:9; Rom. 3:9-23; 8:8; John 15:5; Eph. 2:9; 2 Tim. 1:9. (d) Rom. 5:18; Col. 1:14; John 3:3; Heb. 12:14; 2 Cor. 5:10; Titus 3:5. (e) *see atonement.*

CHAPTER III.
Of Christ.

SECTION I.

[1] The Son of God possesses all Divine perfections. As he and the Father are one, he, in his Divine character,[2] performed all the offices and works of God to his creatures, that have been the subjects of revelation to us.

---

[5] " Deceived " omitted in 9th.
[6] " Of trial " omitted in 9th.
[7] Ninth ed. substitutes " before the fall " for " by creation."
[8] The remainder of the sentence reads " are inclined to evil " in 9th ed.
[9] Ninth ed. inserts " and mere work of his own "; and omits " holy " following.
[10] Ninth ed. substitutes " obedience " for " holiness."
[1] Ninth ed. has " Jesus Christ the Son," etc.
[2] " Nature " for " character " in 9th ed.

As man, he performed all the duties toward God that we
are required to perform, the repentance of sin [3] and from
dead works excepted.

His Divine perfections [4] are proved from his titles, his
attributes, and his works.

1. *His titles.* The Bible ascribes to Christ the titles
of Saviour, (a) Jehovah, (b) Lord of Hosts, (c) the
First and the Last, (d) God, (e) true God, (f) great
God, (g) God over all (h) Mighty God, and the everlasting Father. (i)

2. *His attributes.* He is eternal, (j) unchangeable,
(k) omnipresent, (l) omniscient, (m) omnipotent, (n)
holy, (o) and is entitled to Divine worship. (p)

3. *His works.* By Christ, the world was created;
(q) he preserves (r) and governs it; (s) [5] he has redeemed men, (t) and he will be their final Judge. (u)

(a) Isa. 45:21, 22; Hos. 13:4; Isa. 43:10, 11; John 4:42; Acts
4:12; 5:31; Eph. 5:23; Phil. 3:20; 2 Tim. 1:10; Tit. 1:4;
2:13; 3:6; 2 Pet. 1:11. (b) Isa. 40:3; Lu. 1:76; cf. Ps. 68:17,
18 with Eph. 4:7, 8; Jer. 23:6 and 1 Cor. 1:30—Isa. 42:8. See
also Rev. 1:8. Cf. Joel 2:32 with Rom. 10:3-13; also Ex. 6:3
and Gen. 17:1 with Ex. 3:2, 4; Isa. 63:9; Mal. 3:1 and Rom.
10:4-9; Isa. 48:8; Ps. 83:18. (c) Isa. 8:13, 14; 1 Pet. 2:4-6.
See also Eph. 2:20-22; Mt. 21:42. Cf. also Isa. 6:5 with John
12:41. Ps. 24:7-10. (d) Rev. 22:13. Cf. Rev. 1:8 with Isa.
44:6. Rev. 1:11; 21:6; (e) 1 Tim. 3:16; Acts 20:28; 1 John
3:16; Jude 25; John 1:1; 20:28, 29; Heb. 1:8; Col. 2:9; Tit.
2:10; Heb. 3:4. (f) 1 John 5:20; Jer. 10:10, 11. (g) Tit.
2:13; Rev. 22:12; 2 Thes. 1:7-10; 2 Tim. 4:1. (h) Rom. 9:5.
(i) Isa. 9:6; 45:5; (j) Col. 1:17; Mic. 5:2; John 1:1; 8:58;
Prov. 8:22-32; Heb. 1:12; 13:8; Rev. 1:8, 17, 18; 17:5, 24. (k)
Heb. 13:8; 1:12; 2 Tim. 2:19. (l) John 3:13; Mt. 28:20;
Eph. 1:23. (m) Rev. 2:23; John 2:24, 25; 16:30; 1:18;
10:15; 21:17; Acts 1:24. (n) Col. 2:8, 10; Ps. 45:3, cf.
with v. 2 and Rev. 19:16; Mt. 28:18; 1 Cor. 1:24; 15:24, 25;
John 10:18; 17:2; Eph. 1:21; Heb. 1:3; Rev. 1:8; 1 Cor. 4:5.
(o) Acts 3:14; Mk. 1:24; Lu. 1:35; Heb. 7:26; Rev. 3:7. (p)
Heb. 1:6; John 5:23; Phil 2:10, 11; Mt. 28:9; Lu. 24:52; Mt.
2:2; 8:2; 9:18; 28:19; John 9:38; Rev. 1:5, 6; 5:9-14; 7:9,
10; 2 Pet. 3:18; Gal. 1:5; 1 Cor. 1:2; 2 Cor. 13:14; Acts 7:59,
60; 1 Cor. 1:2; Acts 1:24. (q) Heb. 1:8, 10; John 1:3, 10; Col.
1:16; John 5:19; Eph. 3:9; 1 Cor. 8:6; Heb. 3:3, 4; Isa.
44:24; 45:12; Heb. 3:4; 2 Kgs. 19:15. (r) Heb. 1:3; Col.

---

[3] " And from dead works " omitted in 9th ed.
[4] For " Divine perfections " 9th has " divinity."
[5] Ninth ed. has " He has provided redemption for all men " for this clause.

1:17; Mt. 28:18. (s) Isa. 9:6; 1 Pet. 3:22; Col. 2:10; Eph. 1:21; 1 Cor. 15:24. (t) Eph. 1:7; Heb. 9:12; Isa. 54:5; Gal. 3:13; Ps. 19:14; 78:35; Isa. 43:14; 44:6; 49:26; 60:16; Jer. 50:34; Gal. 4:4, 5; 1 Pet. 1:18, 19; Tit. 2:14; Rev. 5:9. (u) 2 Tim. 4:1; Mt. 25:31-46; John 5:22; Ps. 50:6; 75:7; Heb. 12:23; 1 Chro. 16:33; Ps. 82:8; 96:13; John 5:27; Acts 10:42; Rom. 2:16; Rev. 1:7.

SECTION II.—THE INCARNATION OF CHRIST.

The Word, which in the beginning was with God, and which was God, by whom all things were made, condescended to a state of humiliation in [6] becoming united with human nature, or a body like ours, pollution and sin excepted. (a) In this state, as a subject of the law, he was liable to [7] all the infirmities of our nature; (b) was tempted as we are; (c) but lived our example, (d) and rendered perfect obedience to the Divine requirements. (e) As Christ was made of the seed of David according to the flesh, he is called " The Son of Man; " (f) and as the Divine existence is the fountain from which he proceeded, and was the only agency by which [8] his body was begotten, (g) he is called the Son of God; (h) being the only begotten of the Father, (i) and the only incarnation of the Divine Being.

(a) John 1:14; 1 Tim. 3:16; Phil. 2:6, 7, 8; Heb. 2:14, 16; Gal. 4:4; Lu. 2:52; 2 Cor. 8:9; Isa. 9:6; Heb. 10:5. (b) Mt. 8:17; Heb. 2:17; Mt. 4:2; 21:18; 27:50; John 6:6; 19:28; 11:33, 35; Isa. 53:3; Mt. 8:24; Lu. 22:14. (c) Heb. 4:15; Mt. 4:1-11. (d) 1 Pet. 2:21; Rom. 15:5, 6. (e) Isa. 42:21; Mt. 5:17; 3:15; Gal. 4:4. (f) Lu. 19:10. (g) John 16:27, 28; Mt. 1:18, 20. (h) Lu. 1:35. (i) John 3:16; 1:18; 1 John 4:9.

CHAPTER IV.

Holy Spirit.

1. The Scriptures ascribe to the [1] Holy Ghost the acts and attributes of an intelligent being. He is said to

---

[6] For " becoming . . . like ours," ninth ed. has " being united with human nature, and becoming like us."

[7] " All " omitted in ninth.

[8] Ninth has for " his body," " he."

[1] Ninth ed. has " Holy Spirit " uniformly.

guide, (a) to know, (b) to move, (c) to give information, (d) to command, (e) to forbid, (f) to send forth, (g) to reprove, (h) and to be sinned against. (i)

2. The attributes of God are applied to the Holy Ghost; such as eternity, (j) omnipresence, (k) omniscience, (l) goodness, (m) and truth. (n)

3. The works of God are ascribed to the Holy Ghost; creation, (o) inspiration, (p) giving of life, (q) and sanctification. (r)

4. The same acts, which in one part of the Bible are attributed to the Holy Ghost, are in other parts said to be performed by God. (s)

5. The apostles assert that the Holy Ghost is Lord and God. (t)

From the foregoing, the conclusion is, that the Holy Ghost is in reality God, and one with the Father in all Divine perfections. It has also been shown that Jesus Christ is God, one [2] in essence with the Father. Then [2] in essence these three, the Father, Son, and Holy Ghost, are one; [3] though they are three in respect to their agency and relation to man. Hence the words found in 1 John 5:7 are true: " For there are three that bear record in Heaven, the Father, the Word, and the Holy Ghost; and these three are one."

The truth of this doctrine is also proved from the fact, that the Father, Son, and Holy Ghost are united in the authority by which believers are baptized, and in the benedictions pronounced by the apostles, (u) which are acts of the highest religious worship.

(a) John 16:13. (b) 1 Cor. 2:11. (c) Gen. 1:2; Acts 8:39. (d) Acts 21:11; 10:19; John 16:14, 15; 14:26. (e) Acts 13:2. (f) Acts 16:6. (g) Acts 13:4. (h) John 16:8; Gen. 6:3. (i) Mt. 12:32; Isa. 63:10; Acts 7:51; 5:3, 4, 9; Eph. 4:30; 1 Thes. 5:19. (j) Heb. 9:14. (k) Ps. 139:7. (l) 1 Cor. 2:10, 11. (m) Neh. 9:20; Ps. 143:10. (n) John 14:17. (o) Job 26:13; 33:4; Ps. 104:30. (p) 2 Pet. 1:21; Acts 28:25. (q) 1 Pet. 3:18; John 6:23. (r) 1 Cor. 6:11; Rom. 15:16. (s) Cf. Isa. 6:8, 9 with Acts 28:25, 26; cf. Christ Son of God with Mt. 1:18. (t) 2 Cor. 3:17; Acts 5:3, 4. (u) Mt. 28:19; 2 Cor. 13:14.

[2] " In essence " omitted in 9th ed.
[3] 9th ed. has " one God," and omits the remainder of the paragraph.

CHAPTER V.

Atonement and Mediation of Christ.

1. ATONEMENT. As sin cannot be pardoned without a sacrifice, and the blood of beasts could never actually wash away sin, Christ gave [1] his life a sacrifice for the sins of the world, (a) and thus made salvation possible for all men. (b) He died for us, suffering [2] the penalty of the law in our stead, to make known the righteousness of God, that he might be just in justifying sinners who believe in his Son. (c) Through the redemption effected by Christ, salvation is actually enjoyed in this world, and will be enjoyed in the next, by all who do not in this life refuse obedience to the known requirements of God. (d) [3] As for the body, no provision was made for its redemption from the consequences of the fall, till the resurrection. (e) Then the bodies of the saints will be raised, and made like the body of Christ. (f) An atonement for sin was necessary. (g) For present and future obedience can no more blot out past sins, than past obedience can remove the guilt of present and future sins. Had God pardoned the sins of men without satisfaction for the violation of his law, it would follow that transgression might go on with impunity; government would be abrogated, and the obligation of subjection to God would be, in effect, cancelled.

2. MEDIATION OF CHRIST. Our Lord not only died for our sins, but he arose for our justification, (h) and ascended to heaven, (i) where, as Mediator between God and man, he will make intercession for [4] us till the final judgment. (j)

(a) I John 2:2; Isa. 53:5, 10, 11; Rom. 4:25; Mt. 20:28; I Pet. 3:18; John 1:29; Heb. 9:26; Gal. 1:4; Tit. 2:14; Eph. 5:25; Rom. 5:6, 8. (b) Heb. 2:9; I Tim. 2:6; Tit. 2:11; Rev. 22:17; Isa. 45:22; 2 Pet. 3:9; Acts 17:30; 2 Cor. 5:14, 15; Ps. 145:9; I Tim. 2:3, 4; 4:10; Isa. 55:1, 7; Ps. 86:15. (c) Rom. 3:25, 26; 13:39; 5:9, 18; Mt. 26:28; Eph. 1:7; Col. 1:14,

[1] For "his life," 9th ed. substitutes "himself."
[2] 9th omits "the penalty of the law."
[3] 9th ed. omits the two following sentences referring to the body.
[4] For "us" 9th ed. has "men."

20; Heb. 1:3; 9:14, 22; Rev. 5:9.   (d) Rom. 5:18; 8:1; 4:15;
2:14; Lu. 18:26.   (e) Rom. 8:21-23; Eph. 1:14.   (f) Phil.
3:21; 1 Cor. 15:49, 52-54.   (g) Heb. 9:22; Eph. 1:7; Rom.
5:19; John 1:16; Mt. 26:39.   (h) Rom. 4:25; 1 Cor. 15:17.
(i) Acts 1:11; Eph. 4:8; Mk. 16:19.   (j) Heb. 9:24; 1 Tim.
2:5; Heb. 7:25; Rom. 8:34; 1 Cor. 15:24; Isa. 53:12.

CHAPTER VI. [1]

The Gospel Call.

By virtue of the atonement, which is designed to
counteract the effects of the fall, man is placed in a sal-
vable state; (a) the grace of God, (b) the influences of
the Holy Spirit, (c) and the invitations of the gospel are
given to all men, (d) and by these they receive power to
repent and obey all the requirements of the gospel. (e)
Hence it appears a perfect inconsistency to suppose that
God would provide salvation for a less number than he
really loved. As his love extended to all mankind, if he
provided salvation for one, he must necessarily for all,
there being nothing in his nature, nor in man's nature,
whereby this provision should be limited. (f) The facts
being admitted that God loves all men, that Christ died
for all men, that the Holy Ghost reproves all men, that
the gospel invites all men, and that, by virtue of these,
all men have the ability to repent and believe, what other
conclusion can be drawn than that the salvation of all is
possible? We mean only to say, that salvation is *possible,*
for though in its provision it is free and absolute, (g)
yet in its application it is expressly conditional. (h) Salvation, then, being freely provided, and man being capable, through grace, of obtaining it, if he perish whom
can he blame but himself? The charge must fall upon
him with aggravated weight, " *Thou hast destroyed thy-
self.*"

(a) Mt. 18:11; John 17:4; Gal. 3:13; Rom. 5:18; John 3:17;
1 Tim. 4:10.   (b) Tit. 2:11; Rom. 5:20, 15.   (c) Joel 2:28;
John 16:8; 1:9; Acts 2:17, 18; Job 32:8; Rev. 14:6.   (d) Prov.
8:4; Isa. 45:22; Mk. 16:15; Rom. 10:18; Rev. 22:17; Mt.

---

[1] For this chapter 9th ed. substitutes the following: " The call of the
gospel is coextensive with the atonement to all men, both by the word
and the strivings of the Spirit; so that salvation is rendered equally possible to all; and if any fail of eternal life, the fault is wholly their own."

24:14; Col. 1:23; Isa. 55:1. (e) Phil. 1:29; 1 John 5:3; Isa. 5:4; 1 Pet. 1:22. (f) Acts 10:34; Ezek. 18:25; 33:11; 2 Pet. 3:9; 1 Tim. 2:4. (g) John 3:16; Rom. 5:8; 2 Cor. 5:14, 15. (h) John 3:36; Mk. 16:16; John 8:24; Acts 13:39; 16:31.

CHAPTER VII.

Repentance.

¹ The repentance which the gospel requires is a deep conviction, a penitential sorrow, an open confession, a decided hatred, and an entire forsaking of all sin. (a) This repentance God has enjoined on all men, and without it in this life the sinner must perish eternally. (b)

(a) Rom. 3:20; 7:9; 2 Cor. 7:10; Ps. 51:17; Joel 2:12, 13; Prov. 28:13; Ezek. 36:31; 14:6; Isa. 55:7; Ezek. 18:30, 31; Ps. 38:18; Hos. 5:15; John 12:25. (b) Acts 17:30; 2:38; 3:19; Mk. 6:12; Lu. 13:5; John 9:4; 2 Thes. 1:7, 8, 9; Acts 24:20; Mt. 4:17; 11:20-22; 12:41; 21:31, 32.

CHAPTER VIII.

Faith.

¹ True faith is an assent of the mind to the great and fundamental truths of revelation; (a) an ² act of the understanding in giving credit to the gospel, through the influence of the Holy Spirit; (b) and a firm confidence and trust in ³ the living God. (c) The fruit of faith is obedience to the gospel. (d) The power to believe is the gift of God; (e) but believing is act of the creature, which is required as a condition of pardon, and without which the sinner cannot ⁴ be regenerated, nor obtain salvation. (f) All men are required to believe,⁵ and those who yield obedience to the obligation become the children of God by faith. (g)

(a) Heb. 11:6; John 5:46, 47; Heb. 11:1; John 16:27, 30; Ps. 119:66; Rom. 10:9. (b) Rom. 10:10; 1 Cor. 12:8, 9; Gal. 5:22; Rom. 10:17. (c) 2 Chr. 20:20; Prov. 14:26; Rom. 4:20, 21; Eph. 3:12; 1 Tim. 4:10. (d) James 2:17, 20-24, 26; Gal. 5:6; 1 Tim. 1:5. (e) Phil. 1:29; Acts 14:27; 2 Pet. 1:1; Eph.

---

¹ For " true " 9th ed. has " saving."
² For " act . . . gospel " 9th ed. has " acceptance of the gospel."
³ For " the living God " 9th ed. has " Christ."
⁴ " Be regenerated, nor " omitted in 9th ed.
⁵ After " believe " 9th ed. adds " in Christ."

2:8. (f) John 6:29; Mk. 16:16; Acts 16:31; John 3:36; 8:21, 24; Heb. 11:6; Mk. 1:15. (g) Acts 10:43; John 1:7; Gal. 3:26; Rom. 16:26; 5:1; John 3:15.

CHAPTER IX.

Regeneration.

[1] As God is a holy Being and heaven a holy place, man must be regenerated before he can enter a state of happiness. (a). This change is an instantaneous [2] renovation of the soul by the grace and Spirit of God, (b) whereby the penitent sinner receives new life, becomes a child of God, (c) and [3] is enabled to perform spiritual service. (d) It is called [4] a being born again, born of the Spirit, (e) being quickened, (f) passing from death unto life, (g) and a partaking of the divine nature. (h)

(a) Heb. 12:14; Rev. 21:27; Mt. 5:8; Gal. 5:19-21. (b) John 3:5; Ezek. 36:26, 27; Tit. 3:5; Eph. 2:10. (c) John 5:25; Eph. 2:10; 1 John 3:9; Rom. 8:16; John 1:12; Jas. 1:18; 2 Cor. 5:17; Gal. 6:15. (d) 1 Pet. 2:5; Ezek. 11:19, 20; Phil. 2:13; 1 Pet. 4:11. (e) John 3:6; 1:13; 3:5, 8; 1 John 3:9; 4:7; 5:1, 4, 18. (f) Eph. 2:1; Ps. 119:50, 93; Eph. 2:5; Col. 2:13. (g) John 5:24; 1 John 3:14. (h) 2 Pet. 1:4; Heb. 3:14.

CHAPTER X.

Justification and Sanctification.

Personal justification implies that the person justified has been guilty before God; and that, in consideration of the [1] righteousness of Christ, received by faith, the sinner is pardoned and absolved from the guilt [2] and punishment of sin. (a) Though the [1] righteousness of Christ is the foundation of the sinner's redemption, yet without repentance and faith it can never give him justification and peace with God. (b)

[1] In 9th ed. the first sentence reads: " As man is a fallen and sinful being, he must be regenerated in order to obtain salvation."
[2] " Renovation . . . God " reads in 9th ed. " renewal of the heart by the Holy Spirit."
[3] " Is . . . service " reads " disposed to serve him."
[4] After " called " 9th ed. adds " in Scripture."
[1] For " righteousness " 9th ed. has " atonement."
[2] " And punishment " omitted from 9th ed., while " and restored to the divine favor " is added at the end of the sentence.

³ Sanctification is a work of God's grace, by which the soul is cleansed from all the pollutions of sin, and is renewed after the image of God. (c) Though in regeneration the soul is sanctified, yet, while the Christian continues in a state of trial, he has to contend with the corruptions of nature, and is liable again to be defiled. (d) Sanctification is also a setting apart the soul and body for holy service. (e) It is a progressive work, by which the Christian obtains victory over every temptation, corruption, and sinful inclination; and in which his will is brought into entire resignation to the will of God. (f) The attainment of entire sanctification in this life, is both the privilege and duty of every Christian. (g) For as sin is odious in the sight of God, Christ died to save his people from it, and the gospel has sufficient power to complete the work during this probation. (h)

(a) Rom. 5:16, 17; Acts 13:39; Rom. 5:1, 9; Isa. 53:11; Rom. 8:22-26. (b) Acts 3:19; Heb. 4:2; 11:6; Rom. 9:31, 32; 3:25-30; Acts 13:38, 39. (c) 1 Cor. 6:11; Heb. 10:10; John 17:17; Col. 3:10; 2 Cor. 3:18; Eph. 5:26. (d) Gal. 5:17; Rom. 8:13; 7:18-25. (e) Ps. 4:3; Rom. 12:1; Gen. 2:3; 1 Tim. 4:5. (f) Heb. 6:1; 2 Pet. 3:18; 1 John 5:4; Heb. 13:20, 21; Col. 4:12; 1:9; Prov. 4:18; Eph. 6:12. (g) 1 Thes. 5:23; 4:3; 2 Cor. 7:1; Gen. 17:1; Deut. 18:13; Col. 3:14. (h) 5:25-27; 1 John 1:7, 9; Mt. 5:48; 1 Pet. 1:16; 1 John 5:3; Col. 1:28; Phil. 2:14, 15; 2 Pet. 3:14; Jas. 1:4; John 1:47; 2 Cor. 13:11; Phil. 3:15; 2 Tim. 3:17; Mt. 19:21; 1 John 2:5; 1 Pet. 5:10.

¹ CHAPTER XI.
Perseverance.

As the regenerate are placed in a state of trial during this life, their future obedience and final salvation are neither determined nor certain. (a) It is, however, their duty and privilege to be steadfast in the truth, to grow in

³ For the remainder of this chapter 9th ed. substitutes the following: "Sanctification is a work of God's grace, by which the soul is cleansed from all sin, and wholly consecrated to Christ. It commences at regeneration, and the Christian can and should abide in this state to the end of life, constantly growing in grace and in the knowledge of our Lord Jesus Christ."

¹ Ninth edition has this chapter as follows: "There are strong grounds to hope that the truly regenerate will persevere unto the end and be saved, through the power of divine grace which is pledged for their support; but their future obedience and final salvation are neither determined nor certain; since, through infirmity and manifold temptations, they are in danger of falling; and they ought therefore to watch and pray, lest they make shipwreck of faith, and be lost."

grace, persevere in holiness, and make their election sure. (b)

(a) Ezek. 18:24; 33:18; John 15:6; Heb. 6:4, 5, 6; 2 Pet. 2:20, 21; Heb. 10:26; 2 Pet. 1:10; 1 Cor. 10:12; 2 Pet. 1:9; 1 Cor. 9:27; 1 Tim. 4:1; Heb. 12:15; 4:1, 11; 12:15; 2 Pet. 3:14. (b) 1 Cor. 15:58; 2 Pet. 3:18; Phil. 3:14; Mt. 24:13; Rom. 2:7; 1 Cor. 9:24; 2 Pet. 1:10, 11; Rev. 2:7, 11, 17, 26; 3:5, 12, 21; 21:7.

[1] CHAPTER XII.

The Sabbath.

This is a seventh part of time, which from the creation of the world, God has set apart for a day of sacred rest and holy service. It was included in the ten commandments written on tables of stone, and given to Moses on Mount Sinai. (a)   Nature itself teaches the necessity of its observance.   Its obligation is taught both in the Old and New Testaments, and is to continue with that of the other commandments till the end of time.   As the law of the Sabbath was at first given to the whole world, it requires all men, on this day, to refrain from all servile labor, and devote themselves entirely to the service of the God that made them. (b)

(a) Gen. 2:3; Ex. 20:8-10. (b) Jer. 17:21; Lu. 23:56; Isa. 58:13, 14; Ex. 16:23, 29; Mt. 5:19; Mk. 10:19; 1 John 2:4; Mk. 2:28; Lu. 24:1, 6; Acts 20:7; 1 Cor. 16:2; Rev. 1:9, 10.

CHAPTER XIII.[2]

The Church.

A Christian church is an assembly of persons who believe in Christ and worship the true God, agreeably to his word. (a)   In a more general sense, it signifies the whole body of real Christians throughout the world. (b)

[1] In ninth ed. this chapter is as follows: " This is one day in seven, which from the creation of the world, God has set apart for sacred rest and holy service.   Under the former dispensation the seventh day of the week, as commemorative of the work of creation, was set apart for the Sabbath.   Under the gospel the first day of the week, in commemoration of the resurrection of Christ, and by authority of the apostles, is observed as the Christian Sabbath.   On this day all men are required to refrain from secular labor, and devote themselves to the worship and service of God."

[2] Chapter XIII is so greatly altered in the ninth edition that it is here given entire as follows:
" CHAPTER XV.   *The Church.*   A CHRISTIAN CHURCH is an organized body of believers in Christ, who statedly assemble to worship God,

The church being the body of Christ, (c) none but the regenerate, who obey the gospel, are its real members. (d) Believers are received into a particular church, on their giving evidence of faith and being baptized. (e)

SECTION I.—OFFICERS OF THE CHURCH.

The officers in the primitive church were apostles, bishops, and deacons. (f) The apostles were the especial *witnesses* of the works and sayings of Christ; (g) and of course this office ceased when their work was accomplished. The *gifts* perpetuated in the church are evangelists, pastors, teachers, helps, and governments. (h) These, however, do not appear to be distinct officers; but they imply different kinds of duties, which are performed by bishops or elders, deacons, and others.

1. *Bishops* are overseers, (i) who have the charge of souls—to instruct and rule them by the word. (j) They are called *elders,* (k) and they perform the duties of pastors, teachers, and evangelists. (l) The qualifications required in a candidate for this office, are as follows:—He must be guiltless and the husband of but one wife. He must be watchful, prudent, and have the regular exercise of cool, dispassionate reason. His conduct

and who sustain the ordinances of the gospel agreeably to his word. In a more general sense it is the whole body of Christians throughout the world, and none but the regenerate are its real members. Believers are admitted to a particular church, on their giving evidence of faith, being baptized, and receiving the hand of fellowship.

"CHAPTER XVI. *The Gospel Ministry.* 1. QUALIFICATIONS OF MINISTERS. They must possess good natural and acquired abilities, deep and ardent piety, be specially called of God to the work, and ordained by the laying on of hands.

"2. DUTIES OF MINISTERS. These are, to preach the word, administer the ordinances of the gospel, visit their people and otherwise perform the work of faithful pastors.

"CHAPTER XVII. *Ordinances of the Gospel.* 1. CHRISTIAN BAPTISM. This is the immersion of believers in water in the name of the Father, the Son, and the Holy Spirit, in which are represented the burial and resurrection of Christ, the death of Christians to the world, the washing of their souls from the pollution of sin, their rising to newness of life, their engagement to serve God, and their resurrection at the last day.

"2. THE LORD'S SUPPER. This is a commemoration of the death of Christ for our sins, in the use of *bread* which he made the emblem of his broken body, and the *cup,* the emblem of his shed blood; and by it the believer expresses his love for Christ, his faith and hope in him, and pledges to him perpetual fidelity.

"It is the privilege and duty of all who have spiritual union with Christ thus to commemorate his death; and no man has a right to forbid these tokens to the least of his disciples."

and manners must be decent, orderly, and grave. He
must be a lover of hospitality and of good men; ready to
communicate, and able to teach. (m) He must be temperate; not quarrelsome; nor desirous of base gain. He
must be meek; not contentious, neither a lover of money.
(n) He must govern his family well; he must not be a
young convert, but experienced in the things of God,
and have a character not justly liable to reproach. (o)
He must be especially called of God to the work; (p) ad-
here closely to the doctrine of Christ, (q) and be ordained by the laying on of hands. (r)

The duty of an elder or bishop is, 1. To be an ensample
to the flock in all things. (s) 2. To examine into the
spiritual state of all the souls under his care, and suit all
his instructions, entreaties, and admonitions, to their condition. In this work is included the duty of a pastor. (t)
3. To study, preach the word, baptize, and administer the
Lord's Supper. (u) 4. To do according to his ability
the work of an evangelist. (v) 5. As a steward he receives authority from Christ to rule the flock by the word.
Therefore, he should neither act as a lord over God's
heritage, nor yield to the doctrines and wickedness of
men; but see that gospel discipline and holiness are enforced and practiced in the church. (w) He should
assist in ordaining elders and deacons, committing the
things which he has learned of God to faithful men, who
shall be able to teach others also. (x) The care and the
salvation of souls being more important than every thing
else, he should, as far as possible, avoid engaging in any
temporal concerns which will divert his attention from
his great calling, and devote himself wholly to the
work. (y)

2. *A deacon* is a regular or stated servant of the
church. As the bishops were appointed to take the
charge of souls, it is inferred that the seven appointed to
minister to the saints (Acts 6: 1-6) were *deacons;* and
that as the former have the oversight of the spiritual concerns of the church, the latter have the charge of its temporal affairs, particularly in serving the tables of the
needy. (z) Though there is no scriptural evidence that
serving the *Lord's table* at communion was required of

deacons, it appears that by common consent they have long performed this service in several denominations.

The *qualifications* required in a candidate for this office are the following. He must be sober, honest, temperate, not desirous of unrighteous gain, holding the mystery of the gospel in a pure conscience. Being first proved he must be found blameless. His wife must also be serious, not a defamer, but sober, and faithful in all things. He must have but one wife, and rule his children and his own house well. (a) He should be a wise man and filled with the Holy Spirit. (b) Having been selected by the church, he should be appointed by prayer and the laying on of hands. (c)

Duties of a Deacon. He should attend to the temporal wants of the poor members of the church, that those called to labor in the gospel may give themselves to prayer and the ministry of the word. 2. As the design of his appointment was that the ministry might be freed from temporal care, the inference naturally follows that it is his duty to see that *their* wants also are supplied, lest they should be compelled to leave the word of God to serve their *own* tables. 3. There being no other officer in the church to superintend its *temporal affairs,* it is inferred from the nature of his office that the deacon should attend to all the concerns essential to its prosperity, which do not devolve on a bishop. 4. From the important nature of his qualifications, it has been considered his duty to take the lead of religious meetings in the absence of the minister.

(a) I Cor. 1:2; Acts 2:47; 2 Cor. 8:5; Rev. 2:1, 7, 8, 12, 18; 3:1, 7, 14. (b) Eph. 5:23; 1:22; 3:10; 5:25, 27; Gal. 1:18, 24. (c) I Cor. 12:27; Col. 1:18. (d) I Pet. 2:5; 2 Cor. 6:14; John 18:36; Gal. 4:28, 31; Rom. 9:8; Ps. 50:16; John 15:2, 6. (e) Acts 2:41; Gal. 3:27. (f) Eph. 2:20; Phil. 1:1; Lu. 6:13; I Cor. 4:9. (g) Acts 10:39; 1:8; 5:32; Lu. 24:48.

(h) Eph. 4:11; I Cor. 12:28; 2 Tim. 4:5; Acts 13:1. (i) Acts 20:28; I Tim. 3:1-6. (j) I Tim. 3:5; I Pet. 5:2; Acts 20:28. (k) Tit. 1:5-7; I Pet. 5:1; Acts 14:23; cf. Acts 20:28 w. v. 17. (l) 2 Tim. 4:5; Eph. 4:11, 12; I Tim. 3:2, 1; Jer. 3:15; I Cor. 4:1; Ezek. 3:17; I Pet. 5:1; Eph. 4:11; 2 Cor. 5:20. (m) I Tim. 3:2; 1:8; 2 Tim. 2:24, 25. (n) I Tim. 3:3.

(o) I Tim. 3:4-7; Tit. 1:5-7; 2:7, 15. (p) Heb. 5:4; Acts 20:28; I Cor. 9:16; 2 Cor. 3:5, 6; I Tim. 1:12; Acts 13:2;

Rom. 10:14, 15; 1 Cor. 9:17. (q) Tit. 1:9; 2:1, 7, 8; 1 Tim. 1:3; 4:16; 2 Tim. 1:13; 1 Tim. 6:3, 4. (r) 1 Tim. 4:14; 5:22; Heb. 6:2; Acts 13:3. (s) 1 Tim. 4:12; 1 Pet. 5:3; Tit. 2:7; Phil. 3:17. (t) Heb. 13:17; 1 Pet. 5:2; 1 Tim. 4:6 Acts 20:28; 2 Tim. 4:2; Jer. 3:15. (u) 2 Tim. 2:15; 1 Tim. 4:15, 13; 2 Tim. 4:2; 2 Cor. 4:5; Mt. 28:19; Lu. 22:19; Acts 20:11; 27:35. (v) 2 Tim. 4:5; Mk. 16:15; 2 Cor. 8:19; 10:15, 16; Acts 9:32; 15:41. (w) Tit. 1:7; 1 Pet. 5:3; Tit. 2:15; 1 Tim. 1:3; 4:16, 11; 5:17; Tit. 1:5; Lu. 22:25, 26; Heb. 13:7, 17, 24; 2 Tim. 2:14; 1 Tim. 4:6. (x) Tit. 1:5; 2 Tim. 2:2; Acts 6:3, 6.

(y) 2 Tim. 2:4; 1 Tim. 4:15; Acts 6:4; Isa. 62:6; Ezek. 3:17-21. (z) Acts 6:1-4.

(a) 1 Tim. 3:8-12. (b) Acts 6:3, 5. (c) Acts 6:6.

SECTION II.—ORDINANCES OF THE CHURCH.

The following ordinances or institutions were appointed by Christ or his apostles, and are obligatory on the church.

1. *Christian Baptism.* (d) This is the immersion of believers in water (e) in the name of the Father, Son, and Holy Ghost, (f) in which are represented their death to the world, the washing of their souls from the pollutions of sin, (g) their resurrection to newness of life, the burial and resurrection of Christ, their resurrection at the last day, (h) and their engagement to serve God. (i)

2. *The Lord's Supper* is designed to commemorate the sufferings of Christ, and to represent, in the use of bread and wine, the communion which saints have with him, and with each other. (j) Every *true believer* in Christ, being a member of his body, and a part of his visible church, has not only a right to partake of his body and his blood in the communion, but is under obligation thus to commemorate his death. (k)

3. *Washing the saints' feet* is an example that was set by our Lord, and enjoined on his disciples to teach them humility. (l)

4. *Public worship.* This is that service which the church or its members publicly render to God, agreeably to his word. (m) Hearing the gospel signifies " listening, attending to, and obeying " the revealed will of God,

as contained in the Scriptures, and preached by his ministers. (n)

(d) Eph. 4:5; Acts 10:5, 6, 44-47. (e) Col. 2:12; Rom. 6:4,5; Acts 8:38, 39; Mt. 3:16; John 3:23; Mk. 1:5; Mt. 3:6; 1 Cor. 10:2; 15:29; Acts 16:13, 15, 32-34; Mk. 16:16; Acts 8:37; 2:41; 16:33; Mt. 28:19. (f) Mt. 28:19; 1 Cor. 1:13. (g) Col. 3:3; Tit. 3:5; Heb. 10:22. (h) Col. 2:12; Rom. 6:4; 1 Cor. 15:29; Rom. 6:5. (i) Gal. 3:27; Heb. 6:1, 2. (j) Mt. 26:26-28. Lu. 22:19; 1 Cor. 11:23-26; 10:16; Lu. 14:22-24. (k) Eph. 1:22, 23; 1 Cor. 10:17; Col. 1:24; Acts 2:42; 20:7.

(l) John 13:14-17; 1 Tim. 5:10. (m) Heb. 10:25; Acts 3:1; 16:13; 1 Thes. 5:11; Heb. 3:13; 1 Cor. 14:31, 3, 5; Acts 2:18; Phil. 4:6; Col. 3:16; Eph. 4:11-14; Mt. 18:20; 1 Cor. 11:18, 20; Acts 4:31; 11:26; 15:25; 12:5; Eph. 6:8; 1 Thes. 4:18; Rom. 12:6. cf. Acts 1:13, 14 with 2:1, 4; Lu. 2:36-38; Eph. 5:19; Mk. 14:26. (n) Mt. 7:24; 1 John 4:6; Jas. 1:22; Mk. 4:24; Rom. 10:14, 17; 2:13; Jas. 1:25.

SECTION III.—DUTIES OF THE CHURCH.

The duty of the church is that obligation which the revelation of God enjoins upon it, collectively, or as individuals, for the manifestation of his manifold wisdom, (o) the perfection of the saints, (p) and the conversion of the world. (q) In this obligation are included the observance of the ten commandments, (r) entire obedience to the influences of the Spirit, (s) to the institutions of the gospel, and to all the instructions and precepts of the Scriptures. (t) Among the latter are the following particular requirements: Christian fellowship, (u) secret & family prayer, (v) domestic and social duties, (w) watchfulness, (x) administering to the necessities of the poor and afflicted, (y) the support of those that preach the gospel, (z) and the exercise of church discipline. (a)

(o) Eph. 3:10, 11. (p) Eph. 4:1-13. (q) Mt. 5:16; Rom. 16:26; Mk. 16:15; Mt. 5:13. (r) Mt. 5:17, 19; Lu. 23:56; Mt. 22:37-40; Mk. 10:19; Rom. 13:8-10. (s) 1 Thes. 5:19; Eph. 4:30; Rom. 8:1; Gal. 5:16. (t) 1 John 5:3; Mt. 19:17; 5:48; Jas. 1:4; 2 John 6; Isa. 8:20; 1 Cor. 7:19; John 14:21; Eccl. 12:13. (u) 1 John 1:7; Acts 2:42; Eph. 5:11; 1 John 1:3; Phil. 1:5. (v) Mt. 6:6; Lu. 6:12; Dan. 6:10; Acts 10:9; Jer. 10:25; Acts 10:2, 30; Ps. 55:17. (w) Eph. 5:25; Col. 3:19; Eph. 5:28; Col. 3:18; Eph. 5:24; 1 Pet. 3:1; Eph. 6:4; Col. 3:21, 20; Eph. 6:1, 2, 5, 9; Col.

3:22; Eph. 5:21; Rom. 12:10; Col. 3:13; Rom. 12:18; Mt.
5:44; Mk. 11:25, 26; Rom. 12:20; Tit. 3:1. (x) Mk. 13:37;
Mt. 26:41; 1 Cor. 16:13; 1 Pet. 4:7; 5:8. (y) Lu. 18:22; Mt.
19:21; Prov. 28:27; 19:17; Lu. 11:41; 12:33; Deut. 15:7, 11;
John 12:6; Rom. 15:26; Gal. 2:10; 1 Cor. 16:1, 2; Jas. 1:27;
Mt. 25:26; 1 Tim. 5:10. Acts 6:1; Phil. 4:14. (z) Mt. 10:
9, 10; Lu. 10:7; 1 Cor. 9:4, 6, 11, 13, 14; Gal. 6:6; 2 Cor. 11:8,
9; Deut. 12:19; Phil. 4:16, 18. (a) Mt. 18:15-17; 1 Tim. 5:20;
Gal. 6:1; 2 Thes. 3:6; Jas. 5:16; 1 Cor. 5:11, 13; Rom. 16:17;
2 John 10; Tit. 3:10; 1 Tim. 5:19; 2 Cor. 2:6, 7, 8; 1 Cor. 5:4,
5; 1 Tim. 1:20; 6:3-5.

CHAPTER XIV.[1]

Death.

The bodies of men being subject to the calamities of
the fall, all have died, or will die, excepting Enoch,
Elijah, and the saints that shall be in the earth at the last
day. (a) But the soul, spirit, or the immaterial part,
survives the dissolution of the body, and immediately
after death enters a state of happiness or misery. (b)

(a) Rom. 5:12; Heb. 9:27; 11:5; 2 Kgs. 2:11; 1 Thes.
4:17; 1 Cor. 15:52; Ps. 89:48; Eccl. 8:8. (b) Eccl. 12:7;
Lu. 23:43; Phil. 1:23; Mt. 17:3; 22:31, 32; Acts 7:59; Rev.
6:9; Mt. 10:28; 2 Cor. 5:8; Lu. 16:22, 23, 24; Jude 7.

CHAPTER XV.[2]

The Resurrection.

As the transgression of Adam secured temporal death
to all his posterity, so the obedience and resurrection of
Jesus Christ render it certain that the bodies of all men
will be raised from the dead. (a) The doctrine of the

---

[1] Ninth edition has this chapter as follows:
"*Death and the Intermediate State.* 1. DEATH. As a result of sin,
all mankind are subject to the death of the body.
" 2. THE INTERMEDIATE STATE. The soul does not die with the
body; but immediately after death enters into a conscious state of happiness or misery, according to the moral character here possessed."
This chapter is then added:
" CHAPTER XIX. *Second Coming of Christ.* The Lord Jesus, who
ascended on high and sits at the right hand of God, will come again to
close the gospel dispensation, glorify his saints, and judge the world."

[2] Ninth edition has this chapter as follows:
" The Scriptures teach the resurrection of the bodies of all men at the last
day, each in its own order; they that have done good will come forth to
the resurrection of life, and they that have done evil to the resurrection of
damnation."

resurrection is not only taught in the Scriptures, but it is intimated in the natural world. (b) The saints will be raised in the likeness of Christ; but the wicked will awake unto shame and everlasting contempt. (c)

(a) 1 Cor. 15:21, 22, 13-19; Acts 24:15; Job 19:25, 26; Isa. 26:19; Mt. 22:30; Acts 26:8; John 5:28, 29; 2 Tim. 2:18; Acts 26:8; Rom. 8:11. (b) Job 14:7, 14, 15; 1 Cor. 15:36. (c) Phil. 3:21; 1 Cor. 15:53; 1 John 3:2; Ps. 17:15; Dan. 12:2; John 5:28, 29; Mt. 25:32-46.

CHAPTER XVI.[1]
The General Judgment.

As men do not receive the due reward of all their deeds in this life, there will be a general judgment, when time and man's probation will close forever. (a) Then all men will be judged according to their works; (b) the righteous will enter into eternal life, (c) and the wicked will go into a state of endless punishment. (d)

(a) Acts 17:31; 2 Pet. 2:9; Mt. 11:24; 2 Pet. 3:7; Jude 6; Rev. 10:6; 1 Cor. 15:24; Mt. 12:41, 42; 25:31, 32; 1 John 4:17; 2 Pet. 3:11, 12; Rev. 20:11, 12. (b) 2 Cor. 5:10; Rom. 2:16; Eccl. 11:9; 12:4; Mt. 12:36; Rev. 20:13; Rom. 2:6, 7-9; 14:10, 12; Eccl. 3:17. (c) Mt. 25:34, 46; 2 Pet. 1:11; Rev. 3:12; 1 Thes. 4:17; Rom. 6:22; Rev. 1:6; 3:4; Col. 3:4. (d) Mt. 25:41, 46; 2 Thes. 1:9; Mk. 3:29; 9:44; Jude 7; Rev. 14:11; John 8:21; Rev. 20:10, 15; 21:8, 27; 22:11; Mt. 13:41, 42; Ps. 9:17; 11:6.

[1] Ninth edition has this chapter as follows:
"*The General Judgment and Future Retributions.* 1. THE GENERAL JUDGMENT. There will be a general judgment, when time and man's probation will close forever. Then all men will be judged according to their works.
"2. FUTURE RETRIBUTIONS. Immediately after the general judgment the righteous will enter into eternal life, and the wicked will go into a state of endless punishment."

Part Five

CONFESSIONS OF OTHER NATIONALITIES

All the Confessions thus far treated, which can in strict propriety be considered Baptist, were drawn up in English. But in the course of the nineteenth century Baptist churches rose in other lands, propagated for the most part directly or indirectly from England and America. Besides the mission fields, strictly so-called, which have been and are still dependent on English-speaking Baptists for their vitality, doctrines, and practices, there are on the continent of Europe flourishing bodies of Baptists, whose views and practices have been formulated with considerable independence. The most important of these are the German, French, Swedish, Danish, Hungarian, and Russian Baptists. Some of these bodies have drawn up independent Confessions of faith of considerable importance. They are all Calvinistic, but their Calvinism is of a mild type.

I. GERMAN BAPTIST CONFESSION

Of these Confessions, that of the German Baptists is most important, because of the size and vigor of the body, and of the further fact that they have been largely instrumental in planting Baptist bodies in the other countries of Northern and Eastern Europe. They are in no way descended from the old Anabaptists or Mennonites, alongside of whom they live to-day without any intercommunior. The work began at Hamburg, in 1834, with the baptism of J. G. Oncken, a colporter of the

330

Edinburgh Bible Society, who had been converted by independent personal study of the Bible, to the Baptist view of the subject and mode of baptism. April 23 the first Baptist Church of Germany was organized in the house of Oncken, in the great commercial city of Hamburg. Through much persecution and over great difficulties, Baptist work gradually spread to all parts of the country, until at present (1909) there are some forty thousand Baptists in the empire.

Early in the history of the movement, Julius Köbner, a Danish Jew, and G. W. Lehmann, of Berlin, were converted and threw in their fortunes with the Baptists. These two, with Oncken, form the famous " Clover-leaf " of German Baptist history, and for years shaped the views and policies of the body. They drew up that statement of doctrines which continues to the present to be the sole Confession of the whole body of German Baptists. As in the case of the early English Baptists, their purpose was to disprove the slanderous accusations constantly circulated against them, and to afford a brief text-book for indoctrinating the churches in the teachings of the Bible.

As early as 1837 such a Confession was drawn up by Oncken and Köbner to be laid before the government of Hamburg. When it was presented to the Hamburg church, some of the members rejected it because of its outspoken doctrine of the election of grace, and were excluded in consequence. It was then adopted as the doctrinal belief of that church. A transcript copy was sent to the church in Berlin, where Lehmann enlarged and modified the Confession, and the Berlin church then adopted it. In this form the brethren at Hamburg would not receive it. For nine years it was impossible for the two parties to agree upon any common statement. Finally, in 1845, during a visit of Lehmann in Hamburg, the brethren, after struggling for days and nights with the subject, reached a statement in which all parties could find their views. The doctrine of the Lord's Supper is Calvinistic rather than Zwinglian. Köbner, who was the leading literary representative of the Baptists, was charged with the duty of giving literary form and providing Scripture references for the whole. This work was not finished until 1847, when the Confession was printed, and at the urgent demand of Oncken, was laid before all the churches for adoption. This was done, and henceforth all who were received into the churches were required to give assent to the Confession. Not only were the Scripture references given, but many of the passages were printed in full, thus placing before the reader's eyes the Scripture proof of every position (Lehmann, " *Gesch. d. deutschen Baptisten*," I, 254f). The opposition the German Baptists encountered not only cemented their union but made them especially careful in regard to the standards of their faith which they sent forth.

When the Baptist Union was formed, in 1848, it was agreed that the " Foundation of this Union is the Confession of Faith adopted by all the churches which enter this Union."

As before stated, this Confession remains the common bond of the German Baptists to the present time. But in 1906 a committee was appointed by the General Conference to consider its revision. A carefully prepared revision (printed in " *Die dreijährlichen Berichte*" for 1909) was brought in in 1909, but after considerable discussion action was postponed for another period of three years. The original Confession therefore continues in force. A translation with Scripture references attached follows:

CONFESSION OF FAITH

and

CONSTITUTION

of the

CHURCHES OF BAPTIZED CHRISTIANS

commonly called Baptists.

With Proofs
out of the
Holy Scripture.

13th Edition.

Kassel.
Publishing House of the German Baptists, G. m. b. H.
1908.

Article 1.

OF THE WORD OF GOD.

We believe that the holy Scriptures of the Old Testament [books named], together with the holy Scriptures of the New Testament [books named], are truly inspired of the Holy Spirit (1); so that these books as a whole make the only true divine revelation to the human race and the sole source of the knowledge of God, as they must be the sole rule and plumbline of faith and practice (2).

1) 2 Tim. 3:16. Ex. 19:9. 2 Sam. 23:2. Isa. 1:2. Jer. 1:9. John 10:35. 2 Pet. 1:20, 21. Heb. 1:1, 2. Lu. 10:16. Mt. 10:20. 1 Thess. 2:13. Gal. 1:11, 12. [1 Cor. 2:9, 10]. 1 Cor. 2:13.
2) 2 Pet. 1:19. Ps. 119:105. Lu. 16:29-31. 2 Tim. 3:15-17. (Jno. 5:39. Act. 17:11.) Rom. 1:16. 1 Cor. 14:37. Gal. 1:8. (Rom. 16:25, 26. 3:21. Rev. 22:18.)

———

Article 2.

OF GOD.

We believe that there is only one living, true and eternal God (1): the Father, the Son and Holy Spirit (2), in their natures and attributes complete, eternally alike and inseparable (3), so that the Father is true, eternal God (4), the Son true eternal God (5), the Holy Spirit true eternal God (6), and yet we do not believe on three Gods, but only on one eternal (7), almighty (8), all-wise (9), omniscient (10), omnipresent God (11). To the knowledge of this God can man attain only through the divine revelation of the holy Scripture and the Holy Spirit(12).

1) Deut. 6:4. (1 Cor. 8:4, 6. 1 Tim. 2, 5.)
2) Mt. 28:19. (Gen. 1:26; 3:22. Isa. 61:1. Mt. 3:16, 17. Jno. 14:26. 2 Cor. 13:13. 1 Jno. 5:7.)
3) 1 Jno. 2:23. Jno. 10:30. Jno. 14:7-10. (Jno. 16:13, 14.)
4) Eph. 4:6. (Mt. 6:9.)
5) Rom. 9:5. Jno. 1:1-14. Jno. 20:28. 1 Jno. 5:20. Heb. 1:3-10. (Isa. 9:6. Jer. 23:5, 6. Jno. 5:23. 8:58, 59.)
6) 1 Cor. 2:11. Mt. 12:32. Acts 5:3, 4. 2 Cor. 3:17, 18. (Gen. 1:2. Ps. 33:6. Acts 20:28. 1 Cor. 3:16, 17. 12:11. Eph. 4:30. 1 Pet. 4:14.)

7) Ps. 90:2.   (Exodus 3:14.   1 Tim. 1:17.)
8) Rev. 4:8.   (Gen. 17:1.)
9) Rom. 16:27.   (Rom. 11:33, 34.   Isa. 40:28.)
10) Acts. 15:18.   Heb. 4:13.   (Ps. 139, 2-4.)
11) Jer. 23:24.   (Ps. 139, 7-10.)
12) 1 Cor. 1:21.   1 Cor. 2:14.   Jno. 14:26.   (Mt. 11:25, 27.
Rom. 10:17.)

Article 3.
OF SIN.

We believe that God created the first man after his own
image (1), an upright, holy and innocent creature (2),
able to glorify his God, and, united with Him, to be saved
(3). Through the deceit of Satan (4) man sinned, fell
away from God, lost the image of his Creator, and fell
immediately, body and soul, into the state of death (5).
Since now all men sprang from the seed of Adam, so
they likewise became partakers of the same fallen and
wholly corrupt nature (6), so that they were conceived
and born in sins (7), are children of wrath (8), wholly
incapable and undisposed to all good, but susceptible and
inclined to all evil. (9).

1) Gen. 1:27.
2) Eccl. 7:30.   (Gen. 1:31.)   Gen. 2:25.
3) Gen. 3:8.
9) Gen. 3:13.   Rev. 20:2.   Jno. 8:44.
5) Gen. 2:17.   Mt. 8:22.   Eph. 2:1.   Rom. 8:6.   (Rom. 6:23.
Col. 2:13.)
6) Jno. 3:6.   Rom. 5:12, 18.   Gen. 6:3.
7) Ps. 51:7.   58:4.
8) Eph. 2:3.
9) Rom. 8:7.   Gen. 8:21.   Jer. 17:9.   Mk. 7:21, 22.   Lu.
24:25.   Mk. 16:14.   Rom. 3:10-18.

Article 4.
OF REDEMPTION.

We believe that God could redeem man from the
frightful consequences of his fall in no other way than
through a complete and valid pacification and satisfaction of his holy justice (1); therefore he, from eternity,
destined his only begotten Son, Jesus Christ, to be a

sin offering (2). As a consequence of this, at the time
chosen by God, Christ, the Son of the living God (3)
appeared in the form of sinful flesh upon earth (4), and
united in the same his eternal Godhead with human nature (5), a truly human soul and a human body (6),
which, however, were and remained completely pure and
spotless, so that never either in the heart of Jesus or in
his outer life did sin appear (7). So he rendered an
active obedience in that he fulfilled for us the whole
divine law (8), and a passive obedience in that he laid
down his body and his soul as an offering for us (9).
He became a curse for us (10), since he bore the wrath of
God, the punishment of our sins (11).—We believe that
this eternally complete and valid redemption (12) of the
Son of God is the sole cause of our salvation (13), and
that we out of the same forgiveness of all our sins and
transgressions (14), become partakers of justification
(15), an eternal righteousness (16), redemption from
death, the devil and hell (17), and of eternal life (18),
as also that we thereby attain power to hate sin, to die
to it (19), to will and accomplish the good (20).—After
Christ accomplished his redemption through his death
(21), he rose from the dead on the third day (22),
ascended to heaven (23), sat down at the right hand of
the Majesty on High (24) and sent us his Holy Spirit
(25), who makes us willing to accept the blessings of
this glorious redemption in faith (26). As high-priest
he represents us with the Father (27), is with us all the
days unto the end of the world, and will finally lead us
to heaven where he has prepared the place for us (29).

1) Heb. 9:22. 10:5-7.
2) 1 Pet. 1:20.
3) Gal. 4:4. Mt. 16:16. 3:17.
4) Rom. 8:3.
5) Col. 2:9. 1 Tim. 3:16. (Rom. 1:3, 4.)
6) Mt. 26:38. Heb. 2:14. (1 Tim. 2:5.)
7) Jno. 8:46. 1 Pet. 2:22. Heb. 4:15.
8) Mt. 5:17. Gal. 4:4. Rom. 10:4. 5:19. Ps. 40:8, 9.
(Mt. 20:28. Isa. 42:21.)
9) Isa. 53:4. Heb. 5:8. Phil. 2:8. Lu. 22:19. Ps. 22:15,
16. Isa. 53:11. Mt. 26:38. Lu. 22:44. Heb. 9:28. (Heb.
9:14, 26. 10:12, 14.)

10) Gal. 3 : 13.
11) Zech. 13 : 7. Mt. 27 : 46. 2 Cor. 5 : 21. Isa. 53.
12) Heb. 9 : 12. (Isa. 45 : 17)
13) Heb. 5 : 9. Isa. 53 : 5.
14) Eph. 1 : 7. (Col. 1 : 14.) 1 Jno. 1 : 7. Mt. 26 : 28. Acts 20 : 28.
15) Rom. 3 : 24. 5 : 1.
16) Isa. 61 : 10. Jer. 23 : 6. 2 Cor. 5 : 21. (Dan. 9 : 24).
17) 1 Cor. 15 : 26, 54, 55. Jno. 6 : 40. Gen. 3 : 15. Col. 1 : 13. (Col. 2 : 15.) 1 Jno. 3 : 8. (Heb. 2 : 14, 15.) Eph. 4 : 8. 1 Thess. 1 : 10.
18) 1 Jno. 5 : 11, 12. Jno. 11 : 25, 26. (Jno. 3 : 36. 10 : 28. 2 Tim. 1 : 10.)
19) Titus 2 : 14. Rom. 6 : 14. 1 Jno. 3 : 3. Acts 15 : 9.
20) Phil. 4 : 13. 2 : 13. Rom. 7 : 21, 22.
21) Jno. 19 : 30.
22) (Mt. 28. Mk. 16. Lk. 24. Jno. 20.). Acts 2 : 32.
23) Lu. 24 : 51. (Mk. 16 : 19. Acts 1 : 9.)
24) Mk. 16 : 19. Heb. 1 : 3. 8 : 1.
25) (Acts 2. Jno. 15 : 26. 16 : 7-14.)
26) Acts 16 : 14. Rom. 5 : 5. 8 : 14. Jno. 16 : 13, 16. (Gal. 5 : 5.)
27) Heb. 4 : 14. Rom. 8 : 34. 1 Jno. 2 : 1.
28) Mt. 28 : 20.
29) Jno. 14 : 3. 17 : 24.

———

Article 5.
OF ELECTION TO SALVATION.

We believe that it has been from eternity the free and independent good pleasure (1), the definite purpose of God to redeem sinners (2). Therefore, as before the foundation of the world, it was, out of unfathomable, compassionate love, determined in the Godhead that Jehovah, the Anointed, should through his incarnation and his death be the Redeemer (3), so were the persons of the lost human race to whom redemption should in the course of time be really communicated also chosen by the Father (4), their names written in heaven (5), they themselves given over into the hands of the Redeemer (6), as his people (7), as the sheep of his pasture, for whom he would lay down his life (8), as his inheritance (9), as the booty of his death struggle (10) and as his bride (11). To these persons was the eternal life in Christ apportioned (12), and likewise were all the means decreed which should bring them to faith in Christ, to holiness

w

and finally to eternal salvation (13). Such decree of
God is unchangeable and eternally fixed (14) so that
those to whom it refers, the elect, cannot be torn out of
the hands of Christ (15) ; rather through the power of
God in faith and in love to Christ they remain guarded
until they become fellow-heirs of his glory.

1) Eph. 1 : 11.   (Rom. 11 : 34.)
2) Jno. 3 : 16.
3) Acts 2 : 23.   3 : 18.   (Eph. 3 : 10, 11.)
4) Acts 13 : 48.   Mt. 25 : 34.   Mk. 13 : 20..   Jno. 6 : 37.   6 : 65.
15 : 16.   Acts 16 : 6.   18 : 9, 10.   Rom. 8 : 28, 33.   9 : 11-16.   9 : 20.
11 : 4, 5, 7.   Eph. 1 : 4.   2 Thess. 2 : 13.   2 Tim. 1 : 9.   Ps. 65 : 5.
(Mt. 20 : 16.   Lu. 18 : 7.   1 Cor. 1 : 26-29.   Eph. 2 : 8, 10.   Col. 3 : 12.
Ps. 33 : 12.)
5) Rev. 17 : 8.   Dan. 12 : 1.   (Lu. 10 : 20.   Phil. 4 : 3.   Rev.
20 : 12, 15.
6) Jno. 17 : 6, 9, 11, 24.
7) Mt. 1 : 21.   (Acts 18 : 10.   Isa. 53 : 8.)
8) Jno. 10 : 15, 16, 26, 27.
9) Eph. 1 : 18.   (Ps. 28 : 9.)
10) Isa. 53 : 12.
11) Rev. 21 : 9.   (Ps. 45.)
12) Jno. 17 : 2.   (Jno. 10 : 28.   Rom. 5 : 21.   6 : 23.   1 Jno. 5 : 11.)
13) Rom. 8 : 29, 30.   1 Pet. 1 : 3.   (Eph. 1 : 19.   Isa. 43 : 5-7.)
14) Rom. 11 : 29.   Phil. 1 : 6.   Isa. 54 : 10.   Ps. 89 : 31-35.   (Isa.
65 : 17, 19.)
15) Rom. 8 : 35-39.   Mt. 24 : 24.   Jno. 6 : 39.   Jno. 10 : 28.
(Rom. 7 : 23-25.)
16) 1 Cor. 1 : 8.   1 Pet. 1 : 3-5.

————

Article 6.

OF THE MEANS OF GRACE AND THEIR ORDER.

We believe that God has ordained means of grace
through which he draws sinners to himself and com-
municates to them the salvation which Christ has earned.
With respect to the same God has arranged a definite
order which can not be changed by us without transgression of the divine will (1).   There comes into use (a)
the word of God (2).   Those converted thereby under
the working of the Holy Spirit are then added to the
church of Christ through (b) baptism (3), and the members of this church celebrate in the same (c) the Supper
(4) as a proclamation of the death of Christ and as an

intimate fellowship with him (5). In this supper the communion of saints likewise finds its highest expression (6). However, prayer is the soul of all these means (7) and of the state of grace in general (8). It begins with the first moment of the new life (9) and never again ceases.

1) Jno. 8:31. Jno. 14:21, 23. Mt. 28:20. Col. 2:5.
2) Mk. 16:15. Acts 2:14. 8:5. 8:35. 16:13. 16:32. (Acts 10:34-44, 18:4, 5.)
3) Mk. 16:16. (Acts 2:41. 8:12, 37, 38. 16:15, 33. 10:48.)
4) Acts 2:41, 42. (Acts 20:7.)
5) Jno. 6:56.
6) 1 Cor. 10:17.
7) Lu. 3:21. Acts 22:16.
8) Acts 2:21. (Rom. 10:11-14.)
9) Acts 9:6. 9:11.

Article 7.
OF THE CONVERSION OF THE SINNER THROUGH THE WORD OF GOD.

The way of salvation is this, that man, through the word of God which is living and powerful, (1) is awakened out of his sinful sleep; (2), recognizes his sins and his guilt and heartily repents (3). In the feeling of his danger he has recourse to Christ (4) as his only Deliverer and Saviour (5), and receives through faith in him the forgiveness of his sins (6) and the witness in his heart that he is a child of God and heir of eternal life. (7) This great change in the heart and in the knowledge of the sinner is exclusively the work of the Holy Spirit (8), who according to the gracious will of God accompanies the word with his almighty, successful working (9), thereby effects the regeneration of the fleshly minded sinner (10), opens his heart (11), enlightens his soul (12), and begets living faith in Christ (13).

1) Heb. 4:12. Jer. 23:29.
2) Acts 2:37. Isa. 55:10, 11. (Lu. 16:29-31.)
3) 2 Cor. 7:10. Lu. 18:13. Ps. 51:6. Acts 17:30. (Lu. 7:37-48.)
4) Jno. 6:37. Mt. 11:28.

5) Acts 4:12. Jno. 14:6. (Jno. 3:36.)
6) Rom. 3:24, 25, 28. Acts 26:17, 18.
7) Rom. 8:16, 17. Gal. 4:6. 1 Jno. 5:10, 11. (Eph. 1:13, 14. 4:30. 2 Cor. 1:21, 22.)
8) 1 Cor. 6:11, 1 Cor. 12:3. Jno. 6:45.
9) 1 Thess. 1:5. 1 Cor. 2:4, 5. Jno. 6:63. Acts 10:44, 46.
10) Jno. 1:13. 3:3, 5, 6, 7. Jas. 1:18. 1 Pet. 1:23. Gal. 6:15.
11) Acts 16:14.
12) Eph. 5:8. 1 Cor. 2:14.
13) Eph. 2:8.

Article 8.

OF HOLY BAPTISM.

We believe that according to the definite declarations of the New Testament holy baptism, which was ordained by Christ, and is to continue for believers until his reappearance (1), consists in this, that the candidate is dipped one time under water in the name of the Father, of the Son and of the Holy Spirit (2) and again raised out of the same by a minister of the Lord appointed for that purpose. Only so is the divine command fulfilled (3), and the ordinance of Christ retains its deep original significance (4). The persons who should subject themselves to this ordinance and receive with thankful heart this means of grace are also very definitely defined in Holy Scripture, viz., only such persons, no matter to what people they may belong, as have previously been converted from their sins to Christ through the gospel and God's free grace, and believe with the whole heart on him as their Redeemer (5).

Baptism is a first-fruit of faith and love to Christ, the entrance into obedience toward the Lord (6) and his church (7). It is the solemn declaration, the confession of the sinner (8), who has recognized the frightfulness of sin and the damnability of his whole being (9): that he sets all his hope solely on the death and the resurrection of Jesus Christ his Saviour (10), and believes on him as the Redeemer from the curse and wages of sin (11),— that he consecrates himself with body and soul to Christ and puts him on (12), as his righteousness and strength

(13),—that he gives his old man to death and wishes to walk with Christ in a new life (14).

Baptism is, moreover, the solemn declaration and assurance of God to the believing candidate that he is swallowed up in Christ Jesus (15), and so with him dead, buried and risen again (16); that his sins are washed away (17), and that he is a beloved child of God, in whom the Father is well pleased (18). Baptism should call forth the consciousness of his deliverance and salvation in the candidate more definitely and powerfully (19), and such will God work through a sealing with the Holy Spirit (20), though only where he has previously brought forth through this Spirit true saving faith in the Son of God in the power of his death and his resurrection (21).

Baptism has the peculiarity that it should be administered only once, while the other means of grace are repeated and renewed throughout the whole life of the Christian; therefore it is especially necessary that this ordinance should be rightly performed.

1) Mt. 28:19, 20.
2) Mt. 3:13-15. Mk. 1:9. Mt. 3:16. Jno. 3:23. Acts 8:36, 38, 39.
3) Eph. 4:5. Rom. 6:5.
4) Col. 2:12, 13.
5) Mk. 16:16. Acts 2:37, 38, 41. 5:14. 8:12. 8:37. 18:8. Gal. 3:26, 27. Acts 10:42-48. 16:13-15, 29-34. Mt. 3:1, 2, 5, 6, 7-9. Mk. 1:5. Lu. 3:3. Acts 13:24.
6) Acts 2:38, 41. 9:6. 22:16. Jno. 15:10, 14. (Mk. 16:16.)
7) 1 Cor. 12:13. Acts 2:47.
8) 1 Pet. 3:21. Heb. 10:22, 23. 4:14.
9) Acts 2:36, 37. 9:5, 6, 9. 16:29, 30. (Mt. 3:6.)
10) Acts 2:38. Rom. 6:3, 8. 2 Cor. 5:14.
11) Rom. 6:23. 6:10, 11. (Isa. 53:5. Acts 8:35.)
12) Gal. 3:26, 27.
13) Isa. 45:23, 24.
14) Rom. 6:4-6.
15) Rom. 6:3.
16) Rom. 6:4, 8. (Col. 2:12, 13.)
17) Acts 9:9. 22:12, 13, 16. (Acts 2:38.)
18) Mt. 3:17. Eph. 1:6.
19) 1 Pet. 3:21. Acts 8:39. 9:19, 20. 16:31-34. **Rom.** 6:3-11.
20) Mt. 3:16. Heb. 1:9. 2 Cor. 1:21, 22. (Acts 2:38.)
21) Eph. 1:13.

Article 9.

OF THE HOLY SUPPER.

This ordinance, so full of grace, given by the Lord to his church, which we regard as an inestimable means of grace and of which we should make frequent use (1), consists in this, that bread is broken by one appointed thereto in the church with the pronunciation of the words of institution, and after a solemn prayer of thanksgiving, and this then, as afterwards also wine out of the cup, is partaken of by the members of the church (2).

According to the holy and blessed command given to them the redeemed of the Lord should through this meal proclaim his death, till he come again, as the sole ground of their life and salvation (3). Through this proclamation the memory of the Son of God becomes living anew in their hearts, he appears to their soul anew in his bloody beauty (4).

We believe that in these holy symbols Christ gives his body and his blood to believers to be partaken of in a spiritual manner (5). The communion of the body and blood of Christ in the enjoyment of the holy supper (6) should be to the believer a divine pledge, through which the consciousness of his part in Christ and his offering, is heightened and strengthened (7), and through which the forgiveness of sins, appropriated by him in faith, is constantly renewed and assured (8).

The holy supper is exclusively and only for such as through God's converting grace have become his possession (9), and have received holy baptism (10).

1) Acts 2:42, 46. 20:7.
2) Mk. 14:22-24. (Mt. 26:26-28. Lu. 22:17-20. I Cor. 11:23-25.)
3) I Cor. 11:26. Jno. 6:51. Isa. 53:5.
4) I Cor. 11:23-25. 2 Tim. 2:8.
5) Ps. 42:3. Isa. 55:2. (Jno. 6:57.)
6) I Cor. 10:16.
7) Lu. 22:19, 20. Jno. 6:57. I Jno. 5:12. Jno. 17:23. Rom. 8:32.
8) Mt. 26:26, 28.
9) I Cor. 10:16-18, 20, 21. 5:11. Mt. 7:6. (2 Cor. 6:14-18.)
10) Mt. 28:19, 20. I Cor. 12:13.

ARTICLE 10.

OF THE CHURCH OF THE LORD.

Through baptism we are taken up into the church of Christ on earth (1), and the Lord has ordained this as a means of grace for us (2). In accordance with the command of Jesus Christ and his apostles, (3) as also the example of apostolic times (4), and in order to be able to bring all the ordinances of the New Testament into operation (5), it is the duty of every believer converted to God not to stand alone for himself, but to unite himself with other disciples of the Lord as a member of a body (6) and as the living stones of a house of God (7), in order mutually to edify one another, to comfort and help each other on the way of salvation (8), in order to continue in the apostles' doctrine, in fellowship, in the breaking of bread and in prayer (9). Such a union of the true disciples of Christ, regulated according to the word of God, is a Christian church (10). The unchangeable rule and plumb-line of the church remains the New Testament (11).

Offices in the Church

Only the Lord Jesus Christ himself is the head of the same (12); it knows no visible heads on earth (13).

The church itself chooses its elders, preachers and ministers (14), who are clothed with their office through ordination.

By *ordination* we understand the usage, which the holy Scripture teaches us, that the persons chosen by the church for service are set apart by the elders and preachers of this or some other church, by the laying on of hands and through prayer, to the work of their calling (15).

With regard to their manner of life they remain afterwards as before, like every other member, subject to the discipline of the church. This must be done, however, in accordance with 1 Tim. 5:19 (16).

Elders and Preachers

We do not recognize any distinction in rank among elders and preachers (17), but hold that the designations

of holy Scripture: bishops, presbyters, etc., do not indi-
cate distinctions in rank.

Learning we hold to be desirable for these offices, but
not absolutely necessary (18), but above all the condition in Jno. 21:15-17 (19) and the characteristics and
qualifications demanded in the Epistles of Paul (20).

The *elders* preside in the church meetings whose leadership they undertake. They are thereby obligated to
carry into effect the conclusions of the church. Besides
this they are obligated to a true and special care of souls
(21).

The *preachers* are authorized and obligated to preach
in the assemblies for worship (22).—In respect to the
evangelical purity of their teachings they stand under the
oversight of the united church (23), which in case a
preacher departs from the doctrines of the gospel as they
are conceived in this Confession of faith, and persists in
his departure notwithstanding all warnings, can remove
the same from his office (24).

Holy baptism and the holy supper may be administered
as well by the elders as by the preachers (25).

The office of elder and that of preacher are frequently
united in one person.

It is entirely in harmony with his office for an elder or
preacher also to follow some temporal calling; though
it is under certain circumstances desirable that he should
devote himself exclusively to his spiritual office (26). In
case the church wishes this, it is obligated according to
the divine commands to give him a respectable support in
accordance with their abilities (27).

Servants

The deacons or servants of the church must possess the
characteristics indicated in Scripture (28). They assist
the elders and preachers in their office and the temporal
affairs of the church are specially committed to them
(29).

Duties of the Members

The duties of the church members consist in a mutual
hearty love (30), in a living, active participation as well

in the spiritual salvation as in the bodily welfare of all (31), and in a conscientious use of the means of grace and a following of those things prescribed, as the Lord, as Head of the church, has given them (32). Especially is it the duty of each member to unite in the celebration of the holy supper (33), and to attend regularly the stated assemblies of the church on Sunday as well as on a week day (34). Only in cases of the greatest necessity or because of sickness may a member of the church absent himself from the celebration of the holy supper or from attendance upon the assemblies for worship, but especially upon the business meetings (35).

Voting

In the deliberative assemblies of the church all matters of business, insofar as possible, are to be determined by voting (36).

In voting all members have equal voices (37), and the decision will be determined by a majority of the votes. To such a decision the minority must then willingly submit, since freedom and order in the house of God can be preserved only in this manner (38).

Reception [of members]

The reception of a new member can take place only by vote, after previous acquaintance with his spiritual condition and the submission in person before the church of a confession of faith (39). In such voting it is highly desirable that unanimity of voices take place.

Discipline of the Church

The order of Christ in the 18th chapter of the Gospel of Matthew, from the 15th to the 17th verses, is to be strictly followed by every member without distinction. It is the duty of every one to accept an admonition in love, or, where it is necessary, to give it in love, without permitting any knowledge of it to come to a third party. Not until after exclusion may a brother or a sister be considered and treated by the members as no longer belonging to the church or to the people of God (40).

Exclusion

The church is, in accordance with the rule of its Founder, authorized and obligated to exclude by an orderly vote those of its members whose walk contradicts their confession, who transgress some one of the divine commands, and will not be led to hearty public penitence and the resolution for genuine improvement through the admonitions given them, but continue in sin, and to withdraw from them the rights of members (41). Members who have been guilty of gross sins, causing public reproach, or oft repeated sins, and whose bare word for the time deserves no confidence, are to be excluded in the same way without regard to assurances of penitence (42).

The restoration of an excluded member, like every other reception, takes place by vote after examination and a confession of sins made before the church (43).

1) 1 Cor. 12, 13.
2) Eph. 4:15, 16. Heb. 10:24, 25. (Rom. 12:5.)
3) Jno. 17:22. 1 Pet. 2:5. 2 Cor. 6:16, 17.
4) Acts 4:32. (Acts 1:14. 2:1, 41, 46, 47. 4:24.)
5) Mt. 18:15-17.
6) 1 Cor. 12:27. (1 Cor. 12:12-27.)
7) Eph. 2:19-22. (1 Pet. 2:5.)
8) 1 Thess. 5:11, 14. Col. 2:18, 19. (Jud. 20.)
9) Acts 2:42.
10) Jno. 10:27. 8:31.
11) 1 Cor. 3:9-11. (Eph. 2:20.)
12) Eph. 1:22. Col. 1:18. (Eph. 4:15.)
13) Mt. 20:25-27. 23:8.
14) Eph. 4:11, 12. Acts 14:23. 15:22, 25. Acts 6:2-5.
15) Heb. 6:2. Acts 14:23. 13:3. 1 Tim. 5:22. Tit. 1:5.
Acts 6:6.
16) 1 Tim. 5:19.
17) Mt. 20:25-27. Mt. 23:9-11. (1 Cor. 4:9. 3:8.)
18) 1 Cor. 1:17. 2:1-5. (Mt. 4:18-22.)
19) Jno. 21:15, 16.
20) 1 Tim. 3:1-7. Tit. 1:5-9.
21) Acts. 20:28, 31. Heb. 13:17.
22) Jas. 3:1. 1 Tim. 4:13. 2 Tim. 4:2. 2:15.
23) Mt. 7:15. 1 Jno. 4:1. Rev. 2:2. Col. 2:8.
24) Gal. 1:8, 9. Rom. 16:17, 18. (1 Tim. 6:3-5.)
25) 1 Cor. 4:1.
26) Acts 18:3. 20:33, 35. (2 Thess. 3:8.) 1 Cor. 9:13, 14.
Lu. 10:7, 8.
27) Gal. 6:6. 1 Tim. 5:17, 18. (1 Cor. 9:7-14.)

28) Acts 6:3. 1 Tim. 3:8-12.
29) Acts 6:1-4.
30) Jno. 13:34, 35. 1 Jno. 3:11. 1 Pet. 1:22. (Jno. 15:12, 17. Jas. 2:8.)
31) 1 Jno. 3:16-18. Rom. 12:15. (Gal. 5:6. 1 Thess. 5:14.)
32) Eph. 5:24. 1 Jno. 2:4. 2 Jno. 6.
33) Mt. 26:27. Mk. 14:23.
34) Heb. 10:25. Acts 1:14. 2:1. 2:42. 4:24. Ps. 27:4. 122:1. 84:1.
35) Ps. 116:18.
36) Acts 15:22, 25. 21:21-23. (Mt. 18:17.)
37) Mt. 23:8, 11.
38) 1 Cor. 14:40. 14:33. Col. 2:5. Eph. 5:21. 1 Pet. 5:5. Mt. 18:17, 18.
39) 1 Tim. 6:12. Heb. 4:14. Rom. 10:9, 10. (Mt. 10:32.)
40) Mt. 18:15-17.
41) 1 Cor. 5:1-13. 2 Thess. 3:6. Tit. 3:10, 11. 1 Tim. 1:19, 20. (1 Tim. 6:3-5.)
42) 1 Cor. 5:1-13. Mt. 3:8.
43) 2 Cor. 2:6-8.

Article 11.

OF SANCTIFICATION.

We believe that without sanctification no man will see the Lord (1). It is a consequence of the justification of the sinner before God through faith in Christ, and stands in inseparable union with the same (2).

It consists in this, that, after the dominion of sin in the heart of the regenerated one has been brought to an end (3), he now through the constant influence of the Holy Spirit (4) uses all diligence to die to the sin which still constantly clings to him (5), to fulfill the law of his God (6) and to bring his soul as well as his body as a living sacrifice well pleasing to God (7), through which God is glorified (8). In this striving, however, he can still be overtaken by many weaknesses and sins (9) which he will never excuse (10), rather will deeply regret (11), because he thereby offends his gracious God (12) and destroys his peace with him (13). He will in such a case find no rest again until he obtains forgiveness anew (14) and will for the future walk all the more carefully (15).

A holy filial love to God and his commands is the most essential quality in sanctification (16), and this love, which

is begotten, preserved and nourished in the heart by the
Holy Spirit (17), transforms the man by degrees into
the image of God (18). We hold that sanctification
should go on throughout our whole life (19), and that
we also even in the most holy living constantly need the
forgiving grace of God through the blood of Christ (20).

1) Heb. 12:14. I Pet. 1:15, 16. I Thess. 4:3, 7. (Eph. 1:4.)
2) I Cor. 1:30. Rom. 6:2. Jno. 15:2. (Jas. 2:17. Mt.
7:17. Gal. 5:22. Eph. 2:10.)
3) Rom. 6:14, 22.
4) Rom. 8:14.
5) Rom. 7:21. 8:13. Col. 3:5-10. Heb. 12:1. (Eph. 4:22-
32. Tit. 2:11, 12.)
6) Heb. 8:10. Rom. 7:22. Ps. 119:29, 111-113. (Ps. 119.)
7) Rom. 12:1.
8) I Cor. 6:20.
9) Rom. 7:19, 23, 24. Gal. 5:17. I Jno. 1:8, 9. (I Jno. 3:3.
Prov. 20:9. Eccl. 7:21.)
10) Ps. 51:5.
11) 2 Cor. 7:9. Ps. 51:19. (Ps. 38:5-7.)
12) Ps. 51:6. Mt. 26:75.
13) Ps. 38:4.
14) Ps. 32:3-6. Mt. 6:12.
15) Eph. 5:15, 17. Ps. 51:14, 15.
16) 2 Cor. 5:14. I Cor. 13:1, 3, 13. I Cor. 14:1. Eph. 4:15.
(2 Thess. 3:5. I Jno. 4:19; 5:3.)
17) Rom. 5:5.
18) Eph. 4:23, 24. 2 Cor. 3:18. (Col. 3:10.)
19) 2 Cor. 7:1. (I Cor. 9:24-27. I Tim. 2:15.)
20) Heb. 4:16. I Jno. 1:7. Jas. 2:10. Dan. 9:18. (Rom.
3:27, 28. 4:4-8. I Pet. 1, 2.)

Article 12.

OF THE DIVINE LAW.

Of Law in General

We believe that although we live under the dispensation of the grace of the new covenant, yet the divine law,
as already given in paradise (1), further explained on Sinai (2), and glorified in the clearest manner by our Lord
Jesus Christ (3), has not been deprived of power and
effectiveness (4), but now as formerly, has its value and
right use (5). This is, however, three-fold:
a. It should put bit and bridle into the mouth of the

raw, unruly passions of men, and preserve God's holiness and righteousness on earth in respect.

b. It should give knowledge of sin (7) and become a school-master to bring us to Christ (8), in that it, in its holiness and inviolability (9), in its great scope (10) and its spiritual significance (11), shows the sinful man the impossibility of keeping it (12), and therefore awakens the need of grace and forgiveness.

c. It should be a light to the regenerated one (13), who as such takes pleasure in God's law according to the inner man (14), so that he may not miss the right way (15) nor fall into self-righteousness (16), and that he hold constantly in view that glorious end to which he was destined, to be renewed completely in God's image (17); all on account of the weakness of his flesh which still constantly cleaves to him on earth (18).

With regard to the ceremonial part of the law we believe that the same was completely fulfilled by Christ (19), and since in him the essence for the shadow has appeared (20), so this is put aside (21), and in the offering of Jesus, laid hold of by faith, lies the fulfilling of that part of the law (22). With regard, however, to the ethical, moral part of the law, as it is found in the ten commandments, we believe that therein the essence and the will of God is expressed for all times (23), and that heaven and earth will pass away before even one tittle shall fail from the law (24).

Of the Sabbath in Particular

All the commands of God among the ten are, therefore, of equal dignity and holiness, and this we believe especially of the 4th commandment regarding the sabbath (25). According to its content (26) we hold ourselves obligated to work for six days with persevering diligence and great conscientiousness in the business affairs of our civil calling, using all the powers of our body and spirit for the benefit of the world (27). But no less does the command obligate us to sanctify one out of the seven days of the week wholly to the Lord and on the same to rest from labor (28), i. e., to cease unqualifiedly all activity which has to do with our livelihood, as also from every

other purely worldly work which is not absolutely necessary (29) or demanded by love, according to the example
of Christ (30). The day of the Lord shall, according to
the custom of the first Christian churches, be kept as the
Christians' sabbath (31), for the promotion of Christian
knowledge and true godliness, for the hearty union of the
members of Christ, as also for work for the kingdom of
God. We hold further that everyone should on this day
frequently read the Holy Scripture, that the children
should be instructed out of the same, and that men should
attend church services regularly.—We regard this day as
a precious gift of our God (32), absolutely necessary for
the existence of a Christian church.

1) Hos. 6:7. 1 Jno. 2:7.
2) Rom. 13:9. (Gal. 5:14.)
3) Mt. 5:17. Gal. 4:4, 5. Phil. 2:8. Isa. 42:21.
4) Rom. 3:31. 1 Cor. 7:19. Rom. 7:25.
5) Rom. 7:12. 1 Tim. 1:8.
6) 1 Tim. 1:9, 10.
7) Rom. 3:20. Rom. 5:13. 7:7. 7:13.
8) Gal. 3:24.
9) Gal. 3:10. Rom. 2:23. (Jas. 2:10.)
10) Mt. 5:22, 28. 1 Jno. 3:15.
11) Rom. 7:14.
12) Rom. 3:19, 20. 8:3.
13) Ps. 119:6. Ps. 1:1, 2.
14) Rom. 7:22.
15) Ps. 119:101, 104, 128. (Jos. 1:8.)
16) Col. 2:18.
17) 1 Jno. 2:3.
18) Heb. 12:1.
19) Mt. 5:17.
20) Heb. 10:1. Col. 2:17.
21) Heb. 7:18, 19. Acts 10:13-15. 15:28, 29. (Eph. 2:14, 15.)
22) Gal. 4:1-5. Rom. 10:4.
23) Mt. 19:17, 18. 22:36-40. Eph. 6:1-3. Jas. 2:8, 11, 12.
(1 Jno. 2:7.)
24) Mt. 5:18.
25) Gen. 2:1-3. Mt. 24:20. Isa. 56:1-7. 58:13, 14.
26) Ex. 20:8, 9.
27) 2 Thess. 3:10-12.
28) Acts. 20:7.
29) Mt. 24:20.
30) Mt. 12:10-12.
31) Jno. 20:19, 26. Lu. 24:13, 33, 34, 36. Acts 20:7. 1 Cor.
16:1, 2. Rev. 1:10. Ps. 118:22-24.
32) Mk. 2:27.

Article 13.

OF MARRIAGE.

We believe that marriage was instituted by God (1) for mutual help between man and woman (2), for the increase of the human race (3) and for the avoidance of unchastity (4); also that the man may take only one woman for wife, the woman only one man for husband, while both are still alive (5).

We hold that Christians may marry only in the Lord with believers (6).

As a divine and civil ordinance marriage must be confirmed in both ways. The last must accord with the laws of the land (7), the first occurs through the word of God and prayer in the church of the Lord (8).

We regard divorce, if it occurs on grounds which do not agree with the word of God, and remarriage of such divorced persons, as unallowable (9). In cases of adultery, however, (10) and of malevolent abandonment we believe that a separation and the remarriage of the innocent party may take place according to the word of God. In divorce as in marriage the provisions of civil law must be carefully observed (12).

1) Gen. 2:24. Heb. 13:4. (Eph. 5:5, 22-33.)
2) Gen. 2:18.
3) Gen. 1:27, 28.
4) 1 Cor. 7:2, 9.
5) Mt. 19:4-6. 1 Cor. 6:16.
6) 1 Cor. 7:39. 9:5, 6. Gen. 6:1-3. Jos. 23:12, 13. (1 Kings 11:1-8. Ezra ch. 9 and 10. Neh. 13:23-28.)
7) Mt. 1:18. (Mt. 25:1-10.) Jno. 2:1, 2. Mt. 22:2-12.
8) Col. 3:17. 1 Tim. 4:3-5.
9) Mt. 19:6-8. 1 Cor. 7:10, 11.
10) Mt. 19:9.
11) 1 Cor. 7:12, 13, 15.
12) 1 Pet. 2:13.

Article 14.

OF CIVIL ORDER.

We believe that magistracy is ordained of God (1), and that he clothes it with power for the protection of the righteous and the punishment of the evildoers (2). We hold ourselves obligated to render unqualified obedience to all its laws (3), if these do not curtail the free exercise of the duties of our Christian faith (4), and through a quiet and peaceful life in all godliness to lighten their heavy task. Also we hold ourselves obligated according to the command of God to pray for magistrates (5), that they may so administer the power entrusted to them, according to his will and under his gracious protection, that peace and righteousness may thereby be preserved.

We hold that the misuse of the oath is forbidden to Christians (6), but that the oath—viz., the reverent solemn appeal to God as a witness of the truth—rightfully demanded and given, is only a prayer of an unusual form (7).

We believe that magistrates, which also under the New Testament bear the sword not in vain, have the right and the duty, according to the divine law, to punish with death (8); also to use the sword against the enemies of the land for the protection of the subjects entrusted to them, and hold ourselves, therefore, obligated, if we are required to do so by the government to render military service (9). Yet we can also unite heartily with such as do not share our conviction with regard to the oath and military service.

We do not regard ourselves as hindered by our faith from administering civil office (10).

1) Rom. 13 : 1, 2.
2) Rom. 13: 3, 4. (Deut. 16: 18.)
3) Rom. 13: 5-7. Tit. 3: 1. 1 Pet. 2: 13, 14, 17.
4) Mt. 22: 21. Acts 4: 19, 20. 5: 29, 42.
5) 1 Tim. 2: 1-3.
6) Mt. 5: 34-37. Jas. 5: 12.
7) Rom. 1: 9. 2 Cor. 1: 23. Gal. 1: 20. Phil. 1: 8. 1 Thess. 5: 27. Rev. 10: 5, 6. Heb. 6: 13, 16-18. (Heb. 7: 20, 21, 28.) Gen. 24: 3, 9. Ezra 10: 5. Deut. 6: 13. (10: 20.) Isa. 65: 16, 17. (Jer. 12: 15, 16.)
8) Mt. 26: 52. Gen. 9: 6.
9) Lu. 3: 14. Acts 10: 1, 2. 23: 12-24. (Mt. 8: 5-13.)
10) Lu. 3: 12, 13. Rom. 16: 23. Phil. 4: 22. (Acts 13: 7, 12. 16: 34-36.)

Article 15.

OF THE RETURN OF THE LORD, THE RESURRECTION OF THE DEAD AND THE LAST JUDGMENT.

We believe in the return of our Lord Jesus Christ (1) in power and glory (2). We hold the day of his revelation for the crown of the redemptive work (3); for on this day will the eyes of all the world behold the truth and wonderful greatness of this work (4); they will see the King crowned with honor (5), and with him his bride, the Church (6); for the dead in Christ will rise bodily (7) in incorruptible glory (8), will see him as he is, be like him and reign with him (9).

We believe also in the resurrection of the godless (10) and in the judgment of the world (11), that all men must be brought publicly before the judgment seat of Christ that they may receive according to that which they have done in the life of the body (12). As the Son of God will give eternal salvation to all those who in faith served and followed him (13), so will he pronounce on all the godless the judgment of eternal damnation (14). We hold fast on the definite and clear expressions of the Holy Scripture which picture the salvation or lost condition of man after this life as unchangeable and believe that both states are eternal (15), so that no passing out of the one into the other takes place, and no rescue is possible after death (16).

We are mindful of the word of our Lord: "Behold I come quickly!" and with the Spirit and the bride of which we regard ourselves as an essential member we cry "Amen. Yes, come, Lord Jesus."

1) Acts 1:10, 11, 12. Zech. 14:4, 5. 1 Cor. 11:26. (Rev. 1:8. 3:11. 22:7, 20.)
2) Mt. 16:27. 25:31. 2 Thess. 1:7. Ps. 24:7, 8.
3) 1 Cor. 1:7, 8. Phil. 3:20. Jas. 5:7, 8. Heb. 9:28. 1 Jno. 2:28. Tit. 2:13. 2 Pet. 1:16. 1 Pet. 1:7-9. 5:4. (Phil. 2:16. 1 Thess. 1:10. 2:19. 2 Pet. 3:12, 13.)
4) Rev. 1:7. Mt. 24:30. Mt. 25:31, 32. Phil. 2:9-11. Rom. 14:10, 11.
5) Rev. 11:15, 17. Isa. 24:23. (Zech. 14:9.)
6) Lu. 21:27, 28. 2 Thess. 1:10. Col. 3:3, 4. Rev. 19:6-9. (Jno. 17:24. Rev. 21:9-27.)

x

7) 1 Thess. 4: 13-18. Rom. 8: 23. 1 Cor. 15: 16-20, **23. Job** 19: 25-27. (Jno. 6: 40, 54. Rom. 4: 17. 2 Cor. 4: 14. Isa. 26: 19. Hos. 13: 14.)

8) 1 Cor. 15: 42, 43, 53. Phil. 3: 21. (1 Cor. 15: 12-57.)

9) 1 Jno. 3: 2. Ps. 17: 15. Rev. 20: 4, 6. 22: 5. Rev. 5: 10.

10) Jno. 5: 28, 29. (Acts 24: 15. Dan. 12: 2.)

11) Acts 17: 30, 31. (Jud. 14: 15. Rev. 20: 11-13.)

12) 2 Cor. 5: 10. (Rom. 2: 6, 14. 10: 12. Gal. 6: 8. Rev. 22: 12. Eccl. 12: 14.)

13) Mt. 25: 34. (Rom. 9: 23. Rev. 14: 13.)

14) Mt. 25: 41. (Rom. 2: 5, 9, 22. 1 Thess. 6: 10. 2 Pet. 2: 9. Rev. 6: 16, 17. 20: 15.)

15) Mt. 25: 46. Mt. 3: 12. 25: 10-12. Mk. 9: 43-48. Lu. 13: 25-28. 2 Thess. 1: 7-9. Jud. 7: 13. Rev. 14: 11. Rev. 20: 10, 15. (Prov. 1: 24-32.)   16) Lu. 16: 24-26. Heb. 9: 27.

2. French Baptist Confession

The first Baptist church in France was organized in Paris in 1835. Through much persecution and overwhelming difficulties the Baptists have made some progress, but they are still few in numbers. Their first Confession was very brief, and was drawn up by Missionary Willard, and printed at Douai in 1848. Naturally it reflects American opinion. A second Confession was published a few years later, probably based on the first, and drawn up by Willard, assisted by some French brethren. In 1879 a third Confession was published at Chauny (Aisne). It was drawn up by six French Baptist preachers, of whom Rev. A. Ramseyer and Rev. H. Andru were the leading men. It may be regarded as an independent production of the French Baptists, though the covenant was taken from the first Confession. A second edition was printed by Pastor Saillens, in Paris, in 1895, under the title, " Confession of Faith and Ecclesiastical Principles of the Evangelical Churches called Baptist." It is a reprint of the first edition, except that the last section, " Of the Congregation," was omitted. This Confession is now received by all the Baptist churches of France, Belgium, and Switzerland. A translation of the first edition of 1879 follows.

CONFESSION OF FAITH

AND

ECCLESIASTICAL PRINCIPLES

OF

THE UNION

OF THE

BAPTIST CHURCHES OF FRANCE.

———

Chauny
Imprimerie Bugnicourt, rue du Pont-Royal, 72
1879

CHRISTIAN COVENANT.

In consequence of the truths which we fully receive and which are expressed in the following articles, and of the conviction which we have that we have been brought by the grace of God to receive the Lord Jesus Christ and to give ourselves to Him, relying upon His aid we together make a solemn covenant, and promise:

That we will walk together in brotherly love, as is becoming to the members of a Christian church; that we will exercise an affectionate watchfulness over one another and that we will warn one another and exhort one another mutually and faithfully on all occasions, in order to stimulate one another to charity and to good works;

That we will never neglect the assembling of ourselves for mutual edification, nor fail to pray for one another and for all;

That we will always exert ourselves to bring up the children who have been committed to us in the discipline of the Lord, nourishing them with His Word, and that we will give to all our kinsmen and friends the example of pure conduct in order to bring them to the love of the Savior, to holiness and to life eternal;

That we will rejoice in the happiness of each other and will strive with tenderness and sympathy to bear one another's burdens and sorrows;

That we will live with circumspection in the world, renouncing impiety and worldly lusts and setting a good example, remembering that, since we have been voluntarily buried in baptism and raised with Christ, a special obligation rests upon us henceforth to lead a new and holy life;

That we will do all that is in our power to contribute of our means to the faithful preaching of the gospel in the midst of us;

That according to our power and in all circumstances, as worthy stewards of the Lord, we will do good to all men, and especially in aiding the propagation of the gospel in its primitive purity and power throughout the whole earth.

Finally, that, during the whole course of our earthly pilgrimage, in evil report and in good report, we will seek humbly and ardently to live for the glory of Him who has called us from darkness into His marvelous light.

CONFESSION OF FAITH

AND

ECCLESIASTICAL PRINCIPLES

OF

THE UNION OF THE BAPTIST CHURCHES OF FRANCE.

DOCTRINES.

I

OF THE TRUE GOD.

We believe that there is only one God, Father, Son and Holy Spirit, Creator of all things, infinite, eternal, omnipotent, and meriting in the highest degree confidence, love, obedience, praise and adoration.

Gen. 1 : 1, 2; Deut. 6 : 4; 2 Sam. 23 : 2; Job 33 : 4; Ps. 24 : 8-10; 45 : 7, 8; Isa. 11 : 2; 40 : 3; Dan. 9 : 24; Mt. 12 : 28; 28 : 19; Mk. 12 : 29-32; Lk. 2 : 10, 11; Jno. 1 : 1-14; 10 : 30; 14 : 9, 10 ; Act. 1 : 16; 5 : 3, 4; Rom. 8 : 9-11, 14; 2 Cor. 13 : 13; Eph. 4 : 4-8; Col. 2 : 10, 11; Rev. 4 : 11.

II

OF THE HOLY SCRIPTURES.

We believe that the canonical Scriptures of the Old and of the New Testament are the word of God and are to be the sole and infallible rule of faith and of Christian life, by which we shall be judged, and the sole touch-stone for testing every tradition, every doctrine, and every religious system.

Ex. 24 : 4, 12; Deut. 18 : 18; 2 Sam. 23 : 2; Ps. 78 : 5, compared with Rom. 3 : 2; Isa. 8 : 20; Mat. 4 : 4; Jon. 5 : 39, 46; Act. 1 : 16; 3 : 21; 17 : 11; Rom. 1 : 2; 1 Cor. 14 : 37; Gal. 1 : 6-12; 2 Tim. 3 : 16; Rev. 22 : 18.

III

OF THE FALL OF MAN AND OF THE CONSEQUENCES OF SIN.

We believe that Adam, our first father, was created innocent and good, but that having voluntarily violated the commandment of his Creator, he lost his first estate; so that all his descendants, inheriting his nature, are inclined to evil. We believe, also, that all those who have transgressed the law of God are justly liable to eternal death.

Gen. 1 : 27, 31; 3 : 6, 24; 5 : 3; Deut. 24 : 16; Ps. 51 : 7; 53 : 4; Isa. 53 : 6; Dan. 12 : 2, 3; Mat. 25 : 46; Rom. 3 : 19, 22; 4 : 15; 5 : 13; 2 Cor. 5 : 10; 2 Thes. 1 : 9; 1 Jno. 3 : 4; Rev. 20 : 14, comp. Ezk. 18 : 20.

IV

OF JESUS CHRIST AND OF HIS WORK.

We believe that Jesus Christ, the Word made flesh, born of a virgin, conceived by the power of the Highest, is the Son of God, and that after having been tempted in all things as we are, He remained holy, innocent, without spot; that He suffered and that He died upon the cross to make atonement for our sins; that He rose again and ascended to heaven, where He is the sole Mediator between God and men, and whence He will return to judge the living and the dead.

Isa. 53 : 4, 5; Mat. 24 : 15-42; Lk. 1 : 26 : 35; Jno. 1 : 14; Act. 1 : 11; 3 : 18-21; 10 : 42; Rom. 1 : 4; 3 : 25; 14 : 9; 2 Cor. 5 : 14, 15, 19; Gal. 4 : 4; Phil. 2 : 8; 1 Thes. 3 : 13; 1 Tim. 2 : 5; 2 Tim. 4 : 1; Heb. 1 : 2-6; 4 : 15; Rev. 1 : 7.

V

OF SALVATION BY FAITH IN JESUS CHRIST.

We believe that, in order to be saved, the sinner must repent of his sins, accept the work of Jesus and be united to Him by faith. This union produces justification, regeneration and sanctification, without which no one shall see the Lord. We believe also that true faith always manifests itself by works pleasing to God.

1 Kgs. 8 : 47, 48; Ps. 51 : 3, 4; Lk. 13 : 3, 5; Jno. 1 : 12, 13; 3 : 3, 16, 36; Act. 20 : 21; Rom. 5 : 1, 9; 1 Cor. 1 : 30, 31; Eph. 2 : 8; Heb. 12 : 12-17; Jas. 2 : 14, 18, 26; 1 Pet. 2 : 1, 2, 11, 12; 1 Jno. 3 : 4-9; Mat. 7 : 17-21.

VI

OF THE WORK OF THE HOLY SPIRIT.

We believe that it is the Holy Spirit who, applying to the heart the truths of Scripture, produces in those who have been elected according to the foreknowledge of God the Christian life in its principle and in its effects, and renders them capable of persevering therein to the end.

1 Sam. 10 : 6; Ezk. 37 : 14; Zach. 7 : 12; Jno. 3 : 5, 6; 16 : 8; Rom. 5 : 5; 8 : 9, 14, 16; 1 Cor. 3 : 16; Gal. 5 : 16, 18, 22; Eph. 1 : 4, 5; 5 : 9; 1 Pet. 1 : 2, 22, 23.

VII

OF THE MINISTRY OF THE WORD

We believe that God instituted a ministry of the Word composed originally of prophets, apostles, evangelists or missionaries, of elders or pastors and teachers, for the purpose of leading sinners to conversion and of directing them in the Christian life. This ministry, in those of its branches which were to come down to us, that is, the work of pastors and that of evangelists, is to continue till the return of Christ.

Deut. 4 : 5; Isa. 58 : 1; Amos 7 : 15; Mt. 28 : 18-20; Mk. 3 : 13-15; Lk. 10 : 1-20; Acts 6 : 5; 8 : 5; 13 : 1; 15 : 6, 22, 23, 33; 20 : 17-28; 21 : 18; 1 Cor. 12 : 28, 29; 14 : 29, 30; Eph. 4 : 11; 1 Tim. 3 : 1-7; 4 : 15, 16; 2 Tim. 2 : 2; 1 Pet. 5 : 1·5.

VIII

OF LOCAL CHURCHES

We believe that a local church constituted according to the Word of God is an assembly of baptized believers, independent of all authority other than that of Jesus Christ, the sole head of the Church universal, which is His body.

The members of the local church, associated in a voluntary agreement, are governed by the laws of Christ, and exercise, in the general interest, the duties which are imposed upon them according to the gifts which they have received.

The Christians who have a special charge in the local church are the pastors, the deacons and the deaconesses, whose duties are indicated in the New Testament.

Mt. 18 : 17, 20; Act. 2 : 33, 41; 6 : 2-5; 11 : 24, 26; 14 : 23, 27; 15 : 3, 22; 19 : 9; 20 : 17-28; 1 Cor. 5; 16 : 1, 3; 2 Cor. 8 : 19, 23, 24; Phil. 1 : 1; 1 Thes. 5 : 12; 2 Tim. 2 : 2; Tit. 1 : 5; Heb. 13 : 17; 1 Pet. 5 : 1·4.

IX

OF BAPTISM

We believe that baptism is, for Christians voluntarily dead to the world and to sin, the striking and solemn emblem of burial and of resurrection with Christ, to whom they are united by faith, to live in Him a new and holy life.—We believe, after the order of Christ, His example and that of the apostles, that the immersion of believers must precede admission into the local church and participation in the communion.

Mat. 28 : 19; Mk. 1 : 5, 9, 10; 16 : 16; Jno. 4 : 1, 2; Act. 2 : 38-41; 8 : 36-59; 10 : 47; 16 : 33; Rom. 6 : 3, 4; 1 Cor. 1 : 13-17; Gal. 3 : 27; Col. 2 : 12; Tit. 3 : 5; 1 Pet. 3 : 21.

X

OF THE SUPPER

We believe that the supper, instituted by our Savior Jesus Christ, is to be observed in the churches until He returns; that the bread and the wine, in which all the members of the church participate, are the symbols of the body and the blood of our Savior; that by this communion, the members, in participating therein, profess to form the same body with Christ, and to be united to one another in the same Spirit.

Mt. 26 : 26-29; Mk. 14 : 22-25; Lk. 22 : 14-20; Act. 2 : 42; 20 : 7; 1 Cor. 10 : 16, 17; 11 : 23-29.

XI

OF THE RETURN OF CHRIST AND OF THE RESURRECTION.

We believe that the Lord Jesus Christ will return from heaven as He ascended thither, conformably to the declaration of the Scripture. We believe in the resurrection of the dead, both of the just and the unjust, and in the final judgment, where will take place the eternal separation of the good and the evil, these going away to eternal punishment and the just to life eternal.

Dan. 7 : 13; Mat. 13 : 49; 24 : 30, 31; 25 : 31-46; Mk. 8 : 38; Lk. 21 : 27; Jno. 14 : 3; Act. 1 : 11; 24 : 15; Rom. 2 : 5; 1 Cor. 15 : 12, 20, 42-58; 1 Thes. 4 : 14-17; 2 Thes. 1 : 6-12; 2 Pet. 3 : 10-13; Rev. 1 : 7.

XII

OF THE SANCTIFICATION OF SUNDAY

We believe that, conformably to the example of the apostles and of the first Christians, the first day of the week is to be considered as the day of the Lord, in memory of the resurrection of Jesus Christ, and that, in consequence, we ought to employ Sunday for the edification of our souls in our holy assemblies and for works of charity, thus preparing ourselves for the rest which remaineth for the people of God.

Mt. 28 : 1; Mk. 16 : 1; Lk. 24 : 1; Jno. 20 : 1, 26; Act. 20 : 7; 1 Cor. 16 : 2; Heb. 4 : 3-11; Rev. 1 : 10.

XIII

OF CIVIL GOVERNMENT

We believe that civil government was ordained of God for the interest and good order of society and that it is necessary to pray for magistrates and the constituted authorities, to honor them and obey them in all things which are not contrary to the teachings of the holy Scriptures, according to the words of the Savior: "Render unto Cæsar that which is Cæsar's, and unto God that which is God's."

Mt. 17 : 24, 27; 22 : 21; Lk. 20 : 25; Rom. 13 : 1-7; 1 Tim. 2 : 1, 2; Tit. 3 : 1; 1 Pet. 2 : 13-17.

THE CHURCH

I

FORMATION OF LOCAL CHURCHES

The apostles, or their companions in labor, after having baptized the first believers, organized them to form the local churches, to which they communicated the divine laws which they were to follow. It is thus that the churches of Jerusalem, of Antioch, of Corinth, of Philippi, of Ephesus, of Rome, of Colossae were formed. This was the apostolic rule.

To-day still, in order to form a local church, it is necessary that the missionary begin by baptizing those who have accepted the evangelical doctrines. Once constituted, this association continues to add to itself as new members the baptized believers who desire to unite with it.

Baptism, which is the entrance into the church, constitutes between the new member and the old ones a true covenant with reciprocal engagements. The candidate in submitting to baptism accepts publicly the evangelical doctrines, pledges himself to put them in practice, in accord with those to whom he is united ; and the church, on its part receives him into its bosom as one of its members and makes him partaker of all its spiritual privileges.

Mat. 28 : 19;
Jno. 4 : 1, 2;
Act. 2 : 38, 41,
47; 5 : 13, 14;
6 : 1, 2, 5; 8 :
12; 9 : 26; 11 :
19-30; 13 : 1, 3
(comp. Act. 14 :
26, 27); 14 : 23;
15 : 3, 4, 22, 30;
16 : 14, 40; 18 :
8, 10; 19 : 1-5;
Rom. 12 : 5; 1
Cor. 12 : 13;
Phil. 1 : 1.

II

NOMINATION TO THE OFFICES OF THE CHURCH

After having founded in person the first churches the apostles while still living committed the continuation of their work in the Christian assemblies to pastors and teachers, whom the Scripture denominates without distinction bishops, elders or pastors, who, as well as their successors, were to build upon the foundation which has been laid. They were installed in their functions by prayer and the imposition of the hands of the elders.

After the death of the apostles the choice and nomination of pastors always appertained to the churches. We preserve their principle.

Act. 1 : 15-23;
6 : 3-6; 11 : 30;
14 : 23; 15 : 2-
4, 12, 22, 23; 16 :
4; 20 : 17, 28;
21 : 18; 2 Cor.
8 : 18, 19; Phil.
1 : 1; Col. 4 : 17;
1 Thes. 5 : 12-14;
2 Thes. 3 : 12-15;
1 Tim. 3 : 1-6;
4 : 14; 5 : 17-22;
2 Tim. 1 : 6; 2 :
2; Tit. 1 : 5, 7;
Rev. 2 : 2, 15, 16.

III
PASTORS AND TEACHERS

The Scripture establishes no distinction of rank or of authority between pastors and teachers, nor between bishops or overseers and elders or pastors, except such as are due to greater age.—The elders, as overseers chosen by the church, are charged with the administration of baptism and the supper, direction of worship and the deliberations of the church, and with the execution of its decisions. They are never to lord it over the church of God, but to make themselves models of the flock, watching over their souls as having to render an account.

Relative to their conduct, the pastors are subject, like all the other members, to the discipline of the church, but always in accordance with 1 Tim. 5: 19.

A pastor charged with the direction of a church can at the same time devote himself to secular occupations; but it is desirable that he give himself exclusively to his spiritual vocation.

Act. 20 : 17-28; 1 Cor. 3 : 5-8; 4 : 1; 9 : 6; 2 Cor. 1 : 24; 11 : 7-10; Phil. 1 : 1; 2 Thes. 3 : 9; 1 Tim. 3 : 1-6; 4 : 12-16; 5 : 1, 18; 6 : 3-10; Tit. 1 : 5-9; 1 Pet. 5 : 3.

IV
DEACONS AND DEACONESSES

Besides elders or pastors, the sole functionaries of a local church are the deacons and deaconesses. They should be elected by the assembly and installed in their charge by the imposition of hands. They should possess the qualities required by the Scriptures; their office is to assist the pastors in their ministry, to serve the church in consecrating to it the gifts they have received from the Lord, and in charging themselves with all that which has relation to the material wants of the assembly.

Act. 6 : 1-6 (comp. vs. 5 with 8 : 5-13, 26-40, and 21 : 8); Rom. 16 : 1, 2; Phil. 1 : 1; 1 Tim. 3 : 8, 13.

V
VOTE AND ADMISSION

Each local church ought itself to attend to its own affairs independently of all political or religious authority. In the reception of candidates for baptism, as in questions for discussion, everything ought to end as far as possible by a vote. All members, whatever may be their sex or their position, have the same voice in the church, and the decision is determined by the majority of the votes cast.

Mat. 18 : 17; Act. 1 : 15-26; 6 : 5; 9 : 26, 27; 11 : 2, 4, 22, 29; 15 : 3, 4, 12, 22, 23, 30, 32; 18 : 27; Rom. 16 : 1, 2; 1 Cor. 5 ; 16 : 3; 2 Cor. 2 : 6-8; 8 : 19-23.

The admission of a new member coming from another church of baptized believers takes place upon the presentation of a letter of recommendation from the church he has left. When he has no letter of recommendation the brother who is a stranger should confess his faith, make known his principles, and the church decides.

VI

CHURCH DISCIPLINE

According to evangelical teachings, the church ought to exclude from its bosom all its members whose profession of piety is contradicted by their conduct; who transgress knowingly one of the commandments of God and who reject the fraternal exhortations which are addressed to them with a view of bringing them to repentance and abandonment of their sins.

Mat. 18 : 15-20; Rom. 16 : 17; 1 Cor. 5; 2 Thes. 3 : 6-15; 1 Tim. 1 : 19, 20; 6 : 3-6; 2 Tim. 3 : 1-5; Tit. 3 : 10, 11; 2 Jno. 9, 11; Rev. 2 : 11, 20.

The rejected member is excluded from th supper and deprived of all his rights in the church, but is not rejected from the public meetings for worship.

VII

RESTORATION

The excluded member can, upon his request, be re-admitted into the church, if his conduct proves that he has become again pious and faithful.

2 Cor. 2 : 1-11.

VIII

INDEPENDENCE OF THE CHURCHES AND DUTIES OF THE MEMBERS TOWARD THEIR PASTORS

Our churches being, according to the apostolic example, separated from the State and accepting no pay, it is the duty and the privilege of the members to sustain their pastors, to second them in their efforts, and to have for them love, esteem and respect, for the sake of the work which they do.

1 Cor. 9 : 11-14; Gal. 6 : 6; Eph. 5 : 23, 29; Phil. 4 : 14-16; 1 Thes. 5 : 12, 13; 1 Tim. 5 : 17, 18; 1 Pet. 5 : 5.

OF THE CONGREGATION

I

THOSE WHO HAVE PART IN IT

Outside of the church which is composed of baptized believers who participate in the supper, is "the congregation" which is composed of all those who are not members of the church, but who attach themselves to the flock by frequenting the evangelical worship or by requesting the visits of the pastor, without being converted or baptized.—All those are admitted who declare themselves to be attached to evangelical worship, who request to be enrolled upon the register of "the congregation" and whose conduct does not dishonor the gospel.

II

RIGHTS OF THE MEMBERS OF THE CONGREGATION

Those who are considered members of the "Congregation" have the right:

1. To the presentation or consecration of their children to God by the prayer of the pastor and of the church;
2. To the religious instruction of their children; and for themselves, to the particular instruction given to adults;
3. To the visits of the pastor;
4. To the benediction of their marriage;
5. To the religious ceremony of burial.

III

DUTIES OF THE MEMBERS OF THE CONGREGATION

The members of the "congregation," even as the members of the church, ought to consider it a duty and a privilege to contribute according to their means to the general expenses of the worship and to the work of evangelization.

IV

EXCLUSION

In the various cases mentioned below the name of the member is erased from the register of the "congregation":

1. When he requests its erasure;
2. When he abandons the worship;
3. If he conducts himself in a disgraceful manner.

3. SWEDISH BAPTISTS

One of the most vigorous and prosperous of the younger Baptist bodies is that of the Swedish Baptists. The first church was organized in 1848, and they now number nearly fifty thousand, despite the fact that they have suffered much persecution, and have lost hosts of members by emigration. Their churches are not legalized by the government, and there is, therefore, no legally recognized Confession. Moreover, they have not laid any emphasis on Confessions, and commonly say they have no Confession but the Bible.

In 1868 a country church sought and obtained legalization from the government on the basis of a Confession drawn up by itself. This Confession is described as containing " a few meager statements, just barely sufficient in number and contents to serve the purpose of obtaining legal sanction from the government for the church as a Baptist church. Besides, that church held some tenets which were out of harmony with the views of the Baptists in general." This Confession was never adopted elsewhere, and the church has been dissolved; the Confession, however, figures with the civil and ecclesiastical authorities as *the* Baptist Confession because it is the only one ever presented to them as the basis for legalization.

Shortly before 1861 a Confession was drafted and adopted by the First Baptist Church of Stockholm. This Confession was laid before the Conference of all the Baptist churches in Sweden, held in Stockholm, June 23-28, 1861, and by them adopted as *" The Confession of Faith of the Swedish Baptists, adopted at their general Conference, June 28, 1861."* The above facts and the following translation were communicated by Rev. C. E. Benander:

1. We believe that the Holy Scriptures of both the Old and the New Testament (the commonly so-called Apocryphal Books excepted) are inspired by God and constitute the one perfect rule for our Christian faith and practice.

2. We believe that there is one only living and true God —who is a Spirit infinite in all perfections—; who has re-

vealed Himself in three equal persons, the Father, the Son, and the Holy Ghost.

3. We believe that the first man Adam was created holy, in the image of God, but fell by voluntary transgression of the law of God into a state of sin and death; and that in consequence of his fall all his natural posterity have inherited his corruption, are void of all will to turn to God, and without power perfectly to keep his law, and therefore they are guilty before the wrath of God and condemned to eternal punishment.

4. We believe that our Lord Jesus Christ in his one person united true Godhead and true manhood, that he through his perfect obedience before the law of God and through his atoning death has opened for all a way to redemption and salvation from this lost state, and that every one who from his heart believes in him will become a partaker of this redemption and salvation without any merit or worthiness of his own.

5. We believe that the gospel—viz. the glad tidings of the salvation which is acquired through Christ—ought to be preached to the whole world; that every one who hears the gospel is under obligation to repent—viz. with a sincere grief before God to confess and abandon his sins, and at the same time to believe in Christ as his only and all-sufficient Savior—, and that whosoever may refuse to do so will incur upon himself a worse condemnation.

6. We believe that saving faith is a gift from God and entirely a fruit of the working of the Holy Spirit through the word; that all who are to be saved have been given by the Father to the Son and were chosen in him for salvation and sonship before the foundation of this world was laid; and that we ought with utmost diligence to seek to obtain assurance of our own election.

7. We believe that the law of God has for its end to be: 1) a restraint for the ungodly to restrain them from performing all the evil purpose of their heart; 2) a schoolmaster to bring sinners to Christ, in as much as it sets before them the just claims of God and his wrath over sin, shows them their inability to fulfil these claims, and thus awakens in them the need of grace and forgiveness of sin; 3) a rule for the walk of believers to be fol-

lowed in the spirit of the new covenant;—and that, therefore, with these ends in view the law ought to be inculcated in all.

8. We believe that baptism ought to be administered only to such as have personally by a trustworthy confession given evidence of possessing a living faith in Christ; that it is properly administered only through the immersion of the whole person in water; and that it should precede admittance into the fellowship of the church and participation in the Lord's supper.

9. We believe that a true Christian church is a union of believing and baptized Christians, who have covenanted to strive to keep all that Christ has commanded, to sustain public worship, under the guidance of the Holy Spirit to choose among themselves shepherds or overseers, and deacons, to administer baptism and the Lord's supper, to practice Christian church-discipline, to promote godliness and brotherly love, and to contribute to the general spread of the gospel;—also that every such church is an independent body, free in its relation to other Christian churches and acknowledging Christ only as its head.

10. We believe that the first day of the week was kept holy by the apostolic churches as the Lord's day, instead of the Jewish Sabbath, and that we specially on this day are together for common worship and to exercise ourselves in godliness.

11. We believe that civil government is ordained by God, and regard it our duty to honor and pray for the King and the magistracy and in all things to obey the laws of the land, unless they plainly are in conflict with the law of Christ.

12. We believe that this world is to come to an end; that our Lord Jesus Christ will again appear on the earth on the last day, wake up the dead from their graves, and execute a general judgment in which all wicked men will be irrevocably condemned to eternal punishment, while all believing and righteous men will be solemnly established in their possession of the kingdom which was prepared for them from the beginning of the world.

4. In Other Lands

Of Baptist Confessions in other lands, there is little to say. On the mission fields the churches naturally reflect the opinions of the missionaries from whatever land or party they come.

The Canadian Baptists have laid no stress on confessional statements, and now circulate no recognized Confession. The same conditions probably prevail in South Africa, New Zealand, and Australia. Hungary has nearly twelve thousand and Russia nearly twenty-five thousand Baptists, while many other countries have a few churches and members, but nothing has been learned as to their confessions.